Rowing in Eden

Rowing in Eden:
Rereading Emily Dickinson

MARTHA NELL SMITH

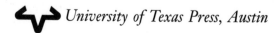 University of Texas Press, Austin

The author gratefully acknowledges permissions to reprint manuscript, previously published materials, and photographs from Amherst College Library, Houghton Library of Harvard University, and the The Belknap Press of Harvard University Press. "Love Letter" by Bonnie Hayes, Copyright © 1989 by Monster Music/Bob-A-Lew Songs (ASCAP), P. O. Box 8649, Universal City, California 91608, all rights reserved, is used by permission. Full citations appear in the author's acknowledgments.

Requests for permission to reproduce material from this work should be sent to Permissions, University of Texas Press, Box 7819, Austin, TX 78713-7819.

ⓧ The paper used in this publication meets the minimum requirements of American National Standard for Information Sciences—Permanence of Paper for Printed Library Materials, ANSI z39.48-1984.

Library of Congress Cataloging-in-Publication Data

Smith, Martha Nell, date
    Rowing in Eden : rereading Emily Dickinson / Martha Nell Smith. —
1st ed.
        p.   cm.
    Includes bibliographical references and index.
    ISBN 0-292-72084-X (alk. paper).—ISBN 0-292-77666-7 (pbk.: alk. paper)
        1. Dickinson, Emily, 1830–1886—Criticism and interpretation.
I. Title.
PS1541.Z5S67   1992
811'.4—dc20   92-6368
                                                                 CIP

for M.L.

Contents

Abbreviations of Frequently Cited Sources

A   Manuscripts at Amherst College will be indicated by this initial and the library catalogue number. The Amherst College numbering system usually designates leaves of a given manuscript, beyond the first, by the main number followed by *a*, *b*, *c*, etc., and references to specific leaves will reflect this system (e.g., of L 233 the first leaf is numbered 828, the second 828a, etc.). Occasionally, however, the verso of a leaf will be lettered (e.g., Prose Fragment 19 is A 743 and 743a). In all cases I have followed the actual numbering, indicating the verso of a leaf by superscript *v*.

AB   Bingham, Millicent Todd. *Ancestors' Brocades: The Literary Debut of Emily Dickinson*. New York: Harper & Brothers, 1945.

"Annals"   Dickinson, Susan. "Annals of the Evergreens." Box 9. Dickinson Papers. Houghton Library, Harvard University, Cambridge, Mass.

Editing   Franklin, R. W. *The Editing of Emily Dickinson: A Reconsideration*. Madison: University of Wisconsin Press, 1967.

F   Franklin, R. W., ed. *The Manuscript Books of Emily Dickinson*. Cambridge: Harvard University Press, Belknap Press, 1981. References to this edition will use this initial and cite fascicle number only.

FF   Bianchi, Martha Dickinson. *Emily Dickinson Face to Face: Unpublished Letters with Notes and Reminiscences*. Boston: Houghton Mifflin, 1932.

"Fascicles"   Franklin, R. W. "The Emily Dickinson Fascicles." *Studies in Bibliography* 36 (1983): 1–20.

H   Manuscripts at the Houghton Library, Harvard University, will be indicated by this initial and the library catalogue letter and/or number.

Home   Bingham, Millicent Todd. *Emily Dickinson's Home: Letters of Edward Dickinson and His Family*. New York: Harper & Brothers, 1955.

L   Johnson, Thomas H., and Theodora Ward, eds. *The Letters of Emily Dickinson*. Cambridge: Harvard University Press, Belknap Press, 1958. References to this edition will use this initial and give the number assigned by Johnson.

LF   Wylder, Edith. *The Last Face: Emily Dickinson's Manuscripts*. Albuquerque: University of New Mexico Press, 1971.

LL   Bianchi, Martha Dickinson. *The Life and Letters of Emily Dickinson*. Boston: Houghton Mifflin, 1924.

Life   Sewall, Richard. *The Life of Emily Dickinson*. New York: Farrar, Straus and Giroux, 1974.

ML   Franklin, R. W., ed. *The Master Letters of Emily Dickinson*. Amherst, Mass: Amherst College Press, 1986.

P   Johnson, Thomas H., ed. *The Poems of Emily Dickinson*. Cambridge: Harvard University Press, Belknap Press, 1955. References to this edition will use this initial and give the number assigned by Johnson.

PF   This refers to the Prose Fragments printed in *Letters*, vol. III, pp. 911–929. Citations will use these initials and give the number assigned by Johnson.

Revelation   Bingham, Millicent Todd. *Emily Dickinson: A Revelation*. New York: Harper & Brothers Publishers, 1954.

Set   This term is used to refer to the unbound fascicle sheets, which can be found in *Manuscript Books* vol. 2. Franklin used the term to distinguish these sheets of poems grouped but not sewn together from the poet's "completed books."

YH   Leyda, Jay. *The Years and Hours of Emily Dickinson*. New Haven and London: Yale University Press, 1960.

Acknowledgments

As a little girl growing up in the West Texas town of San Angelo, I attended Santa Rita, an elementary school named after the saint of the impossible, and was fortunate enough to have teachers who encouraged me to "dwell in possibility" well before I knew very much about Emily Dickinson. Thus it was probably fated that the University of Texas Press editor Frankie Westbrook should pick up where those teachers left off, and I cannot thank her enough for her belief in me and my project. Other Texans who must be thanked are the members of my family, who always encouraged me to ask questions and look for opportunities. I am especially grateful to my parents, Earl and Mozelle Smith, whose unstinting support taught me that nothing is impossible and helped make the dream of this book a reality.

I would like to thank the National Endowment for the Humanities for providing both monies for travel to the archives as well as a fellowship which afforded me a year in which I could devote all my time and energies to this and related projects, the American Council of Learned Societies for providing a grant which enabled me to complete work in the Dickinson archives, and the General Research Board at the University of Maryland at College Park for providing travel funds and stipends for summer research and a semester's leave. I would also like to thank John Lancaster, Special Collections Curator, Amherst College Library, and Rodney G. Dennis, Curator of Manuscripts, Houghton Library of Harvard University, as well as staff members of both libraries; without their cooperation and careful assistance locating documents, this study would not have been possible.

Without loving and patient constancy of dear friends both near and far this project would have never reached fruition, and I am especially grateful to Martha Foy, B. Z. Palubinsky, Paul and Lori Madden, Mike Arnold and Lisa Honaker, Debra Burns and Bill Malloy. Thanks, too, to Greg Marcangelo for his persistence in locating an obscure text and to Carol Sanders and Ann Steinecke for indexing. Many colleagues have read drafts of *Rowing in Eden* or offered critical insights that contributed substantially to my work, and to those who feel they were involved and who do not find themselves mentioned here, I offer both my apologies and gratitude. I am also heavily indebted to many theorists and critics of textuality and sexuality, as well as to a century's worth of Dickinson scholars and biographers. I would especially like to thank Alice Crozier for her early encouragement and tough critiques of this study in its infancy; Susan Howe and Cris Miller for their insightful questions over the past several years; Suzanne Juhasz, Jane Eberwein, and Rachel Blau DuPlessis for careful readings and vital suggestions regarding oversights in an earlier draft; and Ellen Louise Hart for incisive commentaries and for sharing her own insights regarding examination of Dickinson's holographs. Both for their careful scrutiny of the manuscript and years-long enthusiasm for the project, I thank Jim Bloom, Vivian Pollak, Ruth Stone, Wendy Barker, Joe Wittreich, Katie King, Susan Stanford Friedman, Neil Fraistat, and Linda Kauffman. For critiquing several manuscript versions and encouraging and exhorting me when my own spirit flagged, I thank Alicia Ostriker, who believed in this study from its beginning as well as in my ability to succeed. And for her generous debates, tireless editing, unfailing wit, and faith that Eden is no superhuman site but always within our grasp, I am ever indebted to Marilee Lindemann.

Emily Dickinson's manuscripts are quoted by permissions of the Trustees of Amherst College and by permission of the Houghton Library of Harvard University. Emily Dickinson's poetry is reprinted by permission of the publishers and the Trustees of Amherst College from *The Poems of Emily Dickinson*, Thomas H. Johnson, ed., Cambridge, Mass.: The Belknap Press of Harvard University Press, Copyright © 1951, 1955, 1979, 1983 by the President and Fellows of Harvard College, and from *The Complete Poems of Emily Dickinson*, Thomas H. Johnson, ed., Copyright 1929, 1935 by Martha Dickinson Bianchi; Copyright © renewed 1957, 1963 by Mary L. Hampson: Little, Brown and Company, Boston, and reprinted by permission of the publishers from *The Manuscript Books of Emily Dickinson*, 2 vols., R. W. Franklin, ed., Cambridge, Mass.: The Belknap Press of Harvard University Press, Copyright © 1981, © 1951, 1955, 1978, 1979, 1980 by the President and Fellows of Harvard College, © 1914, 1924, 1929, 1932, 1935, 1942 by Martha Dickinson Bianchi. Emily Dickinson's letters are reprinted by permission of the publishers from *The Letters of Emily Dickinson*, Thomas H. Johnson and Theodora Ward, eds., Cambridge, Mass.: The Belknap Press of Harvard University Press, Copyright © 1958, 1986 by the President and Fellows of Harvard College. Susan Dickinson's "Annals of the Evergreens" is quoted by permission of the Houghton Library. Versions of chapter 1, "To Fill a Gap," have been previously published in *San Jose Studies* and *Women's Studies Quarterly*.

Rowing in Eden

A nd on the sand would I make signs to range
These woofs, as they were woven, of my thought;
Clear, elemental shapes, whose smallest change
A subtler language within language wrought. . . .

—SHELLEY, *THE REVOLT OF ISLAM*

He who draws noble delights from the sentiments of poetry is
a true poet, though he has never written a line in all his life.

—"GEORGE SAND"

I have decided that the trouble with print is, it never changes
its mind.

—URSULA K. LE GUIN, *DANCING AT THE EDGE OF THE WORLD*

Introduction

Writing about Emily Dickinson, one cannot possibly hope to please every reader. As the often contradictory images of her in books, articles, on stage, and even on television suggest, critics and biographers often maintain strong, practically immutable convictions about her personality, her preferences for living, and her poetic intentions. To foreground (as I do) Dickinson's unconventional regard for her sister-in-law and her equally unconventional attitudes toward the publishing industry is perhaps certain to meet resistance, yet these stories need to be told, retold, revised, and connected to each other. The stories of her relations with and regard for men—her father, brother, Thomas Higginson, "Master," Charles Wadsworth, Samuel Bowles, Otis P. Lord—have been told time and again, and the importance of men emphasized to such an extent that one critic even claims, "When she has a man for 'Master,' she says she can 'speak': she then has 'power' and 'art.'"[1] Though the stories presented here necessarily attend to her relationships with women, especially "Sweet Sue," and are in that sense partial, that is because I want to emphasize what has previously been devalued by or excluded from most Dickinson studies. Let me say at the outset that to underscore the literary importance of Sue and other women to Dickinson in no way denies the significance of men whom she held in high regard. Likewise, stories about her relationships to the world of publication have been repeatedly told, and almost all, conveying some version of the traditional "partially cracked poetess" (L 481n) and stressing her social disappointments or lack, have speculated what she would have done had she elected (indeed, been able to elect) to publish her poems conventionally or have concluded that her refusal to publish was conventionally feminine in the extreme. Thus mine, meditating on the possibility that her chirographic "publication" was not simply "part of an unusual and painful strategy that signaled privacy and alienation,"[2] but was instead a consciously designed alternative mode of textual reproduction and distribution, is a rarely told, underdeveloped critical story.

One question—"What did Emily Dickinson think she was doing when she sent out at least one-third of her poems in her letters?"— prompted this study. Another question—"What does it signify when Thomas Johnson records '*words erased*,' '*one line erased*' (L 57), '*half a page cut out*' (L 80), '*several words erased*' (L 113), and '*seven lines erased*' (L 116)?"—directed my examinations to the manuscripts and to issues of textual transmission and reproduction that dramatically enriched this project. Like Alice walking through the Looking-Glass or Dorothy opening the door to Oz, I found my study of American poetic culture, of literary materiality, and of gender relations serendipitously enhanced by this tighter focus on issues raised by the Dickinson documents. Among my discoveries was that similarly motivated oversights and excisions contributed to erasures of both Dickinson's textual and sexual prerogatives. Trying to explain the censorious receptions led to such questions about the poet's intentions as, "Is it possible that unconventional aspects of Dickinson's identity gave her a sense of freedom and flexibility that in turn influenced her literary vision?"[3]

Perusing triangular intertextualities, or the influences of biography, reception, and textual reproduction upon one another, *Rowing in Eden*, my story of reading Dickinson in manuscript, explores critical concepts about literary authority and the poet's sexual/textual preferences by restructuring customary methods of reading her writings that separate poems from the letters and packets in which they were enclosed. The first chapter introduces the kinds of issues that will be investigated in various ways in the subsequent five chapters. It begins by examining Dickinson's avowal that she refused standard publication, and conjectures that editorial misunderstandings contributed significantly to her decision, thus arguing that Dickinson "published" herself in her letters and in the forty manuscript books (or fascicles) left in her drawer. Then I propose that we repattern Dickinson study by systematically reading her writings in the context of those correspondences, for, by manifesting a poet carefully shaping her written performances, such reorganization of critical inquiry significantly alters both our perceptions of the works and the woman who made them. I adduce transmission of a few key poems and letters translated into print and isolated from the correspondence or fascicle in which Dickinson presented them to show how my hermeneutics, the chief principles of which are to privilege holographs over print translations, discloses "two factors— gender and politics—which," until the past couple of decades, have been disguised, denied, or otherwise "suppressed in the dominant models of reading," editing, and interpreting her works.[4] Thus, highlighting intersections of reading, gender, and language as well as examination of gendered influences on both the poet's production and her reception are central to this investigation.

The second chapter outlines my methodology for interpreting Dickinson's texts by describing why I use her phrase "Rowing in Eden" to describe new strategies for studying her works and lives. The phrase is appropriate for describing how, by challenging some traditional conceptions of literary and critical authority, her poetic production suggests new patterns, elaborated in the chapter, for receiving and interpreting her "books" of poems and letters. Framed by tracing a century of reader response, the third chapter investigates to what extent gender-inflected assumptions that perpetuate interpretations similar to those of her contemporary editors—who gave "He fumbles at your Soul" the title "The Master" (F 22; P 315; Mabel Loomis Todd, ed., *Poems by Emily Dickinson*), and placed it in the middle of the section "Love"—continue to inspire infatuation with the three unfinished pieces known as "The Master Letters." My examination of those documents critiques them not as biographical notes but as records of literary process. Then, considering the context of her letters and poems (or "publications") to women, as well as those to Thomas Higginson and other men who were important friends, I scrutinize her "publication" to her mentor Susan Dickinson. The fourth chapter muses on the limitations of attempting to reconstruct any personal association on the basis of surviving documents; the fifth surveys their lifelong correspondence to analyze their epistolary relationship and describes aspects of their poetry "workshop" by examining their exchange over "Safe in their Alabaster Chambers" (F 6, F 10; P 216; L 238); the sixth examines Sue's obituary for Dickinson, her role as editor transcribing three-score poems and making notations throughout the fascicles, and her letters to editors about the printings of Emily's poems. Analyzing these volumes of correspondence to "Master" and Sue, I interrogate, among other subjects, the role of the book in literary study; the supposed but never substantiated relationship with "Master" is so privileged in Dickinson study that the three mysterious missives are reproduced separately in facsimile, in a book all their own, while the three hundred or so poems and one hundred and fifty or more letters to Sue lie dispersed throughout six volumes of poems and letters edited by Johnson or Johnson and Theodora Ward and seven volumes edited by Martha Dickinson Bianchi or Bianchi and Alfred Leete Hampson. Following this plan, *Rowing in Eden* examines

Dickinson according to literary presentations in her major correspondences, those which provided her primary contemporary forum, as well as those with which posthumous readers have been most preoccupied.

This story of reading distinguishes itself from other Dickinson studies in two primary and vital ways: first, by arguing that Dickinson "published" herself, thereupon comparing and contrasting her various presentations to different audiences accordingly; and second, by placing Dickinson's thirty-five-year literary relationship with Susan Huntington Gilbert Dickinson at the center of inquiry. Throughout the book, all interpretations of Dickinson's texts will be illuminated by relevant comments to, from, and about her most influential audience, "Dear Sue," upon whom the poet lavished much attention and more poetic and epistolary works than any other contemporary, and at whose behest Dickinson actually revised at least one poem (while we know, for example, that she routinely ignored the advice of Higginson, prominent editor and arbiter of American poetic taste). Feminist applications of tenets of reader-response and poststructuralist literary theory, as well as of theories about the principles for textual editing, inform my analyses.

Though the significance of "Rowing in Eden" will be more fully elaborated throughout the book, especially in the second chapter, it is important to commence this story by summarizing reasons for foregrounding the phrase. Long recognized as an important Dickinson expression, "Rowing in Eden" comes from the poem that elicited the most well-known early reader's response to her work. Considering it for inclusion in *Poems by Emily Dickinson: Second Series* (1891), Thomas Higginson remarked:

> One poem only I dread a little to print—that wonderful "Wild Nights,"—lest the malignant read into it more than that virgin recluse ever dreamed of putting there. Has Miss Lavinia any shrinking about it? You will understand and pardon my solicitude. Yet what a loss to omit it! Indeed it is not to be omitted.

(AB 127)

As Rebecca Patterson observed, "all but the prudish" recognize this text's eroticism.[5] The phrase is important for my purposes because it yokes the sexual and textual and foregrounds woman's problematic relationship to both. Also, over the course of her forty-four-year writing career (counting from the date of her first known letter), Dickinson returns again and again to the imaginative place Eden, continually revising this site of humanity's mother's seduction. When she is but fifteen, she muses:

> I have lately come to the conclusion that I am Eve, alias Mrs. Adam. You know there is no account of her death in the Bible, and why am not I Eve? If you find any statements which you think likely to prove the truth of the case, I wish you would send them to me without delay.

(L 9, JANUARY 12, 1846)

In this she highlights the fact of Western culture's pervasive amnesia regarding women's history. This study, which offers many reasons that Dickinson may be considered a literary Eve, restores part of literary history that has been nearly forgotten and that needs to be explored far beyond the scope of the present project. By tasting the forbidden fruit, Eve tested God's dictum and introduced critical inquiry, or the quest for knowledge, into the world. In analogous ways, Dickinson's extraordinary poetic project continues to test dicta about literary production and reception.

"Letters speak volumes, where volumes can engulf and stifle the persona portrayed."[6] Epistles printed and widely available (edited by Loomis Todd, Bingham, Dickinson Bianchi, Johnson, Sewall) offer a context for reading the correspondences I have elected to study. I draw my sketches of Emily Dickinson from her writings themselves, especially her letters, knowing such study is of the poet's *autograph*, not her autobiography. With Domna C. Stanton, I excise *bio* from *autobiography* to "bracket the traditional emphasis on the narration of 'a life,' and that notion's facile presumption of referentiality."[7] Like her, I do not do this to take the life completely out of the literature, but to emphasize such complexities as the fact that any writing of a life involves that which an "I" chooses not to inscribe as well as that translated into words. Dickinson's epistolary record includes not only her omissions, but also writings that others cut out and pretended she had never written and writings that are lost.

There are many absences, created both willfully and by oversight—whole correspondences are missing (e.g., Dickinson's letters to Wadsworth), correspondents' letters to Dickinson are mostly missing (exceptions include a letter or two each from Sue and Higginson and one presumably from Wadsworth), parts of correspondences are missing (e.g., poems and letters that Sue deemed too private to print and some letters to Elizabeth Holland), portions of letters are, as the following chapters show, erased or cut or torn away. Stories abound in these censorial handlings.

My surprise to see deliberate scissorings and erasures was at the time and energy expended by "Austin" to preserve parts of holographs even as "he" destroyed other portions, at the trouble "he" took to make holes instead of wholes. In referring to the mutilator as "Austin," all I have is Mabel Loomis Todd's word that Dickinson's brother, Austin, was indeed the perpetrator. So throughout this book I use quotation marks to denote that hearsay. In any case, someone desperately wanted to remove something from Dickinson's written record, expunge part or parts of the story inscribed. Yet the tracks left all over the mutilated manuscripts speak ambivalence about the deletions. Why not do as the Norcross cousins (Fanny and Louise) and simply transcribe, then destroy holographs? Why not do as Willa Cather did and forbid all direct quotation from letters? It is as if "Austin" wanted others to know that erasures of parts of the tale told by Dickinson had been made and, long before Marianne Moore's epigraph, wanted to remind readers that "Omissions are not accidents." [8]

To the woman who mutilated her own Bible, her *New England Primer*, and her father's Dickens, such textual excisions would probably come as no surprise, and since most of our cultural scriptures have been rearranged, tailored, translated, or in some way altered (and presumably "damaged") in handling, the cuttings do not astonish us. Consciousness of the deletions is valuable not to the degree that it answers "Who dunnit?" but to the extent that it sensitizes us to instabilities in all Dickinson texts and to "the play of identity and difference" in all texts. [9] Awareness of other gaps like those Shelley muses upon in *A Defense of Poetry* when he writes of the poetic ideal as "the original conception of the Poet" and of textual fact as the "poetry . . . communicated to the world," which is but a "feeble shadow" of the generative idea, enriches our literary understanding by making us more conscious of the reader's continually repeated role in literary reproduction, thus less likely to reify poems by confusing texts with the artifacts on which they are inscribed. At the same time, readers are likely to be more attuned to the range of meanings—from nuances to radically contradictory connotations—suggested because of different corporealizations of a poem. Similarly, more informed, readers will likely be more self-conscious and more astute when aware of mutilations to Dickinson's work.

By seeking to revamp portraits of the poet and foster some new attitudes toward her holographs in order to expose some of the unusual strategies with punctuation, lineation, and calligraphic orthography, I do not propose this study as the definitive analysis of either Dickinson or her poetic techniques. Yet clearer images of the poet Dickinson and her literary practices will surely emerge from serious dialogic exchanges about her personal preferences and literary performances examined here, though no portion of or position maintained in those dialogues will by itself portray the poet and her work. So what I recommend is that we neither bind Dickinson up in one critical/biographical perspective nor limit our understanding of her poetics to the conventions of print. By interrogating ways in which gender and intentionality shape our reproductions of lives and literature and by offering new strategies for reading Dickinson's poetic practice, I do not propose to obviate previous methods, but to build on what we have already learned. In some ways, this endeavor is "fundamentalist" in that, acting in part on a suggestion by Adrienne Rich, I seek to discover more about the poet and her literary production in words (her own).[10] Yet, like trying to get "back to the Bible" in the age of mechanical reproduction, perusing any printing, including of course facsimiles, is in fact reading in translation. Too, the actual documents, itemized, numbered, catalogued, tucked into individual folders, and housed primarily at the Houghton Library at Harvard and the Frost Library at Amherst College, have been translated from their original states, where they were bound into envelopes or fascicles by Dickinson.

At first glance, it may appear that this project seeks to get as close as possible to the "originary moments" of Dickinson's poetic creation by studying the manuscripts. Or, by acknowledging the importance of facsimiles, I may seem to be impelled by the urge Walter Benjamin describes "to get hold of an object at very close range by way of its likeness, its reproduction."[11] But my aims are not that simple. Benjamin's analysis of the work of art in this age of mass reproducibility and dissemination helps reveal a point at which the much-used metaphor comparing poems to art objects begins to break down, and, in doing so, the great paradox of this manuscript study is also revealed: though the material facts of a poem's reproduction, many of which I examine, are not in fact the poem, they do make vital suggestions about the poem, and, though they should not be idolized, neither should they be trivialized. When Emily Dickinson asks Thomas Higginson, "Are you too deeply occupied to say if my Verse is alive?" (L 260, April 15, 1862), she inquires whether or not the material records she sent him of four poems make tasty enough recipes or pleasing enough scores for a reader to play upon.

Superficially, emphasizing the importance of the holographs may look like an act of textual criticism that "has the effect of desocializing our historical view of the literary work."[12] After all, since Dickinson has grown in stature over a century in which most editions and criticism have simply ignored her stylistic techniques when they are idiosyncratically resistant to mass reproduction, to insist on their significance may look like capitulation to what some have called her "solipsism." Yet the nearer one draws to Dickinson's holographs, the less likely one is to regard poems as closed artifacts and the more one is reminded of just how different a poem is from a painting or sculpture. Adding a brush stroke or chiseling a shard, one irrevocably damages the artwork. In disfiguring poems or letters, editors reproduce their own versions as mediations for readers. But unlike the permanent damage to an artwork, such mediations are part of a reading dynamic.

As shown by her ambiguous punctuation and variants from which readers must choose, the poet who wrote "A word is dead, when it is said / Some say—/ I say it just begins to live / That day" (L 374; P 1212) was well aware that "as soon as the author utters or writes down his work, even for the first time, a mediation has to some degree come between or 'interfered with' the original, unmediated 'text'"[13] and that every subsequent reading is in fact a rewriting, another mediation. The original Dickinson documents emphasize the fact that readers do not "get hold of" or "master" poems, but are themselves part of the poetic process. As we will see, Dickinson's literary productions are themselves theoretical, beginning to critique the idea of the author, the role of the reader, and to elaborate what we now call reception studies. What I will elaborate is how she introduced me to a whole new world of reading, how, studying the manuscripts, I have found myself, time and again, pondering her textual and sexual priorities and, as Dickinson herself might say, "Rowing in Eden—."

Path between the Homestead and the Evergreens, houses in which Emily and Sue Dickinson lived side by side for thirty years. By permission of the Houghton Library, Harvard University.

"**S**he" is indefinitely other in herself. That is undoubtedly the reason she is called temperamental, incomprehensible, perturbed, capricious—not to mention her language in which "she" goes off in all directions and in which "he" is unable to discern the coherence of any meaning. Contradictory words seem a little crazy to the logic of reason, and inaudible for him who listens with ready-made grids, a code prepared in advance.

—LUCE IRIGARAY, *THIS SEX WHICH IS NOT ONE*

It is precisely because her traits, habits, needs, and probable demands are distinct from those of man, that she is not, never was, never can, and never will be, justly represented by him.

—THOMAS W. HIGGINSON, *WOMEN AND THE ALPHABET*

Readers will be struck by the frequency with which her variants show that her line spacings and stanza divisions follow no pattern. Much of the irregularity clearly suggests a conscious experimentation.

—THOMAS H. JOHNSON, *THE POEMS OF EMILY DICKINSON*

All men say "What" to me, but I thought it a fashion—

—EMILY DICKINSON, L 271

One *To Fill a Gap: Erasures, Disguises, Definitions*

When Emily Dickinson wrote Thomas Higginson, "I had told you I did not print," she enclosed a clipping of "The Snake," the version of "A narrow Fellow in / the Grass" (Set 6c; P 986) which had appeared in the *Springfield Weekly Republican* two months earlier, to demonstrate her reasons for choosing not to do so. She comments on the printed version: "Lest you meet my Snake and suppose I deceive it was robbed of me—defeated too of the third line by the punctuation. The third and fourth were one—I had told you I did not print—I feared you might think me ostensible. . . ." (L 316, early 1866.)[1] She appears angry because editors, presuming to know how the poem should be punctuated, inserted a question mark she had purposely omitted. By 1866 she had seen at least ten, very probably more, of her poems in print. The *Republican* had printed most of them, and in most of the printings Dickinson had seen alterations of her poems.[2] According to her, such editorial interference dissuaded her from conventional publication. So distressed by the changes that she employs a language of conquest to describe an apparently minor tampering of the editors, Dickinson remarks that their revision by no means improved the reader's lot but was one that "defeated" her intention that the third and fourth lines be read together, as a unit. Editors had not recognized that her choice of

> You may have met Him – did you not
> His notice instant is

was "defeated" and printed as

> You may have met him – did you not?
> His notice instant is,

(P 986, L 316, SEE ESP. NOTES ON PUBLICATION)[3]

The question mark separates "not" from "notice," spoiling the anaphoric pun. "Not," followed so quickly by "notice," with no pause underscored between, brings to mind "Did you note?" On the other hand, the divisive punctuation discourages the punning and ambiguity made possible in its absence. By emphasizing the break between lines, the punctuation mark practically insists on a particular reading, whereas its omission makes the relationship between the two lines more indeterminate, hence encouraging more interaction by the reader and more possibilities to create meaning. Therefore, the poet objects to limits that she herself did not wish to impose being forced upon her poem. If, as Paul Valery suggested, "a poem, like a piece of music, offers merely a text, which, strictly speaking, is only a kind of recipe," then Dickinson becomes exasperated because editors changed the instructions for performing or cooking up readings.[4]

A Story about Reading

That is one story to tell about the meaning of her remarks. Certainly the combative language of assault and thievery, Dickinson's own more violent metaphors for editorial intervention, argues for such an interpretation. Elsewhere her metaphors are claustrophobic; Dickinson writes as if a poetic impulse has been shut up in prose (F 21; P 613), as if she has been "robbed" of a room in her literary house of "fairer" possibility (F 22; P 657). To construct a narrative about her reaction to editorial interference, the reader fills several key gaps in the letter's passage: she asserts the cause-effect relationship implied by Dickinson's placing a statement about conventional editorial practices beside her professed attitude toward standard published forms; the reader assumes, therefore, that the particular incident Dickinson describes is representative of her general experience with the world of mechanical literary reproduction and that Dickinson found the printed transformations of her work dissatisfying; most important, the reader concludes that, because of her disappointments, Dickinson chose not to distribute her work in the mass-produced ways to which most unknown authors aspire. Concurring with Joanne Dobson's recent study, other readers might choose to literalize the last clause in the passage and maintain that "in conformity with the attitudes of her female contemporaries toward the private nature of personal lyrics, she herself chose not to publish."[5] Such interpretation concludes that internalized codes of femininity constrained Dickinson more than editorial interference and her ambitions for her poetic project. Yet as Richard Salter

Storrs Andros's preface to *Chocorua and Other Sketches* (1838) as well as many other statements by male authors contemporary to Dickinson show, proclamations of authorial deference were conventional for both men and women: "The author of the following pages is not, perhaps, the first who has been dragged before the public against his own will." Deciding whether Dickinson's refusal is a personal response, a convention of authorial or feminine codes of behavior, or none of the above, readers must acknowledge the problem of distance in time and would do well to heed Hans Robert Jauss's observation that "distance in time is to be put to use and not—as historicism would have it—overcome, that is, abolished through a one-sided transplanting of the self into the spirit of the past."[6]

The author's preferences are clearly important to both stories of reading outlined above. Equally vital to the narrative is a reader's willingness to accept her role in scripting Dickinson's text. Thus intentionalities of both the author and readers play central roles. To determine preference among her variants, Thomas Johnson invokes Dickinson's intention time and again, for example to privilege a commaless first stanza version of "A narrow Fellow" (see P 986n, particularly the last comment on its transmission through "Publication"). Indeed, a century of stories told about reading this poet and her written expressions are predicated on convictions about her intentions: Thomas Higginson's "virgin recluse" kept to her father's ground and to the editor's preconceptions of what she meant to imply in "Wild Nights – Wild Nights!" (*AB* 127); Clark Griffith's Emily Dickinson lived "on the outskirts of sanity"; Cynthia Griffin Wolff's Emily Dickinson sat in the corner of her most recent biographer's study waiting for her to tell how her subject's "poetic mission" was "an explicit reenactment of Jacob's struggle with the Lord"; Adrienne Rich's Emily Dickinson practiced "necessary economies" on "her own premises"; and John Hollander's Emily Dickinson did not punctuate her poems.[7]

The willful Emily Dickinson of this chapter's opening paragraph is the poet central to this book. As in that tale, her intentions are important considerations for this practice of interpreting her statements, though, as will become evident, they are not necessarily the final arbitrating factor. Important too is the reader's awareness that through various elliptical strategies, this Dickinson invites readers to author connections between her texts and patterns within texts. Whether writers acknowledge their participation or not, readers will construct texts, but the Dickinson of these pages is conscious of the inevitability of the reader involved in such play.[8] But print reproductions often erase significant textual experimentations directed toward prospective readers and their performances. Because of these erasures, recovery of the designs Dickinson created in her hand-made poetic productions (and presumably intended for the reader's plea-sure) is vital to our reading. Contemplating my consensus with and depar-ture from Hollander's reading of "those things that are reproduced as dashes" reveals a particular manifestation of the paradoxes that emerge in my reading of Emily Dickinson. Though I agree with Hollander that "like all great poets Dickinson turns every reader into a poet" and that, in order to understand a poem of hers, every reader is "implicitly punctuating it," I do not dismiss as "scholarly nonsense" conjectures about her unusual ho-lograph experimentations. Nor do I concur with his conclusion that had someone "in the local printer's shop" insisted that she print a volume, she would have "probably done what Higginson did, rather better"; in other words, Hollander agrees with a century of readers who argue that had Dickinson published conventionally, she would have of her own volition smoothed her poetic forms and rendered them much more conventionally. Like Hollander, John Updike, also widely published, maintains that John-son's transcriptions of Dickinson's dashes "is a mistaken scholarly fidelity to holograph mannerisms that were never meant by the author to be trans-lated into type."[9] Though I agree that Johnson's translation of the oddly angled marks as dashes may be "mistaken" in leveling many different marks into one kind of representation, I am not so confident about what Dickinson would have intended for typeface. Whether one holds that, as Higginson usually did, she would have opted to translate her marks into commas and periods, or, like Johnson, to straighten them into dashes, one limits conceptions of Dickinson's intentions to the forms and conventions of mechanical reproduction.

Of the Dickinsons named so far, *Rowing in Eden*'s poet is most akin to the resolute woman imagined by Adrienne Rich, having it out "always on *her* premises." However, "cartooning" in her word pictures, in sketches on letters and cutouts framing poems, and in her calligraphy, my Emily Dickinson probably teeters more often on hilarity. Upper middle class, white, Protestant, without the right to vote, this Emily Dickinson without much socially sanctioned public authority was (and still is) nevertheless powerful. That she was privileged by class but disenfranchised by gender is important. Her class standing enabled her to remain comfortably single and afforded her time for writing. Yet as a female, she found her social status and her literary authority compromised. As a woman poet, Dickin-son was not read by her contemporaries and has not been read over the past century without the fact of gender having significant influence. Nor did she read her cultural situation as a man might have. While Whitman printed himself and sent a volume to Emerson, a premier man of letters who wanted "spermatic, prophesying man-making words,"[10] Dickinson established a correspondence with a self-appointed adviser of young writers who championed the rights of women yet recognized that "there is a brutal honesty in this frank subordination of the woman according to the grammar."[11] Higginson admits that a woman's relation to language is not the same as a man's. On the most rudimentary level, all can see that *he* is the paradigmatic pronoun, *she* the variant, and also that women's access to public speech was much more circumscribed than men's. Emily Dickinson was far from oblivious to this.

Yet we need to be aware of the distinction Dickinson and her sister-in-law emphasized between the often synonymously used terms *publish* and *print*. Dickinson did not say, "I had told you I did not *publish*"; she said, "I had told you I did not *print*" [emphasis added]. Also, when she smiles at Higginson's conjecture that she delays "to publish," quotation marks make it plain that she uses his words when she utters the more commonplace term for works produced in the literary marketplace instead of her more precise "to print" (L 265, June 7, 1862). Writing February 18, 1891, to William Hayes Ward, superintending editor of the *Independent*, Susan Huntington Gilbert Dickinson corrected herself:

> . . . I recognize fully all Miss Emily's lack of rhyme and rhythm, but have learned to accept it for the bold thought, and everything else so unusual about it.
>
> I think if you do not feel that your own literary taste is compromised by it, I would rather the three verses of the "Martyrs" ["Through the Straight Pass / of Suffering" (F 36; P 792)] should be published if any. I shall not be annoyed if you decide not to publish at all. I should have said *printed*. . . .
>
> (H LOWELL AUTOGRAPH, AB 115)

Surrounded by lawyers (Dickinson's father and brother), these women are somewhat legalistic in their differentiations, using *publish* in the special sense "to tell or noise abroad" (*OED*).[12] For the purposes of this study and story of reading Emily Dickinson, that is not a negligible fact.

The Story Continued

Suppose we extend the story which takes seriously Emily Dickinson's declaration that she "did not print" (L 316, early 1866) to allow that she was deliberate, not desperate, when she "replied declining" to someone who requested that she "aid the world" by permitting the printing of her poems (L 380, late 1872?).[13] Opening a folder containing one of Dickinson's documents, one cannot help but imagine that this is indeed the case. To see the quiet weave of the fine linen stationery, and the pinholes where those leaves had been so carefully threaded together to make the fascicles, the manuscript books she folded and tucked and left in her drawer (or chest) for posterity, and to see the poems written and rewritten, sometimes even revised after they had been carefully copied onto these pages sometimes edged in gold leaf, sometimes embossed (with a capitol building or a queen's head or flower), enables one to see more clearly the writer for whom the choice of each word mattered, the woman who diligently recorded her words on exquisite paper, then lovingly laid the little books of lyric away in a place where they were sure to be discovered by those willing away that portion of her belongings "Assignable" (F 26; P 465). Old questions come to mind. Had anyone known of the poet Dickinson's bookmaking enterprise? Had anyone seen her threading and unthreading the little fascicles? Had any contemporary suspected all these poems?

To entertain as fact that she devised her own method of publication by sending her poems out in letters moves the locus of study to the manuscripts themselves. After all, if, like Blake, she was publishing herself, but without his access to engraving and printing materials, then her pencil or pen was her printing press and her calligraphic orthography her typeface; and, as Susan Howe has pointed out, holographs like that of "The Sea said / Come to the Brook" (Set 11; P 1210), in which the *S*'s are shaped like waves and the *T*'s formed to resemble choppy seas, indicate that eschewing that foul auction, conventional publication (P 709), freed her to appropriate even calligraphy for her poetic practice.[14] Such strategies are, of course, lost to us in printed transcriptions. Further, to study Dickinson's major correspondences in transcription is made especially problematic by the evidence that—at least according to his lover, Mabel Loomis Todd—Dickinson's brother, "Austin," changed his sister's epistolary record by scissoring and erasing passages about his wife that he regarded as private. These and other gaps have caused distortions in the critical treatment of Emily Dickinson, which in turn directed my critical attention toward the archives.

Sitting in the Frost Library at Amherst College, poring over erasures, surprised by scissorings, I was, quite frankly, aghast at the extent of mutilation to some of Dickinson's letters and poems. Translated into descriptions by Thomas Johnson, the tamperings, like Dickinson's handwritten productions translated into uniform type, "sound" considerably less dramatic than they actually appear. Remarking upon the powerful effect of reading Dickinson's manuscripts, Amy Clampitt declares that "there's something about the way those words go racing across the page, and yet with spaces between them, that changes your idea of everything you've read before. . . . The handwriting is fierce."[15] Likewise, the mutilations are fierce, and, as I said at the outset, readers cannot help but wonder what provoked an earlier reader or readers to responses creating such gaping gaps in the Dickinson documents. Yet especially penetrating was a much more subtle change caused by translating the penciled "like you" that I found in the "Master" letter beginning "If you saw a bullet hit a Bird" (L 233).[16] Three drafts to an addressee or addressees unknown, the "Master" letters are also Dickinson's most well-known correspondences. Some have taken them as documentation that poor Emily had her heart broken by some man. But an apparently negligible detail, noticeable only in manuscript, had raised the vital question of whether the real or imagined addressee of a couple of drafts was indeed, as I and most others had always assumed, male. Despite other difficulties noted by critics in getting Dickinson's writings correctly from her page to the printed one, no printed representations or critical commentary reproduce two very crucial words—"like you"—as they appear on the holograph.[17] Penciled in above the inked line, the phrase is plainly an addition—probably but not necessarily by the poet—to a line once considered finished.

This failure to indicate the nature of the transcriptive interpretation "like you" is especially important, for some critics hinge part of their interpretations of these letters on readings limited by it. These critics accept the idea that these two words seem to confirm that this frustrated love letter could only have been written to a man. Johnson indicates in print that, addressing "Master" as "Sir," this letter's speaker cries, "but if I had the Beard on my cheek—like you—" (L 233). Along with many critics, John Cody recognizes that Dickinson was in love with her sister-in-law, Sue. He also notes, with Richard Chase, Charles Anderson, and Rebecca Patterson, that in Dickinson's love poems, "the figure of the beloved man lacks presence," then proposes a dilemma: "If 'Master' existed and was close enough to Emily Dickinson frequently enough to feel he might proffer offers of sexual intimacy with her, why does he appear so insubstantial and unindividualized in her verse?" But when he evaluates Patterson's "hypothesis" that Dickinson's "lover was, in reality, a woman," an assertion that "would explain the lack of a distinct masculine image in the verse, while at the same time it would account for the sexual fears and reservations" so evident in writings like the "Master" letters, he dismisses this conjecture, saying, "The 'Master' letters alone are sufficient to explode this theory. In these it is clearly stated that 'Master' has a beard; the relationship the letters picture is that between a small, fragile, immature female and an older, parental, kindly, somewhat formidable male." [18] Yet holograph study of these letters that have so often been used to document Dickinson's passionate and unrequited love for a man indicates that his rebuttal is insufficient, for it is not so "clearly stated" that "Master" has a beard.

Why Are Manuscripts Crucial?

Why are those two penciled words so crucial? In a transcription so scrupulous, where another penciled addition, above the line, like this two word emendation, is carefully denoted by parentheses, it is odd that, when the two penciled words "like you" reach print, they are presented as if they were part of the original sentence, when it is absolutely clear that they were not. When the "like you" is treated as a solid part of the letter, the line becomes conventional in that it is necessarily heterosexual. But without it, Dickinson might be saying to a female lover, "If I had the beard on my cheek"—if I were a man—"and you had Daisy's petals"—and you were a woman—if, in other words, ours was a conventional, "normal," heterosexual romance, then would it be acceptable to speak our love? Unfortunately, the possibility that Dickinson, like her beloved Shakespeare, may have been disguising her characters by dressing a woman up in masculine pronouns and names has been made very difficult to recover in all available transcriptions of these drafts, and even Franklin's photographic representation obscures the difference between pencil and pen.

In effect, there is a silence surrounding that penciled change, a subtle erasure that partially hides, as Susan Howe puts it, "Dickinson's brilliant masking and unveiling, her joy in the drama of pleading." This silence, this erasure, obscures unconventional, possibly even lesbian interpretations of these letters in which the imploring rhetoric most resembles not the rhetoric of her letters to Samuel Bowles or her male correspondents, but the beseeching rhetoric of many of her letters to her beloved Sue. Why this silence? Was it merely an oversight? Is there any significance to this gap? Of the letters' design and purpose we can never be certain. These "Master" letters, these most popular of all her epistolary documents, are love letters on the order of who knows what. They might be to a man, they might be to a woman, they might not be to anyone in particular at all. Reading the "Master" letters, we would be wise to remember Dickinson's imaginative power and her amazing ability to transform experience and, of the most familiar (even, as John Crowe Ransom would say, the Mother Goose-y[19]), make the surprising and wonderful. And we would be wise to entertain seriously suggestions like Howe's that the "Master" letters may be modeled on the hysterical letters of Dickens's "Little Em'ly" (written after she has eloped with Steerforth) and "were probably self-conscious exercises in prose by one writer playing with, listening to, and learning from others."[20]

Silence surrounds other editorial changes. Perusing the facsimile printings in R. W. Franklin's *The Manuscript Books of Emily Dickinson*, one concurs with Sewall that her dashes are "not . . . mere eccentricities of penmanship" (*Life* 2 : 349); one sees that Dickinson's directing her dashes up or down was, as Edith Wylder argued, an intentional appropriation of rhetorical notation learned at the Amherst Academy, and not, as Johnson and his assistant Theodora Ward had claimed, an "especially capricious" (P, p. lxiii) accident of emotional "stress."[21] For example, the dash at the end of "I dwell in Possibility ⁄" (F 22; P 657) dances up; when the fly re-enters the text in "I heard a Fly buzz – when / I died – " (F 26; P 465), and the speaker sees the little beast, the dash drags down: "There interposed a Fly ⹁." This comic sensibility is lost to us in conventional transcription, as are Dickinson's unusual experiments with lineation. In the holograph of the much talked about "One need not be a Chamber ⹁ / to be Haunted ⹁" (F 20; P 670), her lineation elicits a chuckle. In this ghost story of a poem about psychic fragmentation, Dickinson has a little fun with the third stanza's scheme:

> Ourself behind Ourself –
> Concealed –
> Should startle – most –
> Assassin–hid in Our Apart –
> ment –
> Be Horror's least –

What we expect is not what we get: the unanticipated mid-syllable line ending, not haphazard, is a deliberate breaking of form. Mimicking the lyric's sense, the lineation acts almost as cartoon. Yet this prosodic experimentation has not previously been transcribed and, until Franklin's *Manuscript Books*, had been lost to Dickinson's public. Seeing so much of the visual impact of Dickinson's cartooning and experimentation with lineation and punctuation silenced in transcription, I wondered what impact might be lost to us in the transcriptions of the "mutilations" (L 80n). Since reading the facsimile printings of the holographs in Franklin's *Manuscript Books* had made such a remarkable difference in my experience of the poems, I reasoned that examining the holographs of the mutilated letters would prove more enlightening than pondering transcriptions.

As "Austin's" work with scissors and erasures shows, not all of the silences imposed on Dickinson's texts are so subtle as the misleading transcriptions of lineation (which to date have assumed that the stanza and not the line is her basic poetic unit[22]), of dashes, and of "like you." A glance at the first couple of fascicles in the *Manuscript Books* provides excellent examples of what a review of Dickinson's correspondence to her brother makes clear: "Austin" sought to expunge every affectionate reference to his wife, the woman whom Dickinson herself acknowledged as, "With the Exception of Shakespeare" (L 757), her greatest teacher. In an effort to blot out a loving poem about Sue, the text of "One Sister have I in the house" (F 2; P 14) is inked over.[23] In this case, "Austin's" attempt proved futile; Sue had her own copy of the poem and it survives, intact. When Loomis Todd's daughter, Millicent Todd Bingham, repeated her mother's story that "Austin" was responsible for mutilations of his sister's work, she conveyed much more important information about the nature of the expressions provoking such seemingly hysterical reader response than the mutilator's identity: ". . . Mr. Dickinson stipulated that if Emily's letters to him were to be used, the name of one of her girlhood friends must be left out—that of Susan Gilbert, his wife. But omitting her name was not enough. Before turning over the letters he went through them, eliminating Susan Gilbert's name and in some instances making alterations to disguise a reference to her . . ." (*Home* 54). Thus many of the letters to Austin are altered, and the changes always appear near adulatory mention of Sue.

Almost all the deletions are made in letters written to Austin during the years Susan grew intimate with the Dickinson family, particularly with Austin and Emily. Between 1851 and 1854, almost half of Dickinson's letters to Austin are mutilated, sometimes extensively (with a half or quarter of a page cut out or several lines erased), sometimes with only a few words erased.[24] After 1854, the record shows only three more letters (written 1861, 1884, 1885) to Austin; none of them is mutilated, not even in mention of "Sister," Susan. Noting that the deletions do not begin to occur until the fall of 1851, when Emily begins to write Sue passionately (see L 56, L 57), and keeping in mind that the passages deleted all refer to Sue, examining the altered letters to Austin in context of the letters Dickinson was writing to Susan Gilbert at the same time substantiates the conclusion that the expurgations clearly seek to expunge the record of Dickinson's affection for this woman she was to call "Only Woman in the World" (L 447, about 1875). It was not, as Johnson declares, simply all references to Sue that "Austin" wanted to excise, for in some letters of this period mention of Sue goes undoctored: Emily's expecting a letter from Sue is not particularly affectionate and remains intact (H L 23; L 87, 1852), as do hoping that Susan appreciates a "blessed" thunderstorm (A 590; L 89, 1852) and telling Austin that their father called on Sue (A 592; L 95, 1852). Though there is an attempt to erase mention of Sue's ability to excite a laugh, an incidental reference in the same letter to her receiving letters from Austin is left alone (A 595; L 108, 1853), as is an apparently unimportant observation of Sue's impending arrival after she has been in Boston with Austin (A 596; L 109, 1853). Passages focused on Austin are generally not defaced: when Dickinson writes of Susie's visit "to supper" and of their walk to the "Old Oak Tree," where they speak primarily of missing Austin, all is intact, as is a paragraph in which Dickinson describes Susie's "carrying" Austin's letter with her, and reading it "over and over" (A 602; L 118, 1853), a remark that Susie is "so disappointed at having no letter from" Austin (A 608; L 128, 1853; a later phrase putting Austin "and Susie and Emily" together has been erased), mention that Susie plans to write Austin (A 612; L 132, 1853), a passage reminding Austin that "Poor Susie hears nothing from you" (A 617; L 144, 1853), and information that Susie, evidently practicing a lawyer's wife's role, "went round collecting for the charitable societies" (A 618; L 145, 1853). If the perpetrator wanted to remove evidence of Sue and Austin's courtship, as some have conjectured, then surely passages like these, especially ones like the dreamy-eyed longings for him beneath the "Old Oak Tree," would be gone. When Dickinson writes of her intense feelings for Sue, the letters are defaced.

Words and Affections Lined Out

A March 7, 1852, letter shows that when Dickinson talks of sending Sue flowers, the words are lined out:

> ~~I have been hunting all over the house, since the folks went to meeting, to find a small tin box, to send her flowers in~~ [*lines missing*] ~~very often and~~ [*line erased*] . . .

(A 587, 587A; L 80)

With bracketed notations Johnson records the erasure but not that the most affectionate words are censored, overlaid with penciled lines. Neither does he note that when "Austin" sought to obfuscate his sister's erotic expressions, the change sometimes borders on the absurd, as an April 16, 1853, letter makes plain. There "Austin" alters the singular pronoun from feminine to masculine, evidently in an effort to disguise reference to Sue. "Austin" erased "her" and wrote "his" over it and erased the *s* from "she," so that a sentence about Emily and Sue reads: ". . . I shant see him [her] this morning, because [s]he has to *bake* Saturday, but [s]he'll come this afternoon, and we shall read your letter together, and talk of how soon you'll be here [*seven lines erased*]" (A 601; L 116). Johnson creates yet another gap when he records that there was a change, but does not note that the apparently hostile "Austin" went so far as to change pronouns and, therefore, in effect, gave Sue a "beard."

After Austin and Sue trysted for the first time at the Revere Hotel in Boston, Dickinson wrote her brother an angry letter. In its most telling paragraph, "Austin" tried to erase "Susie," the name of his sister's love: "Dear Austin, I am keen, but you a good deal keener, I am *something* of a fox, but you are more of a hound! I guess we are very good friends tho', and I guess we both love [S]us[ie] just as well as we can" (A 597; L 110). Although he does not represent it in the text (L 110), Johnson notes that an "attempt has been made to erase 'Sue' in the second paragraph above the signature." His misdescription of the erasure is slight, but what it overlooks about the holograph is significant. It appears that it is "Susie," not "Sue," that is erased from the text. Not all the letters are erased, but only the first one and last two, leaving "us." So the sentence reads "I guess we are very good friends tho', and I guess we both love us just as well as we can." Obviously this is an attempt to remove a record of Sue being at the center of the conflict between brother and sister, and to replace expression of love for the outsider with declaration of sibling affection.[25]

Why was "he" so sensitive about such expressions of woman-for-woman love when, "for centuries, within Western societies women's love for one another was considered to be one of women's noblest characteristics"?[26] Why have so few critics talked about these silences imposed on Dickinson's expression? Is it that "Austin's" self-consciousness is so painfully clear? Does Loomis Todd's declaration that her lover Austin had grown very bitter toward his wife account for his actions? Her unavoidably biased account must be questioned. It is not only that of the mistress, but it is also hearsay: Mabel said that Austin. . . .

As several studies have shown, by the end of the nineteenth century men were no longer "convinced of their own representations of (their) women's basic purity and asexuality," and "Austin," well aware of her intense devotion to his wife, may have simply been trying to protect his sister from the speculations of "the malignant."[27] Widely recognized is the fact that, by the end of the nineteenth century, "the separation of sexuality and reproduction made Americans more conscious of the erotic element" of passionate friendships between women, and "during the 1890s, the labels 'congenital inversion' and 'perversion' were applied not only to male sexual acts, but to sexual or romantic unions between women, as well as those between men." In fact, "when the medical discourse on sexual perversion emerged at the end of the century, . . . the medical labeling of same-sex intimacy as perverse conflated an entire range of relationships and stigmatized all of them as a single, sexually deviant personal identity." Some have argued that the lack of an indisputable record of homosexual acts between Emily and Sue could well mean that such desires never occurred. As John D'Emilio and Estelle B. Freedman astutely point out about the general situation of sexuality in American culture, though there is of course an "absence of procreative evidence" and a paucity of "direct records of homosexual acts," "the condemnation of the practice at the end of the century provides a clue that [homosexuality] indeed existed."[28] Likewise, the censorship of Dickinson's papers at the end of the century suggests that her passionate friendship with Sue was not simply innocent.

Significantly, anxious editing of Dickinson's declarations to Sue persists, even in recent feminist criticism. Lately many have started to turn their attentions to Dickinson's relationship with Sue, but, again, gaps have been created. Thus, in one of the most informative and widely read essays about her love for Sue, a curious silence is imposed which in effect excises not "Austin's" but Dickinson's own self-consciousness. In "Emily Dickinson's Letters to Sue Gilbert," Lillian Faderman chastises Austin and Sue's daughter, Martha Dickinson Bianchi, for editing Dickinson's letters in a way that masks her aunt's love for her mother and points out that post-Freudian Bianchi excises the very sensual "How vain it seems to *write*, when one knows how to feel—how much more near and dear to sit beside you, talk with you, hear the tones of your voice, . . . Oh *what* will become of me? Susie, forgive me, forget all what I say." Yet Faderman's own selective quotation edits out and disguises Dickinson's self-consciousness, which appears long before "Austin's" actions at the end of the nineteenth century. She stops quoting as if the letter ends with "forget all what I say."

But this letter, which, like others of this period, speaks of wanting to hold, kiss, and caress Sue, continues, and Dickinson seems well aware that her feelings for Sue are unacceptable. She urges her beloved to ignore her loving speeches and take up tales of holy virginity: "Susie, forgive me, forget all what I say, get some sweet scholar to read a gentle hymn, about Bethleem and Mary, and you will sleep on sweetly and have as peaceful dreams, as if I had never written you all those *ugly things*" (H L 10; L 73).²⁹

In light of this complete quotation, the fox-hound metaphor in the letter to Austin, somewhat obscured by his editing, suddenly is perfectly appropriate: whereas women's erotic love is, when not denied or silenced, formally or informally punished, and whereas heterosexual love is a conquest and men are the conquerors, Dickinson casts herself as the sly one in her love for Susie, while representing Austin as a bounding, stalking hunter. The most self-conscious part of the sentence is that which encourages Susie to embrace patriarchal normalcy and to act "as if" Dickinson "had never written . . . all these *ugly things*." Significantly, Dickinson's handwritten flourishes point a reader's attention to "*ugly things*." Just glancing at the holograph, a reader's eye is pulled to the phrase, for in both words an exaggerated *g* underscores the letters preceding. Calling remarks about her affection "*ugly*" makes Dickinson's anxiety clear, yet in her attention to Bianchi's self-consciousness, Faderman overlooks the degree to which Dickinson sees her woman-for-woman love as transgressive. The commonplace assertion that nineteenth-century women were not self-conscious enough about their intense romantic friendships to qualify those as lesbian is quite similar to what Faderman proclaims about Dickinson's love for Sue.³⁰ But in order to make sure that Dickinson fits this widely accepted analysis of nineteenth-century culture and its rhetoric, a gap has been created and a silence imposed. Both Peter Gay and Karen Lystra have recently demonstrated that there are significant gaps in our understanding of nineteenth-century sexuality.³¹ Though Lystra is concerned with heterosexual eros in her study of romantic love in America, her persuasive case for women's sexual expression demands a revision of the widely held characterization of woman-for-woman love in the female world described by Carroll Smith-Rosenberg. Since we can no longer blithely proclaim that nineteenth-century American middle-class women repressed sexual desires toward men, any proclamation that passionate friendships between women were nonsexual is also questionable. As Lystra argues, privatization of sexuality is not the same as denial or repression, thus generalizations about an absence of sexuality between women must be skeptically scrutinized. And a consensus on what it means to be lesbian is not so certain as Faderman implies.

Dickinson's Love

When analyzing Dickinson's love for her sister-in-law, it is important to keep in mind both Adrienne Rich's range of "woman-identified experience," which embraces on a "lesbian continuum" many "forms of primary intensity between and among women," and Catharine Stimpson's insistence that lesbianism "represents a commitment of skin, blood, breast, and bone," that "carnality distinguishes it from gestures of political sympathy with homosexuals and from affectionate friendships in which women enjoy each other, support each other, and commingle a sense of identity and well-being."[32] Although the sisters-in-law's desire for one another may have remained unconsummated, with Emily refusing to act on her passion and Sue displacing hers onto Austin (see Cody's *After Great Pain* for a more thorough discussion of Sue's "homosexual panic"), Dickinson's correspondence to Sue, frequently expressing her wanting to caress and kiss her beloved (L 96 is one of the many examples) and imagining orgasmic fusion with her (L 288, about 1864), speaks a carnal as well as an emotional affection. Therefore, even Stimpson's "conservative and severely literal" definition of what can and cannot be called lesbian is appropriate to consider. Yet that this was an emotional devotion of a lifetime is very important, so Rich's insistence on primary emotional intensity between women is also vital to our understanding. If Dickinson herself had not been so self-conscious about it and if Sue had not acknowledged that some of Dickinson's expressions of love for her were "too adulatory to print," this woman-for-woman love might comfortably fit under the umbrella of Smith-Rosenberg's nineteenth-century female world. Yet Dickinson's own words suggest that her participation in the female world of love and ritual is not so innocuous. Because we need to connote both the eroticism and difference of Dickinson's affection, *lesbian*, that loaded gun of a word that both Stimpson and Rich attempt to define, is most appropriate for characterizing this relationship, which has been ignored and trivialized over the last century.

Objections to the use of this term may be swift, with critics insisting that we have no foolproof documentation of a physical relationship between Sue and Emily. But such dissensions miss a very important point. In her study of H.D., *Psyche Reborn*, Susan Stanford Friedman makes a crucial observation, reminding us that the term *lesbian* is not entirely unique in provoking quandaries about meaning:

> Compounding the difficulties of ignorance is the current ambiguity of the labels "lesbian," "bisexual," and "heterosexual" in our culture in general and in the feminist movement much more particularly. . . . All three terms are variously used to describe specific sexual behavior at any point in time; inherent, lifelong sexual preference; socially conditioned sexual preference; erotic attraction and fantasy; sexual and/or psychological identity, including those whose behavior is at odds with their sense of self; and a political perspective, epistemology, and lifestyle.[33]

Though Friedman focuses on the problems with only one of those terms—"within this complex of definitions, 'lesbianism' has been inconsistently equated with everything from sexual intimacy between women, to female friendship and sisterhood, woman's creative center, woman-identification, and the epistemology of the oppressed who exist on the fringes of the patriarchy"—inconsistent equations characterize our use of even the most conventional label. We do not distinguish among all the phenomena coexisting under the term *heterosexuality*, yet are bound not to notice because our contradictory and contesting definitions are so deeply ingrained that we assume they are "natural," hence take them for granted. *Heterosexual* refers to relationships between husbands and wives; men and women engaged to be married; psychosexual familial dynamics between brothers and sisters, fathers and daughters, mothers and sons; affections between boyfriends and girlfriends dating; the muse as the artist's creative center; numerous political positions, epistemologies, and lifestyles. Then, describing erotic experiences and potentially sexual relations, *lesbian*, like *heterosexual*, of course takes on a range of often inconsistent meanings. Whether we see hers as a utopian fantasy of women empowering women is finally not so important, because Rich's idea that all sorts of relationships described by the same term are in fact variously erotic, from practically negligible to irresistible in degree, is crucial to our beginning to understand the many stories we tell about sexuality and its divorce from our other affections. What Friedman's perspicacity forces us to reconsider are the ways in which we schematize our basic attractions. Such reconsideration is essential if we are ever going to get beyond and find some answers to the now very tired question, "How genital must it be to call it homosexual or lesbian?"

Also analyzing H.D., Rachel Blau DuPlessis notes that the modernist's bold concept was that "the erotic" is "played out for spiritual stakes on a historical terrain . . . far beyond the domesticity of depicted relationships, acceptable or taboo," and that H.D.'s response to rigid schematizations provides an enlightening model. In a letter to one of her close friends (possibly a lover), H.D. makes plain her resistance to psychoanalysis when it is in the hands of those who adopt an overly clinical, corrective attitude toward the erotic: "It is hardly a question of your being, as you say, A2 or B3 Lesbian. . . . But it's a matter of something infinitely bigger than Lesbian A2 or anything. The Lesbian or the homo-sexual content is only a symbol—note I did not say a 'symptom.' *That* is not very important. *How* you love is more important than WHO you love."[34] *How* we use this powerful term to convey a sense of relationship is all important, and how intensely Dickinson loved Sue demands such a strong word.

Faderman is right to exhort us to remember that "lesbian history has been buried even more deeply than women's history," that it is difficult to trace its evolution, and that we must be very careful when applying the label to instances of woman-for-woman love in centuries and circumstances different from those of our own. Yet her definition for "the fairly common type of situation which we label 'lesbian' today" could be appropriate for describing Dickinson's relationship with Sue: "two women living together in an affectional relationship over a long period of time and sharing all aspects of their lives." In a well-tempered analysis of the severe limitations imposed by the fact that a number of Dickinson biographers and critics embrace the hearsay testimony of an opportunistic Mabel Loomis Todd while ignoring the "Dickinson revealed in her letters" to her primary correspondent Sue, Dorothy Huff Oberhaus points out that Dickinson's relationship with Sue was "loving and lifelong" and notes that "Sue possessed an understanding of Dickinson's solitary life, her reluctance to publish, the uniqueness of her voice, her wit, her reifying and emblematically visual imagination, the movement characteristic of so many of her best poems, her love of nature, her reading habits, and her religious sensibility and reverential attitude toward life and poetry."[35] As Marilyn Farwell observes, "Although contemporary definitions of lesbian at times seem at odds, feminist theorists have begun to evolve a complex, problematic, and yet flexible image that both deconstructs the heterosexual pattern for creativity and creates a space for redefining the relationship of the woman writer to other woman writers, to readers, and to the text," and such redefinitions are necessary if we are to analyze Dickinson's complex and creative decades-long literary exchange with Sue.[36]

Interpreting her own definition, Faderman insists on twentieth-century terms, for "women living together" means women setting up a separate household together. However, as she points out, in a century so different from our own, where "economic reasons alone" made such arrangements between women "extremely rare," lesbian arrangements would not necessarily resemble the heterosexual arrangements of marriage. Even while Faderman pronounces Dickinson's affection for Sue homoerotic, she masks the degree of Dickinson's self-consciousness about her feeling by excising part of her expression. By erasing, Faderman directs our attention away from the fact that Dickinson's most important lifelong relationship was the one with Sue about which the young poet in her twenties seems to have felt guilty, and yet another portion of lesbian history is left unearthed, for just how important this relationship was to Dickinson is partially disguised. Sue was the most important person, not just for the "five years" that Faderman accounts, but throughout Dickinson's life. The poet sent Sue at least 430 poems and letters, but sent Higginson (after Sue, her most frequently addressed correspondent) only 171, considerably fewer than half as many. Although their situation does not fit our twentieth-century notions, the two women lived close together and shared intimate details of one another's lives for decades.

Gaps like that created by Faderman, inevitable in the enterprise of criticism, can be filled. And when they are, Dickinson's expressions of love for Sue become less mysterious. Indeed, building on the pioneering work of Rebecca Patterson published in 1951, Faderman's study is part of an ongoing project to fill the gap created by downplaying Dickinson's erotically charged relationships with women during the first half-century of critical responses to her work. Significantly, this project has been countered and marginalized by Millicent Todd Bingham's publication of the "Master" letters in full in 1955 and the predictable critical fascination with those three indeterminate documents (*Home* 422–432; "Master" is reproduced in facsimile). Though there has been no formally organized "School of a Lesbian Dickinson," the critics contributing to this body of work over the last four decades have been investigating lesbian connotations of Dickinson's writings. In the sixties and seventies poet/critics who identify themselves as lesbian like Adrienne Rich and Judy Grahn claimed her as a literary forerunner, while throughout the seventies and eighties critics interested in gay/lesbian history and criticism like Faderman and Paula Bennett substantially developed aspects of Patterson's interpretations—Faderman convincingly expanded Patterson's critique of Bianchi's editing while Bennett extensively tested Patterson's hypotheses about Dickinson's use of images and colors to depict homoeroticism. Other critics like Adalaide Morris have interrogated the "essential bonds" of "passion and poetry" between Emily and Sue, while poet/critics like Susan Howe have speculated to what degree Sue fueled Emily's imagination. *Tulsa Studies* closed 1990 with an issue featuring an article by Judith Farr exploring Dickinson's relationship with Sue and its effect on her appropriation of others' writings as well as one by Ellen Louise Hart exploring their relationship and possible influences on Dickinson's formulations of her own literary endeavors.[37]

Most of these interpretations tend to read Dickinson's writings to propose stories of reading that frame the poems and letters as autobiographical accounts of a woman in what DuPlessis has called "romantic thralldom." Some go so far as Nadean Bishop and argue that interpretations of Dickinson's marriage poems must be revised to account for what she argues was a consummated relationship with Sue. As such, these postulations are interpretations appropriative of heterosexual plots which script Dickinson's love for Sue as a variant of the "conventional heterosexual narrative script," thralldom.[38] As we shall see throughout the chapters on Emily and Sue's correspondence, to read their passion for one another as a story of "totally defining love between apparent unequals" in which "the lover [Emily] has the power of conferring self-worth and purpose upon the loved one [Sue]" is, however novelistically entertaining, oversimplifying. Nevertheless, even stories of lesbian thralldom are important steps in our achieving a better understanding of Dickinson's passionately poetic relationship with Sue.

Other gaps concerning erotic expressions can also be filled. Readers contemporary with Dickinson expected a woman writer to be especially capable of profound emotion but to remain undefiled by eros. And "Austin" was not just anxious about Dickinson's affection for his wife. The drafts of letters that "he" brought to Mabel Loomis Todd and said had been intended for Judge Otis P. Lord show that "he" sought to silence more than his sister's erotic woman-for-woman desire. He sought to silence all her erotic desire, apparently even her heterosexual desire. Sacrilegious and sexy, a letter that declares "when it is right I will lift the Bars, and lay you in the Moss – " has a whole top of a sheet cut off just before she writes: " . . . to lie so near your longing – to touch it as I passed, for I am but a restive sleeper and often should journey from your Arms through the happy Night, but you will lift me back, won't you, for only there I ask to be – " (A 739; L 562). The passionately affectionate yearnings in the correspondence to Sue and these bawdily flirtatious remarks in the letters said to be to Lord show, like long overlooked works by Fanny Fern and Louisa May Alcott, that many women's real sensibilities challenged idealized patriarchal molds of proper, chaste femininity. Thus awareness of her unabashedly erotic expressions, as well as of subversive literary strategies in the "American Women's Renaissance," creates a context casting suspicion on overly literal-minded interpretations of Dickinson's works like the "Master" letters and the many poems used to confirm her lovelorn despair. Imbued with the rhetoric of "secret sorrow" and the "literature of misery," such documents should be interpreted in light of Dickinson's cultural context, especially that created by the explosion of literary works by other American women. Readers would do well to admit the possibility that "for Dickinson, all woman's stereotypes," including that of the disappointed spinster given to renunciation and seeking emotional compensation in dedication to her art, "become matters of literary theater and metaphorical play." [39]

Other Gaps

Still other gaps in Dickinson's poetic record contributing to one-dimensional conclusions drawn by those who read her pose in white dress without irony, some of which existed for more than sixty years, can be and have been filled. Yet few have noticed that these erasures of blasphemies of idealized womanhood existed in the first place and few have pondered the significance of such shushings. The publication history of the following shows what I mean:

> A solemn thing – it was –
> I said –
> A woman – white – to be –
> And wear – if God should
> count me fit –
> Her blameless mystery –
>
>   *hallowed*
> A timid thing – to drop
> a life   *purple*
> Into the mystic well –
> Too plummetless – that it
> come back – *return*
> Eternity – until –

I pondered how the bliss would
look –
And would it feel as big –
When I could take it in
my hand –
As hovering – seen – through
fog – glimmering

And then – the size of this
"small" life –
The Sages – call it small –
Swelled – like Horizons – in my
breast – *vest*
And I sneered – softly – *"Small"*!

(F 14; P 271)

A nineteenth-century lady would never utter the final two stanzas, would not be likely to sneer, and, although Thomas Higginson had written "Let us alter as little as possible" during his and Loomis Todd's editing of the first posthumous volumes of Dickinson's poetry in the 1890s, when Loomis Todd printed the poem in 1896 she edited those stanzas out and titled it "Wedded." In the version produced by Loomis Todd, to be married is a holy thing for women, and that "Solemn thing" is a "hallowed" mystery.[40] In Dickinson's version, marriage is a solemn state indeed, and, she is careful to mention, one for which women cannot be blamed. Loomis Todd's changes—omitting stanzas and inserting the variant "hallowed" in a different position than Dickinson's sardonically suggestive placement— are gender-determined in that she edits out the erotic woman poet who blasphemes the social order. As Amy Lowell observed a couple of decades later, to commodify Dickinson and her writings, "the editors of the first three series compiled the books with an eye to conciliating criticism" (*FF* xi). By contrast, in Dickinson's poem, the unmarried speaker ends, not pining to be "A woman – white," but, by comparing her unwed state to what she imagines bridal "bliss" to be, she sneers at those who would pity her. Unapologetic, unashamed, the spinster is made huge and powerful by her unorthodox contentment.

Like Emerson's eye—"the first circle" and "the horizon which it forms," "the primary figure repeated without end"—the speaker's way of seeing makes her "Swell" so "Horizons" are "in" her breast, not somewhere far off, at some rainbow's end. This powerful "She" who snickers at romantic conventions that would usher women through life and make them brides would never make a poetess who celebrates husband and "Wedded" domestic circumference. Like the speaker of "Wild Nights," a woman who says such things is out of society's control. Unlike the ballerina who cannot dance upon her toes (P 326), this woman does not even pretend to be conventionally coy. Nor is her message heavily coded. This voice, like that which utters the breathless sexuality of "Wild Nights," is unequivocal and champions female power.

When the poem was printed in the *New England Quarterly* in 1947, then more widely disseminated by Thomas Johnson in his variorum edition in 1955, that gap created by Mabel Loomis Todd was filled (as many of those created by Johnson himself are now being filled by Ralph W. Franklin). Other gaps, like those imposed by "Austin," can only be partially filled. Although we can see that someone sought to silence her powerful sexuality and produce in print a more conventional woman than Dickinson's written record would allow, we must live with the fact of these gaps. Their context shows what was the nature of the excised expressions, and sometimes, as in the case of "One Sister have I in the house," we can know exactly what is beneath the blot. Yet we must be careful when studying erasures, which, like the elder Hamlet and the nine lost books of Sappho, call out to us though we cannot quite see them. It is well known that Elizabeth Barrett Browning's *Aurora Leigh* was one of Dickinson's favorites, and it offers, perhaps, the best advice to keep in mind when pondering such forced silences. When the poem's Marian Erle learned to read, she had to depend on a "pedlar" to provide mutilated volumes. He would

> toss her down
> Some stray odd volume from his heavy pack,
> A Thomson's Seasons, mulcted of the Spring,
> Or half a play of Shakespeare's torn across
> (She had to guess the bottom of a page
> By just the top sometimes,—as difficult,
> As, sitting on the moon, to guess the earth!)
>
> (III, 972–978)

When forced to sit on "Austin's" moon to guess Dickinson's earth, our crescent of reading lacks (P 909).

When something is cut out of a letter, there is not the same there *there* anymore. Yet to ignore the imposed silences now there is to create another erasure. We do not ignore the "Master" letters because they create more gaps than they fill. In fact, critical attention lavished on them perpetuates the erasures and widens the gaps initiated by "Austin." With the exception of the just-published *Heath Anthology of American Literature*, the most recent anthologies, for example, indicate that Dickinson's primary correspondences were with Higginson and Master, while, by ignoring it, they devalue her most prolific correspondence with Sue.[41]

The Primary Correspondence

So Dickinson's primary correspondence is most often slighted while attention is lavished on the letters written to or about (as in the case of Charles Wadsworth) men; and the word of the other woman, Mabel Loomis Todd, about the wife, "dear Sue," has been treated as fact and, as Oberhaus notes, has worked "to obscure Sue's close relationship with Dickinson." Dickinson's most powerful relationship—personally, poetically, even politically—was with her beloved friend and sister, Sue.[42] Intimate for nearly forty years, their relationship knew anger as well as joy, ambivalence as well as clarity in feeling, periods of intense daily interactions and periods of separation. This singular relationship makes, therefore, a good standard of comparison for all of Dickinson's other relationships. Yet over the past century, one misrepresentation has led to another, and the cycle continues.[43] So many gaps in her texts have been created by efforts to hide Dickinson's blasphemy, be it lesbian or disrespectful of the patriarchal bastion of marriage. And those gaps have been imposed on our reading.

Reminding us that Mary Wollstonecraft was much maligned for exercising sexual freedom and that "Barrett Browning was praised for her blameless sexual life," Sandra Gilbert and Susan Gubar note the eroticism of Dickinson's "A Word made Flesh" and say that traditionally "genius and sexuality *are* diseases in women, diseases akin to madness."[44] From the beginning, those who have loved Emily Dickinson or found themselves somehow invested in her virginal image have sought to excise her powerful sexuality and, by reading the expression of her eroticism as submission, helplessness, and feminine, unrequited emotion out of control, have sought to spiritualize and "normalize" what she says. As the inordinate attention to the "Master" letters evinces, these attempts to hide the range of Dickinson's love and sexuality have not helped to further our understanding and reading of Dickinson. On the other hand, recognizing Dickinson's love as lesbian desire suggests not only different stories about her life, but can clarify and enhance our reading so that her cross-dressing characters and speakers, her impassioned rhetoric to Sue, "Austin's" responses to those inflamed expressions, and the rhetoric of similarity in many of her love poems make a new sense: the "Garnet to Garnet – " and "Gold – to Gold – " of "Title divine – is mine!" (P 1072), images glittering and enticing but hardened and cold, are perfect for articulating lesbian desire thwarted in a heterosexist culture and are both more intelligible and complex when read with that possibility allowed.[45]

Read with Dickinson's love for Sue in mind, Dickinson's "Calvary of Love" poems, replete with a rhetoric of similarity, long noticed and of late getting considerable attention, are no longer so mysterious.[46] In fact, for a woman who was in love with a woman whose exotic religious interests are well known, the poems are most befitting. "Title divine – is mine," the most famous of these, is usually discussed when one is proposing Samuel Bowles as a lover or as a candidate for "Master" because he was one of only two Dickinson correspondents whom we know received the poem. Yet when Dickinson sent Bowles a copy, she appended it with a note of entreaty—"You will tell no other?"—clearly asking him to keep one of her secrets. I propose that, if readers construe the poem as referring to an actual situation, then when she sent Bowles the poem, she was confiding in him, telling him about another situation, not about her feelings for him. Sue was the other recipient of a version of this poem; and Dickinson simply signed that copy "Emily":

> Title divine, is mine.
> The Wife without
> the Sign.
> Acute Degree
> Conferred on me –
> Empress of Calvary –
> Royal, all but the
> Crown –
> Betrothed, without
> the Swoon
> God gives us Women –
> When You hold
> Garnet to Garnet –
> Gold – to Gold –
> Born – Bridalled –
> Shrouded –
> In a Day –
> Tri Victory –

"My Husband" –
Women say
Stroking the Melody –
Is this the Way –

(H 361; P 1072, 1860s)

Obviously this poem is about a love not sanctioned by public vows. Titles are filed in the clerk's office, not worn around one's finger or atop one's head like a crown, that public ornament signifying royalty. Anyone who could write such a poem is self-conscious about certain expressions of love and Dickinson acknowledges that her speaker is not like a woman

> . . . in swoon,
> To whom life creeps back in form of death,
> With a sense of separation, a blind pain
> Of blank obstruction, and a roar i' the ears
> Of visionary chariots which retreat
> As earth grows clearer . . . slowly, by degrees . . .
>
> (*AURORA LEIGH* I, 559–565)

Hers is not the deathlike state that she attributes to conventional marriage where women are enamored with the sounds of their title—"My Husband," Mrs.—and stroke the melody, caressing those rather than the corporeal spouse. Nor is the relationship she describes a completely un-complicated, blissful union. Wedlock is also deadlock, and the speaker says she is "Born – Bridalled – / Shrouded – ." Using terms reflecting her ap-parent ambivalence, in but a day the speaker is both born again and dressed for death when she is adorned like a bride. Juxtaposed here are life and death with the "Bridalled" state sandwiched between them. *Bridal* connotes a wedding feast or festival and the jollity associated with bride-ale. Yet it puns on *bridled*. The newlywed woman may swoon, but in ac-cepting the vows of a nineteenth-century wife—to love, honor, and obey—the bride already has a bit in her mouth. Her desires must be cur-tailed to meet the approval of her husband. Faced with such circumscrip-tion, many a woman bridles. Shroud's connotations are multifarious as well. Women are shrouded behind their wedding veils; the dead are shrouded in winding sheets. Here nuptial images, supposedly full of life, are synonymous with those of death. In "I'm 'wife'— I've finished that —" (F 9; P 199), Dickinson declares women eclipsed by their husbands, and, with shroud, she also calls to mind Polonius hidden behind the arras. In this poem, love is not a happy, publicly celebrated affair, but a secret and a crucifixion.[47]

A Calvary Experience

It is nothing new to recognize that Dickinson depicts love as a Calvary experience. Sewall, among others, has suggested that "Title divine" is possibly a poem in which she is "the imagined wife of Samuel Bowles" (*Life* 2:405), a poem in which a love that can never be realized crucifies her. Sewall observes, "There are scores of poems from the late 1850s, many of them clearly love poems, that Emily did not send to Bowles" (*Life* 2:496). Her loving remarks of the late 1850s and the early 1860s were to Sue. In spite of his intimacy with the Dickinsons, Bowles may or may not have understood the poem that Dickinson forwarded to him. More surely Sue understood the poem when Dickinson forwarded it to her; for in context of their correspondence, the poem makes sense.

In Sue's version, an odd line appears. For her beloved, Dickinson adds "Tri Victory – ." By itself, this alteration befuddles: is Dickinson punning on "try" and recommending that Sue attempt to celebrate her wifely circumference, or is she speaking of some three-way triumph? Considering the line in context of some of her other writing offers illumination, if not an answer.

Around February 1861, when Dickinson tells Bowles that Vinnie, Sue, and she all hope he is recovering from his sciatica, she proclaims it a "tri-Hope" (L 229). If she uses a similar formula in the poem, are the three people involved Bowles, his wife Mary, and Emily? If so, why is the "Tri" line not included in his copy? The most intense triangle in which he was involved was with his wife and her cousin, his intimate, Maria Whitney. Since the poem articulates the reality of secret betrothal, of that which cannot be publicly acknowledged, and since the imagery is, as in "Like Eyes that Looked on Wastes – " (F 32; P 458), where Queens make each other Queens (not Kings), a rhetoric of similarity, not difference, this "Tri" may be punning off the fact of her triangle with her sister-in-law and brother. To speak of a situation of homoerotic/incestuous bonding, such rhetoric is apt, as is the metaphor of crucifixion.

Like Jesus, who had to be nailed to a cross to become a messiah, and like the Queens, who find only a wasteland for their love and "reign" by "perish[ing]," the Empress proclaims her royal realm the site of the Cross.

Thus do crucifying images accompany this rhetoric of sameness. In "Title divine," the poem's speaker says this secret title confers "Acute Degree" and that her Golgotha makes her "Empress." From the columns of the *Republican*, it is clear that Bowles was well acquainted with the women poets of his day, whose work tended to take "secret sorrow" as a major theme. In fact, in 1860 he plainly expressed his doubts about "another kind of writing only too common . . . the literature of misery," written chiefly by "women, gifted women may be, full of thought and feeling and fancy, but poor, lonely and unhappy."[48] Such private pain made women, who were already assumed to be capable of greater feeling than men, even more sensitive. As Cheryl Walker observes, "By defining the poet in terms of the capacity for pain, they implied that women had a special talent for verse."[49] When Bowles and Sue read "Acute Degree," they must have known what Dickinson meant by it. Other Calvary poems explicate her phrase. In three of these, this private pain and its heightening of sensitivity are the theme. In "I dreaded that first Robin, so," (F 17; P 348), nearing the bird "hurts a little," "Pianos in the Woods" sometimes have the "power to mangle," and "Daffodils" can "pierce." But the poem's speaker has grown "some accustomed" to the intense feeling and this "Queen of Calvary –" lifts her "childish Plumes" "in bereaved acknowledgment / Of" nature's "unthinking Drums – ." Here, as elsewhere in Dickinson's work, nature is not particularly hostile, nor are its creatures especially cognizant of her speaker's plight and coming near, as they did for Snow White, to take care of her. They are merely separate from her, and going about their business. It is her perception of them that has been profoundly altered and makes her aesthetic "Acute." Acronymically A.D. the phrase signifies that she lives not "in the year of our Lord," but in a time lorded by her grief; when her anguish was born, the speaker's senses were made raw.

If, as Sewall and others have suggested, this is an epistolary poem referring to real events, considering the kind of copies Dickinson sent to each of them, "Title divine" is more likely to be about Dickinson's decades-long love for Sue than for Bowles. Certainly many of the rest of the "Calvary of Love" poems support such an interpretation (the reader might consult F 33, P 313; F 13, P 322; F 20, P 364; F 31, P 549; F 30, P 553; F 27, P 561; F 28, P 568; F 15, P 577; F 32, P 620; F 36, P 725). Dickinson made fair copies of all these poems in the early 1860s; several show lovers who are equals; all emphasize a love crucified. When Dickinson chooses images in these, the crimson and gold colors that reflect the blood of crucifixion as well as the royal weeds of an empress, they do not reflect the hierarchy and difference of heterosexual relations in patriarchy, but the sameness and equality of lesbian relations. In "There came a Day [perhaps the day she was born, bridalled, and shrouded] __ at / Summer's full – " (F 13; P 322), "Each was to each – the sealed church –" and "Each – bound the other's / Crucifix – ." "Each to each" echoes "We learned the Whole of Love – " (F 28; P 568) and the lines

> Think of it Lover! I and Thee
> Permitted – face to face to be –

of "If I may have it, when its' / dead" (F 15; P 577). As Emily and Sue often mirror one another—in their descriptions of literature's power to make one feel extraordinary (see L 238, L 342a), in Sue's highly allusive obituary of Emily—so do the lovers in these poems. As far as we know, only "Title divine" and "There came a Day" were "published" by Dickinson to any of her contemporaries. Higginson, who received "There came a Day," and Bowles got one poem each; Sue got copies of both poems. This fact, viewed in light of the mutilations to Dickinson's affectionate expressions for and about Sue and of their lifelong intimacy, suggests that, unless Dickinson's Calvary of Love was a fiction, Sue was the primary object of Dickinson's erotic desire.

What it confirms, however, is Sue's ultimate importance as a constant audience for Dickinson's poetry. To read "Title divine" as a biographical document referring to Dickinson's imagining herself as the "wife" of anybody runs the risk of reducing criticism to gossip. What is most exciting, therefore, is not identifying the "real" object(s) of Dickinson's most profound erotic attractions, but the ways in which she transformed homoerotic desires into compelling literature. Like many women writers of her day, Dickinson donned conventional appearances to voice radical departure from official rhetoric extolling wives and motherhood. Unfortunately, the will to conceal the nature of Dickinson's personal affections has clouded perceptions of both her powerful ironic play with nineteenth-century cultural stereotypes and the circumstances she found most enabling for her literary production.

If all these letters and poems and especially the erotic and seductive expressions had been sent to a man, little doubt would remain that he was the "Master" so many have spent so much time looking for. Yet the majority, or "Corporation" (L 233), recoils from Dickinson's powerful lesbian eros. Dickinson sent many poems to Sue about perception and its power, and it seems that the various assumptions that label homosexuality as neurotic, maladjusted, and underdeveloped have determined the way that Dickinson's esteem for her sister-in-law has generally been perceived. At best, it has been seen as "a real tragedy"; [50] at worst, it has been denied and erased. Like any lifelong love relationship, the love between these two women knew its ups and downs. Although tension in such an intense involvement is to be expected, any voicing of friction between these two has been used to discount their thirty years of living side by side. Dickinson seemed aware that such love may well call for defenses and for each woman to be a fortress for the other. In "the Dimpled War"

> Without a Formula we fought
> Each was to each the Pink Redoubt –
>
> (P 1529, ABOUT 1881)

After three decades, when she characterizes their love to Sue, she does not compare it to the adolescent, swept-away passion of Romeo and Juliet, but to the sophisticated, persistent, if tired, love of Antony and Cleopatra. Talking in Shakespeare, Dickinson tells of the problematic relationship of this love between two women, between the woman who claimed to put her dear female friend before all others and the other who loved her friend and sister but took a husband:

> Susan's Calls are
> like Antony's
> Supper –
> "And pays his
> Heart for what
> his Eyes eat,
> only –"
>   Emily '
>
> (H B 24; L 854, ABOUT 1883; SEE
> *ANTONY AND CLEOPATRA II*, II, 225–226)

A Persistent Image and Persistent Questions

Many unanswered and probably unanswerable questions persist about Dickinson's relationship with and affection for her sister-in-law; yet it is certain that the poet's expressions to and about Sue provoked censorship. It can probably never be known who ordered whom to do what when or who did what when; nevertheless, to arrive at some understanding of the nature of the relationship these mutilations sought to occlude is crucial to advance understanding of Dickinson's poetic production and the history of its reception among Dickinson scholars and other readers. These erasures are, in the words of Tillie Olsen, "not *natural* silences" (i.e., neither inevitable nor necessary),[51] and some of the ruptures created by them need not be permanent. From the beginning of the first century of Dickinson study, Sue Dickinson's importance has been downplayed. We are indebted to one of husband Austin's other women, Loomis Todd, for initially editing and translating Emily Dickinson's texts into mass reproducible works. That the adulterous editor would want to deemphasize the importance of her lover's wife to the poet whom Loomis Todd commodified but never met face to face is not at all surprising. Twenty years after the inaugural print volumes, when Dickinson's niece, Martha Dickinson Bianchi, sought to accentuate the importance of her mother Sue to Dickinson's literary production, the great chain of Aunt Emily's poetic being had already been established.

Willis J. Buckingham recently pointed out that much of twentieth-century Dickinson criticism has misunderstood and mischaracterized the late nineteenth-century reponses to her originality as wholly negative, when in fact her fin de siècle publication was at a time when many "could feel, and take pleasure in, the alien force of her voice."[52] However, by writing and editing against the more conservative responses espoused in the "religious family weeklies" which contributed so profoundly to "popular literary tastes," and by writing and editing against Sue's influence on her, certain misunderstandings of Dickinson's first readers have been, as Jauss reminds us, "sustained and enriched in a chain of receptions from generation to generation."[53] One of the most comprehensive, finest biographies of the poet, Sewall's National Book Award-winning *Life of Emily Dickinson* is, as he scrupulously reminds us in the preface, the culmination of studies enriching the Higginson-Todd-Bingham line of reception, for it was written at the request of Millicent Todd Bingham to tell "'the whole story' of her mother's involvement . . . but in the setting of the larger story of Emily Dickinson" (*Life* 1:xiv).

At the advent of a second century of reading Emily Dickinson, scholarly attention may now focus on developing understandings of the poet's most frequent contemporary reader, Sue, filling what gaps we can, with readers well aware that some omissions, both foisted on the written record and inherent in the dynamics of language itself, can never be closed.

To   fill   a   Gap
Insert   the   Thing   that
Caused it –
Block   it   up
With   Other – and 'twill
yawn   the   more –
You   cannot   + Solder   an
Abyss
With   Air –

+ Plug   a   Sepulchre –

(F 31; P 546)

Like Gwendolyn Brooks talking about Dickinson's influence, each reader might respond that to fill a gap, then, "is almost hopeless, because Emily [Dickinson] and I are so absolutely different in the details of our lives." As Brooks continues, however, she discovers that she has much to say about Dickinson's poetic artistry, about her powerful combinations of ordinary words to make extraordinary meanings, which, like magic, transform the reader's way of looking at the quotidian by offering revelation in exhilarating juxtapositions of the routine. In other words, when Brooks stops dwelling on the differences of Dickinson's life and concentrates on her forerunner's literary endeavors, she is, like Dickinson reading Elizabeth Barrett Browning, "absolutely enchanted" (F 29; P 593).[54] As a feminist literary critic, I view Dickinson's biographical circumstances as important, but only for the ways in which they elucidate her poetic career, the poems and letter-poems themselves, and subsequent reception of those documents. To recover what can be known about Dickinson's most sustained literary relationship begins to supply a long-standing missing link in the chain of her poetic being.

Hiding, overlooking, or ignoring Dickinson's love for women, especially Sue, and privileging her affections and regard for men, especially "Master," cloaks Dickinson in mystery, befuddles critics, confuses issues, and closes texts. Some even maintain that of the more than one thousand letters still extant, "three letters, which Emily Dickinson drafted to a man she called 'Master,' stand near the heart of her mystery" (ML 5). Such a declaration replicates the preoccupations of many a scholar and popular reader who seem convinced that identifying the object of this apparent ardor for "Master" would explain Dickinson the poet. There are many stories of "the second story," captivity narratives seeking to explain her much ballyhooed withdrawal, that subordinate Dickinson's literary productions to her personality even as they offer literary precedent for the tale.[55] The literal second story in the Dickinson Homestead, open to tourists certain days and hours of the week, stands as something of a sanctuary for this widely shared nostalgia for a lovelorn spinster writer. The pictures most prominently displayed on Dickinson's bedroom wall are of those men many have supposed was "Master"—Charles Wadsworth, Samuel Bowles, and Judge Lord—and serve as reminders of a brokenhearted virgin driven to writing verse. With her furniture mostly at Harvard and the pictures with which she decorated her walls—of Barrett Browning, George Eliot, and Thomas Carlyle—counterpointed by those men rumored to be most important to her, it is hard to imagine Emily Dickinson walking those rooms. Thus to the commodification of Dickinson Adrienne Rich responds:

> In Emily Dickinson's house in Amherst
> cocktails are served   the scholars
> gather in celebration
> their pious or clinical legends
> festoon the walls like imitations
> of period patterns
>
> (. . . *and, as I feared, my "life" was made a "victim"*) [56]

A century of edition after edition of her poems and letters, numerous biographies, a one-woman-show-of-a-play performed around the country and broadcast for PBS, a sixty-second biographical sketch produced for CBS, a dance by Martha Graham based on her spirit, a place setting at *The Dinner Party* by Judy Chicago, at least two records of readings, numerous musical settings of her poems, a murder mystery, a commemorative stamp, a ceremonial burial in the Poet's Corner at St. John's Cathedral in New York City, a centenary celebration of her work by contemporary women poets reading for two days at Seton Hall University (April 10–11, 1986), a *Peanuts* daily strip all her own (November 21, 1984), *Bloom County* (September 25, 1988) and *Outland* (August 26, 1990) Sunday tributes, a salute on NBC's prime-time comedy series "Cheers" at a Thanksgiving dinner (November 27, 1986), the frequent subject of "Jeopardy" answers, an Emily Dickinson throw pillow, an Emily Dickinson cookbook, and the use of "Because I could not stop for Death" to appeal for organ donors (*Washington Post*, June 3, 1991) all attest to the fact that she is a Hero in American culture. But the Emily Dickinson celebrated often seems to have as much to do with the "type of poetess" as an American "cultural phemomenon" Walker analyzes as it has to do with the flesh-and-blood woman who produced hundreds of poems and letters in a house on Main in Amherst, Massachusetts.[57]

Perpetuating a long-established pattern, editorial license bolsters the image Simon and Garfunkel reiterated of a future Miss Lonelyheart reading her "Em'ly Dickinson" while the seriously agonizing young bard studies his Robert Frost. That one can easily find greeting cards with girlish gushings of a very young woman just beginning to think of herself as a poet hints at what a close look at the two record set, *Emily Dickinson—A Self Portrait*, makes clear: it is the idea of Emily in bridal white (see the cover of *The Marriage of Emily Dickinson*[58]), pining, made especially sensitive by unrequited love, rather than the prolific poet who wrote Thomas Higginson's wife, "I wish you were strong like me" (L 481), who has captured the popular imagination. One of the greeting cards quotes a letter to her brother as if it had been bound and folded into one of her fascicles:

Today is very beautiful
just as bright, just as blue,
just as green and as white
and as crimson
as the cherry trees
in full bloom,
and the half-opening
peach blossoms
and the grass just waving,
and sky and hill and cloud
can make it, if they try.

How I wish you were here.

(L 122, MAY 7, 1853)

Like Thomas Johnson producing "There is another sky" (P 2; L 58, October 17, 1851), the greeting-card editor produces a Rod McKuen–like poem from an early letter that does not feature the unusual line breaks, nor does it, as did so many letters from the 1860s on, look like a lyric poem. A decade later Dickinson herself would begin to experiment with genre and force readers and editors to admit "doubt where the letter leaves off and the poem begins" (L xv). But Johnson produces an early poem from a letter to her brother, while the anonymous editor of the greeting card manufactures a poem befitting a poetess in distress from Dickinson's epistolary expression. In doing so, they attempt to create conditions which, not having existed in the first place, are of course irrecoverable.

Though there is, perhaps, a glimmer of hope in an apparently conventional "thirtysomething" version of Dickinson who rather bitchily tells the whiny untenured English professor—"I don't think I like you. You've got a very poor attitude" (April 10, 1990)—nostalgic impulses permeate the culture grown up around the legends and volumes of poetry and letters, biography, and criticism produced in the name of Emily Dickinson. Starring Julie Harris, who for so long headlined *The Belle of Amherst* as the gingerbread-bearing poet finally enthralled with "Master," the *Self-Portrait* recording offers us a lovelorn lady, obsessed with renunciation and the Father God and Father, whose major accomplishment was that she "domesticated heartbreak" (liner notes). The double album featuring a selection of Dickinson's letters and poems devotes most of its energies to her juvenilia and supposed disappointments in love, and, representing her correspondence with Sue, offers only three letters to her "breath from Gibraltar" (L 722, late summer 1881). Spinning the story between two women in the usual way, these meager few are provocatively edited. One letter that talks of the hard and cold hearts both women bear for the young men and proclaims that "there's a big *future* waiting" for Emily and Sue is, listeners are told, addressed to "my sister-in-law to be." One need look no further than Johnson's scholarly transcriptions to see that this is not the case (see L 85, April 5, 1852). One of Dickinson's longest, the letter is mostly about "big tears," "bitter tears," and missing and loving "Susie." Mentioned only as an afterthought, Austin, Sue's future husband, is tucked into the postscript, as if he is not of any particular interest to Sue. In fact, in this letter, Dickinson never alludes to their relationship as prospective in-laws. In a letter to Austin also quoted on this album, there is a sentence that makes it clear that when Dickinson says she will take his place, she means his place beside Sue. But on the album the remark is torn from the context in which it was written and spliced into a letter in which it does not appear so the listener has no clear idea of what place she means (L 115 edited into L 118, both April 1853).

As does Dickinson's room preserved for tourists, so this record tells more about audience fascinations and the nineteenth-century image consonant with preconceived notions of literary history and women's role in culture than it reveals about her actual poetic production and the actual world of nineteenth-century literary women. It is perhaps no surprise that popular culture conventionalizes Dickinson, but of scholarly significance are the many ways in which these productions parallel how she has been tamed as well by serious biographers and critics who continue to shroud her in sentimental and exclusively heterosexual notions, and see something of a weak, defeated damsel instead of a writer, strong and self-aware. In "The Spirit of Place," Rich continues:

> The remnants pawed   the relics
> the cult assembled in the bedroom
>
> and you   whose teeth were set on edge by churches
> resist your shrine
>
> escape
> are found
> nowhere
> unless in words   (your own)

The examples in this chapter's preceding sections show that in landmarks memorializing her, biographies, and much literary criticism, the shrewd, self-conscious poet who had reasons for her "High Behavior" (L 282, about 1863) is normalized, thus contained for her role as America's premier female poet. As Walker has shown, the white dress, especial sensitivities, unrequited love, and reclusiveness were stock traits of the nineteenth-century poetess widely advertised by real figures like Lucretia Davidson, Lucy Larcom, Anne Lynch, Maria Brooks, Frances Osgood, and even Christina Rossetti, as well as by literary characters like Miss Archer of Longfellow's *Kavanagh*, a favorite of Austin, Sue, and Emily. Following the masculinizing impact of the *Cambridge History of American Literature* (1917–1921) and D. H. Lawrence's *Studies in Classic American Literature* (1923), women writers were neglected,[59] and a cultural amnesia allowed readers and scholars alike to forget just how conventional "stories of the second story," of the withdrawal of the mothlike writer in the white gown, are. Printed in the 1890s to promote the poet, the small, ladylike, white leather gilt-edged volumes with suitable subject categories like "Life," "Love," "Nature," and "Time and Eternity" and the essays by Higginson and Loomis Todd touting Dickinson's reclusion present an image which American audiences were prepared to like. These little books present a woman writer, who, though rather eccentric, was not doing anything especially radical with her poems. These first editors of Dickinson, then, perceived unusual techniques of her poetry as quirks to be amended.

With Jauss and Frost, "knowing how way leads on to way," readers can see that this figure has been reproduced time and again in more or less variant forms to suit the critical moment. In this way, her unusual life and its many aspects which can never be fully explained have been bound into forms that intrigue even as they enable a perception of Dickinson as, however exceptional, within lines already drawn for nineteenth-century American white upper-class women whose most passionate friendships were with other women. Likewise, her literary productions have been bound into increasingly more sophisticated versions that conform to pre-determined ideas of what makes a poem, an edition of poems, a letter, an edition of letters, a book. By reviewing the variously manifested predominance of this "half-cracked" figure, my point has not been to discount those who produced stories of Emily Dickinson's life and her works for other cultural moments, but to set the stage to discover what a different slant of attention uncovers about her writing processes and objectives in this particular moment. In closing this chapter, more reflections on the two most profound issues for Dickinson study, textuality and sexuality, both of which influenced the perpetuation of the "scribbling" virgin, are warranted.

With sexuality so bound up with notions of her intentions and conceptions of texts "proper" enough for reproduction, current attitudes toward eroticism bear more consideration. In the turn toward the twenty-first century, audiences are more willing to accept sexual desires not necessarily substantiating the myth of an unswerving heterosexual highroad. Therefore, confronted with poems in which she sneers at conventional wifehood or letters in which she proclaims her passionate, sexually charged affections for another woman, readers feel less compelled to explain these away in schemes and terms designed within heterosexist discourse. In analogous ways, with so many gender biases acknowledged, readers today are more willing to accept that, throughout history, and certainly in nineteenth-century America, determined women have learned the power of maintaining the appearance of being domesticated even as they go about their business, subverting patriarchal order. As we are beginning to learn the follies of reading many of the women writers contemporary with Dickinson too simplistically, without recognizing their "shifting literary masks," [60] so we should be wary of overly neat interpretations of her erotic appetites. When reading beyond heterosexuality, the prevailing urge has been to discern that which is Not Me from that which is Like Me. Yet such dichotomies may be as overly simple as they are easier and more soothing to read.

As there is for steady demarcation between male and female, there is still a nostalgia, heterosexual and homosexual, which maintains that homoeroticism is entirely different from heteroeroticism and which wants "natural, fixed" differences in sexual desire as well as between the sexes. Though often a strategy for gay and lesbian will to power, such insistence can also be used to brutalize and oppress homosexuals. It has yet to be seen how, like "the promotion of fixed sexual differences," the promotion of fixed differences in sexual desire—"whether they are described as natural or culturally constructed—does anything but maintain an all too familiar system of oppositions and stereotypes."[61] The 1989 legislation stipulating what kinds of artistic enterprises may and may not be funded by the National Endowment for the Arts, approved by a U.S. Senate voice vote on July 26 and passed in slightly modified form in September, justifies itself according to such an ideology of difference. In the first specification of this amendment, which has never been altered, blatant stereotyping equates sadomasochism, homoeroticism, and the exploitation of children: "None of the funds authorized to be appropriated pursuant to this Act may be used to promote, disseminate, or produce—(1) obscene or indecent materials, including but not limited to depictions of sadomasochism, homoeroticism, the exploitation of children, or individuals engaged in sex acts. . . ."[62] Obviously, the thrust of this proposal is to protect the heterosexually pure from any contaminating deviant body. Key to the assumptions delineated is the belief that homoeroticism and sadomasochism can be readily identified, labeled dangerously different, then prohibited.[63] Most dangerous is this faith in consensus and stable definitions that labels the homosexual as Not Like the law-abiding rest of "us." In fact, heterosexist notions of "normality" persist, even within deconstruction.[64] Not surprisingly, some have wanted to protect Emily Dickinson from the contaminating label of homoeroticism.

This belief in an ability to separate pure from profane bodies parallels yearnings for stable definitions of Dickinson's sexual desires as well as for *author*itative printings of her texts. Conversely, though no responsible critic would want to underestimate the significance of homosexual difference, none should make the story of difference the whole, therefore the only, gay/lesbian story. Likewise, none would want to minimize the differences—suggestive dashes, chirography, and lineation—of Dickinson's texts and the impossibility of translating those to print, but neither should one conclude that, so different from mass-produced typeface, these can be noted as such, then dismissed as trivial or something very much other than what can be shared in critical dialogue. Both her sexual desires and textual productions, so variant in form and with so many variants, challenge audience complacency and force readers to ask, "What are the guidelines for reading these matters of sex and texts?" Instead of insisting on determin-

ing discrete bodies—a sexual being who is definitively heterosexual, lesbian, bisexual, or asexual and a textual body for which one variant, stanzaic
division, or scheme of lineation is definitively preferable—readers, remembering the "heteroglossia" of all forms of communication, might acknowledge that in "unfinished" texts so apparently informal, Dickinson
formalizes relationships that already exist between readers and texts.[65] To
put it crudely, while transcription appears to fix texts, and definitions to
delimit the realms of sexual desire, different contexts and different readers
always augment and destabilize meaning, and the documents bequeathed
by the poet with a "Vice for Voices" (A 743a; PF 19), who wrote "A pen
has so many inflections and a Voice but one" (L 470), show that she did
not need poststructural theories to elaborate her consciousness of this.

At issue for those who want to return to a mythical time when sex
was clearly, as H.D. put it, "A2 or B3" and texts were simply like Grecian
urns is the power over (and of) interpretation. As in so many critical
struggles, particularly in disagreements about feminism, "the battle-
ground is representation itself," for "identity and reality are created within
representation,"[66] and interpretations appear easier to control in realms of
definitude. As we have seen, in various ways, editors, critics, and biographers have sought to shore up particular depictions of Dickinson's poems,
letters, intentions, and life. But always multivoiced, representations also
tell stories they do not intend as well as those the author and editors mean
to convey. For example, by representing Dickinson's letters and poems
with changes to excise affectionate reference to Sue, "Austin" unwittingly
yet inevitably points a reader's attention to the loving expressions that
"he" wanted to hide.

This Story of Reading

Joining analyses of her erotic and textual intentions, and explicating
various connections between expressions of unconventional passions and
productions of anomalous works, my story of reading Dickinson's primary
correspondences is precisely the kind of interpretation her first editors
intended to discourage. As we have seen, different kinds of material in-
terventions by others have constituted and created interpretations that
obscure Dickinson's biographical and poetic differences. By changing lineation, punctuation, and spelling (especially her calligraphic orthography),
by deleting sections of poems and deleting sections of letters, by titling
untitled poems, by selectively regrouping poems into "safe" standard cate-

gories or regrouping the documents to divorce poems from the context of their original presentation in letters or fascicles, and even by redecorating the walls of her room to showcase rumors about love unrequited, editors, critics, and biographers have rearranged Dickinson's literary and biographical records to emphasize her timidities and to erase her aggressiveness. Instead of closing off Dickinson's texts and life by translating her irregularities into regular forms easier to read (variously shaped and angled dashes into uniform typeface and reclusion into profound disappointment or neurosis), this study advocates a careful consciousness regarding that which, so obvious, may well be taken for granted: how notions of who the author is (biography) influence the kind of book editors and publishers imagine making from her work (reproduction), and how both in turn influence readers' perceptions of the poet and her role in presenting such poems (reception), which then influence new biographies and reproductions.

To explore these intertextualities, the last four chapters of this book tell a story of reading what may be called Dickinson's "major" correspondences. These chapters consider what the surviving documents to her favorite correspondent and to the elusive character "Master," whom we know only through her writing, suggest about her relationships with her readers and editors and reveal about her creative processes. Since one study cannot examine all the correspondences, I have selected that to Sue, granted the most attention by Dickinson, and that to "Master," granted the most attention by her audiences, to adduce ways in which the cycle of reception can be illuminatingly broken. Like Dickinson's relationship with Sue, which resists easy classification, her literary productions that resist translation into print or challenge our wisdom about cultural history have, "just like" traditional attitudes toward "woman," been devalued. By taking cues from her writing, in this chapter I have outlined collisions between century-old reconstructions of her work and the actual archival record to begin to expand our valuations so that Dickinson herself "mothers" a whole new way of receiving her literary productions. To prepare to interrogate the two correspondences and also to begin to expand our poetic valuations, in the next chapter I shall survey some of the most formidable issues of textual reproduction in light of what can be learned from reading Dickinson reading.

I was in a **Printing house** in Hell & saw the method in which knowledge is transmitted from generation to generation.

—WILLIAM BLAKE, *THE MARRIAGE OF HEAVEN AND HELL*

No further trace
of the printer

IN / HIS / SOLITUDE / To The

Reader the work
Prayers, &c. belonging
to no one without
Reasons

—SUSAN HOWE, *A BIBLIOGRAPHY OF THE KING'S BOOK OR EIKON BASILIKE*

I came to explore the wreck.
The words are purposes.
The words are maps.

—ADRIENNE RICH, "DIVING INTO THE WRECK"

Two Rowing in Eden: Reading Dickinson Reading

Whether consciously considered or not, conceptions of authorial intention inform critical stories of reading, and formulations in the genealogy of Dickinson study are no exception. After discussing why Dickinson's phrase "Rowing in Eden" is appropriate to name new modes of reading and different attitudes toward poetic valuations inspired by the poet's holograph productions, the second part of this chapter interrogates speculations about her intentionalities and their relationships to literary and intellectual property, while the third section outlines some strategies for reading Dickinson anew.

Texts and Territories

Geographical and cartographical metaphors of exploration have for obvious and much discussed reasons been important to New World literature and consciousness and are, not surprisingly, often highlighted in Dickinson's works.[1] Therefore, such a metaphor is especially useful to describe the "new world" opened by new methods for reading devised from studying Dickinson's holograph productions. That "Rowing in Eden"—a phrase from what is widely regarded to be Dickinson's most erotic poem—christens this approach is most fitting since these procedures parallel her activities as reader. Since "Wild Nights – Wild Nights!" (F 11; P 249) couples the sexual with the textual, the lyric's penultimate phrase connotes both action and place in erotic context. While the action is smooth and rhythmic, the place is the site (in Judeo-Christian mythology) of humanity's Mother's seduction and the consequent great Fall into knowledge and sin. Since, like assumptions about Sappho's homosexual or heterosexual desire which presuppose interpretations of the Greek's lyrics, assumptions about her womanhood or her sexual desires often color interpretations of Dickinson's writings, the phrase is at least doubly appropriate.[2]

To row, one must expend energy, extend muscle. Neither an especially contentious nor combative activity (here I do not concern myself with the competition of crews but with the strokes in which they are engaged), rowing nevertheless strains muscles. Like the study of reading, rowing, which can be enacted in the privacy of one's garret with a machine or solitarily in a single-seat kayak or canoe, is also often performed in concert with others. A feat of coordination, even the struggle to row is a relatively peaceful, if strenuous, exercise and an apt metaphor for depicting exchanges Dickinson herself appears to imagine between texts and readers. What the manuscripts tell us about her as a reader suggests that Dickinson expected anything but passivity from her audience. In Roland Barthes' terms, she wanted to inspire readers to be coproducers of texts, "methodological fields" which can be "*experienced only in an activity of production*" (an act of interpretation), not mere consumers of works, artifacts, or "fragment(s) of substance, occupying a part of the space of books (in a library for example)." Her poems are, then, always what he would call *writerly*, oriented toward their futures with readers.[3] That she did not regard works as untouchably sacred is obvious from her own role as reader, for Dickinson sometimes went so far as to cut up others' works to take an illustration or group of words to append her own. Unlike the mutilations to her poems and letters, this is not an angry or hostile act to excise offensive expressions, but a sign of a reader at play or engaged in dialogic drama, combining hers with others' literary productions, remaking both in the process. Nor is this a crude example of the readers Harold Bloom envisions always at war with texts, at best producing strong misreadings. Comparing the author's work of choosing words to quilting, Cristanne Miller muses that "Dickinson's poems are short, often nonlinear and fluid in form," revealing "a consciousness that without anxiety knows itself to be incapable of complete control" as she pieces together fragments of meaning.[4] This just as well applies to the fact of Dickinson's awareness that she is not in control of reader's responses. Imagining readers who interact with works to produce texts, this consciousness does not put anxiety over or battles for meaning center stage, but spotlights the meaning-producing processes of give and take between author and text, text and reader, reader and author, inevitable in reading.

Certainly Dickinson's punctuation marks, "dashes" which have inspired so many debates among critics and editors, suggest an author who expects readers, who must decide whether to regard the marks as substantive or accidental, to engage in textual production and in effect become co-authors. And when Dickinson describes a reading process in her question "Did you ever read one of her Poems backward, because the plunge from the front overturned you?" (PF 30), she does not portray such reading against conventional instructions as a violation. On the contrary, such reading, certainly a movement "from one condition of knowledge to another," seems an almost ecstatic engagement in search of sense.[5] Like Gwendolyn Brooks talking about one of her most famous poems, "The Mother," the interpretation of which resists resolution, Dickinson, hyperconscious of a pen's many inflections (L 470) and a pencil's "awful power" (L 656), is well aware that readers will "take from the poems what they need." Pulling "text from text," "forcing, abbreviating, pushing, padding, subtracting, riddling, interrogating, re-writing," Dickinson takes from others' words what she needs to make a point more "clear" (L 265) or to manufacture a "cartooning" layout.[6] On the surface of things, this may seem inconsistent with, in fact contradictory to, impulses of the principled writer who complained about editorial addition of a punctuation mark. But an editor laboring over a text to make a work for mass reproduction is in a very different position than the common reader, and while Dickinson objects to editors unnecessarily making decisions for readers, she, embracing the inevitable, invites readers to make decisions for themselves. Her manuscripts, with multiple variants and variant punctuation and line breaks, will not let us forget that reading is dialogic drama, always a matter of editing, of choosing what to privilege, what to subordinate. Her consternation toward editorial intervention is at the rather imperious addition of a question mark or comma and the fact that, sealed into print, such changes preempt and circumscribe subsequent readers' choices, which poets like Brooks and Dickinson expect and, by their indeterminate texts, demand.

In sharp contrast to critics or poets who present poems as objects for the initiated, a holy literary priesthood fond of exclusionary poetic politics which pretend to be no politics at all, these American women writers, so different from each other in race, cultural setting, and writerly choices, share an impulse "to define" a poetic "identity which is not merely personal but communal." As Alicia Ostriker has observed, "this impulse commonly extends itself toward the poem's audience, in poems created to function not as closed artifacts but as personal transactions between poets and readers."[7] For example, by making the reader's authorship—connecting variants to places in lines and diacritical marks to meanings suggested by the words and spaces around them—an integral component of the pleasure of reading her texts, Dickinson's project challenges rigid self-other boundaries as the prerogatives and roles of reader and writer mingle. Thus the ways in which Dickinson seeks to involve readers differs markedly from the strategies of a Pound or Eliot who calls upon esoteric or high-brow knowledge to interpret his poem "correctly." While their exclusionary objectives stress "literary traditions in large part the creation of writers who have unapologetically identified themselves as male, patriarchal, and patriotic" to the point of valorizing those with the most such knowledge, Dickinson seems more concerned to involve even the most common of readers by offering a different kind of field for perusal and play, one which privileges reader participation and hard work by which "each and all" may acquire knowledge rather than elitist keys to understanding held by those already "properly" educated.[8] The "rowing" or exchanges among poet, text, and reader emphasized by Dickinson's productions are constitutive parts of the site of reading. Besides her own actions as reader, her commentary on textual transmission shows that she does not consider the reader an outsider to the work (a world already made), but a vital part of a textual world perpetually Edenic as it is continually remade with every reading.

Though paradisiacal, Eden is a rather demanding, if rewarding, place to be and a poignant metaphor for this textual terrain. Of the imagination, this literary place cannot be owned, nor can it be assumed without the reader's participation. Confronted with a New World indeed, their "horizon of expectations" prefiguring reception, her first editors finished and produced works to regularize Dickinson's poetry so that it would conform both in form and content to literary customs and at least some of "the styles and clichés of Atlantic coast magazines."[9] In the turn from the nineteenth to twentieth centuries, many literati, Higginson included, still looked askance at Whitman, whose public revisions and generative printings of *Leaves of Grass* underscored the organicism, development, and continual extension of the work into text. Thus, a product of a critical blindness to the possibility that "unfinished" manuscript works were Dickinson's call to participatory reading which also recognized the text constantly extending itself, the impulse to "complete" her texts appeared unassailably proper. After a century, the new horizons of expectations demanded by her holograph works, which by their variants externalize the facts "that every current horizon gives way to new horizons as one moves along or travels" and that "the producer is always a recipient as soon as he begins to write," still do not have general currency among Dickinson scholars.[10] Yet the last quarter century, inaugurated by Franklin's *The Editing of Emily Dickinson* and Edith Wylder's often overlooked and misunderstood postulations about the slanted dashes in *The Last Face: Emily Dickinson's Manuscripts*, and highlighted by publication of the *Manuscript Books* and *Master Letters*, laid the foundation for altering our aesthetic norms. Instead of perpetuating the cycle of study usually focused on her works in typeface translation, texts in which odd signs like slanted dashes are altered to conform to ruling standards of taste, we are prepared to step out of the critical circumference and into new, Edenic modes of appreciation and interpretation of the holographs.

Dickinson's conjoining sexual and intellectual significance in the symbolic Eden appropriately conveys our involvement with her texts, which Barthes would say are bound to *jouissance* (joy, bliss, delight—all feelings identified with loving). In a letter to Kate Anthon, Dickinson herself identifies rowing with loving—"I am pleasantly located in the deep sea, but love will row you out if her hands are strong" (L 209, late 1859?)—and Dickinson's use of Eden has most recently been discussed in terms of its erotic connotations. As William H. Shurr notes, "Come slowly – Eden!" (F 10; P 211), "Did the Harebell loose her girdle" (P 213), and "Wild Nights – Wild Nights!" all argue for Eden "as the paradise of sexual security and enjoyment." [11] Yet interpretations to explain what Dickinson meant by "Eden" which posit that she, in one way or another and to one degree or another, refers to a state of mind are also buttressed by her writing. [12] In a letter to close friend Elizabeth Holland, Dickinson reports that "Vinnie says you are most illustrious and dwell in Paradise. I have never believed the latter to be a superhuman site. Eden, always eligible, is peculiarly so this noon" (L 391, summer 1873). Obviously, Eden is in the eye of the beholder, or, to elaborate the metaphor, in the eye of the reader. As Barthes elucidates the emotional appeal of reading with a deconstructive sensibility consciously involved in textual production, so Dickinson's account of reading another woman poet, Elizabeth Barrett Browning, emphasizes the erotics of reading: "The Dark – felt beautiful," and the reader no longer passively surveys the world around her, but reads it as a text, producing a new transformative world in which "The Bees" become "Butterflies" and "The Butterflies," "Swans" (F 29; P 593).

For my purposes, then, this garden of Genesis describes a state of mind that is both receptive to novel experience and willing to expend energy acquiring it, acknowledging all the while the erotic and emotional appeals of reading; and rowing characterizes the dynamic processes between the author and her readers, since both parties work to produce texts. Thus Dickinson's poems and letters are not static objects, works demanding passive consumption, but are frontiers to be explored and cultivated, places bustling with activity (since without readers the texts are nowhere). Paradoxically, readers continually both find and make these sites of reading. To put it in contemporary popular culture terms and play a bit on the trope of literary work as musical score, each reader performs her own "dance mix" of a Dickinson text. The maker of a "dance mix" remixes contemporary pop hits—"radically restructuring each composition at the studio console, dismantling some sections of a song to its skeleton, doubling other parts, stretching and extending and bending the record into a danceable commentary on itself."[13] In explication each reader is a textual producer, restructuring, dismantling, and reassembling, and in the process consciously or unconsciously comments on her own activity; with the material copy of the poem existing before intervention always available, on her field of textual play the work also turns into a commentary on itself.

"Whoever you are holding me now in hand" (to borrow from Whitman's "Calamus") need not suppose a return to the confusion of the Tower of Babel or textual anarchy, an ascent or descent into a world where each solipsistically utters unintelligible glossolalia, the speaking in tongues "inaccessible to the general congregation" and "foreign to the known tongues of humankind."[14] Remembering heteroglossia, or "the ability to speak in the multiple languages of public discourse," neither appealing to the Foucauldian notion of "anonymous discourse," nor concluding with Barthes that the cost of the birth of the reader must be the death of the author is quite sufficient to critique Dickinson's challenge to and project for readers. As Tania Modleski, Nancy K. Miller, and Biddy Martin have rightly pointed out, for women to forswear or play with the idea of relinquishing authorial power they have traditionally been denied is a quite different matter than for men to do so. And Emily Dickinson was no "white brain writing alone in a white room," but an author who sowed her works in the fields of unknown and famous contemporary readers and who planted her carefully assembled books where they were sure to be discovered.[15]

Forcing us to rethink our critical methods, interrogate her intentions as well as our own, and even to theorize about authorship, Dickinson's poetic and epistolary holographs, like critical hypotheses and debates, repeatedly remind us that issues of control are always central to reading. When tracing developments and some inconsistencies in reader-response criticism, Jonathan Culler notes a pertinent paradox: "The more a theory stresses the reader's freedom, control, and constitutive activity, the more likely it is to lead to stories of dramatic encounters and surprises which portray reading as a process of discovery." Using the process by which a joke works as an exemplary text, he notes that "the listener is essential to the joke, for unless the listener laughs, the joke is not a joke." But "the listener does not control the outburst of laughter: the text provokes it (the joke, one says, *made me* laugh)." [16] In her apparently "unfinished" productions, Dickinson acknowledges that control is dynamic and temporal. Yet in the first hundred years of studying her, patterns of control over interpretations established through "authoritative" representations finished for print and critical speculations time and again appeal to Dickinson's intentions in order to legitimate and entrench themselves.

Though determining authorial intention raises problems and issues that can never be completely resolved and part of the appeal of applying unrevised Foucault or Derrida is surely the opportunity to dispense with questions for which there are no absolute answers, considering the preferences inscribed in her texts in light of our preconceptions is a crucial critical endeavor. Observing Paul de Man's admission that "the deconstructive impulse is sometimes defeated by an intentionalism built into the very structure of our languages," Annabel Patterson writes that, after the "death of the author" and subsequent conjectures that rumors of such a demise may be considerably exaggerated, on the subject of intention "we are not required to be *regulatory*." [17] Likewise, speculating about Dickinson's intentions, we need not be regulatory and draw inflexible conclusions circumscribing her desires or literary experimentations, but, aware that our horizons of expectations are predetermined by standard histories and literary traditions, should consciously cultivate horizonal change. More than a century ago, Dickinson produced works that call all our modes of textual regulation into question and remind us, as do the tenets of contemporary literary theory, that a control which proposes to fix and finish literary or biographical texts, even if predicated on an author's plainly stated intention, is in fact illusory.

Inevitably then, control has been the central issue for readers and editors of Dickinson. Translated from chirography to print, editors' works have been invested with an authority—privileging one over all other variants, for example—missing from the originals and in which Dickinson does not appear to have been interested. An inevitable consequence of reproduction in the medium, the regularization and uniformity of typography exaggerates parameters of Dickinson's poetic forms and techniques to disguise them as inflexible and without evolution over decades. Widely recognized is the fact that in a world transformed by the printing press, "print . . . both diffused elements of control" and " 'made possible new

kinds of control over people,' based in people's measurement of 'themselves against a widespread norm and . . . doubt [of] their own worth.'"
Via conduct books, autobiographies, and even novels, print culture abet-
ted ideologies of propriety and normalcy through wider disseminations of
depictions of norms and standards. "Print did not cause conformity" but
clarified "what was expected of people and what would be considered
atypical." [18] Likewise, print translations of Dickinson do not cause conformity among her readers, but they do clarify expectations for readers and
demarcate an interpretive territory or horizon of expectations for what
may (her appropriation of the hymnal stanza) and may not (her appropriation of rhetorical notation) be deemed poetically significant.

   In this "fallen" world of reading, an amnesia similar to that which
made readers forget that the poetess in white was a stock character also
makes us forget that the slanted marks of punctuation so unusual to twentieth-century eyes "can be found in almost any nineteenth-century elocu-
tion text," casting "Emily Dickinson's choice of punctuation . . . in a far
more sympathetic light" than one which would relegate it to a sign of
"stress" (*LF* 12–13). Following the call of her "unfinished" texts and
Dickinson's own actions as reader, we need not resign ourselves to a kind
of hermeneutical stalemate, averring that techniques resisting print translation or found to be occasional are insignificant. What we should allow is
a hermeneutics of "Possibility" (F 22; P 657), a story of reading lending
itself to a thousand and more interpretations, all of which may be faithful
to Dickinson's poetic project. [19] Eschewing stasis, readers will want, like
Dickinson, to assert "I am Eve" (L 9) and avail themselves of the ecstasy of
eating fruits forbidden by print reproductions and notions of final authorial intention about finishing a literary product. [20] Mark Schulman reminds us that "outside the male-dominated production and distribution
processes of typographic culture, women have been molding their own alternative print culture for at least a century." Similarly, Dickinson designed an alternative project, reinventing methods of distribution and
some poetic techniques. Interpreting her radical performances, readers
will surrender many forms of control to which we have become accustomed and which, delimiting developments of genre and within certain
historical periods, have made us comfortable. Thus, "Rowing in Eden,"
readers will want, as much as is possible, to adopt an attitude that consciously aspires to be "prelapsarian"—before a fall into knowledge about
how Dickinson was as a poet or woman, and before a fall into opinion of
how her texts should appear in print, where they have been celebrated and
ridiculed, figuratively and literally bought and sold. Since to be absolutely

prelapsarian is not only an impossible dream, but an undesirable retreat into ignorance, readers will want to acknowledge that this Eden is a realm of carefully tended experience, and after Eve started investigating the possibilities of critical inquiry. Listening to Blake, readers will find cultivation of informed "innocence," which eschews the foreclosing prejudices of experience, desirable; and with Robert Frost ("Never Again Would Birds' Song Be the Same"), readers may even decide that never again will poetry—or at least Dickinson's poetry—be the same, and that jolting readers out of passive worship of what other textual producers have made was why Dickinson came. More than a decade ago, Karl Keller maintained that Emily Dickinson "is now strong enough as a writer in our literary history to transform our view of the culture itself. She makes *it* indigenous to *her*. We may understand much of it somewhat differently because of her." [21]

Literary Property and Intellectual Copyright

Translated into printed works, Dickinson's poems and letters have long been treated as properties. In her complaint about "The Snake," the poet herself sounds rather territorial about misplaced punctuation, and in a letter to Dickinson, Helen Hunt Jackson sounds even more proprietary. Maintaining that literature belongs to its audience, in 1876 Hunt Jackson complained that Dickinson had not returned a poem previously sent, "though you wrote that you would. Was this an accident, or a late withdrawal of your consent? Remember that it is mine—not yours—and be honest" (L 444a). Lavinia Dickinson, Mabel Loomis Todd, Susan Dickinson, Martha Dickinson Bianchi, and Millicent Todd Bingham staked competing claims and contested one another over who rightfully possessed Emily Dickinson's poems, and the wars between the houses Dickinson, then between them and the house of Todd, have long been documented and variously rehashed (see *AB*, *Editing*, or *Life*). Likewise, for the past century, critics and editors continually replicate proprietary struggles over what meanings may be properly assigned and how Dickinson's poems may be correctly reproduced. Theories have been proposed about her angled dashes and capitals only to be dismissed as absurd (*Editing* 121), yet those questions remain unsettled; and disputes over how to regard her fascicles and lineation are far from over. Since in its relation to conventional publication Dickinson's poetic career and poetics may be aptly described as "contestatory," all this dissension is probably inevitable. Jerome McGann proclaims, "The retreat of Emily Dickinson is eloquent with social meaning, and her poetic methods—the refusal to publish, the choice of album verse forms, the production of those famous manuscript fascicles—are all part of a complex poetic statement which is explicated in the context of her world, and which carries significance into our day when we are able, not to enter, but to face and come to terms with that world." [22] We must also come to terms with the major arbitrating factor in the struggles to control interpretations in this first century of Dickinson study—intention. Not surprisingly, as Dickinson has become more and more a communal property, stories about controlling readings of her have abounded, and concepts of her intentions become increasingly important to establish "authenticity" of various critical positions. As important as our refusal to discount her intentions entirely, however, is a commitment to resist the overarching claim that would use an understanding of Dickinson's purposes to dismiss contradictory interpretations. Emily Dickinson need not be interpretively imprisoned in the prose of our individual renditions of her works and/or lives (F 21; P 613).

To begin to analyze what she may have intended and the continuing social significance of her poetic production, one should first consider how Dickinson located herself in her literary world. At a time when Emerson claimed there was no circumference (see "Circles"), Dickinson declared circumference—her own terms and premises—her "Business" (L 268). Had she not hailed from the upper classes, she would most likely have not been able to do this. Like "Fanny Fern" (Sara Payson Willis) and her fictional Ruth Hall, women who were Dickinson's literary contemporaries usually had to sell their work: "There tended to be a sort of immediacy in the ambitions of literary women leading them to professionalism rather than artistry, by choice as well as by social pressure and opportunity." [23] Or, to invoke Dickinsonian succinctness: "Publication – [was] the Auction" (F 37; P 709) necessary for economic survival. Dickinson did not have to write to earn her keep, was not expected to make her fortune in order to maintain the family fortune, and that made, if not all, then certainly a most substantial difference. By her handwritten productions, she deprived a primarily male corps of its copyright on what constitutes serious poetic technique. As critics like David Porter acknowledge, when Dickinson refused the world of print for showcasing her poetry, she ensured herself a particular (some may prefer peculiar) sort of autonomy, for "printed versions of the [Dickinson] poems necessarily recreate the figure of the artist" and her poetic objectives. [24] The fact that she did not have to profit from her literary performances enabled Dickinson to establish a place all her own in the artistic world, a territory which otherwise would have been "off limits" and which is "off limits" to any intellectual copyright.

Literary Production and the Shapes of Performance

From this position, Dickinson could afford to complain about editorial intervention because she did not have to fret or agonize about her earning power, and she did not choose to worry about or prove that she could pay her way. Surely the closest opportunity she had to observe a woman supporting herself was her sister-in-law Sue teaching school in Baltimore. To say the least, Sue's was not the most joyous foray a woman could make into the world of work. For whatever reason—to protect her privacy or autonomy—Dickinson did not tame her odd ways and set conventional publication as her primary goal. Though she saw her poems printed in newspapers, Civil War publications like *Drum Beat*, and the anthology *A Masque of Poets* (in which "Success is counted sweetest," attributed by many to Emerson, appeared), Dickinson was not published like Fern, Elizabeth Oakes-Smith, Lydia Sigourney, Frances Osgood, or other nineteenth-century women writers in volumes widely read among the middle and upper classes.

That Dickinson continued to write though she did not produce books for mass distribution meant that everything, including her "typeface," was handmade. Over the many years of this cottage-industry literary production, her experimentation with the rhetorical notation that she learned at school gradually expanded to include other types of poetic experimentation with visual representation. While others shaped their subject matter and poetic forms and, like the early nineteenth-century American poet Sally Hastings, even their complaints about convention-bound critics [25] to fit what editors of publishing houses would support, Dickinson continued to produce many works that did not conform to print standards. Writing in and from this place Emerson christened "the Portfolio," [26] Dickinson developed a poetics in very different ways from her peers who wrote with the printing press and with pleasing editors, reviewers, and the nineteenth-century American consumer in mind. In fact, these developments are so unusual that it is a commonplace to say, as has Sharon Cameron quite recently, that there are no "changes in the style of the poems" and that "there is no development" in the Dickinson "canon," for "the experiences recorded by these poems are insular ones, subject to endless repetition. Indeed, it sometimes seems as if the same poem of pain or loss keeps writing itself over and over."[27] From this view, holograph poetic form is not regarded as commentary on a lyric's content or on the form itself, and the context of a poem's presentation in a letter or a fascicle is not important enough to be taken into consideration. Similarly, representing a document's context, Thomas Johnson regarded chronology as more important than audience, and, representing textual "facts," did not regard her holograph forms as meaningful parts of the poems. About variant versions of "A Death blow – is a Life blow – to Some –" he remarks that "the text of all these is identical; differences are in form only," as if the same instructions for reading would be conveyed by different arrangements (P 816n). His horizon of expectations, created by study of lyrics as printed objects, does not enable Johnson to see changes in holograph lineation and punctuation as deliberate, but only as "accidents" of handwritten manuscripts.

One familiar with the printed representations, from those of Higginson-Todd-Bingham and Dickinson-Bianchi-Hampson to those of Thomas Johnson, would probably be inclined to agree with these interpretations. Yet scrutiny of her chirography alone tends to modify views of Dickinson's poetic evolutions, however unusual or trivial some variations may initially appear to eyes trained to study typeface. In Franklin's *Manuscript Books* (Sets 8–15), one can see that by the 1870s Dickinson was spacing her letters and shaping them much more dramatically than she had in her early fascicles of the late 1850s and 1860s. As Susan Howe reminds us, if one carefully examines just these later documents, one "will see what gets lost in any typeface. In typography's mirror of production, words reflect only the shadow of their inception. Try to copy [Dickinson's] calligraphy; retrace one sweeping *S*, *a*, or *C*, and you will know how sure her touch was/is. Shapes and letters pun on and play with each other. Messages are delivered by marks. All redundancies are cut away to recover the innocence of the eye."[28] Similar handwriting developments can be seen in her letters.

Other stories told about these alterations have simply assumed that Dickinson's holograph "naturally" changed over the years, and thus these variations have nothing to do with her poetic endeavors. Though her holograph undoubtedly matured, I contend that the diversifications in her script signify more than unwitting or "natural" evolutions: they indicate intentional changes in holograph design. The majority of her surviving documents is prepared for Dickinson's style of "publication." Letters and poems for inclusion in those missives or for binding into manuscript books are copied onto linen, often gilt-edged paper. In these, the handwriting exhibits the exaggerated, apparently deliberate characteristics Howe describes. But besides those documents mailed or bound or organized into sets are drafts—some on scraps of paper, backs of grocery lists, even backs of recipes, and a few on fine stationery. In the drafts and scraps, her handwriting is not so dramatic and looks like that of Franklin's second "Master" letter, which he dates "early 1861" (ML 21–29). The first story to explain this is of course that all of those scraps, then, were written earlier than the documents produced in the extraordinary hand indicating Dickinson's later productions (see P, facsimiles between xlviii–xlix). Yet a draft of a letter said to be to Judge Otis P. Lord and dated in the 1870s also looks like the more casual handwriting of the second "Master" letter of 1861 and that of the scraps, while its fair copy looks like documents dated in the mid-1870s or even early 1880s (see *Revelation* 78–81 for facsimiles of A 734, A 735, L 559). Since they are a draft and fair copy of the same letter, one logically concludes that they were written at the same time. Thus the differences in handwriting indicate that Dickinson had a casual hand for scripting drafts, as well as what one might call a "performance script," a more stylized holograph for "publication." In this intentionally produced performance script are the profound changes in letter formation, spacing, and lineation.

Some Limits of the Marketplace and of Intention

So far I have reviewed some ways in which Dickinson's mode of production shaped the physical details of her performances. Implicit in this story is recognition that Dickinson began to challenge the fetters of the printed form. Because no conventional mode of typesetting can ever adequately reproduce their visual nuances, by the fact of their very existence, her literary productions disrupt, even contest, orders established and fixed by the printing press. So to prepare to row in Eden and read her anew, more detailed consideration of how the mechanical modes of production have for the past century shaped reception and editing of her writings is crucial. In the capitalistic world of publication in America, editors often do not want merely to justify but want to make a profit from manufacturing multiple copies of a work. As we saw in the first chapter, Dickinson's earliest editors tailored certain of her poems to make them more palatable to a larger audience. In the case of "A solemn thing – it was –" (F 14; P 271), the editorial "goal" was not "to discover exactly what" the author Dickinson "wrote and to determine what form" of her "work" she "wished the public to have," but rather was to mold Dickinson's work so that it would be acceptable to what Loomis Todd and Higginson presumed the taste of most of the audience to be.[29] This example, in which her marketability superseded the intentions declared by the fact of the poem, reminds us that, in the world of print, "literary [re]production is not an autonomous and self-reflexive activity; it is a social and an institutional event."[30]

Examples of editorial changes also remind us that recovery of intentions is circumscribed by an editor's horizon of expectations. When Higginson prepared "Blazing in Gold and quenching in Purple" in the early 1890s for a place in the second volume they produced, he wrote Loomis Todd: "I have combined the two 'Juggler of Day' poems, using the otter's window of course (oriel!!) & making the juggler a woman, as is proper" (P 228n). His reference to "oriel!!" is to a version transmitted by Dickinson's cousin, Perez D. Cowan, from memory of a copy given him by Sue (another version with the same word choice had also been printed during Dickinson's lifetime in the *Springfield Daily Republican* on March 30, 1864). Having labeled the most likely source of the variant (the author) "Wayward" (L 271), "spasmodic," and "uncontrolled" (L 265) three decades before, Higginson appears to regard "oriel's" a preposterous alternative and indicates as much with his exclamation point and prepositional phrase "of course." Or, aware of and perhaps influenced by the hostilities between Sue and Mabel, he may have considered transmissions of Dickinson's poetry via Sue suspect. Yet as the conclusion of his statement makes plain, his expectations are most shaped by preconceptions of what is "proper." That notions of propriety played a key role in assumptions Higginson made about Dickinson's intentions is indisputable when one reflects on the fact that he worried to Loomis Todd about the conclusions readers might draw from the erotic lyric "Wild Nights."

The stock character—virgin recluse poet—shapes even the relatively liberal Higginson's image of Dickinson and his views of what she meant. One does not need to know that geography, especially the sea, provides Dickinson with metaphors for her landscape of the heart, and that ships were often her vessel of choice when she needed a symbol for the individuals populating her poems about the affections, to see that "Wild Night's" imagery is explicitly sexual. There is no record of this having been sent to any, but it is obvious why no correspondent of hers would have readily identified him or herself as the recipient of such erotic lyric.[31]

Neither is evidence that Higginson would apprehensively deny Dickinson's sexuality at all surprising. But Higginson and Loomis Todd's reproduction of the poem evinces that his perception was circumscribed by conventional poetic form as well as by preconceptions about the proper spinster. In *Poems by Emily Dickinson: Second Series* (1891), they printed

> Wild nights! Wild nights!
>   Were I with thee,
> Wild nights should be
> Our luxury!
>
> Futile the winds
> To a heart in port,—
> Done with the compass,
> Done with the chart.
>
> Rowing in Eden!
> Ah! the sea!
> Might I but moor
> To-night in thee!

Though he says that they should change her word "as little as possible," Higginson gave his nod to this sanitized version of "Wild Nights." The last stanza, for example, no longer boasts unconventional lineation, encouraging readers to passionate pause, consonant with the poem's sensual suggestions. When Wylder published a photograph of "Wild Nights" in 1971, her argument overlooked lineation and drew reader's attentions to the dashes (*LF* first photostat). But as well as some unusual punctuation, Dickinson's version (H 38; F 11) bears an eye-catching stanza of five lines, not the predictable four (see Figure 1).

Erased from any typescript reproduction, which levels the effects of letters, is Dickinson's extraordinary, somewhat seductive, calligraphy—the wide-mouthed *W*, the triangular *T* at the beginning of the sixth line, and the stunning flourish that crosses both *T*'s in "Tonight." Obviously, in their production Higginson and Loomis Todd regularize the minutiae of Dickinson's punctuation to "correct" her ecstatic exclamation mark without a point and to even the long and short dashes by translating them into conventional, equally demarcated signs; then, by altering the lineation, they smooth out the lyric's rhythm, and, in doing so, mask the breathless sexuality conveyed by the holograph, tempering, therefore, her intemperance. Conforming to notions of proper poetic form may have been the

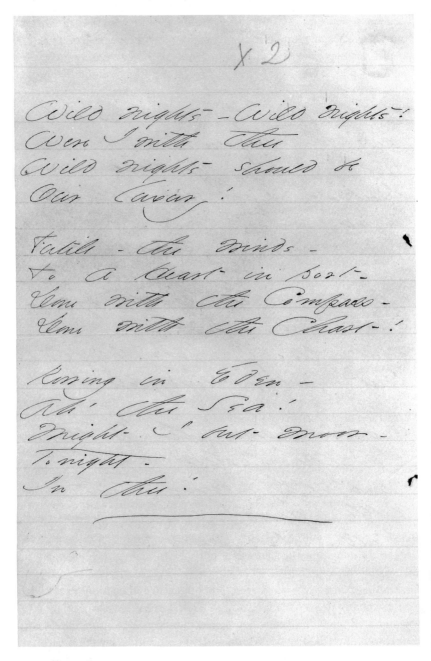

Figure 1
*Fascicle copy of "Wild Nights." By permission of the Houghton Library,
Harvard University.*

only factors consciously urging such editorial changes, since Higginson and Loomis Todd most likely did not imagine that Dickinson meant for the last stanza to be five lines.

Conceptions of what she could have intended continued to limit editorial praxis throughout the first century of translating her holograph works to print. Like Higginson and Loomis Todd, Thomas Johnson does not consider that Dickinson may have intentionally produced a five-line final stanza when he observes that in the earlier editors' version, "the last word of line 11 is arranged as the first of line 12" (P 249n). The idea of a regular four-line stanza dictates the perceptions of these editors. Viewing the Amherst poet's lyric through such a lens has become fairly routine, for, as most anthology headnotes acknowledge, Emily Dickinson's appropriation of the hymn stanza has often been discussed. One of the many ways in which the understanding of the first reader has been elaborated in a chain of receptions from critic to critic, this critical commonplace about Dickinson's form can mediate perceptions of her poetics to such an extent that editors sometimes cannot see more radical experimentations.[32] Privileging the stanza guides the way Johnson sees and reproduces one of Dickinson's most intriguing departures from the constraints of conventional poetic form, the version of "I reason –" (P 301; H 274) that she sent to Sue (see Figure 2).

In this variant Dickinson's poem is not divided into three discrete stanzas of four regular lines each. Instead, she uses the staggered placement of words on sixteen lines to arrest the reader's attention and slow down the process of perusal to a halting pace. In turn, this enables more careful examination of that which could have been rendered in the most standardized form to encourage new, unpredictable ways of reading (another, much more conventional, twelve-line version of this poem is bound into the fascicles; see F 20). By doing so, the thrice-repeated clause "I reason" and the query "But, *what of that?*" redirect the reader and recast her understanding to underscore the *un*reasonableness and irrationality of the Christian assurances Dickinson calls into question here. This version, with its underlinings and dramatic placement of the solitary syllable "*die –*" on a line by itself, seems bitingly sarcastic, while the tone of the more traditionally formulated version is much more muted. Implicitly, this and that regularized twelve-line fascicle version critique one another. Some readers may determine the more unusually lineated copy overdone and, judging them to be more masterful in ironic understatement, prefer conventional lineation and even rhythms for this bold speculation. But the gist of both versions is finally to declare "What does it matter that I reason?" At the

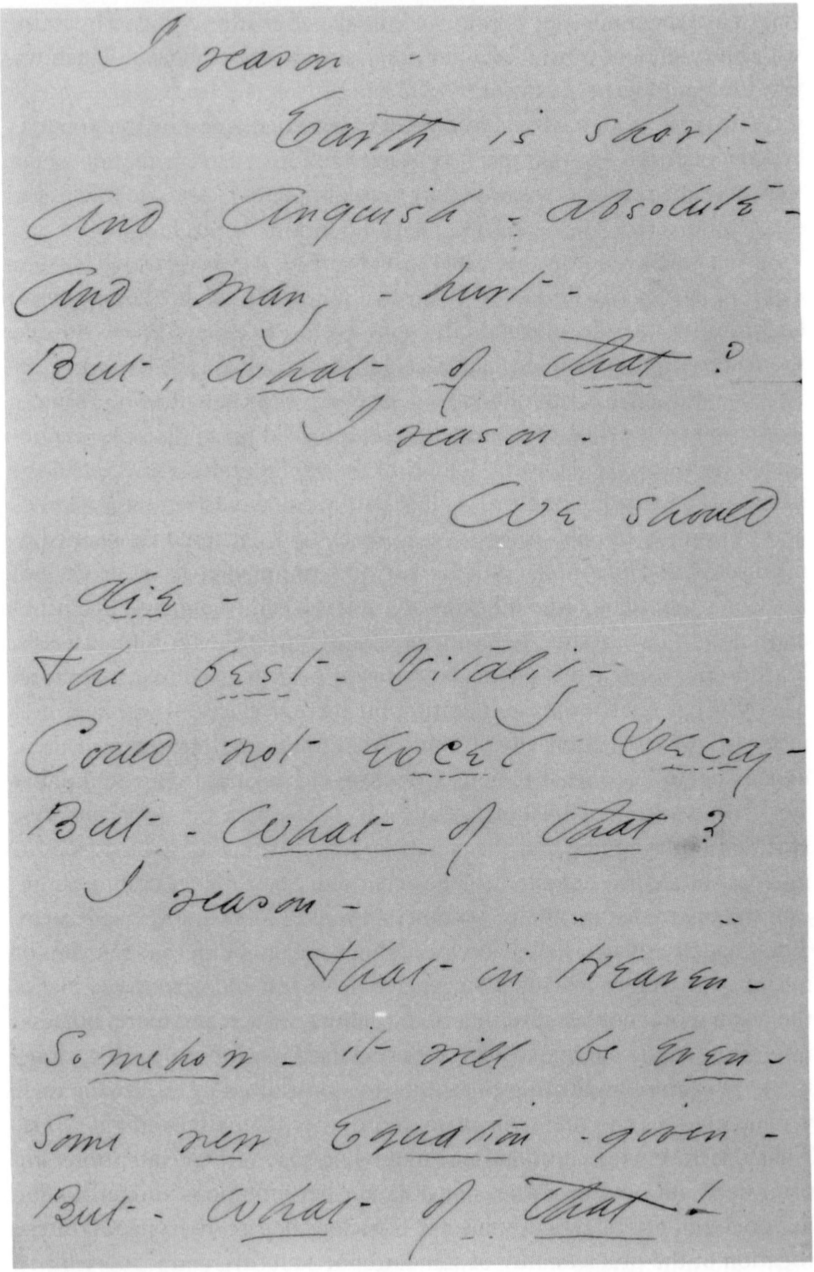

I reason -
Earth is short -
And Anguish - absolute -
And many - hurt -
But, what of that?
I reason -
We should
die -
the best - Vitality -
Could not excel Decay -
But - what of that?
I reason -
That in Heaven -
Somehow - it will be Even -
Some new Equation - given -
But - what of that!

Figure 2
Copy of "I reason –" sent to Sue. By permission of the Houghton Library, Harvard University.

very least, the more exaggerated variant shows Dickinson experimenting with lineation and word placement, therefore with the ways in which unusual forms of written language work upon readers. Her strategies are so novel that the reader attends to every detail, noticing that by this version's end the question "*what of that!*" is punctuated with an exclamation point, thus accentuating the more despairing connotations of "So what, who cares that I reason?"

Yet when Johnson reproduces this version, he obscures Dickinson's extraordinary play with lineation by dividing the poem into three stanzas and printing "*die –*" as if it is on the same line as "We should." His note on the manuscripts reveals that he considers both holographs to be twelve-line poems, and his reproduction of the text indicates that he assumes Dickinson's allegiance to stanzaic form. As G. Thomas Tanselle has observed, questions of authorial intention reflect "legitimate interest in the minds of individual authors as well as in the collaborative physical products of printers and publishers," yet "the texts we encounter in printed or manuscript documents can only be instructions for re-creating works, not the works themselves (the medium of literature being language, not paper and ink)."[33] To examine these documents and try to determine just how Dickinson intended this poem to appear in print (concluding, therefore, what was her final authorial intention for its reproduction) would at best meet with uneasy, editorially presumptive resolutions. But to peruse these documents to learn what they may disclose of Dickinson's poetic mind at work meets with much happier results. To this reader, these variants suggest that both the line and the stanza were forms that Dickinson kept in mind as she shaped her poems. The version to Sue employs odd linear arrangements to disrupt the reassurances offered by reliable stanzaic form. The existence of two forms, each of which suggests different nuances of meaning, therefore leaving a single definitive text indeterminate, makes the poem more, not less, exciting to the general reader, and more, not less, interesting to the literary scholar. Offering itself in various manifestations, the lyric is more fascinating poetically, for scrutinized intertextually each version engages the reader in many more ways than either might alone. That conclusions or postulations about Dickinson's final intentions for print need not be drawn does not discount her intentions altogether, for her doubling of this lyric reveals her conscious departure from and interrogation of the predictability of standard poetic forms, and is more likely than a single print translation to enhance our understanding of her attitudes toward creative processes and the functions of the written word.

Intentions, Ideologies, and the Idea of a Finished Text

Through her variant words and versions of poems, as well as punctuation, lineation, and bookmaking variant from conventional forms, Dickinson extends herself toward her audience, demanding a kind of performance or what Miller calls "actively expectant reading." Dickinson's variant versions work in ways analogous to the word choices left at the end of or between the lines of many lyrics, requiring "the reader's participation in establishing the text of a poem." In such interactions, "the reader must," Miller observes, "continually stabilize the text by choosing what belongs in it and at the same time repeatedly return to account for the other, unchosen, possibilities of the poem's meaning."[34] Like Miller, John Hollander also observes ways in which readers must interact with Dickinson's performances in order to stabilize a text (however temporarily) for interpretation. For example, discussing "a selection of Dickinson's poems" he edited for an anthology and editorial problems with which anyone reproducing her texts must grapple, he proclaims that sometimes one must repunctuate (i.e., substitute conventional marks for "those things that are reproduced as dashes") the poems because they "are so difficult that we have to punctuate them one way to resolve them. . . . This can make difficulties of another sort, because I'm sure that attentive and loving readers of Dickinson's poetry will absolutely and firmly disagree as to the reading of an ambiguous passage that could go either way (but most often not, as in Shakespeare's sonnets, both ways at once). You have to have a very strong sense of what the poem is and what it's doing to be able to resolve these matters of syntax." Absolute and firm disagreements on the part of readers will occur, even when they each peruse the very same marks on the page. Judging from his comments about Dickinson's enjambments of stanzas, Hollander would disagree with my interpretation of "I reason—": "Sometimes she writes out the poem so that if you didn't have an ear you could say, 'Oh, this is in a different experimental form.' But it isn't: she's simply written out two halves of the four-beat line as two separate lines, for example."[35] And I disagree with his apparent conviction that poems demand resolution.

Such differences among readers are not difficulties that need hamper or impede shared or individual readings; on the contrary, "such conflicts and confusions are among the primary motives for intepretation," and, I would add, for the critical dialogue of interpretations.[36] In the rhyming ditty of a statement mentioned in the closing paragraph of the introduction, Dickinson jauntily proclaims acute awareness that her readers, equally versed and equally committed to recovering her meaning, would probably disagree and each have his or her own stories of reading:

> A word is dead, when it is said
> Some say —
> I say it just begins to live
> That day.
>
> (L 374; P 1212)[37]

These words of Dickinson have lived on (without her) in various forms. The sing-song rhyme conveys a jocularity that in self-mocking irony reminds us of Dickinson's consciousness of ambiguity, of the fact that written language is especially rife with variously meaning inflections, and of the reader's contribution to the production of text and meaning. Umberto Eco observes that "to postulate the cooperation of the reader does not mean to pollute the structural analysis with extratextual elements. The reader as an active principal of interpretation is a part of the picture of the generative process of the text."[38] In fact, as Miller observes, in the case of Dickinson, consciously refusing to pollute the structure with extratextual elements like erasure of variants renders poems that directly invite the reader's participation, underscoring her role as "an active principal of interpretation."

Like Gary Lee Stonum, who contends that Dickinson's poems are designed to prompt a reader's imagination without demanding a particular interpretation, Miller recognizes that the reader's involvement is of paramount importance. Observing that the ideas of "literary masterpieces presuppose the idea of author as master," and that "Dickinson's concern is with the effect of poetry, not its production," Stonum concludes that she "can never either fully reject or fully endorse literary mastery as something she is eager to practice."[39] Like William Faulkner, who candidly observed that "when the reader has read all these thirteen different ways of looking at a blackbird, the reader has his own fourteenth image of that blackbird which I would like to think is the truth," Dickinson does not require acquiescence from and dominion over the reader. In his critique of one of her most discussed poems about poets and their value, "I reckon – when I count / at all –" (F 28; P 569), in which poets and their productions inspire the speaker to "write," Stonum notes that, according to Dickinson, the distinctive glory of poets "occasions or stimulates further production on the part of the reader who becomes a writer—part poet, part recording auditor—in her turn. . . . Part of the ultimate business of Dickinson's poetry, in addition to and sometimes in lieu of creating finished spectacles, is producing poems that may then beget from her audience new poems and other forms of free, active response." I would modify Stonum's observations to say that, since it is part of a poem's effect, Dickinson is in fact deeply concerned with the processes of poetic production and reproduction. Recognizing these preoccupations vital to her poetic enterprise leads not to conclusions like R. P. Blackmur's that she was neither professional nor amateur nor to ones like Porter's that her thought is instinctive and formless, but instead to profound questions about the business of literary criticism and our reproductions of interpretations and authors. By leaving alternatives that have forced conventionally motivated editors to pick and choose, thereby refusing to "finish" texts for the printer, Dickinson at least implicitly critiques the processes of poetic production and consumption in the age of mechanical reproduction that discourage individual production and, through automation, "frieze" dynamic texts into static objects.

Whether Dickinson intended her homemade modes of literary production to be part of what Wylder calls her "poetic manifesto" (*LF* 1) and Stonum calls her "literary program" is an obvious and important question to confront. One story of interpretation would answer that her manuscripts exist in these states only because Dickinson did not prepare for publication and that if she had done so, the poems would not have been left in these states (with so many variants), but would have been resolved into final forms. Of course had she published conventionally, her poems would have been reproduced in much more regular forms, whatever her intentions for them might have been. But when Dickinson "published" herself, she did not have to limit her perogatives to a single word choice or particular version. At first glance, that Dickinson chose one among various possibilities when sending a poem to an audience appears to argue for the view that, given the opportunity of print, she would have resolved the most blatant textual indeterminacies by settling on a variant. Yet in an address to the English Institute, Johnson declared that "if any conclusion is to be drawn" from this fact of different versions to different correspondents, "it would seem to be that there are no *final* versions of the poems for which she allowed alternate readings to stand in the packets"[40]; therefore, her fair copy resolutions were occasional and for a particular audience. This fact argues for the opinion that Dickinson's "completions" are always provisional, that she divested herself of presumptions to finish a poem, and that she was highly conscious of diverse, even contradictory receptions. Thus a leap of faith into suppositions about what she would have done to resolve a poem is not necessary. Yet Johnson and subsequent editors do not extend such analysis to conclude that any resolution—whether to construct a reader's edition or to meet prevailing poetic standards—obscures some crucial social import of her literary career.

Though Franklin realized early on that "if we want the poems in a finished state, we must apply other principles of selection [than authorial preference or discernible patterns] and must take responsibility for doing so" (*Editing* 131), he does not speculate that this may have been an important point of Dickinson's poetic project. Like the indeterminate punctuation marks and striking handwriting, the variants and Dickinson's "publications" reveal her regard for language as a dynamic exchange between speaker/author and listener/audience and for poetry as an art fashioned in those processes. Franklin observes that "the manuscript books record many poems in a state of incompletion, whereas when Dickinson went 'public' with a copy to friends, she would produce a fair copy, all alternates resolved. Moreover, the display of alternates in the fascicles is often confusing, with no indication of the words to which they relate, or with indistinct indication." Guided by a notion of finishing a text for publication, his interpretation continues, concluding that the fascicles forestalled "disorder" in Dickinson's manuscripts and their construction served to help her "get control of her poetry in the only way, barring publication, that she had developed" ("Fascicles" 16). If Dickinson had resolved each poem for "publication" to her correspondents in the same way or if we could rest absolutely certain that she never sent the manuscript books out to anyone, then this interpretation that sees the fascicles only as "private documents, copied for her own uses" could perhaps go unmodified. However, an October 1875 letter from Helen Hunt Jackson casts doubt on certainties that the manuscript books were always private documents, as well as on the supposition that Dickinson only sent her poems out one or two or three or four at a time, enclosed in her letters: "I have a little manuscript volume with a few of your verses in it—and I read them very often—You are a great poet—and it is wrong to the day you live in, that you will not sing aloud. When you are what men call dead, you will be sorry you were so stingy" (L 444a). Whether Hunt Jackson had a fascicle or not we can never know, but the possibility that she may have should not be dismissed and raises other important questions. When Hunt Jackson wrote Dickinson ten years later—"I wish I knew what your portfolios, by this time, hold" (L 976a, 1885)—was she referring to Dickinson's "bookmaking" and implicitly asking to see a fascicle or simply using the term "portfolio" conventionally to refer to private writings? How did the solicitous "Miss P—," who requested poems and to whom Dickinson said she "replied declining" (L 380), know to ask for her work? Is it possible that Dickinson sent out more of her work, even some manuscript books, than has been commonly believed? Can we conclusively regard all of the extant fascicles as the same sort of document as Shurr, who believes their addressee is "Master," suggests? In all their variety, what poetic statements are made by their existence?

Challenging the illusions of fixity inspired by printed forms, hermeneutics shaped by conventional conceptions of publication privileging "finished" texts, Dickinson, in her manuscripts, launches an important artistic statement exposing the ideological presumptions driving insistence on textual "resolution." Print culture fosters or abets an ideology of the finished literary piece and the notion that a poem is reified and completed, waiting like a "foster child of silence" on the page (Keats, "Ode on a Grecian Urn"), which in turn reinforces and helps to reproduce the ideology of the autonomous author completing such an object. Though the notion of "finishing" is almost certainly a foregone consequence of poetry evaluated in typographic culture, such convictions originate in hermeneutics developed to produce "authentic" scripture, faithfully transmitting every jot and tittle of the Word of the Alpha and Omega, no more and no less. The Bible promises the most severe penalties for those who interact with scripture in ways Dickinson's poems demand, and Jesus's dying gasp, "It is finished" (John 19:30), reverberates to Revelation's final injunction—"If any man shall add unto these things, God shall add unto him the plagues that are written in this book: And if any man shall take away from the words of the book of this prophecy, God shall take away his part out of the book of life, and out of the holy city, and *from* the things which are written in this book" (Revelation 22:18–19). This imperative threatens that anyone tampering with dead letters pronounced sacred will forfeit her place in the book of life, though of course the facts of translation and transmission have exponentially reproduced texts that can never be resolved into indisputable completion and that often compete with one another as the most authentic Bible.

Nevertheless, determined by a will to control, this concept of Holy Writ, of text as completed object, helped mold concepts of literature and literary reproduction that privilege final authorial intention. Thus the idea of the sealed text resonates to notions of poetic texts as finished, resolved to the most authoritative version. Ironically, in the case of Dickinson, such motivation to control and complete texts contradicts not only her designs but also the original biblical injunction to transmit works as they were written, for many of her works must be changed in order to be "finished."

With the notion of finishing dominating his interpretation of what the variants and versions mean, Franklin makes some important observations about the evolution of Dickinson's poetic project but does not consider the possibility that her intentions may have included critiquing the very idea of final textual resolution. Of the fascicles and the many variants left there, he records:

> Formal aspects of these manuscripts books developed over several years. Among them are the presence and display of alternative readings, underlining and quotation marks, variation in overflow technique, the number of sheets per fascicle, and the use of single leaves. For example, when she began, Emily Dickinson allowed only completed poems into the fascicles. The first unresolved reading does not appear for about a year, and there are only about a half dozen in the first ten fascicles, through about 1860. About 1861, and continuing thereafter, alternative readings became abundant: Dickinson had moved fascicle copying earlier into her poetic process. . . .
>
> ("FASCICLES" 11)

To see the poems with multiple variants as "incomplete" is not only an obvious conclusion to draw, but also a way to control the poems. Yet a poet with such an anomalous style of "publication" viewed the poetic process as much more dynamic than print-determined perspectives have often allowed, and as her conceptions about poetics evolved, authorial presumptions of completion became antithetical to her purposes.

Gender, Poetics, and Intentionality

Like tradition-bound interpretations of Sappho, interpretations of Dickinson have often regarded her productions as masterpieces of unconscious artistry, explaining that the nearly 1,800 poems are by-products of a lonely woman or disaffected intellect who, by scribbling her heart or brain out, coincidentally made literature. Some readers assume that because Dickinson was "a little homekeeping person," "while she had a proper notion of the final destiny of her poems she was not one of those poets who had advanced to that late stage of operations where manuscripts are prepared for the printer, and the poet's diction has to make concessions to the publisher's style-book"; others maintain that she wrote poetry instead of performing household routines, "indefatigably as other women cook or knit," for "her gift for words and the cultural predicament of her time drove her to poetry instead of antimacassars"; still others believe her to have been "a compulsive writer," thus conclude her writing has "something to do with the lack of an advancing, coherent, and complicated intention" and assert that she "is the only major American poet who wrote without a project."[41] Especially since so many assumptions originate in gender-determined pretext about the author, feminist critics bear a special responsibility not only to examine the contemporary social predicament of American women of Dickinson's class and extensions of gender biases into our own time, but also to scrutinize the politics of author recognition and the much-debated idea of the author. If feminist critics do not attempt such complex interrogations, we can, as Cheryl Walker and others have noted, fall into the trap that "assumes no disjunction between poet and speaker" and read poems reductively, as if "the author is the meaning of the text, a personal, autobiographical personage who has a 'true self' that can be embodied relatively transparently in language." Instead, we need to develop "a new concept of authorship that does not naively assert that the writer is an originating genius" creating closed artifacts, but is a textual producer whose enterprise is generative, turning every reader into a coproducer or coauthor.[42] In fact, as the lesbian or sexual continuum makes a useful tool for beginning to understand the highly complex natures of human sexuality, so the idea of an authorial continuum proves a valuable tool for beginning to understand the very complicated symbioses among author, text, and reader. At one pole are those who proclaim that the birth of the reader requires the death of the author, while at the other pole are those whose author-centered aesthetics make them imagine "that reading and writing are neutral or benign and that poems ideally transmit to the audience finished meanings the author has fashioned, devised, or determined."[43] Both ideas are helpful. The former urges readers not only to acknowledge the roles of their own biases and preferences in authoring texts for interpretation, but also, as Walker exhorts, to acknowledge that "ideology will also govern our construction of the author, especially but not only if the author becomes *un sujet a aimer*, a someone to love"; the latter reminds us that "there is an infinite number of presences, or traces, in a given text," some of which are of the originating author. This critical position neither champions anonymous textuality, repressing all critical interrogation of the author's writing identity, nor accepts simple equations between the "I" of her texts and the flesh and blood writing body Emily Dickinson.

Consonant with the critical observations of Georg Lukacs, many critics have observed that lyric poetry—direct, sudden, "like lost original manuscripts suddenly made legible"—fosters illusions of authenticity in depicting moments, as well as, by making the subject appear to be "the sole carrier of meaning, the only true reality," in depicting the lyric "I." [44] Thus Dickinson's choice of form especially lends itself to interpretations that confuse the speaker with the author, and her readers commonly conflate the two. The only times that Dickinson even hinted autobiographical or biographical interpretation might be appropriate was when she incorporated lines of poetry into a letter, which she did with many of her correspondents. Significantly, however, the only reader to whom she sent score upon score of signed lyrics, often prefaced with salutation, was "Dear Sue." By signing and addressing these poems Dickinson complicates our sense of what they are, and they cannot be simply classified as the same sort of lyric as those presented in the fascicles or enclosed as unsigned, unaddressed pieces in letters to others. If Sue chose to interpret these uniquely presented lyrics as referring to actual events or persons, as she and other correspondents probably did when Dickinson incorporated poetic lines into letters, we may reasonably postulate that she was not just responding to the immediacy of lyric form. Yet for the vast majority of readers, Dickinson's poems appear in printed volumes as untitled and unsigned lyrics; in reproduction, even the poems addressed to Sue have been isolated from their salutation and signature. Therefore, it is plain that the effect of the poetic form itself, perhaps in combination with a vague notion of the author frequently labeled "mysterious," impels the relentlessly autobiographical interpretations of readers who never knew or corresponded with Emily Dickinson. Instead of equating unsigned lyrics in a fascicle or enclosed with a letter to Higginson with those addressed "Dear Sue" and signed "Emily" or with those woven into the prose of a letter, as Johnson's presentations in the variorum encourage, readers should take Dickinson's presentation(s) of a poem into account. Deciding that the "I" in a poem clearly addressed to Sue is a "supposed person" is a very different matter from concluding that the "I" in a poem bound into a fascicle is fictional. As will become evident in my discussion of their poetic workshop and literary "self"-presentation, I do not think that such framing of her lyrics to Sue transforms their "I" from a supposed to a real person, but it does demand a different set of critical questions about constructions of the author.

Also, beginning to examine "the process and strategies" by which Dickinson transformed herself into an artist, "taking control of the production of writing to challenge" poetic conventions and traditions—particularly as they relate to gender—raises important questions about the "fundamental tenets" of poetic value, especially that which privileges an ideal of the unified finished product.[45] If her poetic processes, traces of which are recorded in the manuscripts but erased in typographic translations, require us to be done with compass and chart of traditional critical models too limited to analyze them, what are the rules of the game and how do we read the Dickinson documents? If in our efforts to understand we need not regularize nor impose unwonted uniformities on Dickinson's texts, giving precedence to her arrangements over our own, allowing, as M. L. Rosenthal recommends in a review of the *Manuscript Books*, "more consciousness to develop into comprehension" by learning from holographs or facsimile representation of her texts,[46] what are the implications regarding class status and the availability of Dickinson's works? Since profound insights into her poetics like Stonum's are obtainable by studying the print translations, how important to her general audience can manuscript study be? If we do not advocate a program for study open only to those who can afford trips to the archives and the more than one hundred dollars to purchase the photographically faithful reproductions in *Manuscript Books* and *Master Letters*, what then is the point in arguing for the integrity of the "nontranslatables" (elements leveled or otherwise erased in print), especially since most critics depend on one of the Johnson editions or selected representation of the poems in anthologies for both scholarship and teaching? Why not see the experimentations recoverable only in manuscript study as relevant exclusively for a highly specialized field of Dickinson studies, but not necessarily vital for general readers?

The methods for reading Dickinson outlined below begin to address these questions, though they are brief recommendations and in no way exhaustive. First, since serious scholars must and other readers will probably want to acquaint themselves with the facsimiles available, some plans for evaluating the textual facts not obscured through photography are described. Second, since the purview of the book—*The Poems of Emily Dickinson, The Letters of Emily Dickinson*—has shaped our reading, new methods for patterning our perusals will be elaborated. As Suzanne Juhasz has demonstrated, "Undiscovered Continents" (Set 5; P 832), not provinces measured for conventional publication, lie everywhere in the terrains of her texts, even when they are generated by printed works. Last but certainly not least, since most of us have learned to read poems in school or are involved in educational programs, some plans for teaching out of the most commonly used translations of Dickinson's works are mentioned throughout the sections on textual facts and repatterning reading, then briefly delineated at this chapter's conclusion. As scrutiny of the holographs and facsimiles relaxes our presuppositions about what reading Dickinson in particular and poetry in general should be, new patterns for exploring the print translations are inevitable.

A Hermeneutics of Possibility

Textual "Facts"

Discussions about how to value the Dickinson holographs would of course be intertwined with questions about how to regard what appears on the page. Likewise, scholars, faced with the poems produced by representation in *Manuscript Books* and new characteristics of the works must now make many more decisions about what to treat as a vital component of the textual record and what to deem insignificant, what to count as poetic experimentation and what to disregard. Doing so is an editorial act of translation and in calling attention to this teachers have a splendid opportunity to begin to explain why Ezra Pound regarded translation as a superior type of literary criticism. Interpreting Dickinson's marks, editing to emphasize some aspects and practically ignore others are acts of translation that fuse the creative and the critical. By showing how every reader becomes a creator, teachers pass along to students not "correct" interpretations to be memorized and regurgitated in ever more sophisticated narratives about reading, but skills for consciously producing literary art as they read. When Dickinson externalizes the demands for coauthorship every literary text makes of readers, the suggested rules for reading may be called "lesbian" rules—from a mason's rule of lead, which bends to fit the curves of a molding; hence, figuratively, lesbian rules are pliant and accommodating principles for judgment (*OED*). An architectural term is particularly appropriate, punning as it does on intimations of sexuality originally excised from official reproductions of Dickinson's texts while it underscores the building required of the reader. Depending on the work under study, these reconstructions will vary. In Johnson's variorum, for example, variants are numbered and assigned to particular words, while on Dickinson's holographs variants and places for insertion are usually indicated by a cross (+) found in a group at the end of the lyric to be matched with crosses throughout the text and, as Franklin noted, invite readers to experiment with which to insert where. Thus photographic representations of those holographs present the variants very differently than do Johnson's presentations in the variorum. Reflection upon various aspects of the material properties of works made by Dickinson and her editors and their influence on reception are, therefore, significant.

Readers should be self-conscious about differences between Franklin's edition and the actual books left in Dickinson's drawer (or chest). The *Manuscript Books* are not the fascicles themselves, but are pictures thereof, representations by the camera framed in ways the actual documents are not and with features obscured or highlighted by the lens but not the eye. Mutilations to texts, so obvious in the cancellation of "One Sister have I in the house" (F 2; P 14), are in other instances difficult to evaluate via photographs. On "'tis true – They shut me / in the Cold –" (F 30; P 538), for example, Loomis Todd canceled Dickinson's variants at the bottom of the page, then someone erased the penciled marks; in a photograph all this is obscured, and Franklin's note is necessary for readers even to notice the tamperings (F, p. 1383). In these photographs, pen and pencil are often not distinguishable, everything is flattened into black and shades of grey, so that pinholes are the same color as ink, the embossed Queen's head or letters or double-headed eagle are blurred marks in the corner of the page, and the gilded edges of much of Dickinson's stationery are not visible. Testaments to the great respect Dickinson had for her literary productions, awareness of such material facts is important to any assessment of the poet's purposes. Though the photographs obscure some telling features, they picture plainly the diacritical marks, calligraphic orthography, variants, and at least one of the most hysterical mutilations, as well as the fact that, in holograph, Dickinson's poems visually control the page, while in print the white space of the page practically consumes the poems, miniaturizing them in ways the handwritten documents will not allow. After a decade of mass-reproduced availability, these characteristics should be interrogated, and the illusory character of photography's apparent exactitude foregrounded.

"Dashes" and the Question of Punctuation

Echoing editorial patterns for reproducing Dickinson's texts which, accommodating typographic technology, eliminate what will not conveniently translate into typeface, critical wisdom still holds that oddities in punctuation are just as effective when, like her calligraphic designs, they are "normalized" as dashes. Cameron observes that "Dickinson's works will not stand regularizing" and that even Johnson's "variorum is less free of editorial interpretation than one could wish, and the reader's edition is even more burdened with it. This is true first because while any handwritten text must suffer the inexact representation (the regularizing) of the printed word, the problem is particularly severe for Dickinson's texts, punctuated as they are with dashes of varying lengths and perhaps of varying meanings."[47] Though "the general conventions of printing" cannot generate a representation "comformable" to Dickinson's notation, her holographic variations need not be dismissed as "merely habits of handwriting" (*Editing* 120) and banished from study. Nor is it necessary to recommend, as does Miller, that although "Dickinson's punctuation, like her poetry, teaches the reader to trust the play of the mind," we might as well ignore all differences among the marks the poet produced: "To my mind, representing her slanting marks typographically as dashes [straightened out, conventionalized for print technology] . . . reproduces well the effects Dickinson apparently intended."[48] When Johnson levels the slanted marks in a poem like the version of "I send Two Sunsets—" addressed to Sue (H B 154; P 308), he erases not a relatively unfamiliar diacritical mark, but the commonly recognized comma, and in doing so removes a sign that urges important questions about how to regard Dickinson's signed poems. Johnson translates the punctuation at the end of the last line of the poem into a dash when it plainly appears to be a comma. To Sue, Dickinson ends this poem as one closes a letter, turning it into a letter-poem:

> I send Two sunsets –
> Day and I – in com –
> petition – ran –
> I finished Two, and
> several Stars
> While He – was making
> One –
> His own is ampler –
> but as I
> Was saying to a friend –
> Mine – is the more
> Convenient
> To Carry in the Hand,
>   Emily –

In this instance, her choice for punctuation is bound to the occasion, and though on first glance it may appear to be a little matter to recognize the difference between a comma and a dash, it in fact makes subsequent readers conscious of Dickinson's highly selective punctuation and epistolary presentation of her poems. To analyze what appears to be her eccentric punctuation, then, devising "a systematic criticism" which factors in and begins to account for what appear to be the "antisystematic elements" so pervasive in Dickinson's work will be of utmost importance.[49] Considering the context and occasion of Dickinson's "publication" of a poem are necessary elements to formulate this systematic criticism.

By refusing to evaluate the marks simply in the intellectual orb of editor/translators and considering them in the context of Dickinson's world, Wylder initiated an important shift in critical treatment of the poet's stylistic irregularities. Whether or not they are literal guides for declaiming the poems, slanted dashes, a saucy set of quotation marks, an exclamation without a point or with one but upside down (P 159; H 228 to Sue) work very differently on a reader than unexceptional, typographically regular dashes, periods, commas, and semicolons, and critical speculation about their impact could be much more exhaustive. When Dickinson appropriated the more dramatic signals for poetic expression, she was perhaps following an exhortation of Samuel P. Newman, author of one of her rhetoric textbooks: "It should be impressed on the student, that, in forming a style, he is to acquire a manner of writing to some extent, *peculiarly his own, and which is to be the index to the modes of his thinking*—the development of his intellectual traits and feelings."[50] In our "born again," Edenic relations to such poetic techniques, we are constantly reminded that "the notation is always inadequate, by itself, in predicting performance or reading" and that such marks require "multiplicity, freedom, spontaneity" on the part of the reader; thus "much deeper aspects of the Dickinson notation than that which gathers itself in mere punctuation, syntax and grammar" or "in meter, rhythm, and diction" initiate dissolution of the hierarchies of active writer and passive reader. "In this respect the words resemble the notes in music."[51]

Calligraphic Orthography

Stanley Morison's assertion that "typography is properly a department of calligraphy" is important to consider when evaluating whether Dickinson's holograph contributes to poetic expression. The term *orthography* calls attention not only to Dickinson's long recognized deviation from conventional spelling but also to the formation of letters and the relationships of individual characters to meaning. While orthography connotes making meaning through conventional spelling, or arrangements of letters within a word, the term also directs our attention to the power of the letter. A second definition for orthography is "that part of grammar which treats of the nature and values of letters and of their combination to express sounds and words" (*OED*). One of the examples given for this definition is from a text Dickinson mentions in an October 1851 letter to Sue (L 56, H L 5), Lindley Murray's *English Grammar* (5th ed., 1824): "Orthography teaches the nature and powers of letters, and the just method of spelling words" (*OED*). When Dickinson employs the term, she too attends to the individual character, the letter: "Orthography always baffled me, and to 'Ns' I had an especial aversion, as they always seemed unfinished '*M*'s'" (L 806 to Elizabeth Holland, March 1883); and ". . . I used to spell the one [bird] by that name '*Fee Bee*' when a Child, and have seen no need to improve! Should I spell all the things as they sounded to me, and say all the facts as I saw them, it would send consternation among more than the '*Fee Bees*'"! (L 820, spring 1883). In "Many a phrase has the / English language –" (F 12; P 276), the poem's speaker has "heard but one" phrase "saying itself in new inflection –" and "Breaking in bright Ortho- / graphy." Miller suggests that Dickinson puns on the alphabetical letter when she remarks to her Norcross cousins, "An earnest letter is or should be life-warrant or death-warrant, for what is each instant but a gun, harmless because 'unloaded,' but that touched 'goes off'?" (L 656, early September 1880).[52] Like Maggie Tulliver's father, Dickinson "found the relation between spoken and written language, briefly known as spelling, one of the most puzzling things in this puzzling world" (*The Mill on the Floss*, Book 1, Chapter 13). Especially in her later works, Dickinson's letter formation is at least sometimes freighted with meaning, and extraordinary calligraphic techniques that do not conform to expectations created by typeface practically qualify as a new form of spelling.

Sensitized to the visual impact of alphabetic symbols, Dickinson did not only attend to their ornamental aspects. As poet Susan Howe demonstrates in her slide lecture about Dickinson's manuscript techniques, productions like "The Sea said / 'Come' to the Brook" (A 431; Set 11) display her painstakingly careful stroke of the pen.[53] In this instance, Dickinson seems concerned not so much with the beauty or elegance of the letters but with the influence of their formation on expression (see Figure 3). Though they did not investigate possible objectives, the editors of the earliest printed volumes of her poems, in which Loomis Todd and Higginson reproduced a facsimile of "There came a day –" (P 322 in *Poems by Emily Dickinson*, 1891), clearly realized that reading Dickinson in print was a pro-

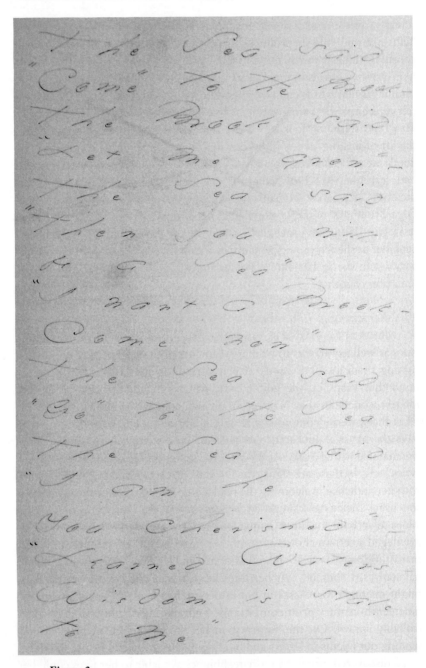

Figure 3
Manuscript of "The Sea said." A 431 from the Emily Dickinson Papers, Amherst College Library, by permission of the Trustees of Amherst College.

foundly different experience than reading her "fossil bird-tracks."[54] In "The Sea said" the sly producer shapes her letters so readers are forced to consider mimesis in the most literal sense. By forming letters that "look like" waves, Dickinson mocks exclusively mimetic goals for language. Her reminders that words can be cymbals as well as symbols, and of language's self-referentialities, are gleefully comic, and her amused and amusing tone shows her self-conscious and ironic stance. By incorporating into a poem the art of making letters into beautiful objects in order to comment on a poet's meaning-making objectives, Dickinson produces a prototype of artistic critiques like Judy Chicago's calligraphic runners symbolizing the greatness of creative women throughout history at *The Dinner Party* and Olga Broumas's "curviform alphabet / that defies / decoding."[55] By these strategies Dickinson urges readers continually to relearn how to read and decipher as she feigns performance of a feminine role of linguistic embroidery while she in fact interroates writerly pretensions to faithful representation of reality.

Variants and Lineation

Readers skeptical of elevating the status of variant stylistic characteristics as well as variants to primary elements of the poetry instead of consigning them as subdivisions of private writing exercises might keep in mind that Franklin, the editor/critic who has studied the fascicles the longest, concludes that "Dickinson did not compose onto fascicle sheets. Even those whose compositional state might be called 'worksheet' do not have the physical appearance of one, for, like other fascicle sheets, they were copied with care sometime after the initial act of composition" ("Fascicles" 12). In these are signs that Dickinson reconceived her relationship with her audience, welcoming the reader's authorship. Thus, though Johnson used Dickinson's supposed breakdown in the late 1850s and early 1860s to account for these unique features as signs of emotional strain and privileged a certain choice over another, regularized representation of her many different "dashes," as well as of her line lengths to conform to hymnal stanzas, I contend that her lines neither accidently spill over (as one might maintain for "Assassin hid in our Apart – / ment") or conform to nineteenth-century print conventions,[56] nor does her handwriting uncontrollably sprawl. On the contrary, in her steady stream of production, sending out poems in letters and binding poems into little volumes, Dickinson discovered more and more techniques available to her than could be offered by a printing press. The many variant components of her texts signal a poet changing (by challenging) the standardized patterns of reading.

"Book" Making: Reading Is Always a Process of (Re)patterning

When M. L. Rosenthal asks a question that should now be central to all Dickinson study, effects on perceptions of macro (e.g., organization of documents) as well as micro (e.g., punctuation, variants) features of production should be of concern: "What, for us, is the real bearing of Dickinson's abjuring publication even while she wrote so intensely and tried her best to organize her poems in richly interactive groupings?" Other questions about the patterns of reading made official by the chain of textual reproductions are necessary to augment this one: "What for us is the real bearing of Dickinson's works having been presented as if they can be definitively divided into discrete genres—poems and letters?" Belknap Press of Harvard University Press has produced eight books—three each of poems and letters and two volumes of fascicles—and readers should keep in mind the authority engendered by The Book. Ideas presented in books seem more important than those proposed in articles; likewise, presenting Dickinson's poems and letters in book form appears to finalize judgments about genre and organization. Their latest production of Dickinson's works, the *Manuscript Books*, faithfully attempts to restore her organization, but the editions of poems and letters overlay her documents with scholarly order. As it did for Blake, mass reproduction created a much wider audience for Dickinson's texts than they otherwise would have enjoyed, yet translating them into impersonal print stripped her productions of their idiosyncrasies and of the place made for each by her ordering of texts. Eager to arrange her poems thematically, early editors removed the threads (strings) from the fascicles and began arranging the poems according to categories they invented. Producing his variorum in the heyday of New Criticism, which defined poems as closed objects, Johnson tore rhythmic lines from letters to make poems from prose (P 2 from L 58, October 17, 1851), divorced poems from letters in which they were enclosed to establish separate editions that assume discrete genres and showcase both letters and poems as isolated units, and, though he traced many poems to their original placement in fascicles, used chronology as his ordering principle instead of trying to restore Dickinson's groupings. Johnson's bringing together the Higginson-Todd-Bingham and Dickinson-Bianchi-Hampson reproductions and imposition of scholarly order (especially the attempt at chronological collation) were valuable and necessary steps to advance Dickinson scholarship. What dismembering Dickinson's organizational units has cost can never be fully measured, even with the advent of Franklin's *Manuscript Books*, for we can never be certain that his meticulous compilations are in every respect those of the poet. Nevertheless, to the extent possible I would like to allow Dickinson to make the "books" herself, to read each of her productions in its connection to the whole corpus to a correspondent or in connection to the fascicle in which it appears.

Besides those volumes Dickinson stitched together are the individual correspondences which, like the epistles of Paul which each make a book of the New Testament, each make a "book." The poems, letters, and letter-poems sent to a single correspondent form a set of stories, apprising us about the literary relationships between Dickinson and her friends and acquaintances. Strategies for reading should follow her highly allusive, contextually oriented lead. Robert Frost remarked that in a book of twenty-five poems, the twenty-sixth poem is the book itself. So in a fascicle of twenty Dickinson poems, the twenty-first poem is the fascicle itself.[57] And a "book" of one hundred letters and poems might be considered the one hundred and first letter-poem, poetic epistle, or even prose romance with verse forms. Since Dickinson's poems have been isolated, numbered, and separated from their placement by the poet since the beginning of their representations in printed volumes, the stories these units tell have been mutilated and obscured. Like Blake, Dickinson manufactures each book—of letters and poems gathered in a correspondence and of poems gathered into a fascicle—individually. For each "book" of letters and poems, she has a specific audience. In contrast, both audience and author of each untitled, unsigned fascicle are "Anonymous." Seeing especially the groups of letters and poems to particular addressees as "books" requires interactive inventive intellectual rhythms. Since their status as books is an imaginary construct of the critic who mentally unites all letters and poems to one correspondent under one rubric, treating them thus is yet another aspect of "rowing in Eden." In dramatic contrast to the capitalist and alienated modes of textual production in the province of book publishing, these personally addressed "books" present a radical alternative.

The subsequent new patterns for reading will likely produce interpretive stories radically different from those about Dickinson's alienation, for Johnson's arrangement makes little plot possible but stories of fragmentation. Indeed, surgically separating poems from their context and referring to them by number makes them appear to be specimens for study of the poet's psyche. In contrast, reading according to the units made by the poet rewards us with the contexture of weaving parts into a whole and encourages reflection upon the power over interpretation wielded by patterns of reading. Learning from intertextualities created by her organization, one considers images and structures, their contrasts and complements, themes, juxtapositions, endings, beginnings. "Because reading is a process of patterning, to read an individual poem in isolation or outside of its original volume is not only to lose the large retroactive sweep of the book as a whole—with its attendant dynamics and significance—but also to risk losing the meanings within the poem itself that are foregrounded or activated by the context of the book."[58] As Neil Fraistat observes, referring to "the contextuality provided for each poem by the larger frame within which it is placed, the intertexuality among poems so placed, and the resultant texture of resonance and meanings," "contexture" connotes all three of these qualities. To see Dickinson's bookmaking strategies as empowered poetic practice enables perception of "contextural poetics," and, as Joseph Wittreich points out perusing the intertextual connections between *Paradise Regained* and *Samson Agonistes*, "meaning itself derives from the concatenation."[59] Richard Sewall wonders if "the fascicles show, perhaps, that she knew herself to be the master of more than the isolated lyric" (*Life* 2:541). Barton St. Armand speculates, "May not Dickinson's art also be an art of assemblage?" His subject focuses discussion on her "'quilting' of elite and popular ideas onto a sturdy underlying folk form, frame, or fabric," and he is most preoccupied with linking her to nineteenth-century American culture at large.[60] While that broad perspective is of vital concern and serves as backdrop for my interpretations, I am most preoccupied with linking poems and letters within a correspondence to one another. For this project, the correspondences to "Master" and to Sue are two "books," and the relationships of individual poems and letters within those bear important similarities to the relationships of individual poems within a fascicle to one another.

When one studies the holographs and sees Dickinson paying more and more attention to the effects of lineation in both her letters and poems, leaving more variants, and shaping her letters more dramatically, one also observes the poet beginning to explore the intertextual possibilities for counterpointing genres—of the letter with that of the lyric poem—around and after her thirtieth year. Sometimes the counterpoint is occasional, for example to mediate potentially offensive statements to Higginson (about poetic expertise) by including "I cannot dance upon my Toes" (P 326; F 19), which proclaims "I know the Art" though "No Man instructed me," in the same letter in which she opines, "All men say 'What' to me" (L 271, August 1862). Perhaps she has a similar strategy in mind when she writes Samuel Bowles, "Because I could not say it – I fixed it in the Verse – for you to read –" (L 251, early 1862). The unsayable "it" more probably refers to poetic philosophy than to some private gossip, especially since Dickinson begins the missive with "If you doubted my Snow." From "Publication – is the Auction" (F 37; P 709), readers are well aware that, in the Dickinson lexicon, "snow" can serve as a metaphor for literary production. Thus her comment does not argue for the poetry as mere private communication or expression. As Dickinson counterpoints poems with letters, so she counterpoints poems within fascicles.

Like Franklin, I am not persuaded by insistence that "severely linear aspects, such as precise balance, unbroken progression, orderly recurrence" or strict "thematic, narrative or dramatic structure[s]" account for intertextualities in the fascicles. Though he acknowledges that "interest has developed in the fascicles as artistic gatherings—as gatherings interrelated by theme, imagery, emotional movement," he concludes that her primary unit for poetic production "had always been the sheet" and that one of her primary motives "in constructing these little books was to reduce disorder in the manuscripts" (F x–xiii). Yet fascicle readers "as a matter of course respond 'to sequential variation, enjoy the play of contrast in return of these, admire a felicitous change, sense the import of positioning—proximities and deferrals, beginnings, articulations, ends." If by the time of the Augustans, poets could presume that, "in light of what was 'normal' in the making and use of books," such reading habits were conventionalized, then surely we can presume it possible that Dickinson bore similar notions in mind when she sewed together her manuscript volumes.[61] Unlike Franklin, I do not conclude that the fact that sheets within the same fascicle were copied in different years is a sign that "no fascicle-level order governed their preparation" ("Fascicles" 17). To the contrary, that she was rearranging poems after copying them suggests consciousness of intertextualities varying according to organization. Time-consuming, deliberate assembly of poems arranged other than chronologically spells premeditation and argues against their functioning merely to reduce disorder.

Perusing Emily Dickinson's "books," then, readers might (1) suppose her self-consciousness concerning the details of organization as well as the details of technique and (2) aggressively recognize (i.e., be on the lookout for) contextures among Dickinson's texts. There are several immediately identifiable types of contexture for the appearance of a Dickinson poem. For the sake of clarity, and because they are two related but different genera of documents, I will describe two notable contextures in which we might find the Dickinson holographs. One analyzes the con-textures within the two correspondences studied for the rest of this book—to "Master" and Sue; the other analyzes contextures within the fas-cicles. Thus I discuss two forums for contexture: when a poem appears in a letter and when a poem appears in a fascicle. Besides the similarities be-tween relationships within a correspondence and those within a fascicle, there are some crucial differences, not the least of which is that the se-quential order of a correspondence may well be less certain than that of the books Franklin has reassembled and the most obvious of which is that Dickinson did not bind a "book" of poems and letters to a single corre-spondent with string but bound documents together by directing them to-ward a specific audience. Among the relationships and correlations we might examine in order to ponder the *contexture of a poem's appearance in a letter* are these: (1) where and when the poem falls in the frame of the en-tire correspondence to the recipient in question, and to what extent that particular sequence established by Johnson or Franklin is reliable; (2) how the poem corresponds to the individual letter in which it is enclosed; (3) how it compares with other poems in the correspondence—whether the poems are similar in subject, in form, and whether there are correla-tions among the poems sent to a particular correspondent; and (4) how the poem compares with types of poems sent to other correspondents. Among the relationships and correlations we might examine in order to consider the *contexture of a poem's appearance in a fascicle* are these: (1) where does it appear in the sequence and scheme of the fascicle—is it first, last, at the center? does it bear images and themes similar to those of the poems by which it is surrounded? if it appears in a fascicle with paired poems gov-erned by clear antitheses, but is not one of those pairs, how is it com-mented on and how does it comment on those correlations? (2) in what different contexts does the poem appear and how does its representation in the fascicle compare with its presentation in other fascicles or in letters? and (3) how does the contexture change when, for poems on which Dick-inson left variants, one substitutes the different choices?

Adducing the rudiments of this reading strategy, one might conclude that the fascicle Franklin numbered 21 describes the career of a "poet of the portfolio."[62] Like "I rose – because He sank – ," almost every poem in this fascicle inverts or subverts ordinary order; and many of these lyrics are explicitly about poetrymaking. "You'll find ˛ it when you / try to die ˛" inverts the expected apprehensions about dying. Death is not absolutely horrible, but is the sensible thing to do. After all, the poem argues, there are "such as went," those who passed away before, whom "You could not spare – you know" and dying too is the only way to see them. "I see thee better – in the Dark," inverts the notion that good things, like this "Love of Thee," for example, are best in the light, and the fascicle continues to disturb conventional assumptions.

In "This was a Poet –" the poetrymaker is so powerful that he can take "the familiar species" and does not need to invent mythic figures to fashion eternal subjects. In "They shut me up in Prose ," the apparently "still[ed]" speaker who makes a habit of mental flight looks "down upon Captivity –" and laughs. "In falling Timbers buried ," and "It would have starved a Gnat ," complement these images of empowering deprivation and prophesy Dickinson's kind of career. Buried by the falling timbers, a man breathes while others make futile attempts to rescue him. He finally dies, and, as in "You'll find , it when you / try to die ,," death is not horrible but gratifying. Death is, in fact, "Grace." As is true of that depicted in the poem, Dickinson's actual death was a kind of release, for it was only then that the volumes to posterity became widely available. Proclaiming that "It would have starved a Gnat , / To live so small as I ,," this poem's speaker asserts, like the speaker of "My life had stood – A / Loaded Gun –" (F 34), that she, unlike the gnat, is without the power to die. Her strength overwhelms her, and even when she feels she cannot, she does "begin – again – ." In these poems, strength keeps asserting itself over apparent weakness. As in her career, that which appears to be failure in the eyes of the world turns into victory. The last two poems in this fascicle plainly describe this power that, for a woman instructed to be submissive and dependent, sometimes felt alien. In a culture singing "Jesus lifted me" and preaching that woman naturally submits to man, "I rose – because He sank –" inverts the usual order of woman depending on the supposedly Herculean strength of man. Like Atlas shouldering the world, the feminine speaker shoulders the helpless, fallen male. Well acquainted with the power of language, it is she, not he, who cheers, sings, and tells. Instead of man articulating experience for woman, this poem describes woman articulating the world for man. Refusing to confirm the cultural myths that perpetuate a hierarchy so stultifying for women, Dickinson articulates experience as it is, not as coercive fairy tales promise it will be. Blatantly championing her power, the female speaker of the final poem, "It was given to me by / the Gods ,," claims that multiple deities grant her talents, wealth, and strength. In a monotheistic, patriarchal culture, such a statement by a woman is multiply (and appropriately) subversive.

In this interpretive process, readers move forward and backward, following patterns created by Dickinson to make up their own instructions for formulating narrative or coherence. The primary project of the fascicles may well be to expose the failure of any narrative to sustain that which is outside itself. After all, any story of interpretation constructed on the evidence supplied by a fascicle cannot be maintained without the storyteller or reader. Yet whatever Dickinson's intention for the fascicles, she was most certainly aware that even for a set of disjointed texts, readers will impose narrative, for it is practically necessary to sustain interpretation.

Some Implications for Teaching

Reconceptualizing notions of "publication" to include Dickinson's circulation of her poems to her correspondents places her in an active, cultured network, and calls into serious question the prevailing image of the isolated, withdrawn poet. Her poems, letters, letter-poems, methods of production, and designs for distribution are all part of her dialogue with the world. As Harold Bloom points out, Dickinson "compels us to begin again in rethinking our relation to poems, and to the equally troubling and dynamic relations of poems to our world of appearances." [63]

When letters shaped like waves, arresting line breaks, and dancing or drooping dashes are no longer presumed to be accidental, propositions about the author's will unfold within and begin to guide the narrative of reading. Even teaching her in print translation, we can call our students' attention to one of the most important points of Dickinson's poetic statement—that poems are not reified objects, but artistic productions that at least implicitly comment on the very processes of reading and representation they set into motion. Perhaps using Shelley's famous proclamation idealizing mental forms or intention as a starting point for describing the processes of transmission, teachers can describe some key elements cut out of translations of Dickinson's poems in order to heighten the self-consciousness of even beginning students and introduce them to matters of textual editing too often (and I think unwisely) reserved for advanced graduate study. For example, a brief explanation of why Dickinson's rhetorical notation has been erased from typographic representations need not scold any editor for having done so, but might serve as a starting point for analyzing the sociology of texts and their print embodiments, as well as the sociology of education by giving them some sense of how the emphases of schooling have changed and will continue to change. Since diacritical marks, underscoring inflection's importance, have never been part of the poetic language shared via the print medium, they have been prejudged by editors as insignificant or private, an argot not intended for or not of interest to most readers.

To elaborate the implications of that vein, teachers might impress upon students problems with overly simple notions of the individual author by asking, "Who made the poems we see on the page? Did the poet Dickinson produce those typographic marks?" Because of the inaccuracies in translating her works into print, even a critic as astutely conscientious about editorial interference as Cameron interprets a poem that Dickinson in fact never wrote. The "I tie my Hat – I crease / my Shawl –" (F 24; P 443) Cameron interrogates is that poem plus nine additional lines incorrectly attached first by Mabel Loomis Todd, then again by Thomas Johnson. Those nine lines probably belong to "A Pit – but Heaven over it –" (F 24; P 1712; see *Editing* 40–46), but they were not part of the poem Dickinson conceived. Analogously, some readers identified her handwritten transcription of George Herbert's "My God, what is a heart?" as Dickinson's own lyric. These misperceptions occurred because the translations of poems and letters into mass reproducible forms involve transcribers, editors, and publishing houses, thus the case of Dickinson can be used to teach students something of the collaborative processes necessary to produce printed volumes. We can hope that such knowledge will incline them to be less susceptible to being seduced by the apparent authority of the printed word and more encouraged to cultivate a healthy skepticism about matters of intention, which Dickinson herself cultivated: "The Fiction of 'Santa Claus' always reminds me of the reply to my early question of 'Who made the Bible'—'Holy Men moved by the Holy Ghost,' and though I have now ceased my investigations, the Solution is insufficient—" (L 794, late 1882).

Learning about and being continually reminded of those group coordinations necessary to produce a book, students must confront the conception of the isolated, completely self-reliant author as a humanistic fiction bound up with faith in the autonomy of the individual. In the age of television, the musical hit, and movies, appropriate analogies between Dickinson's editors and publishers and the movie, video, and record industries' producers, directors, performers, camera operators, and record technicians can be drawn to great effect. Thus like the Apostle Paul telling the Greeks about Jesus by pointing to their memorial to the Unknown God and promising to tell all about him (Acts 17 : 22 – 32), using what our young people already know so well—the Academy and Grammy awards both constantly remind their audience of the collaborative processes necessary to produce a movie or record—can greatly enhance everyone's insights into the social processes of authorial production and automated textual reproduction.

The case of Dickinson especially lends itself to discussion of how matters of textual reproduction are not separate from but are intertwined with hermeneutics. Because of the ways her poems have been printed, many think of Dickinson's poetic production as that of an especially talented occasional poet, as one who writes in response to life's little dramas, like Benjamin Franklin's uncle who "left behind him two Quarto Volumes, Manuscript of his own Poetry, consisting of little occasional pieces addressed to his Friends and Relations." [64] The plots suggested by dismemberment of Dickinson's poems from letters and fascicles also parallel editorial reconstructions like Ted Hughes's arrangement of *Ariel*, which "implies that Plath's suicide was inevitable," while her own "careful sequence" (Hughes's characterization) "ends on a note of hope," and like the arrangements by Emerson, William Henry Channing, and James Freeman Clarke which distorted Margaret Fuller's personality to present her as "arrogant, aggressive," and "unattractive." [65] Whether they intend to be or not, neither the reproductions of texts nor critical interpretations can be innocent of or superior to politics, since both require negotiations among authors, editors, publishers, and readers. Dickinson interpretation will be powerfully enhanced by cultivating constant awareness of the "official" repatternings of the variorum, the three-volume letters, and the separate publication of the "Master" documents. Self-consciousness about those reconstructions cannot, of course, completely negate their impact. However, cultivating reading strategies *un*bound, counting the scholarly order imposed by Dickinson's editorially reconstructed books as valuable but refusing to accept their patterns unquestioningly—reading, for example, each correspondence (not just one) as if it were a book—gives us far more than fresh lenses in our reading glasses. As Shelley would have it, such reading promises to imbue interpretation with Promethean power.

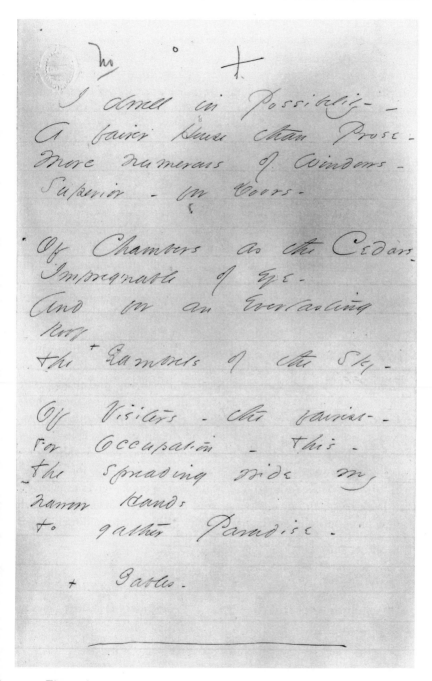

Figure 4
Fascicle copy of "I dwell in Possibility." By permission of the Houghton Library, Harvard University.

The Way I read a Letter's – + this –
'Tis first – I lock the Door –
And push it with my
fingers – next –
For transport it be sure –

And then I go the furthest off
To counteract a Knock –
Then draw my little Letter forth
And + slowly pick the lock –

Then – glancing narrow, at the Wall –
And narrow at the + floor
For firm Conviction of a Mouse
Not Exorcised before –

Peruse how infinite I am
To No One that You – know –
And Sigh for lack of Heaven –
but not
The Heaven God bestow –

+ so + slily + softly + door +

—EMILY DICKINSON, F 33; P 636

Sittin' in front of your house
Light rain and early dawn
Working on a love letter
With the radio on

Got my eye on your window pane
And I smoked a lot of cigarettes
Mercy mercy but love is strange
And you haven't even kissed me yet

—BONNIE HAYES, "LOVE LETTER"; RECORDED BY BONNIE RAITT

Drive your cart and your plow over the bones of the dead.

—WILLIAM BLAKE, *THE MARRIAGE OF HEAVEN AND HELL*

Three All Men Say "What" to Me: Sexual Identity and Problems of Literary Creativity

When Lavinia Dickinson read an account of her sister's life published in the *Boston Transcript* on December 22, 1894, four years after Thomas Higginson and Mabel Loomis Todd's first publication of *The Poems of Emily Dickinson*, she felt compelled to set the record straight and wrote the author, Caroline Healey Dall:

> . . . Emily never had any love disaster; she had the choisest friendships among the rarest men and women all her life, and was cut to the heart when death robbed her again and again. . . .
>
> I was in Washington with her where we found the most delight – [ful] friends.[1] Emily's so called "withdrawal from general society", for which she never cared, was only a happen. Our mother had a period of invalidism, and one of her daughters must be constantly at home; Emily chose this part and, finding the life with her books and nature so congenial, continued to live it, always seeing her chosen friends and doing her part for the happiness of the home.
>
> Our father was the grandest of men, and never hindered our friendships after we were children. Emily had a joyous nature, yet full of pathos, and her power of language was unlike any one who ever lived. She fascinated every one she saw. Her intense verses were no more personal experiences than Shakespeare's tragedies, or Mrs. Browning's minor-key pictures. There has been an endeavor to invent and enforce a reason for Emily's peculiar and wonderful genius. . . .

(*LIFE* 1:153)

This portrait of the poet Dickinson is her fond little sister's, so we should not be surprised at the lack of restraint in its praise. Even while she unreservedly ranks her sibling alongside Shakespeare and the widely admired Barrett Browning, Lavinia is careful to report that "Emily" did "her part for the happiness of the home," thus was properly focused on feminine priorities. But her main objective in writing a letter to one who believed the stories of devastating romance is to disabuse a newspaper gossip of the notion of a lovelorn lady driven to writing verse. She declares that Emily was devoted to language, not a mystery lover.

After a century of literary criticism and scholarly editions of Dickinson's poems and letters culminating in R. W. Franklin's facsimile editions, one would think Lavinia's emphasis on the "verses" would be taken for granted. Thomas H. Johnson's edition of the poems enables critics to compare variants and consider Dickinson's sense of audience; Franklin's facsimile editions help advance such study by affording scholars opportunities to scrutinize her composing process, unique punctuation, lineation, placement of variants, and method of organizing lyrics. Still, a good deal of critical fascination has been directed not at her eye-catching ways of shaping punctuation and lyric form, nor with her method of publishing poems to her correspondents, nor with her arranging them into little books for posterity, but rather with identifying the addressee of fifteen scrawled leaves found among Dickinson's papers and in the drawer cradling the forty manuscript volumes she willed to the world. In fact, interest in the "Master" letters has been so keen that Franklin has published photographic representations of these not only as a separate book, but also in an envelope and on folded sheets, which make of each letter a separate, distinct object; hence his reproductions more nearly resemble the actual documents than pictures on the leaves of a book ever could approximate, and, by printing them on unbound sheets that can be ferried away in an envelope, he emphasizes the interpretation that the drafts were intended for someone real.[2] If deciphered, these three items of writing would tell, many are convinced, the "most important" fact of her life—the tale of Emily's broken heart. Named for the figure many think must have dominated Dickinson, their title is still appropriate, not because it describes one of her relationships, but because it so aptly depicts the power a mere three drafts, among thousands of finished pieces, have had over her readers. The following three sections of this chapter explore the "Master" letters as literary texts, first by recounting the history of their reception and outlining the uses of these documents in Dickinson study to interrogate epistolarity and the writing "I"; second, by analyzing passages in the documents to discuss further the editorial making of particular expressions and genres within the printed Dickinson canon and to develop some of the letters' intertextual connotations; third, by situating the letters as part of her "letter to the World" to recontextualize their skewed impact on critical understanding of Dickinson's literary project.

What's in a Letter?

Gilbert and Gubar cannot resist them. John Cody reads them as "distraught and pathetic" documents of Dickinson's breakdown. Richard Sewall devotes an entire chapter to the "Master" letters and does not think her most voluminous correspondence with the housewife next door, thirty years worth of prose, poems, and poems woven into prose, warrants more attention. Insisting on literal interpretation, Cynthia Griffin Wolff proclaims that the "anguish of these 'Master' letters is certainly authentic" and that "these must be more than epistolary exercises, for certain details are quite specific"; for her, as for Barton St. Armand, their addressee is real—father Edward Dickinson's best friend, Judge Otis P. Lord. To Vivian Pollak, "while it would be naive to assume that Dickinson's prose persona here is spontaneously artless, a random copy of 'real' self, it would be equally naive to ignore the unmistakable desperation of her self-revelations, particularly in the second and third 'Master' letters which make extraordinarily painful reading even at the remove of a century and more." Similarly, for William Shurr, the addressee of the three letters, as well as of the fascicle love poems, is Reverend Charles Wadsworth, and for Sewall, "Master" is probably publisher and family friend Samuel Bowles (*Life* 2 : 5 1 2 – 5 3 1). The personal predicament of Paula Bennett's Dickinson, her rejection by the male Master of these letters, "had a decisive influence on her writing." [3] Dickinson sent hundreds of notes and poems to sister-in-law Sue, but nobody knows if Master breathed, or lived first in Dickinson's, then in the critical world's, and now in "Our Emily's" imagination. Nobody knows whether the Master of each draft is the same character. Readers can only be certain that Dickinson drafted a few sheets to him or her or them. Yet these love letters, attempts at fiction, or private writing exercises, these mysterious drafts whose purpose cannot be positively identified, have drawn more critical attention than any other Dickinson correspondence.

Some reasons for this preoccupation are clear. As conventional notions about poetic strategy moved editors to "correct" Dickinson's verse, conventional notions of romantic tragedy command most readings of the "Master" letters. Unlike the bold, "wayward" woman who fashioned her own style of publication by sending her poems to correspondents, the pleadings of these drafts seem to certify Dickinson's feminine frailty. "Daisy's Arm is small," Master (A 828a^v); and they document her willingness to please: "Would Daisy disappoint you – no – she would'nt – Sir –" (A 828b^v) is apparently addressed to a man and seems to assure that one of the most powerful dramas in the life of the poet Emily Dickinson was first and foremost centered on him. Like Franklin declaring that the letters are "of primary importance" and implying that they could unlock "her mystery" (ML 5), Sewall goes so far as to say that the second draft, unfinished, not prepared for posting, is a microcosm of "Emily Dickinson's whole life . . . the history of what could be called its failures and the reason for them and the prevision of its triumphant success and the reason for *that*" (*Life* 2 : 517). Such extensive discussion of course keeps interest high, and, as the preceding chapters observed, these rough drafts repeatedly usurp the writing to her primary correspondent, Sue Dickinson, which has been talked about since niece Martha Dickinson Bianchi's editions in the earlier part of this century, but, unlike the "Master" letters, never printed separately in a book all its own.[4]

Perhaps that is because, unlike the idolatrous prose and poetry, revised and finished writings addressed to her beloved friend and sister, Sue, the "Master" letters do not seem nearly so bothersome or outrageous as those declarations of unending affection and devotion from one woman to another, effusions which demand not simply explanation but apology. Interestingly, as if to counter Rebecca Patterson's speculations about Dickinson's lesbian attachments in *The Riddle of Emily Dickinson*, published in 1951, Millicent Todd Bingham did not decide to publish the "Master" letters in full until 1955. Predictably, critical fascination with the indeterminate documents ensued. Following the patterns of interpretation set by Loomis Todd, who, besides titling "He fumbles at your Soul" (F 22; P 315) "The Master," puts it in the middle of the section titled "Love," which climaxes with the editorially mutilated version of "A solemn thing – it was –" titled "Wedded,"[5] critics and biographers have often used the "Master" letters to perpetuate a more or less rehabilitative image of this author. Like the misleading stories repeatedly emphasizing the importance of Loomis Todd, to whom we do owe gratitude for producing Dickinson's works for the public forum, speculative stories about the poet's mysterious male lover are conventionally novelistic ways to narrate (and thus contain) a life. And stories of "romantic thralldom"[6] are easier to tell than are interpretations of her very complicated, intense, anomalous, almost impossible to categorize, literarily productive love for Sue. For example, Jay Leyda's "The People around Emily Dickinson," which serves as preface to *The Years and Hours of Emily Dickinson*, groups Susan, her intimate friend and sister of nearly four decades, with "The Gilbert Family," but devotes a separate section to Loomis Todd, whose acquaintance with the poet was secondhand, as well as an exclusive one to "Master" (*YH*, section on the Gilberts is xlviii–xlix; section on Loomis Todd, lxxiii–lxxiv; section on "Master," lxi–lxii).

Since Loomis Todd and her daughter Bingham established many of the terms for subsequent receptions, the dominance of such perspectives on Dickinson has been inevitable. As early as 1894, Loomis Todd included six brief sentences from one of the "Master" letters in the edition she produced of Dickinson's letters, then reproduced them again in 1931, dating them "early 1860s," twenty or so years earlier than her original designation of "1885." Not simply one of Dickinson's editors, Loomis Todd was also the "other woman" in a triangle completed by Austin and his wife Sue; thus her stories of reading Dickinson's works and life continually downplay the importance of Sue, who, after the affair was in full swing, regarded the mistress acrimoniously. Likewise, as has been well documented, daughters Bianchi and Bingham inherited and perpetuated this bitter feud. Though Bingham claimed not to like stories of Dickinson the lovelorn and hastened to point out that niece Bianchi was in fact responsible for tales of Aunt Emily's "youthful love for a married man" (*Revelation* 4), by printing a facsimile of one letter and transcriptions of the other two while mentioning Higginson, Wadsworth, Bowles, and Lord as possible candidates for "Master," she reinforced rumors about the poet's mystery lover. In fact, before Bingham's publication of the documents in 1955, all Dickinson studies "were without knowledge of their existence, text, or apparent recipient" (ML 6). Too, Bingham appears enthusiastic when repeating Loomis Todd's story attributing a report on Emily's romance to Sue:

> . . . Here are my mother's unedited words: "About this time Sue, as
> she was called in the village, began to tell me about a remarkable
> sister of Austin's who never went out, and saw no one who called. I
> heard of her also through others in town who seemed to resent,
> somewhat, her refusal to see themselves, who had known her in
> earlier years. Then came a note from this mysterious Emily's house-
> mate, her sister Lavinia, demanding that I call 'at once, with my
> husband.' Sue said at that, 'You will not allow your husband to go
> there, I hope!' 'Why not?' I asked innocently. 'Because they have
> not, either of them, any idea of morality,' she replied, with a certain

satisfaction in her tone. I knew that would interest my good husband, and pressing her a little farther, she added, 'I went in there
one day, and in the drawing room I found Emily reclining in the
arms of a man. What can you say to that?' I had no explanation, of
course, so I let the subject drop, notwithstanding which I went to
the ancestral mansion in which the two lived a few days later."

(*REVELATION* 59)

This is all hearsay, but understandably Bingham does not question
her mother's account, which serves both to portray a haughty, judgmental
Sue and to encourage belief in a clandestine love affair of Emily's. By repeating the story without skepticism, Bingham reinforces the impression
that this is reliable biographical data. Likewise, she never questioned that
the addressee "Master" was real, for she emphatically states that "it is not
impossible that some hitherto unidentified correspondent might turn up,
one whose power to arouse such fine frenzy as that which throbs in these
letters has not yet been suspected" (*Home* 421). Foregrounding speculation about Dickinson's possible relationships with men as she does in relating information about the "Master" documents, then devoting a book,
Emily Dickinson: A Revelation, to Dickinson's supposed amorous affections
for Lord, was perhaps Bingham's unavoidable priority. In typescript documents titled "Scurrilous but True," Loomis Todd unequivocally declared
that "Emily did enjoy her few weeks in both Washington and Philadelphia, and it is quite certain that in the latter city she met the clergyman
who felt her unusual character and to whom she turned for years after-
ward," then followed that gossip with a paragraph making the point that
Dickinson "felt the urge of genuine love" (*Life* 1:289). Bingham's mother
placed relationships with men above all others, and, it should be remembered, the poet's brother Austin, not the poet, was Loomis Todd's primary
emotional connection to the Dickinson clan.

   Certainly Bingham's arrangements and interpretations placed the
patriarchal family at the center of importance: the subtitle for *Emily Dickinson's Home* is *Letters of Edward Dickinson and His Family*. But, as Bingham
reminded readers, the Todd-Bingham interpretive line was not alone in
insinuating that there was a missing man important to the puzzle of Dickinson's life. Bianchi, who wanted to document the vital significance of her
aunt's relationship with her mother, "Sister Sue,"[7] wrote about Dickinson's "renunciation of the man she loved long before we were born"
(*FF* 47–54). As Lillian Faderman shows, Bianchi's representations of Dickinson's writings to her mother excise what Bingham would call expressions

of "fine frenzy" directed at Sue in order to discourage perceptions of their erotic connotations. Yet as we learn about Bianchi's anxiety from her editing of her aunt's works, and about Loomis Todd's assumptions and anxieties about audience from her editing of the poems and letters, which her daughter acknowledged altered "the wording of some poems" (*AB* 335), the most salient (but perhaps most overlooked because all too obvious) fact to keep in mind is that these women were producing a female poet for the patriarchal world. Most important, then, is consideration of what characteristics of the American cultural climate may have prompted and helped constitute their viewpoints. In patriarchy, the most important facts of a woman's life are her relations to men—father, husband, brother, son, lover. The spinster poet Dickinson had a father and brother, but no husband or son and no male lover, as far as we know. In American culture, soap operas, cheap romance novels, sensationalistic tabloid stories, and the primacy of the Oedipal paradigm testify to our thralldom to heterosexual, usually patriarchal, love stories. These indeterminate drafts to "Master" have served for many as patriarchal icons—domesticating Dickinson, assuring that she has not disrupted conventional conceptions of romantic love, and even "proving" to some that this powerful woman was really under some man's thumb. If one interprets these documents autobiographically, the image of Emily Dickinson is of an author writing passionately, desperately, and just like a woman. From this perspective, Eve's sentence binding women to heterosexual desire—"thy desire *shall be* to thy husband, and he shall rule over thee" (Gen. 3 : 16)—commands Dickinson to a "proper" place in patriarchy.

There would not, perhaps, be a problem with obsessive speculation about the "Master" letters if these texts could positively be classified as nonfiction letters addressed to a particular audience, or if they were fair copies that had been folded, tucked into envelopes, and mailed. But they are not. Though written on fine linen stationery, all three—with words or passages crossed out—are drafts. In focusing on the nature of Dickinson's supposed breakdown and on the identity of the Master who some purport was its cause, critics have asked the least interesting questions, queries designed to perpetuate and enhance legends of the white-clad, "partially cracked," popular-culture "myth" (L 481n), and have therefore missed a spectacular opportunity to study the artist's composing process. In the search for Master yet another candidate has recently been added by Polly Longsworth, who extrapolates a possible romance from Dickinson's rather routine question about guests at a Pelham picnic—"Was Mr. Dudley Dear?" (L 293). Quoting only two of Dickinson's letters, neither of which has any clear preoccupation with John Dudley, she speculates, on the basis of one tidbit of gossipy hearsay, that the poet might have been in love with him. As Longsworth's article shows, the search for Him keeps leading readers away from Dickinson's writing.[8] Most measure Dickinson by the apparent depth of the emotional impulses recorded in these drafts, interpreting the letters as if they are the unconscious of her poems, and ignore the signs of the artist experimenting with and reconsidering her expression.

Turning to the documents themselves immediately raises two questions: What is a letter? And what are these letters? Throughout history, letters have assumed many forms, been written for various occasions, and been of wide-ranging import. In the first century A.D., the Apostle Paul wrote letters to fledgling Christian churches to advise them on conducting both intrachurch and interchurch business as well as to suggest how members should comport themselves; in the days of telephonic, instantaneous communication, we write letters so that correspondents will have a record of what we say: personal letters may record affection, condolence, anger; business letters may record offers, terminations, awards or rejections, intentions to enter into a legally binding contract. As products of mass culture, letters may or may not be read by their addressees: superstars pay others to screen and respond to most fan mail; network executives do not read the many letters that come pouring in, but pass them along to minions who merely record numbers of letters in favor and letters objecting to programming decisions. Similarly, our senators and representatives employ staff members to read their mail and scrutinize very few constituent letters themselves. Still, whether by sheer number or individually by the force of persuasive rhetoric, letters maintain their status as potentially monumental items of writing.

In Dickinson's day, letters were a primary medium of both personal and professional communication, and for many letter writing was a fine art, a literary endeavor. Letters have long played a crucial role in literature, and the novel began as an epistolary form. Dickinson's famous "I'm nobody!" (F 11; P 288) perhaps echoes and extends "I am Nobody's"—the pronouncement of Samuel Richardson's heroine in the epistolary *Clarissa*—to articulate playfully the cold, hard truth of a woman without suffrage, for whom the Fourth of July is a time when "Little Boys are commemorating the advent of *their* Country" (L 650; emphasis added). In *Hamlet*, Claudius sends Hamlet the deceased elder's son off with a sealed letter that, not properly delivered, does not result in the demise the uncle intended for his nephew; in *Othello*, letters found on Roderigo complement Emilia's evidence of Desdemona's innocence and prove Iago's guilt and deceit of Othello. An undelivered letter meant to change everything changes nothing in Willa Cather's *Alexander's Bridge,* for Alexander drowns with a "water-soaked and illegible" letter in his pocket informing his wife Winifred that he is leaving her. She lives on, therefore, aware of the letter intended for her but not of its content, believing in the fiction of their happy marriage.[9]

Of those in the Dickinson canon, none have created more fictions than the "Master" letters. Embedded and subordinated in Bingham's statements introducing them is her most important observation about their significance. After spending a paragraph naming the possible addressees, she muses that "it is wiser to wait awhile longer" before settling on one and concludes: "But whoever the man, or men—for all three letters may not be addressed to the same person—here is further evidence that her own heart [and, I will add, her own mind] was her most insistent and baffling contendent" (*Home* 421–422). The importance of this remark is that it directs readers back to Dickinson's concerns, though of more compelling interest than the poet's struggle with her heart are the writing processes and purposes of these letters.

What specific remarks does Dickinson make about letters? In a late letter to Higginson, written after learning of the death of Helen Hunt Jackson, Dickinson exclaimed about epistolary power, especially if its discourse concerns desire:

> What a Hazard a Letter is!
> When I think of the Hearts it has scuttled and sunk, I almost
> fear to lift my Hand to so much as a Superscription.

(L 1007, AUGUST 6, 1885)

In a literary portrayal about perusing a letter, "The Way I read a Letter's – this – " (F 33; P 636), the speaker Dickinson constructs for the poem selects her own society, chooses to take a letter into a private room, and, in order to read it, closes the door on the rest of the world. Though readers are not told what kind of letter this is, from the fact that the speaker enjoys touching it ("I . . . push it with my / fingers –") and revels in reading it without interruption ("And then I go the furthest off / To counteract a knock –"), it appears that the epistle is one cherished, and of a private nature. In the last two stanzas reading the letter proves to be an anticlimatic, disappointing affair. While the opening couple of stanzas focus on caressing and opening the missive, the last half of the poem jarringly shifts the reader's attention to first the most terrestrial then the most cosmic concerns. In the third, the speaker's wide-eyed anticipation narrows to concern that her house is haunted with a tiny four-legged pest ("For firm Conviction of a Mouse") while the fourth records pining for a "Heaven" for which the speaker must wait ("And Sigh for lack of Heaven"). This heaven is not the the "Heaven" that the presumably Christian "God bestow[s]," and though expected, heaven is not conferred by the letter. "Through letters," Cristanne Miller observes, "the poet can control relationships, meeting her correspondents in a literary or aesthetic union— union that can only with difficulty or by death be taken from her because she has constructed it herself through and in language." [10] Just how present writers or addressees actually are in epistolary relationships is of course an infinitely debatable and highly complex issue, but Dickinson's poem substantiates the gist of Miller's observation. To considerable degree, the writer constructs and controls the terms of relationship expressed by a letter, and in this case, the speaker's eager anticipation of an extraordinarily elevating message remains unrewarded. Thus the sender's control over expression constructing the epistolary relationship disappoints the recipient. Whatever, the letter is important enough to be the subject of a poem and to take the speaker's imagination from the ridiculous rodent to a hoped for but unrealized sublime.

As I have already noted, letters are not only the subjects of poems but are sometimes the substance or the poems themselves. In my earlier critiques which began to interpret "Title divine" (P 1072; see chapter 1), I mused on the significance of the different versions sent to two different audiences and on the most probable subjects and situations to which the epistolary poem refers if it is, as so many have suggested, about real events. When Dickinson writes Samuel Bowles, "Because I could not say it – I fixed it in the Verse – for you to read –" (L 251, early 1862), the most obvious interpretation is that she uses poetry to tell stories of her life, at least to Bowles. But to bring the critical story to such hurried closure seriously underestimates both Dickinson's thought and literary endeavors. When Dickinson sends a poem as a letter, what is most important is her transforming daily correspondence into a field for literature. Similarly, most vital for interpretations of the "Master" letters is their significance as literature, not the stories about her love life that we may read in them.

Though like any other writer Dickinson may use the stories of her life to augment her poetic expression, especially the poems but also her letters are not necessarily autobiography. Moreover, self-conscious autobiography, in which the narrating "I" is also narrated and edited for the audience, does not provide readers with an unbiased, factual history. [11] Yet when read for their autobiographical information, Dickinson's poems and letters are sometimes interpreted as if they are foolproof documentation of actual occurrences. This has been especially true of the "Master" letters as Franklin, Cody, and many others question neither that their addressee was real nor that the intended recipient was male. Thus with her statement that "the achievement of the letters . . . is literary," Suzanne Juhasz crucially modifies her assertions that the poet's "'posing' [in letters] tells us as much about the real person as some kind of absolute candor would" and that "we can indeed read Dickinson's letters as autobiography when we recognize that the mode and manner of self-representation is itself an essential self-revelation."[12] What self, after all, is being represented when, as with those three we have titled "Master" and many of Dickinson's others, including her first to Higginson, the letter is unsigned? By not signing so many letters, Dickinson at least tacitly subverts the ideology of autonomous authorship, therefore demanding that readers question not simply "who" is being represented but the very idea of literary "self"-representation.[13] At the same time, as her speaker in "The Way I read a Letter's – this" pushes the letter "with my fingers," Dickinson pushes the bounds of genre. By presenting letters as poems, poems as letters, and narrating so many of both from the perspective of "I," Dickinson demands that readers question overly neat categories of genre, as she begins to undo "a Western generic practice based on exclusion, limit, hierarchy, and taxonomy, and formal norms" by setting up "a fluid, dialogical relationship" between literary forms.[14] Nevertheless, literal-minded conclusions about these literary matters persist.

In the *Manuscript Books* there are three poems folded as if prepared for mailing: "The feet of people walking home" (F 14; P 7), "Knows how to forget" (F 19; P 433), and "The face I carry with / me – last – " (F 19; P 336). With the name of its addressee "heavily erased," "The face I carry with / me – last –" most suggestively raises questions about the autobiographical import of Dickinson's writings. Is the addressee "the face" of the poem? Does the addressee know "the face"? Or is "the face," like the "supposed person" Dickinson declared the "I" or "Representative of the Verse" to be, fictional (L 268, July 1862)? Though letter-poems like "Title divine" or, as Patterson and Faderman have argued, poems like "Wild Nights" may well be expressions of lesbian or erotic desires like those Dickinson actually experienced, and although poems like "The face I carry with / me – last –" may express hopes of eventual reward for long-suffering devotion similar to ones Dickinson really harbored, these poems should not be read as near-autobiographical accounts. Reading too literally, we may, mimicking Dimmesdale, speak "the very" emotional "truth" expressed by these writings, but by applying it to interpret Dickinson's biography, transform it "into the veriest falsehood" (*The Scarlet Letter*, "The Interior of a Heart," Chapter XI). The selves revealed by her letters and poems, then, are Dickinson's literary identities or ways of being, informed, to be sure, by the emotions of the actual woman who lived and wrote in Amherst but not faithfully representing them or revealing her. If they script an autobiography, it is a portrait of the artist.

What portrait of the artist appears in the "Master" letters? Like the responses evoked by Bonnie Hayes's "Love Letter," made popular by the performance of Bonnie Raitt, what kind of story emerges deciphering or interpreting these depends very much on the desires of the reader (see epigraphs for this chapter). The house of the song's first line is variously imagined in the minds of the audience, as is the beloved to whom the house belongs, as is the car in which the speaker sits, as are the songs the speaker hears from the crooners on the radio. In this song, the audience constructs the beloved, and the song's main subject is not a lover longed for but the passionate longing itself; thus the love object is not so much the possible lover but the passion presently enjoyed. Similarly, interpreting the "Master" letters, each reader scripts his or her own beloved object. Since most readers are heterosexual or expect heterosexual amorous discourse and since Dickinson uses the male pronoun or "Sir" as the addressee of two of these, most interpretations confirm conventional expectations. But Rebecca Patterson's extensive study of Dickinson's letters and poems led her to quite different conclusions regarding the gender of a mysterious beloved's identity and to speculation about the poet's passion for Kate Anthon and Sue. Besides the context of erotic letters to those two women, textual facts of the documents themselves throw the gender identity of the beloved into question as well as raise more questions about genre. Briefly and document by document, I will scrutinize each of the drafts, specifically as records of her writing process.

A "Beard," As You Like It

Apparently written between 1854 and 1858, the first letter, which I shall call "Dear Master" and whose addressee is never gendered through pronoun reference, is written in ink. The few emendations are also inked, and appear just above the line for which alternative words are suggested (A 827; ML 11–19; L 187). "Dear Master" provides fine examples of one way in which Dickinson began to weave poems into her prose and to experiment delightedly with punctuation. Franklin's third, Johnson's second letter, which I will call "Master" and would date somewhere between 1858 and 1864, is also in ink with many pencil emendations that may have been made any time from soon after the letter was penned to the late 1870s–1890s (A 828; ML 31–46; L 233). The changes include the cancellations of quite a few lines (by crossing out) as well as alternative wording. From "Master" one can learn Dickinson's liberties with gender-determined conventions of language, and, by reading it in the context of parallel writings, one sees the tremendously literary nature of her correspondence. From Franklin's second letter, Johnson's third, which I shall call "Oh' did I offend it" and which is written in pencil with several pencil alterations, one sees the problems of dating Dickinson's texts and, if a reader desires a real addressee, of assigning the title "Master" to any one correspondent (A 829; ML 21–29; L 248). Since all three letters passed through the hands of her brother Austin and his lover Loomis Todd but were not made available in full until Bingham chose to make them so more than half a century after their discovery, they remind us of problems inherent in the transmission of all of Dickinson's poems and letters. And all serve as reminders that, as did Johnson, Franklin considers his own excellent and painstaking work as something to be improved upon and not as the final word on transcribing the writings of Emily Dickinson.[15]

Commencing "Dear Master," the first draft expresses concern for the recipient's health, acknowledges receiving and giving flowers, and concludes declaring that writing is painful. No printing of this letter reproduced a very important aspect of its composition, now available in the photographic representations. In thanking her correspondent for flowers, Dickinson weaves a bit of verse into her prose and plays with punctuation in a way that enhances the skating rhythm of her syllables:

> The Violets are
> by my side . The Robin
> very near, And "Spring"
> they say, Who is She,
> going by the door,
>
> (A 827A; ML 14; L 187)

Dickinson directs the quotation marks toward the left margin and the dash following down and away from "Spring." On the next line, she does the same after "She." In manuscript the punctuation makes the words sashay across the page and delight in a way that is lost to us in conventional printing. As is true of punctuation strategies involving dashes that dance up or down, this is not verbal signification in the usual sense. Punctuation serves simultaneously as grammatical sign and as visual mimicry of a spring that seems, with its blossoms bobbing and birds returning, to dance. To reproduce the giddy punctuation of the holograph with words translated into uniform typeface highlights the punctuation and discounts the significance of the chirography. Thus my editorial formulation retains the least conventional aspects of the letter's details and ascribes literary importance to that characteristic of the Dickinson manuscripts most widely recognized as unusual but most often ignored as merely idiosyncratic—her oddly designed "dashes."

Translating these lines of Dickinson into a typeface poem, I could, like Thomas Johnson editing an October 1851 letter to Austin (L 58) to create "There is another sky" (P 2), make a much more conventional lyric, with four units lineated predictably in iambic tetrameter, trimeter, dimeter, tetrameter:

> The Violets are by my side
> The Robin very near
> And "Spring," they say,
> Who is she, going by the door.

Retaining Dickinson's lineation produces a much more interesting poem than this one. Yet both poems have to be made from a text originally embedded in prose—not even space between lines or indentations from margins signal the reader. So both poems are editorial constructions like Johnson's creation of "There is another sky," and not like the later "letter-poems" (H, Lowell Autograph; Sue Dickinson to William Hayes Ward, February 8, 1891) or verse-letters which, at a glance, look like lyrics. "The Violets are / by my side" is a poem produced according to the editor/reader's prerogative, just as conventional letters, relineated by editors to meet expectations for prose, have been made of the many distinctive letter-poems Dickinson began producing in the 1860s.

Johnson observes that the "style and rhythm" of Dickinson's letters "begin to take on qualities that are so nearly the quality of her poems as on occasion to leave the reader in doubt where the letter leaves off and the poem begins" (L xv). Yet in print translation, much of her experimentation with traditional forms has been lost to us. To work with the manuscripts themselves and see so many dashes directed up and down in the middle of a line is to see how much of Dickinson's visual notation has been lost to us in print; likewise, even in translations like Johnson's, where he will sometimes print lines according to iambic tetrameter or some other traditional poetic scheme though Dickinson's manuscript does not represent them that way, her blurring of the distinctions between poetry and prose are hinted at but finally lost to us. For example, he separates "'*Speech*' – is a prank / of *Parliament* –" (A 691a; L 252), woven into a letter to Samuel Bowles, and "Silence is all / we dread" (H B 123; L 397), woven into a letter to Sue. In each case, the entire letter, not just the lines he isolates as poetry, looks like a lyric poem. Johnson's decision is not without its logic: one of the Norcross sisters made a transcription of "'*Speech*' – is a prank / of *Parliament* –" from documents Dickinson sent them, and the last two lines of "Silence is all / we dread" appear on a worksheet draft of Dickinson's.

Yet whether Dickinson saw these lines as discrete poems, separate from the letters into which she so carefully wove them, is highly questionable. Barrett Browning, one of Dickinson's literary heroes, called *Aurora Leigh*, one of the poet's favorites, "Her Novel in Verse"; it would be wise to bear that in mind when pondering Dickinson's designs in blending poetry with prose, making poems of letters and letters of poems. In some ways, such moves constitute the ultimate democratization of poetry, integrating it into quotidian production. In an age when Emerson, declaring "We have listened too long to the courtly muses of Europe" (see "The American Scholar"), called for America's literary independence and yearned for a truly American poet while Whitman worked hard to fulfill such a dream, these "letter-poems" were, as Sue Dickinson seemed to realize, part of that same cultural and artistic project. By producing letter-poems Dickinson makes her poetry seem immediate, part of everyday experience, and attests to what Gary Lee Stonum calls her ambivalence toward poet as master[16]; as part of a letter the poetry is inviting, accessible to the common reader. Therefore, instead of normalizing her strategies in order to separate a few lines and make conventional poems, we should interrogate the political significance of the letter-poems as well as the aesthetic potential Dickinson recognized in them.

Though they look more like conventional prose than the later letter-poems, the "Master" letters are poetic. That they have been read for biographical information is not simply a consequence of their appearing to be items of conventionally heterosexual amorous discourse. Both the spilled ink on "Dear Master" (A 827a, ML 17, L 187) and the rhetoric of the letters themselves tender an immediacy, an illusion of authorial presence, as do references to exchanges of flowers, apparent answers to questions like "You ask me what my flowers said –" (A 827ᵛ; ML 15; L 187) and "I dont know what you can do for it" (A 828aᵛ; ML 39; L 233), and entreaties like "Could you come to New England – [this Summer] – [Could] would you come to Amherst – Would you like to come – Master?" (A 828bᵛ; ML 42; L 233). At the same time, the letters' existence reminds readers of the author's absence. Similarly, the letters suggest that one is reading something extraordinarily personal and, through mention of Amherst in "Master," events definitely real. Yet Dickinson's characteristic ellipsis, indeterminate reference, and use of geography to articulate distance between hearts—a strategy characteristic of many nineteenth-century writers (like one of her favorites, George Eliot)—underscore the fact that one can never know just what confidences are being read. Nor can the possibility be dismissed that, like a late letter to Maria Whitney, these to Master are "also fiction" (L 969, 1880s). In fact, as the many revisions of "Master" and "Oh' did I offend it" demonstrate, the letters' hysterical, urgent tone and the relentless present tense of their pleading, which both recall excruciating emotional pain and admit it is ongoing while the speaker utters impossible dreams of happy union, are not spontaneous, but carefully constructed.

Inked, the draft "Master" has extensive pencil alterations. Many words are crossed out; clauses, sometimes several in a row, are canceled; suggested revisions are penciled above the line. There are certain things about this letter that seem to confirm that it could only have been written to a man. In fact, these elements seem to make a heterosexual interpretation of this frustrated love letter almost indisputable: Dickinson, or the speaker, is a stabbed Daisy (A 828; ML 33) and wants to occupy "the Queen's place" (A 828a; ML 37). Addressing Master as "Sir," she cries, "but if I had the Beard on my cheek—like you—" (L 233), and asks "What would you do with me if I came 'in white'?" (A 828bᵛ; ML 42). Flowers have long represented women; stabbing certainly seems a phallic maneuver and brings to mind the male figure bee. But in Dickinson's world, flowers stab each other:

> That any
> Flower should
> be so base
> as to stab
> my Susan,
> I believe un-
> willingly – . . .
> Choose Flowers

that have no
Fang, Dear – . . .

(H B 106; L 911).

Not simply receptive, flowers can even bite. Conventionally, queens are coupled with kings, but since in Dickinson's scheme of things a rhetoric of similarity often casts the story, a queen may very well take her place beside another queen instead of a king: "One Summer," two "Queens" were "Wed" (F 26; P 631); two women will either make each other royal or "Neither" will "be a Queen" (F 32; P 458).

When Dickinson first penned "but if I had the Beard on my cheek," she did not add "like you—." In two of the more meticulous transcriptions to date, neither Johnson nor Sewall (L 233; *Life* 2:514–515) in any way advises us that "like you ," (A 828b) is penciled above the line, apparently an afterthought, certainly a revision. Redundant, it is an uncharacteristic sort of addition for the expressively compact poet, and the handwriting is different enough from the inked script of the main body of the letter to suggest that the addition was made at a much different time—chronologically or psychically. Whenever, however, by whomever made, the revisionary phrase insists on a particular reading and signals anxiety over the ambiguous interpretation allowed in its absence.[17] This brief fantasy, or "What if," to which it is added immediately follows a paragraph smoldering with sexuality waiting, but not daring, to erupt: "Vesuvius" and "Etna" "dont talk," no longer articulate their power in this world (A 828a^v). If at one point Dickinson envisioned her addressee beardless, or a woman, this might be asking "What if I were a man and our love a usual heterosexual arrangement?" Some of Dickinson's poems make such an interpretation more than plausible; in fact, they encourage such readings. In "Rearrange a 'Wife's' affection," Dickinson's speaker tells of a "*bandaged*" secret and says that "Seven years of troth" to an addressee whose gender remains unclear have taught her "More than Wifehood ever may!" To rearrange her love, she wails a suggestion—"Make me bearded like a man!"—then rejects that idea (F 11; P 1737). Also, in a poem Sue marked with an "L," possibly for love, a feminine "Cactus splits her Beard," and the poem's speaker is "Thy Daisy – / Draped for thee!" (F 18; P 339).[18] Yet throughout the letter the only variant for Master is "Sir" and the rest of the paragraph seems to indicate that it is a man who has left her love behind:

I dont know what you can
do for it – thank you – Master -

– but if I had the Beard on
    (like you ,)
my cheek – and you – had Daisy's
petals – and you cared so for
me – what would become of you?
       (me)
Could you forget in fight, or
flight ,   or the foreign land?

(A 828A^{V}–B; ML 38–41; L 233)

A conventionalizing interpretation of this passage would maintain that "you" has a beard and does not have Daisy's petals, therefore is a man. Yet in Dickinson's world of words it is not extraordinary for her to approach a beloved woman with masculine address, and the speaker may simply be returning a literarily cross-dressed female to her original state. Another poem that Sue marked with an "L," "The Moon is distant from / the Sea –" (F 19; P 429), portrays gender as fluid and gender roles as easily reversible when by the last stanza the "Signor" has become the feminine moon. Significantly, the gender of the poem's speaker, who is led by that moon, remains undifferentiated, further suggesting that gender need not be fixed nor precisely determined. In an 1859 letter to Elizabeth Holland, Dickinson refers to herself as "a Bachelor" (L 204), then in an 1866 letter calls herself "Uncle Emily" (L 315), and in an 1878 letter to nephew Ned, she masculinizes herself again: "You know that Pie you stole – well, this is that Pie's Brother – Mother told me when I was a Boy, that I must 'turn over a new Leaf' – I call that the Foliage Admonition – Shall I commend it to you?" (L 571). As late as the early 1880s, Dickinson masculinizes Sue by equating her with the male figure sun[19]:

Thank her
dear power
for having come,
An Avalanche of Sun!

(H B 188; L 755, ABOUT 1882)

By that time, addressing Sue as male was a long-established pattern. As early as June 1852, pining for Sue's return, she writes, "Why, Susie, it seems to me as if my absent Lover was coming home so soon – and my heart must be so busy, making ready for him," and follows up with a long self-conscious paragraph about not being able to pay full attention to a minister's sermon because she "was trying to make up" her "mind" which dress "was prettiest to go and welcome" Susie (L 96). Here Sue is masculine, and after she has become sister-in-law Dickinson characterizes Sue, who is away spending the summer with her sister, Martha Smith, as a man who flees his powerful feeling:

> . . . Ah – Dobbin – Dobbin – you little know the chink
> which your dear face makes. We would'nt mind the sun,
> dear, if it did'nt *set* – . . .
>
> (L 194, SEPTEMBER 1858)

Calling her Captain Dobbin of *Vanity Fair*, who even while he loves silently and for years, takes flight and runs to fight, Dickinson identifies Sue with a lover who, "a coward in heart," absents himself and runs after heroic valor. When Dobbin leaves his beloved Emmy the first time, he leaves her "in a white morning dress," and when he leaves her the second time he leaves her "not caring for society, and moping there a great deal" and "not very happy after her heroic sacrifice" (chapters 30 and 67). Dickinson's parade in white is famous and the "Compact" between her Queens, "Misery" (F 32; P 458). And this "Master" draft beseeches:

> What would you do with me
> if I came "in white"?
> Have you the little Chest – to
> put the Alive – in?
>
> (A 828B^V; ML 42; L 233)

Women may or may not have large breasts, but it is usually men who pump iron with hopes of becoming barrel-chested; and it is women who keep hope chests. Whether she refers to dainty physique or prenuptial habit or something else, "little Chest" signifies the feminine, as well as the role-playing of dramatic performance. Thackeray's "A Novel Without a Hero" concludes: "Ah! *Vanitas Vanitatum!* which of us is happy in this world? Which of us has his desire? or, having it, is satisfied?—Come children, let us shut up the box and the puppets, for our play is played out" (chapter 67). Fond of Shakespeare, and probably *Twelfth Night*, certainly *As You Like It* and *The Merchant of Venice* (see L 545, L 882, L 48, L 958, P 247), Dickinson was familiar with cross-dressing and with a disguised heroine serving as a page to her beloved, in which case the beloved would be "Master." Here Dickinson may well be appropriating such techniques for her gender-destabilizing purposes. At first glance, the speaker appearing "in white" seems surely to allude to a woman who wants to be a bride. But as Emmy appeared to Dobbin, Dickinson's female speaker may have been suggesting that she appear before one with "the little Chest," a female addressee, her Dobbin, "in white." To interpret the pronouns and symbols of this letter singlemindedly by insisting that we can be certain of the addressee's gender robs only the reader.

Critics have looked far and wide and concocted credible, as well as some of the most preposterous, hypotheses imaginable to identify a masculine Master. But the Dickinson lexicon, in which a powerful *she* is *he*, and in which queens are coupled with queens, offers compelling challenges to conventional interpretations, literal or literary, of Master's identity. Though the comparison has usually been overlooked, in her essay " 'The Love of Thee—a Prism Be,' " Adalaide Morris notes the striking similarities between the drafts to "Master" and the letters to Sue; however, because she does not admit the possibility that the "Master" letters might be lesbian literature, she reads the differences that the feminine speaker notes between herself and Master simply as gender differences. Thus she does not consider that the letters may be revisionary mythmaking, articulating anxieties over separation from or rejection by a same-sex lover by translating them into the hierarchical conventions of amorous discourse.[20] If she indeed uses heterosexual discourse for expression of lesbian love, Dickinson equates woman-for-woman desire with that legitimized by mainstream culture. In "Dear Master," the speaker never identitifies himself or herself as male or female, nor identifies Master's gender. The reader/listener must construct the sexual identities of the characters, and the audience of "Dear Master" has usually presumed that Emily Dickinson's letter features a female speaker conventionally addressing a male as "Master." But as Dickinson does throughout the correspondence to Sue, her speaker may be addressing a literary female with terms customarily reserved for males; thus the apparently indisputable heterosexual discourse of "Oh' did I offend it" and "Master" could, as the addition of "A Beard" suggests, be elaborate cross-dressing.

As Margaret Homans has observed, "It may be that Dickinson's greatest originality is in her breaking out of the terms of gender altogether." Though she refers to poems featuring a rhetoric of similarity, "in which the mind appears to be divided into identical halves and in which identical terms replace the expected terms of opposition or complementarity,"[21] her analysis may be usefully extended to discuss Dickinson's bold inversions of gender dynamics and of gendered symbols. The speaker in these letters is not merely a tiny daisy, but also allies herself with the potent Etna. And, as Rebecca Patterson and Gilbert and Gubar remind us, even if "Master" is seen as a male muse, he is curiously passive. Not content to explore power relationships simplistically, in "I make His Crescent fill / or lack –" (F 40; P 909) Dickinson's ungendered speaker subverts our expectations and declares control over a male figure: "He holds superior in the Sky / Or gropes, at My Command." As the lyric's closing verse shows, Dickinson's point when she ponders power is not the expected one, for, like an American Hegel, she concludes the poem to shatter an illusion some have about dominance—that the one in control is all powerful:

> But since We hold a
> Mutual Disc –
> And front a Mutual Day –
> Which is the Despot,
> neither knows –
> Nor Whose – the Tyranny –

The ruler is as enslaved as the ruled, for those in control need those who obey to maintain their command. As Gilbert and Gubar point out when examining poems that they connect to the "Master" myth, especially "My Life had stood – a / Loaded Gun –" (F 34; P 754), "As in Blake's 'The Mental Traveler,' master and slave continually trade places."[22] Thus as she breaks out of the terms of gender, Dickinson also breaks out of overly simplistic terms of dominance and submission, which are not just inverted but are equated. "Mutual," each needs the other in order to be. Also, throughout the Dickinson canon, symbols like the sun, traditionally masculine, are sometimes identified with powerful females like Sue, and symbols like the moon in "The Moon is distant from / the Sea –" (F 19; P 429), traditionally feminine, are sometimes identified with the male title "Signor," which may refer to a male character or to a cross-dressed female. Besides calling herself a boy, a bachelor, and Uncle Emily, to her Norcross cousins Dickinson signed an 1871 letter "Brother Emily" (L 367) and in 1870 referred to a visitor's "son Elizabeth" (L 656). Since her gendered rhetoric bears no consistent relation to actual male and female persons, in the "Master" letters Dickinson may, therefore, be appropriating the power struggles often encoded within conventional stories of romance not simply so her "undoing of rhetorical dualisms becomes a model for a revised pattern of relations between the sexes" (as Homans contends), but in order to script an unconventional tale of romantic love between members of the same sex. More contextualizing of the ostensibly heterosexual rhetoric of the

"Master" letters in light of literary works with which nineteenth-century readers were familiar as well as of the poet's correspondence to Sue proves elucidating and casts more doubt on interpretations which take the pronouns simply at face value.

That these are grieving letters and might be called a little insane most critics agree. But they are certainly not the only letters in the Dickinson canon bearing hysterical rhetoric. To Sue she writes, "In thinking of those I love, my reason is all gone from me, and I do fear sometimes that I must make a hospital for the hopelessly insane, and chain me up there such times, so I wont injure you" (L 77); and, just when Sue is going to her first tryst with Austin, "One would hardly think I had lost you to hear this revelry, but your absence insanes me so – . . ." (L 107). With histrionic expression, twice Dickinson says she will lay her love, which she thinks "may be wrong" (L 85), her love for Sue, in her "box of Phantoms" (L 177) or her "casket" (L 194), and in "Master" she implores the addressee to inter her, alive, in the "little Chest." Besides recalling riddles of true love like Bassanio's winning Portia's hand by choosing the leaden casket housing her portrait (instead of the more materialistically enticing silver and gold chests), such hyperbolic, literary rhetoric should be recognized as part and parcel of the era's sentimental love religion.

In the "concept of romance" that was "a fundamental element of Dickinson's popular culture," "death, love, the afterlife, nature, and art were all bound in fealty to the great idea of romance, whether it was found in theology, history, fiction, or real life." As St. Armand observes, "All the Dickinson children engaged in this romantic kind of mythmaking" and used the rhetoric of passion "endemic to a romantic age."[23] Indeed, the trope of the little casket occurs repeatedly in Dickinson's letters of this period, as a "box of Phantoms" to John Graves (L 186) and "a little box" (L 192) to Mary Emerson Haven. Read against this backdrop, the similarities between the dramas of the "Master" letters and those of love stories by the Bronte sisters, Browning, Longfellow, Thoreau, Stowe, Coventry Patmore, and many others are of utmost importance for any analysis of the Dickinson documents. At a time when the "Good News" was that patriarchal Calvinism was being replaced with sentimentalism, thus elevating feeling itself to a redemptive capacity, these passionate discourses are, like those of Little Em'ly to her family after abandoning Ham for Steerforth, preoccupied with writing desire and with telling some of middle-class American culture's favorite kind of love stories.

In *My Emily Dickinson* Susan Howe reminds us that in *David Copperfield*, "Master" Davy is "Daisy" to Steerforth and that Little Em'ly writes "disjointed, pleading letters after eloping with Steerforth, addressed to her family, Ham, and possibly Master Davy/David/Daisy—the recipient is never directly specified, and the letters are unsigned."[24] Howe compares the beseeching "Oh, if you knew how my heart is torn" (*David Copperfield*, chapter 31) rhetoric of Little Em'ly's letters to that of the "Master" letters. Her suggestion that "these three letters were probably self-conscious exercises in prose by one writer playing with, listening to, and learning from others" seems much more in keeping with the Emily Dickinson who with pink thread attached clippings of *The Old Curiosity Shop*'s Little Nell to "A poor – torn Heart – a tattered heart" to make a "cartoon" of one of her most sentimental lyrics (see Figure 5).[25] Framing her poem with these cutouts, Dickinson implicitly demands that the reader consider how the pictures comment on her lyric and how it in turn comments on one of the most celebrated scenes in nineteenth-century British fiction. The layout seems designed to amuse, challenging singular and sober-minded interpretations of both Dickens's scene and Dickinson's poem. When unfolded like a letter, the illustrations of Little Nell being comforted by her grandfather and Little Nell being ferried to heaven by angels immediately demand attention, urging readers to interpret the "poor – torn Heart" as that of Nell. Since the layout was folded in thirds like a letter and the illustration attached to the bottom was folded up, Little Nell midst the angels popped out—in a fashion similar to that of our pop-up greeting cards—as the reader "pushed it with" her fingers to peruse the contents. Thus the cartooning cutout works to undercut any culturally predetermined insistence that this is a poem articulating Dickinson's miserable flight into angelic rescue. What might be read all too solemnly when divorced from the illustrations cannot be read without humor with her original context restored. Half a century later the death of Little Nell prompted Oscar Wilde to remark that one must have a heart of stone to read about it without bursting out laughing. Judging by the response evinced by the use she made of it to design a pop-up "cartoon," Dickinson anticipated such exhortations to read well beyond convention. The poet's production shows that Dickinson depended on the readers' intertextual interpretive powers and literary play to make sense of the "some supposed persons" of "A poor – torn Heart." The images of "A poor – torn Heart – a tattered heart" (HB 175; P 78) bear striking resemblances to the "childish bosom," "stabs," and "gashes" of "Oh' did I offend it" and "Master," and in contexts such as this, to pore over the missives in morbid fascination, admitting no possibility for irony, says more about our need to believe in a woman's romantic thralldom than it does about Emily Dickinson.

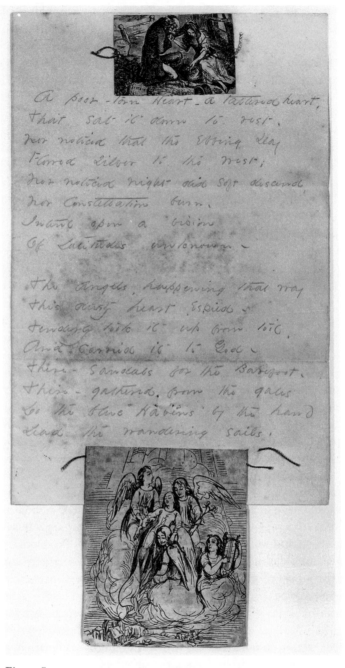

Figure 5
Copy of "A poor – torn Heart" sent to Sue. By permission of the Houghton
Library, Harvard University.

Dickinson's letters to various correspondents show page after page of the poet presenting herself as bard, as comic, as counselor, as friend in need, but always as writer, and, as this layout suggests, she in turn expected writerly readers. By attaching pictures from *The Old Curiosity Shop* to her poem echoing both the rhetoric of *David Copperfield*'s Little Em'ly's letters and one of her own "Master" letters, Dickinson appears to encourage readers to develop multifarious intertextualities. Interestingly, in *The Old Curiosity Shop* Dickinson had a model for destabilizing conventional assumptions about gender as Dickens highlighted ways in which sexual differences are rhetorically constructed. Through appellation and attitude, for all practical purposes Mr. Brass turns his sister Miss Brass into a man. "In fact she bore such a striking resemblance to her brother, . . . that had it consorted with Miss Brass's maiden modesty and gentle womanhood to have assumed her brother's clothes in a frolic and sat down beside him, it would have been difficult for the oldest friend of the family to determine which was Sampson and which Sally. . . ." In fact, her brother's rhetoric cross-dressed this "kind of amazon of common law": "It may be observed in this place, lest the fact of Mr. Brass calling a lady a rascal, should occasion any wonderment or surprise, that he was so habituated to having her near him in a man's capacity, that he had gradually accustomed himself to talk to her as though she were really a man" (chapter 33). This surely intrigued the writer who frequently played with gendered language, and whom Bowles apparently called his "Rascal" (L 515) while she nicknamed herself "Marchioness" and him "Swiveller" (L 241; the latter two are characters in *The Old Curiosity Shop*).

Likewise, a fallen woman entangled in a relationship not quite sanctioned by society, Dickens's Little Em'ly surely must have fascinated Dickinson, and there are other indications that his rhetoric permeates the "Master" letters. In "Master," "Vesuvius dont talk – Etna – dont – [They] said a syllable – one of them – a thousand years ago, and Pompeii heard it, and hid forever – . . ." (A 828a[V]). "Vesuvius" enjoys a certain prominence throughout *David Copperfield*, especially in a disjointed passage of interrupted, halting expression when Micawber is speaking to Copperfield: "I'll partake of no one's hospitality, until I have—a—moved Mount Vesuvius—to eruption—on—a—the abandoned rascal—. . ." (chapter 49). Pollak remarks that "Dickinson was fully capable of constructing a fictive correspondence, had she wished to. That she would have constructed an *incoherent* fictive identity for herself seems improbable, nor is there any other known instance of her use of the prose letter for this solipsistic purpose alone."[26] Indeed, as is characteristic of Dickinson's epistolary performances, the writing is strong enough to create the illusion that the speaker earnestly means what she says and that the addressee must in fact be real; as Aristotle, Mikhail Bakhtin, Roland Barthes, Linda Kauffman, and others have observed, using language to make the beloved palpable is a common characteristic of discourses of desire, fictional and nonfictional.[27] Thus in her production of these love letters, the writer Dickinson participates in a long-established literary tradition by making both the addressee and the writer seem real, even present to readers. Studying the letter "Master" in the context of one of her favorite Dickens's texts, which sports similar incoherent epistolary rhetoric, argues for interpreting the letter as consciously paralleling fictional expressions of the period and not simply as authentic emotional exclamation. But for the most part these letters have been read soberly, as if Emily Dickinson, not Little Em'ly, "was took bad with fever, and, what is very strange . . . is,—maybe 'tis not so strange to scholars,—the language of that country went out of her head, and she could only speak her own, that no one understood" (*David Copperfield*, chapter 51).

The fiction of her time was rife with the terminology found in the "Master" letters, with Rochester pulling baubles and trinkets from his "casket" during his masquerade, Jane Eyre calling him "Master," and Ham calling Copperfield "Mas'r Davy," and Dickinson repeatedly alludes to contemporary writers in both her letters and poems. In "Trudging to Eden" (Set 7; P 1020), "Somebody's" little boy calls himself "Trotwood," thus designating the "Lady" addressed in the line following as "Miss Betsey." As the poem takes revisionary liberties with the characters of *David Copperfield*, the "Master" letters are not literal reiterations of little Em'ly's missives nor of Jane's mode of address for Rochester, but revisionary appropriations for writings whose classification as fiction or nonfiction remains stubbornly indeterminate. When in "Oh' did I offend it" the speaker writes that she grieves "her Lord," Dickinson possibly calls the Judge's name. But this popular religious term is found elsewhere in her sensuous correspondences. When her friend becomes unresponsive and ceases "indeed to talk," Dickinson asks if she should bear Kate Anthon "just as usual unto the kind Lord" (L 209). Yet in "Oh' did I offend it" she may be addressing her audience directly, as she seems surely to be doing in another of the letters supposedly written to Judge Lord. There the speaker remarks, ". . . a Night is *so* long, and it snowing too, another barrier to Hearts that overleap themselves – Emily 'Jumbo'! Sweetest name, but I know a sweeter –" and calls herself "Emily Jumbo Lord –" (A 748b; *Revelation* 88; L 780). As critics have demonstrated time and again, on the basis of such circumstantial evidence, persuasive (and mutually contradictory) arguments can be made to qualify a variety of candidates for "Master," but the highly imaginative world represented in these letters can never be said to bear exact correlation to events in Dickinson's relationships.

So neither their addressee nor their genre can be precisely determined, and definite dating of the "Master" letters is equally questionable. Elements like the fact that the lines span the page, making each letter resemble a conventional prose epistle that is radically different from the letter-poems that begin to emerge later in the 1860s, argue for dating the letters in the late 1850s and early 1860s. Franklin's reasons for dating the documents in 1858 and 1861 are logical, though he interprets references to spring, summer, and Amherst literally. However, much about the handwriting of the pencil draft "Oh' did I offend it" matches, when one compares letter to letter, detail to detail, a rough draft of a letter traditionally regarded as one written to Judge Lord "about 1878." For example, the word "cannot" in the tenth line of "Oh' did I offend it," which Franklin dates "1861," matches that of the "cannot" in the fourteenth line of "My lovely Salem smiles," dated more than a decade and a half later (compare A 829, A 829a, ML 22–29, L 248 to A 735, L 559, and *Revelation* 78–81, esp. the rough draft on 80–81; see also A 748a, A 748a^V, L 780, L 800). Yet several formations of "the" in "Oh' did I offend it" also match those in the pencil revision of "Safe in their Alabaster Chambers," which Dickinson sent to Sue sometime in the early 1860s (H B 74; *Life* 1:203). As Franklin notes, Dickinson's formation of the word "the" has been viewed as a significant clue for dating her documents (ML 9). Rather than speculate that the "Lord letter" (L 559) is dated too late or that "Oh' did I offend it" and the draft of "Safe in their Alabaster Chambers" are dated too early, scholars would do well to note that assigning precise, indisputably accurate dates for these letters is as enigmatical as trying to determine a real addressee. An even more important critical shift would be for scholars to emphasize the fact that the many revisions in the letters heighten our awareness of Dickinson's painstaking care in epistolary production.

This Text Is Not Conclusion

As were the letters supposedly written to Judge Lord, the "Master" letters were passed along to the world by "Austin." When Bingham framed them by presenting them in *Emily Dickinson's Home*, she represented them as letters to a real addressee, never suggesting that they might be fictional. Johnson followed suit by accompanying "Dear Master" with the note, "She may have had the Reverend Charles Wadsworth in mind as 'Master'" (L 187), then placing a letter presumably from Wadsworth to Dickinson immediately after "Oh' did I offend it" (L 248). Yet whether or not Dickinson would have contextualized them that way for public presentation remains an open question. By binding cutouts from *The Old Curiosity Shop* to the top and bottom of one of her most sentimental poems, Dickinson gleefully frames her reiteration of a popular tale about Little Nell into a witty greeting card for her beloved Sue. Her production of the "Master" letters may well parallel her production of "A poor – torn Heart – a tattered heart," and this possibility is of ultimate importance for readers who, in framing interpretation of the "Master" letters, set the terms and range of critique. Scrutinizing the "Master" manuscripts and emphasizing similarities between their rhetoric and that of letters to Sue, as well as similarities between Dickinson's writings and ones fictional with which she was plainly familiar, frames the study of them so that the field for interpretation presupposes the critical importance of acknowledging the indeterminacies of author (or the "I" of the missives), audience, and genre. Those ambiguities can lead us to no positive conclusions except that the manuscripts reveal that the process of writing these letters was not hysterical, overly emotional, or out of control, but carefully manipulated.

Yet within the most widely shared horizon of expectations or critical field of vision in Dickinson studies, overly determined interpretations of the "Master" letters have inspired many stories about the author which have done little to advance critical understanding of her poetic project and have proven to be something of an Achilles' heel for the body of Dickinson's writings, toppling interrogations of her literary works so they lie as clues about her life's story. Targeting the "Master" letters as keys to understanding the author inevitably leads to speculation about Dickinson's personality, and poems, especially the seven directly referring to "Master," begin to be interpreted as if they supply biographical data.[28] On such a field, literary criticism can easily degenerate into canards about the author's life. Any interpretation of the author or these three works, even (or perhaps especially) one revisionary, must take the significations of that critical scar into account, acknowledging that, suppressed for a half century, once rescued from their premature burial, these letters have been celebrated as personal, not literary, evidence. To read the "Master" letters to identify who "He" is with the hope that, by coming to a better understanding of her heart's desire, readers might more intimately analyze her poetic mind, brackets her artistic objectives as autobiographical. Readers attempting to construct an interpretation of the documents as fiction will want to ask why autobiographical interpretations have not only prevailed but primarily go unchallenged. Readers wanting to construct interpretations substantiating these letters as nonfiction will also want to pose such questions. In their questions, both kinds of readers will want to decide whether their horizons of expectations are closed—so that understanding is "the recognition and interpretation of a professed or revealed truth"— or open, thus making understanding "the search for or investigation of a possible meaning." [29] Allowing critical travel, thus new horizons continually unfolding, critics investigate the body of Dickinson's works in different lights illuminating various possibilities of meaning. But if the critical horizon is fixed, only its singular light renders point of view, and readers resign themselves and their interpretations to hermeneutical stasis.

Franklin underscores his packaging the "Master" letters in envelopes to appear as real love letters by declaring in his introduction that "Dickinson did not write letters as a fictional genre" (ML 5). But that Dickinson may have written fiction was not an untenable idea to her contemporaries who speculated that she may have written the "Saxe Holm" stories (*YH* 2:295–297). Nevertheless, since all of her other surviving letters are addressed to real flesh-and-blood audiences, Franklin's characterization appears to be an authoritative—a more than credible, in fact a probable— contention. Omitted from this reconstruction, however, are the levels of fictionality—for example, various "I's" who were each constructed for a particular correspondence and a particular time—comprising all writings, even those unequivocally purporting to be autobiographical. Thus Franklin delimits possibilities for interpretations that he might formulate not by a statement of indisputable fact, but by an informed critical opinion. Any subsequent critical formulation should include and interrogate his horizon of expectations, not to foreclose interpretation of these documents either as certainly nonfictional or as positively fictional, but to generate more and more aesthetic questions about their designs. Dickinson may not have written letters as a fictional genre, but on the other hand these three drafts may be all that remains of an extensive literary project devoted to fictional epistolary experimentation. Or, like overly neat demarcations between the homoerotic and the heterosexual, and between the roles of the author and her readers, crisp, clean distinctions between fiction and nonfiction may fall woefully short of describing Dickinson's writings.

That degrees of fictionality blend practically indistinguishably with degrees of nonfictional expression in ways that parallel Dickinson's long-recognized (if inadequately reproduced) commingling of poetry and prose should be kept in mind when analyzing all of her epistolary productions. Dickinson's characterization of her own letter to Maria Whitney as fictional (L 969) and remarks to Elizabeth Holland that nephew Ned "inherits his Uncle Emily's ardor for the lie" (L 315), to Higginson that her Dresden friend promises to send "a Meadow that is better than Summer's" (L 513), and to Bowles that she will give him "mountains that touched the sky, and brooks that sang like Bobolinks" in the letter she is writing (L 189), as well as her familiarity with literature often incorporating epistolarity, show that she was well aware of the letter's possibilities as a fictional form. But questions should extend beyond discovery of her own commentary and expression of consciousness, for those are not the only factors constructing our critical views and reception of works like these letters.

Incorporating Franklin's critical position into our own, we should recognize how methods of reproduction unavoidably promote certain interpretations, not because editors or textual reproducers are conspiratorial but because any translation of a text into mass reproducibility is a product shaped by editorial opinion. As were Higginson and Loomis Todd, who produced a facsimile for the 1891 presentation of *Poems by Emily Dickinson, Second Series*, Franklin is sensitive to the fact that Dickinson's handwriting produces texts markedly different from reading their translations into typeface. Thus as he did with the *Manuscript Books*, he reproduces the "Master" letters photographically. Similarly, the accompanying reproductions in an envelope reflect his opinion that the three letters belong together and that they are nonfiction. Once again, the reproductions themselves remind readers that conventional publication is a sociological, not an individual, enterprise, created according to editorial conjectures and beliefs about the author, authorial goals, the critical community, and perceived goals for the study of literature, as well as by limits and possibilities imposed by the mechanical means of production and methods involving printers, paper type, proofreaders, copy editors, and much more. The obvious facts—that all of these factors shape how one sees texts, thus how one forges interpretation—play a vital role in constituting critical consciousness. Hence our analyses should embrace recognition of these influences.

Long ago, Lavinia Dickinson identified the mode of questioning that most impedes Dickinson study—the desire "to invent and enforce a reason for Emily's peculiar and wonderful genius." Instead of inventing reasons by seeking to answer the question "Who is Master?" we might further our inquiry by asking questions like "What are these?" Why have we paid so little attention to their extensive revisions and not asked what such careful composition and recomposition signify, and why should we continue to ignore the revisions' import, especially now that they are represented photographically? Interpreting the works of a poet who sometimes assumed masculine roles as a boy or uncle, and who addressed at least one other woman with masculine metaphors, why foreclose interpretation of these letters by insisting that they be read without irony or without cross-dressing in mind? If we read these letters and the poems associated with them as pleading statements of fact, do we then want to suggest that in the act of writing her heart out Dickinson coincidentally produced literature? In a patriarchal culture like ours, which interpretations are more easily formulated and received, and which are more likely to be resisted? How has broader acceptance of women's and gay and lesbian studies framed new questions, and how might those new rubrics for reception resist precluding other oppositional but viable perspectives? For the poet who wrote, "This World is not Conclusion" (F 18; P 501), why should we construct a critical world that draws conclusions for her? These are rudimentary, for the possibilities for posing questions are countless. Of vital importance to this questioning attitude is the recognition that each fresh interpretation realigns (not invalidates) those by which it has been preceded. Anytime we deny ourselves the prerogative to postulate anew, we begin to turn interpretation into doctrine. In effect, we relinquish the role of master to particular interpretations of the text. Static and idolized, such fixed interpretations function like masters who reserve for themselves the privilege to question and bolster their power by attempting to restrict both the right and means of subordinates to do so.

For if Chloe likes Olivia and Mary Carmichael knows how to express it she will light a torch in that vast chamber where nobody has yet been. It is all half lights and profound shadows like those serpentine caves where one goes with a candle peering up and down, not knowing where one is stepping. And I began to read the book again, and read how Chloe watched Olivia put a jar on a shelf and say how it was time to go home to her children. That is a sight that has never been seen since the world began, I exclaimed. And I watched, too, very curiously. For I wanted to see how Mary Carmichael set to work to catch those unrecorded gestures, those unsaid or half-said words, which form themselves, no more palpably than the shadows of moths on the ceiling, when women are alone, unlit by the capricious and coloured light of the other sex.

—VIRGINIA WOOLF, *A ROOM OF ONE'S OWN*

But first the notion that man has a body
distinct from his soul, is to be expunged; this
I shall do by printing in the infernal method by
corrosives, which in Hell are salutary and me-
dicinal, melting apparent surfaces away, and
displaying the infinite which was hid.
   If the doors of perception were cleansed
every thing would appear to man as it is: Infinite
   For man has closed himself up, till he sees
all things thro' narrow chinks of his cavern.

—WILLIAM BLAKE, *THE MARRIAGE OF HEAVEN AND HELL*

"The Poems" will ever be to me marvellous whether in manuscript or type.

—SUSAN DICKINSON TO THOMAS HIGGINSON, *AB* 86

Four With the Exception of Shakespeare: Reconstructing Dickinson's Relationship with Susan Huntington Gilbert Dickinson

Unlike those to "Master," which force readers to wonder and question whether their addressee can ever be identified as other than imaginary, the letters and poems to Susan Huntington Gilbert Dickinson were sent to a real flesh-and-blood respondent.[1] Almost no one would dispute that one of the powerful facts of Emily Dickinson's life is that she was in love with Sue. But, as we have seen from examining the tradition of excisions initiated by the early editing of her poems and letters and by surveying the half-century of studies preoccupied with the "Master" letters as biographical documents, the extent to which this emotional and intellectual entanglement with a woman exerted influence over Dickinson's poetry remains insufficiently explored and examined. With Cheryl Walker I concur that, "for Emily," Susan "became the embodiment of female power" and "that Emily Dickinson's poetry was inspirited in important ways by women." Walker also recognizes that "so much has been made over the identity of the 'Master,' Emily's supposed male lover, that this fact" of women empowering Dickinson "has . . . been overlooked." In 1979 Dorothy Oberhaus lucidly described how hearsay, the testimony of the other woman Mabel Loomis Todd about the wife "dear Sue," has been treated as fact and has worked "to obscure Sue's close relationship with Dickinson."[2] And we have also observed that, because of its longevity and intensity, Dickinson's nearly forty-year involvement with Sue makes a good standard of comparison for all of Dickinson's other relationships. The most important characteristic about this powerfully sensual relationship was its very literary nature and the direct impact it had on Dickinson's poetic compositions. Emily Dickinson was not only in love with Sue, but, as is evinced by their voluminous correspondence, the two participated in a literary dialogue that lasted for decades, and the better part of Dickinson's life.

I will examine Emily and Sue Dickinson's epistolary relationship in this chapter by discussing some of the problems with reconstructing an accurate sense of it on the basis of surviving documents; by tracing evolutions of tone and substance of those writings over thirty-five years and by scrutinizing the evidence of their creating a poetry workshop in the next; and by analyzing Sue's role as posthumous editor of Dickinson's life stories and poems and as respondent to the holograph books in the last. To investigate the relationship's reconstruction in this chapter I will examine issues of contextualization that are at least threefold: to significant degrees, social attitudes toward gender, artistic traditions modeled on conventional heterosexual relations, and editorial procedures by producers of Dickinson's works and by their readers all create frameworks which predetermine interpretations. First, contextualizing Emily and Sue's status as women and considering what bearing it once had and still has on fundamental aspects of social custom and language and on subsequent critical reception are necessary; after all, it is not simply homophobic responses to their eroticism or the manipulations of Loomis Todd but also the most basic ways in which our society is organized that have obscured Sue's importance to Dickinson's literary project. Like John Humphreys controlling both Ellen Montgomery's reading material and her interpretations in Susan Warner's *The Wide, Wide World*, patriarchal customs of naming and defining exert profound influence over and tend to contain "readings" or interpretations of women's identities. As we shall see from her response to her own name, Sue Dickinson was sensitive to such facts of life for women in patriarchy. Second, the fact that woman has functioned culturally as muse or as object to be represented and not as artistic producer complicates receptions not only of her creative endeavors but also of her imaginative resources. Third, contradictory interpretations generated by editors and readers who privilege various characteristics of Emily and Sue's written exchanges underscore the complexities of constructing any reliable stories about theirs as well as about any of Dickinson's relationships.

What's in a Name?

Tania Modleski argues for "the importance of real women as interpreters" because all females share something men do not in the ways in which their subjectivities are and continue to be constructed. To further interpretation of her poetic project at this critical moment, study of Dickinson's commentaries to, as well as the scant record of commentaries by, real women who knew her should no longer be undervalued in favor of reports by the woman who edited her texts posthumously but never met her face to face.[3] Of all of her correspondences with women, that offering the most detailed story—the most poems, letters, and letter-poems from Dickinson and the most writing to and about Dickinson from the addressee—is that "book" containing her correspondence with Sue. As we embark on a study of her literary exchanges with Sue, what needs to be highlighted is an underemphasized fact of Dickinson's creative life: that contemporary women readers were vitally important to her poetic project. Not only was her primary audience a woman, but, as in the case of H.D., the erotic power of Dickinson's intense feelings for women could also be creative power. While the personal conflicts between the "other woman" and the "wife forgotten" may in large part account for the fact that until the last couple of decades Dickinson's literary exchange with Sue has usually been minimized, sometimes altogether repudiated, that situation does not explain why her epistolary relationships with cousins Frances and Louise Norcross, dear friend Elizabeth Holland, passionate friend Kate Anthon, niece Martha Dickinson Bianchi, and even with sister Lavinia (to whom she wrote at least eight letters) have been similarly downplayed. As even the casual reader is likely to be aware, Dickinson's relationship with her mother is consistently characterized as at worst relatively insignificant, at best a continuing source of disappointment.[4] According to our present tabulation, Dickinson "published" 401 poems to women and 184, or less than half as many, to men, but critical emphases on her immediate audience have been on men—Higginson, Samuel Bowles, Judge Otis P. Lord, "Master." Correspondingly, Johnson's descriptions and lists of recipients of Dickinson's letters (L, Appendices 1 and 3) and poems (P, Appendices 1 and 2), the fact of the separate publication of the "Master" letters, and Camille Paglia's recent criticism which maintains that "the historical repugnance to woman has a rational basis: disgust is reason's proper response to the grossness of procreative nature," thus concludes that Dickinson had to "jettison" femaleness in herself "to be free," testify to woman's peculiar status in nineteenth-century culture and to the continuation of that problematic ranking into our time.[5]

Continuing her argument, Paglia rightly points out that it would be "a sentimental error to think Emily Dickinson" [or any other woman] simply "the victim of male obstructionism." Yet with her naked assertion that "male conspiracy cannot explain all female failures," she reveals her tendency to reduce feminist criticism and theory to simpleminded postulations about men scheming. Widely recognized by all but those who stubbornly deny gendered influences on women's artistic productions and their subsequent receptions is the fact that if a woman artist in patriarchal culture is to produce and create literature, she must grapple with her relatively underprivileged position as woman in society's hierarchies, especially in systems of language. Likewise, critical responses to the work of women creators can be tremendously enhanced by considering the fact of gender and its various (and often subtle) manipulations of experience and writing. Charges that male conniveries keep women in their place grotesquely portray as they grossly oversimplify gendered experiences. In the artistic cultures of America and most of the Western world, patriarchal systems work complexly and quietly and rarely have to rely on brute force—mental or physical. In their myriad diversities, American feminist theoretical and critical positions all maintain that, however common and taken for granted, "no representations in the written and visual media are gender-neutral" and they thus interrogate the many consequences of that fact for constructions of knowledge and understanding that may otherwise go unnoticed.[6] For example, useful for furthering our understanding of the relative diminishment in literary history of Sue and other women correspondents important to Dickinson is interrogation of the purportedly "objective" presentations of bibliographical data, for these reveal how patriarchal biases quietly but effectively encroach upon the very rudiments of study.

Scrutiny of the editorial apparatuses of *The Poems of Emily Dickinson* and *The Letters of Emily Dickinson* demonstrates how easily women are overshadowed by standards for record-keeping that are by and large taken for granted. Johnson's indices reiterate the degree to which Dickinson's female contemporaries were overshadowed by the men in their spheres, usually husbands or fathers. On these lists, the given names of thirteen women have disappeared. Totally eclipsed by their husbands, these women are known only as "the wife of." Sentenced to linguistic mortality, "instead of being graphed by distinguished inscriptions, women leave indistinguishable traces." Thus in their critique of Ruth Stone, Sandra Gilbert and Susan Gubar emphasize what the most authoritative record of Dickinson's correspondences manifests—that such systemic erasure is not a trivial matter, but distorts our history as it translates all characters and relationships into terms making males primary. In "Names," Stone writes:

> My grandmother's name was Nora Swan.
> Old Aden Swan was her father. But who was her mother?
> I don't know my great-grandmother's name.[7]

The convention compelling wives to take husbands' surnames symboli-
cally parallels marriage with the biblical creation story and the "proper"
gender hierarchy delineated there. As Gerda Lerner observes, in that story
Adam's prerogative to name "not only is a symbolic act of creativity, but it
defines Woman in a very special way as a 'natural' part of man, flesh of his
flesh, in a relationship which is a peculiar inversion of the only human relationship for which such a statement can be made, namely, the relationship of mother to child."[8] Long-recognized literary masterpieces reiterate
this reversal of facts:

> Bone of my Bone, Flesh of my Flesh, my Self
> Before me; Woman is her Name, of Man
> Extracted; for this cause he shall forgo
> Father and Mother, and to his Wife adhere;
> And they shall be one Flesh, one Heart, one Soul.
>
> (*PARADISE LOST* 8:495–499)

Likewise, our Judeo-Christian patriarchal system of naming perpetually
reinscribes Adam's privilege to bestow meaning and order by naming not
only the animals but also his counterpart, Woman, and by defining himself, or Man, from whose body she came, as her "mother" (Gen. 2:23).

In Johnson's lists of Dickinson's epistolary cast of characters, then,
female recipients are identified primarily by their husband's name or by
their most significant patriarchal relationship—as "daughter," "wife,"
"second wife," "mother," "niece," and "aunt"—and no matter which family member was Dickinson's primary correspondent, male heads of households or clans usually "rule" the biographical blurbs. Even when men are
seen as "son," "eldest son," "brother," "favorite 'Cousin Peter,'" or
"uncle," descriptions tend to ponder accomplishments rather than familial
ties, while we are several sentences into the brief biography of the quite
accomplished Helen Hunt Jackson before discovering that this daughter,
wife, mother, and widow "turned to writing." Of Emily Fowler Ford, a
childhood friend of Dickinson's, we learn that "herself an author of
poems, stories, and essays," she was also "the mother of two well-known
writers" (Paul Leicester and Worthington Chauncey Ford). Her characterization in these lists reminds us of the impact marriage and motherhood have traditionally had on the perceptions and official recognition
of the salient features of women's lives. In a Judeo-Christian paradigm that
has designated the body as a lower order of being than the higher order of
spirit or soul, woman's primary purpose or highest calling has been de-

fined according to her bodily capabilities—to copulate with men and give birth to children—both functions of the "lower" order. Constructed within a culture in which patriarchal order and nomenclature were incontrovertibly normative and before feminist inquiry inspired more and more questions about even the details of social organization, Johnson's critical horizon was not one where questions about the naming of women and its significations of gendered social standing would have been apparent. Most important for our present consideration are these questions: What difference do all these general facts about naming make in Dickinson study? To what extent, if any, have they influenced critical receptions of her friends and family? What was her relation to her own name and what does that signify?

Unlike most of the women mentioned above, Emily Dickinson left this life with the same name given her at birth. Of course, her name was not particularly special. In 1852 there were almost twice as many Dickinsons as there were Smiths registered to vote in the Amherst area: 44 Dickinsons, 23 Smiths (*YH* 1 : 249). In 1881, Dickinson complained to the Norcrosses that the postmaster had been misled by their addressing a letter to Vinnie and herself "Misses Dickinson": "He failed of the intellectual grasp to combine the names. So after sending it to all the *Mrs.* Dickinsons he could discover, he consigned it to us" (L 727). Also, not only were there several other Emily Dickinsons in the area in nineteenth-century Amherst (*YH* 1 : lxxx–lxxxi), but there was another Emily Dickinson residing under the same roof as the poet: her mother. Their names reflect their respective circumstances and choices. Emily Norcross Dickinson bears two surnames, her father's and her husband's; Emily Elizabeth Dickinson sports two given names for women, her mother's and her aunt's. Therefore, Emily Dickinson's name symbolizes the importance she attached to the women around her, as well as the contrast of her life to that of other women writers like Helen Fiske Hunt Jackson and Emily Fowler Ford. Of all these women, however, her beloved Susan's experience with her name is perhaps the most telling about a woman's appellation and what it indicates about gendered circumstance.

Not many women who married only once have quite the parade of surnames that Susan Huntington Gilbert Dickinson has. "Sister Sue" entered this life as Susan Huntington Gilbert and went through her early years as Susan Gilbert. Though she added Dickinson when she married, and of Gilbert kept only the initial G., styling herself Susan G. Dickinson, she dropped her married name for a while and was, though a wife, again Susan Gilbert; then she used Susan Gilbert Dickinson or dropped her father's name and was Susan Dickinson; finally she reassumed her middle name and died as Susan Huntington Dickinson. That Sue could not settle on a surname hints at a greater degree of resistance to genteel domesticity than the cultural mandate for women to marry and the popular rhetoric about the prescription would lead us to expect; both would assure us that a woman of her situation could only be happy and fulfilled (unless, of course, there was something "wrong" with her). After all, Susan did not just marry; she married well. Her prosperous husband was also a man of position, so her marriage bestowed more status on her than that of Wife: she wedded local gentry. Her house was a showplace and she could afford to cultivate just about any taste—for example, in travel or in art—that she wished. By all of culture's promises, her marriage should have made her constantly happy. Yet it did not.

As women in general have been remembered primarily by their relationships to parents, husbands, and children, so Sue has been remembered primarily as Dickinson's in-law, who also happened to be the poet's best friend, at least for a time. As a relative, Sue, the wife eventually forgotten by Emily's brother Austin, has been characterized in literary history by his mistress, Mabel Loomis Todd, and, writing Sue into literary history, Loomis Todd's gossip has supplanted documentation. Thus Sue is often remembered as the unhappy sister-in-law for whom Dickinson harbored immense affection. Many regard Dickinson's love for the reportedly tempestuous, pretentious Sue as a mystery, but even more perplexing to the majority of critics and biographers has been the poet's apparent respect for Sue's literary opinions, for at best, Sue's critical abilities have been questioned. By 1979, Sue was not only aligned with the figure of the unhappy, unappreciative wife, but also with those sentimental figures comprising the "mob" of nineteenth-century literary women, whose "sophomoric intellect[s]" could not discriminate between "oversweet tone" and more sophisticated expressions of "nihilism."[9] Both archetypal female characters are leading players in the drama generally known as "The Woman Question," and both characters have been considered a problem.[10] Framing interpretations of Sue's personal and literary abilities in this way perpetuates long-standing positions assumed to evaluate women in general.

Traditionally, as have most women throughout history, American women have been graphed not only by patriarchal customs of naming, but also by patriarchal postulations about and definitions of their capabilities. As poet/critic Wendy Barker astutely observes, considering its traditional connotations, Higginson's label for Dickinson's poetic ways, "Dark" (L 265), is the appropriate metaphor as it conventionalizes the poetic productions of a woman whose works and selves are so often characterized as "mysterious": "Luce Irigaray's demonstration that Plato's parable of the cave, with its contrast between a dark maternal womb and a divine paternal *logos*, represents just one in a series of philosophical categories that have relegated the feminine to a position of subordination" and to an unintelligible dark.[11] In keeping with this tradition of diminishment, throughout Emily and Sue's thirty-five-year relationship, the women writers so popular then were routinely characterized in periodicals and newspapers as not really producing literature. In 1865, the *Republican*, a staple in both Dickinson houses, featured an article entitled "Employment for Women," which advised "young women of the present day": "What you need is to be set to work at some useful occupation, the homelier the better, till such foolish notions as you now indulge are driven out of you. . . . You feel hurt if you are asked to mend a coat or wash the dishes, do it poorly and sulkily, and then go and write some stuff that you call poetry, about your 'Unanswered Longings,' or 'Beautiful Visions,' or what not!" (*YH* 2 : 103). Two years later the same newspaper ran "Women as Artists," which emphatically editorialized, ". . . it will be no more terrible to have the country flooded with mistaken women-artists, so called, than with mistaken women-poets, who are so numerous lately" (*YH* 2 : 126). Emily Stipes Watts points out that Rufus Griswold's "definition" is "the first to assert that women are probably incapable of 'intellectual' poetry," as his preface to *The Female Poets of America* (1849) maintains that "the conditions of aesthetic ability in the two sexes are probably distinct, or even opposite."[12] According to Griswold's formulation, men reasonably command abstract thoughts while women are compelled by emotion. Not surprisingly, widely read reviews of anthologies of female poets like those produced by Griswold, Caroline May (1848), and Thomas Buchanan Read (1849) posed such questions as "What is to become of us, if all the men emigrate to California and the women to Parnassus?"[13]

Thus Dickinson's "Sister – We both are Women, and there is a Will of God –" (H B 78; L 312) resonates with specific connotations: in nineteenth-century American culture, women were, no matter what name they took or life choice they made, finally ruled by patriarchy and "legitimately" identified, remembered, and defined by it codes. Writing their histories, most of the time this is still the case; Emily and Sue were surrounded by well-known critics and thinkers (including even the suffragist Higginson) who frequently lectured on "Woman's nature," thus "named" and defined female capabilities and shortcomings. Such essentialist speculations persist among contemporary (feminist and nonfeminist) thinkers.

In turn, all this has influenced ways in which their relationship has been written into literary history. Though a few have been instrumental in pushing Emily and Sue's relationship to the foreground of study, feminist critics have not necessarily done so nor have they as a matter of course found this lifelong rapport between two women any easier to analyze than have those with little or no interest in gender's impact upon women's lives.

As feminist historians have been learning that "the writing of women into history necessarily involves redefining and enlarging traditional notions of historical significance, to encompass personal, subjective experience as well as public and political activities," so writing Dickinson's experience as a woman writer into literary history involves a conscious horizonal shift of critical expectations that accepts the profound influence of a nonprofessional literary woman even as it accepts, as we saw in the second chapter, the personal, subjective mode of the poet's "cottage-industry" literary production and distribution.[14] Traditional frameworks that have inclined scholars to remember Sue as a dissatisfied, temperamental wife before remembering her as a young teacher in Baltimore especially adept at mathematics or as a critic to whom Dickinson sometimes listened have functioned hand in hand with traditional frameworks that privilege mechanical reproductions and publishing-house distribution. Recognizing what such outlooks have obscured is an important foundation not only for beginning to understand Dickinson's revisionary mode of textual production but also for beginning to reconstruct the history of Emily and Sue's creative exchanges. As Virginia Woolf pointed out more than sixty years ago, and as the conventions of our record-keeping make obvious, to write about an alliance between two women is never a simple matter. Since feminist inquiry has moved the horizon of critical expectations so that Dickinson's passion for Sue no longer seems as anomalous as it might have even a quarter-century ago, and thus must no longer be categorized only as sisterly or as heterosexual foreplay—like the passionate prelude to marriage between Alice Archer and Cecilia Vaughn in Longfellow's *Kavanagh*—to be accepted, one might reasonably assume that a similar reappraisal of Sue's literary talents has become a primary objective of feminist criticism.[15]

Yet as Nancy Walker's recent essay makes plain, even feminists still characterize Sue's critical skills as "deficient."[16] Concomitantly, an earlier feminist readership that found in Dickinson something of an ideal subject did not, by and large, interrogate her responses to women and female figures but to men and male figures. By 1984, Pollak points out, the most quoted letter from Emily to Sue had nothing to do with their mutual interest in literature but, written when both were in their early twenties, is a reverie on the masochism of feminine flowers that is at least partly focused on male power. Recycled frequently by feminist critics, many readers can probably recite the clauses:

> . . . those same sweet flowers at noon with their heads bowed in
> anguish before the mighty sun; think you these thirsty blossoms will
> *now* need naught but – *dew*? No, they will cry for sunlight, and pine
> for the burning noon, tho' it scorches them, scathes them; they have
> got through with peace – they know that the man of noon is *mightier*
> than the morning and their life is henceforth to him. Oh, Susie, it is
> dangerous, and it is all too dear, these simple trusting spirits, and the
> spirits mightier, which we cannot resist! It does so rend me, Susie,
> the thought of it when it comes, that I tremble lest at sometime I,
> too, am yielded up. Susie, you will forgive me my amatory strain – it
> has been a very long one, and if this saucy page did not here bind
> and fetter me, I might have had no end.

(H L 20; L 93)

Often using this passage to demonstrate her "phobic sexuality," earlier discussions of Dickinson have, like earlier more general feminist critiques, focused primarily on her anxieties over being a disenfranchised female in a patriarchally licensed world.[17] Likewise, not only for male feminist critics like Keller but for others like Joanne Feit Diehl, Dickinson's "precursor becomes a composite male figure" and such hypotheses situate the poet to interrogate her responses to primarily masculine poetic traditions.[18] While it is certainly true that Dickinson fretted over male prerogatives and power, read and responded to many male writers, and cared what some men and some professionals thought of her, those influences are, however, only part of the story of her personal and literary relationships.

To write about how an erotically charged dynamic of care and tension between two unprofessional women (like that between Emily and Sue) informs understanding of a major poet's literary project is especially complicated, because that is to tell an anomalous story the critical community has in several ways not been prepared to receive and, buttressed by culture's prioritizing of relationships, may still be likely to resist. Just as some critics repudiate feminist analyses in general, so some have dismissed as impossible any feminist intention by Dickinson, suggesting that these positions have been superimposed by readers. Of course such contentions are not preposterous, for, as Dickinson well knew, readers will always impose their views upon texts to greater or lesser degrees. Similarly, as some feminists have emphatically separated themselves from lesbians and vice versa, so feminist Dickinson critics have squabbled over whether her love for Sue and/or other women can be called lesbian, what same-sex attractions and affections mean, as well as what is the import of her heterosexual affections. A feminist reader who does not countenance calling Dickinson's same-sex love "lesbian," Margaret Homans maintains that "Like Eyes that Looked on Wastes" (F 32; P 458) is proof that "where the relation between two individuals, like the relation between elements of the self, is structured not by oppositeness and hierarchy, but by sameness and equality, the resulting stasis often becomes a violent stalemate." On the other hand, in the earliest book-length study highlighting Dickinson's lesbian affections, Rebecca Patterson launched an argument that contemporary critics like Adalaide Morris have furthered—that this poem does not reflect the static similarity between same-sex lovers but highlights the impossibility of achieving a union between equal selves in a heterosexist world, however "mutually empowering" it may be.[19] As feminist and non-feminist readers might assert to discount each other's conclusions, those who find lesbian interpretations of Dickinson's work and those who do not might each charge the other with inventing intentions for her. Too often left out of the interpretive formula when critics accuse one another of projecting biases onto texts is that this is to some extent unavoidable.

What is conspicuous and important for our consideration is that general critical trends—feminist and otherwise—can be traced in critical responses to Dickinson and have influenced readings of her relationship with Sue. Equally obvious is that both her intentions and critical impositions inspire competing interpretations. Thus, difficulties in characterizing Dickinson's primary relationship result both from the fact that systems of language, culture, and society have not been especially amenable to depicting same-sex love, and from the fact that the poet herself characterized her passion for Sue variously—as loverlike, sororal, filial. Indeed, the poet described their affection as that of best friends and her disappointments in Sue as that approximating the chilliness between near-enemies.

Elaborating and building upon work like that of Cheryl Walker and Emily Stipes Watts, Joanne Dobson chooses to study the importance of literary women to Dickinson's poetic project against the backdrop of the complex milieu within which nineteenth-century women writers created, and in doing so contends that "her intensely idiosyncratic reconstruction of received feminine images constitutes at once an attraction to and a critique of those modes of being, suggesting a deeply rooted conflict in her own sense of identity."[20] Noting conflicts in and multiple aspects of her identity (or identities) is important, and, in investigating Dickinson's poetic enterprise through her correspondence with her primary audience, I would like to make a similar point. By examining Dickinson's poems, letter-poems, and letters to her beloved Sue, I do not wish to suggest an always empowering, easily identified, completely positive, consistently nurturing relationship. Like any lifelong intimates, these women were both attracted to and critical of one another. Nor do I wish to suggest that male conspiracy impelled Dickinson to make Sue her primary audience, though I obviously think that the patriarchal organization of culture has contributed significantly to their relationship being relatively overlooked until recently. I argue that, whether harmonious, conflicted, inspiring, or frustrating, Dickinson's intense involvement with Sue was no wasteland but proved to be her most fertile poetic plain.

A Pen Has So Many Inflections

Like H.D., who says that she sees the "writing on the wall" through and together with Bryher, "for without her, admittedly, I could not have gone on," Dickinson unequivocally acknowledges that her relationship with Sue is important to her creative insight and sensibilities.[21] Intriguingly, both poets go beyond merely challenging male depictions of women and go so far as to signify other women as their imaginative resource, which recalls Louise Bernikow's assertion: "Modernism was not a male enterprise. We need the women, but not each in isolation. We need them in their connection, which were many forms of love."[22] Prefiguring that critical statement poetically, the speaker of "To pile like / Thunder to / its' close" (H 364; P 1247) unequivocally states that love and poetry "coeval come"; poetic production, for Dickinson a lifetime occupation, is an enterprise neither male, mechanical, nor isolated, divorced from her personal relationships. Thus that one of her primary emotional involvements would serve as a vital forum for presentation of her poetry is to be expected. Though Karl Keller describes her declaration as "facetious," Dickinson nevertheless proclaims that she tastes and feels through her beloved Sue much as H.D. sees through Bryher:

> I could not drink
> it Sue,
> Till you had tasted
> first –
> Though cooler than

the Water – was
The Thoughtfulness of
Thirst.

(H B 139; L 287, P 818, ABOUT 1864)

That Keller would receive this as Dickinson's bemused response to Sue's limitations is almost unavoidable, for, as we saw at the outset of this book, he sees a poet who manipulates conventional womanhood in order to gain her artistic power by submitting to male "Masters." In his story of reading, "the one she finds the most secure and creative is the Puritan woman she plays," who is "fulfilled in her wifely devotion to man," and thus finds her value in submitting to patriarchal order: "Hee for God only; shee for God in Him" (*Paradise Lost* 4:299).[23] As does Keller, makers of culture have traditionally perpetuated the fantasy that, like Eve, women are most satisfied submitting to patriarchal hierarchy: "God is thy law, thou mine: to know no more / Is woman's happiest knowledge and her praise" (*Paradise Lost* 4:637–638). A reader operating with such assumptions is predisposed to view Dickinson's writing that the idea of tasting "water" was "cooler" or more soothing than the fact of following Sue's having done so as banter that is finally dismissive of Sue. Through his critique, then, Keller aligns Dickinson with Western culture's relentlessly heterosexual philosophical, psychological, and poetic patrilineage.[24] In contrast to Keller's poet, who likes the role of a submissive woman, the Dickinson I see finds many other roles just as exciting—or more so. Like H.D.'s story of seeing through Bryher, Dickinson's story of tasting after Sue refuses to portray the other woman as a passive muse but depicts her as an active coparticipant. Through my critique, I align Dickinson with an alternative philosophical, psychological, and poetic matrilineage that has long been evident on the margins of patriarchal culture through stories like that of Ruth's devotion to Naomi (Ruth 1:11–17). Significantly, to proclaim her fidelity to Sue, Dickinson borrows Ruth's vow to Naomi that exceeds even the lifetime promise of marriage—"for my father will be your father, and my home will be your home, and where you go, I will go, and we will lie side by side in the kirkyard" (H L 18, L 88, 1852). In sharp contrast to traditional ways of defining creative dynamics and energies, the interpretation I posit radically revises that symbolic order by reading Dickinson's letter-poem as one signification (among many) of a collaborative aesthetic between women.

Traditionally, woman's symbolic function for men has been as passive female muse, and a correlation between creative production and procreative reproduction has been assumed. Formulation of a literary dynamic as a collaboration of a woman writer with another woman is alien to conventional symbology linking heterosexual desire and poetic inspiration. By her description of Emily's writing to Sue—"The written condition of this relation is leviathan. Every line touched down in ink or pencil on every scrap of paper sent to Susan Gilbert Dickinson inscribes a dialectic of infinite Desire"—Susan Howe ranks it with literature produced by women whose love for other women as well as for literature played central roles in their lives.[25] The scraps of poetry left by Sappho of Lesbos script desire for women and remind us that tales (like Ovid's) of the ancient lyric poet pining for the boatman Phaon are nothing but others' fancies; the "Boston marriage" of Sarah Orne Jewett and Annie Fields was a mainstay for the former's literary production; Willa Cather's forty-year partnership with Edith Lewis provided the writer with the stability and freedom necessary to create; at Vassar, Elizabeth Bishop founded a literary magazine with Mary McCarthy, then, a couple of decades later, for fifteen years anchored her otherwise rather peripatetic existence with Lota Costellat de Macedo Soares in Brazil and in her last years found support in her relationship with Alice Methfessel; and, as Gilbert and Gubar observe, collaborative lesbian literary relationships like those between Renee Vivien and Natalie Barney, H.D. and Bryher, and Gertrude Stein and Alice B. Toklas marked the endeavors of expatriate American and British women writers in the early twentieth century.[26]

Though Jean McClure Mudge has concluded that Emily and Sue wrote poetry together, and though some of Samuel Bowles's writings to Sue appear to suggest as much, the extent to which Sue's involvement in Dickinson's alternative aesthetic of poetic production can be described as collaborative remains to be discovered and, especially since only part of their written exchanges survive, will to a great extent remain irrecoverable.[27] Whether or not the unusually lineated version of "I reason" sent to Sue (P 301, discussed in chapter 2) indicates that they were discussing experimental forms remains hidden from literary history. Though their relationship is a link in a line or, to use a more appropriate metaphor, a pane in a quilt telling a history of women's artistic enmeshments with other women, it cannot be characterized in precisely the same way as any of those other female alliances. Just as all of those collaborations are different from one another and as each varies over time in degree of intensity, so the story of Emily and Sue is distinctive and distinctly evolves.

Any characterization of pieces of their literary exchange like the statement about tastes explained away by Keller should not be evaluated in isolation, but in context of the many startling expressions like that found in the following letter-poem to "Sweet Sue":

> Take back that
> "Bee" and "Buttercup" –
> I have no Field
> for them, though
>   for the Woman
> whom I prefer,
> Here is Festival –
> Where my Hands
> are cut, Her fingers will be
> found inside –
>
> (H B 56; L 288, ABOUT 1864)

Superficially, this appears sadomasochistic, but Dickinson quickly overturns the obvious. Fusing images of giddy, presumably literary (signified by the quotation marks) nature and celebration, then oxymoronically presenting a usually destructive and separative act—cutting—as one of consummate union, Dickinson, on the creative field in her Eden of experience, appropriates the site of crucifying wounds to rewrite the biblical myth of human creation and tell a story about relations between two women who, like Adam and Eve, are flesh of one another's flesh, limbs of one another's limbs. In contrast to the perpetual reinscription of the myth evident in the patriarchal system of naming, Dickinson's letter-poem revises the story and its characters.[28] Though she penned fantastically erotic letters to Kate Anthon, marvelously comic and loving ones to the Norcrosses and Elizabeth Holland, and friendly enough letters to Hunt Jackson, Dickinson did not write any other woman in quite this way, describing an emotional and intellectual engrossment in terms that transform what promises to be a gory scene of bloodletting into that of female figures who cannot be crucified.[29] In fact, when Dickinson writes the Norcrosses—"I know I love my friends—I feel it far in here where neither blue nor black eye goes, and fingers cannot reach" (L 382, winter 1877)—she underscores just how monumental is the orgasmic suffusion of selves described in her letter to Sue. Thus her own writing in the "book" to Sue contextualizes "I could not drink / it Sue" to encourage interpreting it without diminishing irony.

The tone ascribed to any expression predicates interpretation, and Dickinson's many remarks about voices and inflections indicate her sensitivities to modulation's power over meaning and are useful to keep in mind as we formulate interpretation of her declarations to Sue. Though some maintain that Dickinson produced her poetry only for writing and never for speech, especially in the context of her statements like "The Ear is the last Face. We hear after we see" (L 405, January 1874; *LF* 1–7), accounts of those closest to her suggest that she may have tried out various tones of her written expressions by reading aloud to a trusted audience. In a March 26, 1904, letter to the editors of the Boston *Woman's Journal*, Dickinson's beloved Louise Norcross makes it plain that she knew about her cousin's literary work and provides a rare portrait of the woman poet at work, writing and reading aloud amid the duties of housekeeping: "Mrs. Harriet Beecher Stowe wrote her most wonderful sentences on slips of paper held against the kitchen wall while she was hovering over culinary formations. And I know that Emily Dickinson wrote most emphatic things in the pantry, so cool and quiet, while she skimmed the milk; because I sat on the footstool behind the door, in delight, as she read them to me. The blinds were closed, but through the green slats she saw all those fascinating ups and downs going on outside that she wrote about." Here "Loo" promotes her cousin by placing her in the company of the nineteenth century's most widely read American author. Having described herself earlier in the letter as "an ardent crusader for women, a whole-souled suffragist," even while defending housekeeping in this response to an editorial by Charlotte Perkins Gilman, Norcross simultaneously calls attention to the domestic demands on women's time and to the fact that most women had to write in their pantries, not their studies. Briefly interpreting Norcross's letter about the joys of her cousin reading to her, Gary Scharnhorst makes several important points: that the account calls into question the commonplace that Dickinson wrote only at night in her room; that "Norcross was privy to her cousin's secret" and "the writing of her poems was common knowledge between them"; and that, if "Dickinson sometimes declaimed her poetry, the dashes she used to punctuate her lines may have been elocutionary guides."[30]

While the "ups and downs" to which Norcross refers do not necessarily argue for the dashes as elocutionary guides, her anecdote does make more credible any contention that the direction of the marks was not slapdash, but intentional. But most significant is Norcross's choice of "emphatic" to describe her cousin's writing, thus highlighting Dickinson's concern for tone. If they indicate anything, the angled marks appear to serve as suggestive reminders of tone's importance. When Dickinson wrote "a Pen has so many inflections," she continued, "and a Voice but one" (L 470). Besides seeming to demonstrate Derrida's contention that Western culture privileges speaking (voice) over writing, her remark is an accurate description of the fact that, modulating her voice, a speaker stands a better chance of eliciting a particular response from listeners than does a writer who relies on words flattened onto the page.[31] Sarcastic intonation, for example, can transform the welcoming "I'm so delighted to see you" into a nasty, distancing slur. Or so it seems. Left out of Dickinson's formula is the fact that such sarcasm is only delivered when the listener is prepared to receive it. Moved by her desires, the listener may misconstrue causticity as ironic endearment or vice versa.

Since the reader invents the voice of the written text and can return to the work time and again to generate new texts, thus "hear" new voices, the tone of any writing seems infinitely variable. This has been especially true of one of the most well-known letters to Sue. Sometime around their fifty-second year, Emily Dickinson wrote:

> Dear Sue –
> With the
> Exception of
> Shakespeare, you
> have told me of
> more knowledge
> than any one living –
> to say that sincerely
> is strange praise –
>
> (FF 176; L 757, ABOUT 1882)

Devoting a chapter to Sue's importance to Dickinson as well as repeatedly returning to consideration of their relationship, Pollak interprets this straightforwardly and foregrounds it by using the quotation to inaugurate her chapter "Susan Gilbert." Pollak situates this in the context of Dickinson's many writings to Sue, yet this strategy has not been the rule for evaluating the extraordinary statement, which is often read out of context of their other correspondence and sometimes interpreted in a context that seems fabricated in order to explain it. Paglia follows her citation of the letter with "So Susan is also Iago to her Othello. Susan has provided her with the full range of emotional experience, from love to hate."[32] When cited, this brief but stunning letter is often interpreted as having a nasty or embittered edge but not the range of emotions Paglia asserts. Since no one can relate the letter to any particular event, the context created by Johnson in the editorial note attached to it probably accounts, more than the wording of the letter itself, for interpretations hearing betrayal voiced in the adverb "sincerely" and the phrase "strange praise."

Johnson's note makes plain the fact that he reads the comment as sarcastic. Though to rank anyone at any time with Shakespeare is exceptional and strange enough to demand our attention, he takes "strange praise" as evidence of "strain between the two houses." To substantiate his conjecture, he retells Bingham's hearsay anecdote recounting the story her mother attributed to an allegedly scandalized Sue about finding "Emily reclining in the arms of a man" (L 757n). Besides drawing his example from a source that can hardly be considered objective, he never explains the relevance of a tale that has nothing to do with Shakespeare or with Dickinson's commentary to anyone about her relationship with Susan. Thus his conclusion—"It is probable that Sue's resentment concerning the attachment of Emily to Judge Lord was made clear to Emily, and may account for this note of 'strange praise'"—implicitly constructs an argument for a particular interpretation of the letter merely by the editorial apparatus attached to it. Yet the apparatus and conclusion seem unjustified. Not only does Johnson frame this particular letter with a gossipy tidbit citing thirdhand accounts—Mrs. Bingham said that her mother Mrs. Todd said that Susan Dickinson had said—but he also presumes to articulate the emotions of these two women without really documenting how he concluded what the nature of their feelings was. Merely the fact that Loomis Todd dates her anecdote in 1881, about the same time as the letter, is not enough to yoke the two. In his biography of Dickinson, Johnson remarks (about this note): "The praise is indeed strange. One can only speculate what Sue has taught her about the human heart." He does not elaborate or imagine that when Sue does this, it is as a poet, as Shakespeare, teaches. Though he considers Higginson's response to "Safe in their Alabaster Chambers" in some detail, he ignores the fact that when Dickinson wrote several second stanzas for the poem, it was apparently at Sue's bidding. And he does not make the point that Sue wrote some verse herself.[33]

Stories of reading Dickinson's relationship with Sue have often been edited in this way, their context provided by Loomis Todd anecdotes alleging Sue's vituperative description of the woman she would dress for death or provided by some neighborhood denigratory gossip alleging Sue's alcoholism. As Sewall points out, neither Loomis Todd nor Mary Lee Hall, who made the charge of alcoholism and who wrote Bingham that "the awful spirit rises in me whenever Sue and Mattie are in my thoughts" and "never have I fallen so desperately low as to follow Mattie's [Martha Dickinson Bianchi] black flag of spiritual illiteracy" can be viewed as sources who could write "without prejudice" about Sue or her daughter Martha (*Life* 1:230–231, 253–254). Such hearsay should be placed in the context of other hearsay, and especially important is awareness of the fact that not all Amherst gossip slanders Sue and Martha. In an early 1930s interview, "Miss Marian," a Dickinson seamstress, replied, when asked if Emily had any friends, "She was fond of Sue as I remember. She lived on part of the Dickinson land. She and Emily were great friends" (*YH* 2:479). But all of the competing chatter, some favoring Loomis Todd, some favoring Sue, is best reserved for cocktail chitchat and should never be used as reliable documentation. More trustworthy are Dickinson's writings themselves, and from those documents readers know that she sent hundreds of poems, letters, and letter-poems to Sue; of the ten or eleven notes she sent to Loomis Todd, six are thank-you notes.

As we have seen, the context or frames provided by Dickinson's writings for whatever documents are under study should be more thoroughly examined. Interpreting the "Master" letters—sentimental documents with striking parallels to hysterical letters in *David Copperfield*—in light of her production of the cartooning layout for "A poor – torn Heart – a tattered heart –" suggests literary instead of literal conjectures about the missives' meanings. Likewise, by counterpointing poems with letters—for example, by enclosing "A Death blow is a Life blow to some" (Set 7; P 816) in the letter reminding Higginson that she "did not print" (L 316)—Dickinson creates and augments meaning through juxtapositions. Undoubtedly, the context created by editors should be separated from the context created by Dickinson's own writings, and her frame should, when possible, be the first scrutinized to formulate analysis of a particular document. The writings to Sue are no exception to this principle.

However, mutilated, impossible to order with absolute surety, and with many documents missing, Dickinson's writings present a whole new set of problems even as they provide important contexts. Evaluating the "With the Exception of Shakespeare" letter, for example, readers will want to keep in mind the fact that the bottom of the sheet on which it is written is torn away (see photocopy in *FF* 176). This presents several possibilities: that more writing clarifying the remark's sarcastic or sincere tone was removed either to protect Sue, Emily, or both; that the bottom, written upon or not, was torn away through careless handling; that the bottom on which nothing was written was torn away to use for a shopping list, bookmark, or some other relatively insignificant purpose; that the bottom, bearing Dickinson's signature, was torn away and given to someone as a souvenir[34]; that the bottom was torn away by Dickinson herself who, as with many other documents addressed to Sue, grabbed whatever paper was readily available in order to write a message, a poem, an allusion and send across the lawn. The following note, complete with a little drawing of heavenly bodies and a staff with notes, featured on the book jacket of Judy Jo Small's *Positive as Sound*, is on a piece of paper torn from a larger sheet:

> Dear Susie – I send
> you a little air –
> The "Music of the Spheres."
> They are represented above
> as passing thro' the sky.

> (H B 75; L 134, OCTOBER 1853)[35]

That Dickinson herself tore the rectangular piece seems obvious from its neat folds and her address, "Susie," written diagonally across and within one of the quarters. Similarly, though the bottom of the paper on which "With the Exception of Shakespeare" is written is torn away, the sheet itself has been neatly folded into thirds, as if for enclosure in an envelope. Thus the hypothesis that Dickinson made the tear herself is probable, though, since others mutilated her documents, scholars can never be certain beyond all reasonable doubt.

Mutilations strip away information, context, and connections, creating holes in our reading that can never be restored. Inverting this relation of holes to text, many cryptic comments to Sue, surrounded by no letter or poem, appear to emerge from a black hole and cannot be connected with absolute surety to any event or aspect of their relationship. Instead of being riddled with holes, these isolated statements are surrounded by them. Frequently alluding to the bard of Avon, Dickinson might be said to be "talking in Shakespeare" when she writes Sue, and some of the isolated quotations she sends are perfect examples of these expressions leaping out of a vacuum. About 1874, Dickinson sent a deceptively simple message of three words:

> "Egypt – thou
> knew'st – "

> (H B 25; L 430)

To this, Johnson attaches, without commentary, the rest of Antony's speech from *Antony and Cleopatra*:

> Egypt, thou knew'st too well,
> My heart was to thy rudder tied by the strings,
> And thou shouldst tow me after. O'er my spirit
> Thy full supremacy thou knew'st, and that
> Thy beck might from the bidding of the gods
> Command me.
>
> (III, XI, 56–61)

About 1875, she forwarded an equally enigmatic allusion, but Johnson appends his citation of the Shakespeare play with an explanatory conjecture:

> "For Brutus,
> as you know,
> was Caesar's
> Angel."
>
> (H B 34; L 448)

Johnson notes that "the private association of this quotation from *Julius Caesar* (III, ii, 183) is not known, but may have reference to a local situation wherein some member of the family, in ED's opinion, was 'betrayed' by a friend." Another quotation was sent about 1876 by Dickinson without commentary:

> "Doth forget
> that ever
> he heard
> the name
> of Death."
>
> (H B 168; L 484)

For possible interpretation Johnson speculates a bit more boldly:

> Though the occasion that prompted this note is not known, the quotation from *Coriolanus* (III, i, 256–258) leads one to conjecture that the message followed an angry outbreak of feeling on the part of someone.
>
> His heart's his mouth:
> What his breast forges that his tongue must vent;

> And, being angry, does forget that ever
> He heard the name of death.

The lines are spoken by Menenius Agrippa, Coriolanus's friend, in defense of Coriolanus. The context strongly suggests that ED wrote this as a tender note of apology for one whose heart was frequently her mouth, perhaps for Lavinia.

(L 484N)

Readers can never be sure if these passages allude to real events or, if so, to what incidents or circumstances, public or private, she may have referred in these quotations, or if they are part of a literary game the two played, but Sue surely knew. Several critics, most recently Paglia, Judith Farr, and Paula Bennett, have argued that "Egypt – thou / knew'st –" is Emily speaking directly to Sue, proclaiming her continuing devotion and calling Sue her "Cleopatra."[36] For a reader like myself, whose present study takes as a primary goal analysis of Dickinson's correspondence with Sue and who argues that their emotional ties can be characterized as "lesbian," such autobiographical interpretations are tempting.

However, they depend on readers producing a story which assumes that the "thou" in the quotation is Sue. But when such expressions are placed in the context of other writings to Sue, it is not clear how they fit into the patterns of the many effusive and devoted declarations plainly referring to her. They may be documents from some elaborate game the two concocted because of their mutual love for Shakespeare, perhaps around quotations from "a daily Shakespeare calendar" (*FF* 29). With these lines torn from Shakespeare, Dickinson may or may not be addressing Sue directly. These isolated quotations are markedly indeterminate compared with the clearer references in the "With the Exception of Shakespeare" letter, the "I could not drink it" letter, the "Where my Hands are cut" epistle, and many others others, such as:

> To own a
> Susan of
> my own
> Is of itself
> a Bliss –
> Whatever
> Realm I
> forfeit, Lord,

Continue
me in this!
   Emily.

(H B 4; P 1401; L 531, ABOUT 1877)

Dickinson indisputably addresses this epistolary ditty to Susan and signs it, identifying herself as its speaker. In contrast, the quotations are neither addressed nor signed. Like speculations about what kinds of expressions were removed by the mutilations, or hypotheses about "Master," the interpretations offered to attach the references to real situations are guesswork. What tone Dickinson expected Sue to receive from these isolated citations and what tone Sue attached to them, we can never know. But that does not mean the quotations reveal nothing. What they suggest is a private code through which the two communicated or at least Dickinson's presumption that Sue would understand her meaning, and thus they appear to evince Dickinson's faith in Sue's intimate knowledge of her riddling allusiveness or at least her faith in Sue's active role as reader. Of vital importance, then, is recognition that, like her poems, the quotations are generative and turn every reader into an author. First a citation directs the reader to Shakespeare's text, then to develop their intertextualities and narrate their significance, the reader will author connections between Dickinson's reiterative utterance to a particular correspondent and its origins.

Reconstructing a Relationship

Analogously, whether one concludes that Sue is Dickinson's Iago, her Cleopatra, her "Master," friend, estranged friend, embittered friend, or enemy, a reader must first consider what it means to be characterizing a relationship on the basis of the surviving correspondence of record. The "book" of Emily and Sue Dickinson's written record currently consists of the more than four hundred poems, letters, and letter-poems from Emily, three letters and an especially poignant inscription from Sue to Emily, a few letters from Sue to various editors like William Hayes Ward and Higginson, and a few score more by Emily to Sue's husband Austin and her children—Ned, Martha, and Gilbert.[37] Whether studying all this can give one an accurate picture is seriously questionable. Missing are entire documents destroyed by Sue, reportedly "in accordance with Aunt Emily's request" (*FF* 176). Missing, too, are many of Sue's notes to Emily unless she wrote only three or four; yet from Emily's letters to her and Austin in the 1850s and a complaint by Sue to Austin of Emily's failure to write, we can be reasonably sure that there were more than a handful (see, for example, "I had a long letter from Sue last Thursday," L 71, and "I have heard from Sue three times," L 76). About the content of a skipped or blank page Dickinson would suggest, "*That* page is fullest – tho'" (L 247); critics and biographers have filled reams of blank pages with speculations about aspects of her life—like her religious views and sexual practices—that are finally irrecoverable and will always be contestable.[38] Also, how closely the character a writer affects to compose a letter resembles the person actually involved in the relationship is endlessly debatable. Thus, even if we had available all the letters, poems, notes, inscriptions, cards, and shopping lists the two exchanged, as well as all their written comments about one another, what would the written records illuminate about the actual relationship and its influence on Dickinson's literary production?

As my discussion of the material facts—types of paper, signs of others' tamperings, writing instrument employed—has already suggested, they are among the important elements to consider when evaluating the significance of Dickinson's written expressions to Sue. The mostly ink copies of poems in the fascicles (some variants are penciled) both complement and provide a telling contrast to the many penciled productions sent to Sue. Their complementarity is in the fact that both the manuscript books and correspondence show a poet intent on performing at her best. In the fascicles we find poems carefully copied, and calligraphy and spacing highlighted more and more so that in the "sets" (the groupings of the late 1860s and 1870s not threaded together) the alphabetic letters and their placements on the page are carefully exaggerated. In the correspondence to Sue, the notes and poems are not always copied on fine stationery, but are on paper of all sorts. Scraps from shopping bags and cheap paper appear to have been grabbed as she went about her quotidian chores. The contrasts between the correspondences to others and the correspondence to Sue begin with this fact. Though some of the correspondence is missing, the famous exchange over "Safe in their Alabaster Chambers" survives and indicates that at least sometimes Dickinson put her poetic performances through dress rehearsals by sending them to Sue. Comfortable, familiar, Sue's commentary on this poem does not appear the exception in their relationship but the habit. All this makes plausible the suggestion that Dickinson considered Sue's commentaries part of her writing process and an important activity and stage of her workshop procedures for producing poetry.

Turning to individual poems, letters, and letter-poems to Sue, readers should take care to consider contexts Dickinson herself provides, beginning in the following ways: Is the document addressed? Is it signed? What tone does the reader immediately perceive? How has that tone been created? By the reader's desires? By something in the written expression? By the editorial apparatus attached to it? By the ordering in its presentations in the *Poems* and/or *Letters*? By attaching a letter Charles Wadsworth presumably sent Dickinson to the "Master" letter "Oh' did I offend it," how has Johnson foreclosed interpretations of both (L 248, L 248a)? Similarly, by paraphrasing Dickinson's answer to Sue's response to "Safe in their Alabaster Chambers" at the same time he edits out the end of Sue's letter for presentation in the variorum edition of the *Poems*, then not presenting Sue's letter in full until the three-volume edition of the *Letters* three years later, how have interpretations of that exchange been quietly prefigured (P 216, L 238; B 74, H 11, H 203)?

Thus perusing the "book" of documents upon which one attempts to formulate an accurate sense of a Dickinson relationship, readers must accept that such reconstructions will always be significantly limited.[39] Readers should be aware that even bibliographies can never be as objective as compilers' aspirations for them are. Literary criticism in general, but especially, it seems, criticism of Emily Dickinson, seems prey to devolving into gossip, armchair psychoanalysis, or everybody's autobiography. Dickinson critics should, therefore, especially heed Paul de Man's exhortation to "safeguard a discipline which constantly threatens to degenerate into gossip, trivia or self-obsession."[40] In the chapters that follow, I do not pretend to have a disinterested stance, but I do attempt to cast a skeptical eye about drawing hard and fast conclusions, knowing that almost all judgments must remain provisional, since they reflect the desires of readers as well as "truths" about the subjects under study.

"**U**ncle Sam" Bowles was urgent for more. The third verse amused him most:

> He likes a boggy acre,
> A floor too cool for corn.
> Yet when a child, and barefoot,
> I more than once at morn,

> Have passed, I thought a whip-lash, etc.

"How did that girl ever know that a boggy field wasn't good for corn?" he demanded of "Sister Sue," holding Emily guiltless of farming lore.

"Oh, you forget that was Emily '*when a boy*'!" was the reply.

—MARTHA DICKINSON BIANCHI, *FF* 27

My Mother was blessedly busy in her home and Aunt Emily's light across the snow in the Winter gloaming, or burning late when she remained up all night, to protect her plants from chill, was often a mute greeting between them supplemented by their written messages.

—MARTHA DICKINSON BIANCHI, *THE SINGLE HOUND*

Five To Be Susan Is Imagination: Dickinson's Poetry Workshop

If we compare the printings Dickinson witnessed of the ten or more poems mechanically reproduced in her lifetime with the versions her mentor Susan had in her possession after the poet's death, and remember that the latter's home, the Evergreens, hosted many an editor, specifically those of the *Drum Beat*, the *Republican*, and the volume *A Masque of Poets*, all of whom printed Dickinson's verse, it is reasonable to speculate that Dickinson refers to Sue's action when she tells Thomas Higginson that "A narrow Fellow in / the Grass" (Set 6c; P 986) was "robbed" of her and forwarded to publishers. As Thomas Johnson points out, "The fact that Sue lacked a copy [and had to ask Dickinson for one about 1872] tends to confirm the conjecture that it was Sue who had forwarded her own copy to Samuel Bowles because he had expressed his admiration for it" (P 986n). Equally reasonable is the hypothesis that Sue passed along other select poems in her possession for publication. Sue's version of "A narrow Fellow in the Grass" reads "His notice instant is," as did that published by the *Republican*, and the version of "Blazing in gold, and quenching in purple" that Perez Cowan says Sue gave him most nearly matches that published by the *Republican* March 30, 1864 (see P 986n and P 228n). Thus Sue, as would Helen Hunt Jackson a couple of decades later, appears to have actively promoted Dickinson by seeking a wider audience for her poetry while the poet was still living. In fact, Sue continued to promote Dickinson's poetry beyond the 1860s and was the first to introduce it to Mabel Loomis Todd, for in 1882 the latter records in her diary: "went in the afternoon to Mrs. Dickinson's. She read me some strange poems by Emily Dickinson. They are full of power" (*YH* 2:361). In their immediate circle, Sue's handling of Dickinson's poems certainly appears to have been recognized long before her reading them aloud to Loomis Todd. In 1862, editor and friend Samuel Bowles writes Sue and implores her to "tell Emily to give me one of her little gems!" (*YH* 2:68). One of his 1864 letters even appears to substantiate Jean McClure Mudge's assertion that Emily and Sue were writing together: "Speaking of writing, do you & Emily give us some gems for the '*Springfield Market*,' & then come to the Fair. As Lincoln says—classical for 'big things'—*Res magna est*" (*YH* 2 : 93). Over the years, Sue's admiration for Emily did not wane. Besides introducing her poems to Loomis Todd, in 1883 Sue thought enough of one of Dickinson's observations to record it in a memorandum: "Emily speaking to Ned of some one who was a good scholar, but uninteresting said, 'She had the *facts* but not the *phosphorescence* of books—'" (*YH* 2 : 392).

Though strong and affectionate declarations of praise for Sue and her literary opinions are myriad throughout Dickinson's writings to her, much has been made of the discord between them that is rumored to have characterized the later years of their relationship. "For the last fifteen years or so (the number varies) of her life, Emily Dickinson did not have face-to-face contact with Sue." Or so the story usually goes. But as Mudge, who reminds readers that Emily and Sue were born only eight days apart and "were nearly twins," points out, "Emily's notes document regular and happy rendezvous with Sue in the Mansion [the Homestead] until 1883. . . . After 1883, it appears, Sue did not come to the Mansion anymore. She had two good reasons. That year, her eight-year-old son Gilbert died and she withdrew from society for months. At the same time, Austin began his affair with Mabel Loomis Todd, often meeting her in the Mansion. Sue could not cross the path as before."[1] Over the years, Dickinson's letters allude to the pleasures of Sue's visits and of taking coffee together in the Homestead (H B 10, L 346, 1870; H B 150, L 392, August 1873); apologize to Sue for Emily's untidy or "gross" appearances (H B 153, L 383, 1873; H B 11, L 554, June 1878); declare that she must wait before seeing Sue (H B 181, L 581, 1878; H B 7, L 660, 1880) as well as that she would have made an appearance if she had known Sue was there (H B 63, L 662, 1880); and exclaim with pleasure at hearing Sue's voice (H B 89, L 722, 1881). Thus the correspondence suggests regular, casual, face-to-face contact throughout adulthood. An 1885 note from Sue to her daughter Martha indicates that she and Emily may have continued to talk regularly, suggesting that Sue may have visited the Homestead even after 1883. To Martha, Sue writes, "Your letters to Aunt Emily and account of Mr Barny [?] are very amusing" (*YH* 2 : 443). Since Emily may have sent Martha's letter next door for Sue to enjoy, this does not prove direct contact. However, a long-established Dickinson habit was to read letters aloud to one another. Thirty years before, Emily had written Austin about the family reading his letters as a group, and in late 1884 Sue wrote

Martha, "We laughed over your letter last night till I lost off my glasses. Even Papa broke down and for a moment forgot, that he does not allow himself to applaud his family" (*YH* 2:434). In these last couple of years of her life, whether Dickinson read Martha's letter to Sue as she read her writings to Louise Norcross and whether she handed a letter to her nephew Ned directly to Sue to enclose with one of hers (*YH* 2:454) or sent them over with the almost daily deliveries across the path between the two houses can never be known for sure. Likewise, it can never be positively determined whether Dickinson refers literally to physical absence or figuratively to Sue's turning away in anger when she writes, around the right and left edges of the page so the reader has to turn the document all around, "how could I woo / in a rendezvous where there / is no Face?" (H B 77; L 856, about 1883). What is certainly documented in these accounts is that Sue and Emily's regular and intimate exchanges did not cease but were continuous, from the time they were girls together to Dickinson's death at the age of fifty-five.

In the 1850s, early in their relationship, Emily and Sue took long walks, baked cookies, sewed, talked about books and their dreams, and, according to Dickinson, pleased themselves "with the fancy that we are the only poets, and everyone else is *prose* . . . " (L 56). In the late 1850s and early 1860s, after Sue and Austin married, Emily spent many a riotous evening next door at the Evergreens, and at least on one occasion was scolded by her father for staying too late (L 214, about 1859). According to Kate Anthon, on those "celestial" and "blissful evenings . . . full of merriment, brilliant wit, and inexhaustible laughter" Austin and Sue's guests were sometimes treated to Emily "at the piano playing weird & beautiful melodies, all from her own inspiration" (*YH* 1:366–367). Not only in these middle years, but over their more than thirty-five years of intercourse, Emily and Sue shared many cultural delights, exchanging food, recipes, writings, tips for reading, and enjoying a mutual passion for gardening. Like Emily, Sue read voraciously, and those around her were well aware of her intellectual pursuits. In an 1863 letter to Austin, Bowles writes, "There waits at the office the book Sue wanted to read—Jean Paul's great novel. They say it is hard reading" (*YH* 2:78). Sue's library was well stocked with the likes of works by Shakespeare, Milton, Tennyson, Elizabeth Barrett Browning, the Brontës, Lydia Maria Child, George Eliot, William Dean Howells, and Henry James and collections such as Griswold's *The Sacred Poets of England and America*—to name a random few. Not surprisingly, literature was central to much of the discourse between the two women. When Dickinson nicknamed herself "Thoreau" in a letter to Sue, she also recounted dreaming of Sue "meeting Tennyson in Ticknor and Fields" (L 320, August 1866). For Christmas 1859, Sue gave Emily *Adam Bede*, and when the first installment of *Daniel Deronda* appeared in the March 1876 *Scribner's*, Sue sent it over to Emily (*YH* 2:244). For Christmas that same year, Sue gave Emily Thomas à Kempis's *Of the Imitation of Christ*, which influenced Eliot's character Maggie Tulliver (*The Mill on the Floss*, Book IV, chapter 3). That both loved music is plain from accounts of Dickinson's turns at the piano and Sue's writing her brother about the thrill of opera (*YH* 1:221). Besides their mutual love for literature and music, both shared a love for flower cultivation. In October 1859, the *Express* reported: "A basket and a vase of flowers were at once recognized by some of the Committee, as from the splendid garden of Mrs. W. A. Dickinson, whose diligence and success in the cultivation of flowers is only equalled by her surpassing skills in arranging them" (*YH* 1:374). Thus when Dickinson characterizes "Blossoms and Books" as "those solaces of Sorrow" (L 963, January 1885), she may be speaking for Sue as well as for herself.

The primary goal of this chapter is to examine the surviving correspondence between Emily and Sue in order to further understanding of the latter's participation in Dickinson's literary project. Though this is not a biography, I do attempt to study carefully the written products of a biographical situation—Dickinson's decades-long relationship with the woman who shared so many of her literary and cultural interests, who resided literally a stone's throw away for virtually all of Dickinson's adulthood, and whom the poet loved intensely throughout her womanhood. Thus my project contrasts with one like Sewall's in two important ways. While his relies heavily upon the documents produced by and in response to Loomis Todd, I rely heavily on documents to and by Sue, by Mabel's own account, her "most bitter enemy" (*Life* 1:291). Also, as biographer, he properly concerns himself more with factors extraneous to Dickinson's writings than with the writings themselves. As literary critic, I concern myself with Emily and Sue's surviving writings and survey them to see how each characterizes herself and her correspondent in the letters they compose for and about each other. What these characterizations tell about biography will ever be open to question, but these literary and epistolary exchanges do reveal much about Dickinson's immediate presentation of herself and her immediate reception as writer.

In the three sections that follow, I divide study of the "book" of their correspondence rather conventionally into early ("Why Susie!"), middle ("Sue, Dear Sue, Sweet Sue, Sister"), and late ("To Own a Susan of My

Own") periods in order to trace developments of tone and substance in the writings; I title the sections with Dickinson's exclamations because she wrote the vast quantity of the surviving documents passed between them, and I am most concerned with her attitudes and their consequences upon her literary production. Such divisions are of course somewhat arbitrary, especially since the dating of manuscripts must usually remain in some measure inexact. The earlier documents can often be dated by postmark or reference to Sue's location—for example, in Baltimore or in Michigan. Yet fairly reliable dating of even the later documents is possible, for Dickinson's handwriting does identifiably evolve over time and can be used to date manuscripts within more general periods of five to ten years.[2] Though I am less certain than they in our ability to date Dickinson's handwriting within a particular year, I usually concur—give or take a year or so—with Thomas Johnson's or Ralph Franklin's dating. My logic for delineating and defining periods can be summarized as follows: Dickinson's writings between 1850 and 1855, when Emily and Sue were young single women together, are studied in the section titled "Why Susie!"; these letters are often embarrassingly effusive, lengthy, filled with puns and repeated references to the act of writing, yet include little poetry; though triangulation with both Austin and Sue's sister Martha marks these early letters, his and Martha's presences grow more and more dim as the relationship evolves, and while Dickinson's expressions of her love for Sue mature, they do not become less intense. Covering the period when Dickinson saw most of her poems printed and the time between Austin and Sue's marriage and the birth of Gilbert ("Gib"), their youngest child, the writings between 1858 and 1875 are studied in "Sue, Dear Sue, Sweet Sue, Sister"; in general, Dickinson's letters, poems, and letter-poems are far more elliptical, thus more concise than writings of the earlier period, and, significantly, the vast majority of poems is signed; in this section, Sue's lengthy response to "Safe in their Alabaster Chambers" is also interrogated. Covering the time just after Gib's birth and through his heartbreaking death, the poet's apparent passion for Judge Lord and his death, and her own death, the writings between 1876 and 1886 are examined in "To Own a Susan of My Own"; these writings feature many of Dickinson's most radical personal statements and dramatic holographic techniques—extravagant declarations to Sue's "power" as well as extravagant calligraphic orthography.

The first two sections are the longest. The early effusive letters and a couple of plaintive poems in the next section have probably been the most discussed over the past century. Youthful, repetitive, and exaggerated, they present perplexing problems of interpretation even as they record literary efforts of a budding poet. The second section examines the record of Dickinson's most striking exchange over one of her most suggestive poems during what is generally recognized as her most productive period. Outlining her continued literary devotions to Sue, the last section serves as an epilogue to the other two. All of these writings could bear much more scrutiny than those rendered previously and than my examinations here.

Why Susie!

Of all her writings to Sue, these early letters most resemble the passionate epistles Carroll Smith-Rosenberg describes as routine in the female world of love and ritual of nineteenth-century America's upper middle class. As Vivian Pollak observes, some similarities can also be drawn between these and Dickinson's letters to other female friends:

> During the winter of 1851–52, Dickinson's friendship with Sue had become the vehicle for a set of rich and intensely gratifying fantasies. Her relationships with Jane Humphrey, Abiah Root, and Emily Fowler had anticipated some of its component features, just as her subsequent attachments to Elizabeth Holland and perhaps Kate Anthon were to reiterate them, though in a significantly attenuated form. Among these features were her fantasies of subsequent meetings, which included hurried kisses and whispered good-byes; the exclusion of those routine obligations represented by "the worthy pastor"; the creation of a new sacred text, which would also release the sly and derisive laughter enjoyed by the members of a superior, secret society; a freedom of verbal invention to celebrate its mission; and the transcendent pleasure of having effectively circumvented the authority of a monolithic community of elders, while remaining physically present within it. No dancing girl in a pasha's harem, no slave in an antebellum mansion, and no homosexual in a resolutely heterosexual society could have conceived a finer scheme.[3]

With the exception of that to Sue, none of the correspondences incorporates all of these elements to intense degree. The characteristics Pollak delineates can be usefully augmented to identify more traits of Dickinson's early correspondence to Sue: besides inscribing fantasies of kisses, Dickinson repeatedly writes of actually caressing Sue and litters these letters with signs of her devoted blood, sweat, and tears; often accompanying these desirous expressions are revisionary applications of the Bible or of traditional heroes, which continually expand her "new sacred text" and legitimate her love and physical passion by identifying them with holy affections; intimations of a secret society and of a world of clandestine or hidden unions clearly portray a world of US VS. THEM; complaints about domesticity and housekeeping are frequent, implicitly arguing against the life of a wife supposedly coveted by women; and, perhaps most important, Dickinson repeatedly offers Sue three kinds of excuses for not reciprocating writing and love—most obvious are the excuses Dickinson supplies for Sue not writing back as many letters as Emily; then there are the excuses Dickinson gives for herself and for writing so often; and finally, by identifying her love for Sue with guilt, insanity, or disaffection, she furnishes Sue with yet another excuse for not loving her in quite the same way. Most important, over these first several years of correspondence, Dickinson begins to "publish" poems to Sue (whereas she apparently did not do so to Root, Fowler, or Humphrey). Much can be learned by surveying the surviving missives to Sue of this period according to these topics.

Though it would be tedious to cite all of these early letters, extensive quotation is necessary to formulate analysis in this section. First, it is the only means by which one can convey a sense of the staggering number of early loving epistles to Sue. Between 1850 and 1855 Emily wrote at least twenty-five letters to Sue alone, while the combined number to Abiah Root, Jane Humphrey, and Emily Fowler totals twenty-four. The great number of surviving letters to Sue over the years is one of the distinctive elements that marks this correspondence as primary. That Sue saved so many of the letters testifies to their value in her eyes and to her regard for Dickinson as a writer; the fact that the poet sent so many to be saved of course says something about Sue's value as audience to Dickinson.

His sister's letters to Sue never fell into the possession of Austin or Mabel Loomis Todd. Those extant remain mostly intact. Yet the end of an emotional October 1851 letter to Sue written within hours of the first mutilated letter to Austin is "missing," and the letter itself features many elements characteristic of Dickinson's early writings to her dear friend, especially histrionic effusions to prove desire, and offers clues about what both "Austin" and probably Sue herself tried to remove from Dickinson's epistolary record. Dickinson opens the letter declaring, "I wept a tear here, Susie, on purpose for *you*," a strategy common in discourses of desire, and one she would repeat throughout these first years of correspondence (H L 5; L 56).[4] By that statement Dickinson seeks to prove her love and at the same time literally present both evidence and a part of herself in the tearstain on the page.

Dickinson devotes her entire third paragraph to comparing their relationship to the "perplexities about marriage" of a single man recounted
in Ik Marvel's romantic bestseller, *Reveries of a Bachelor* (1850):

> It is such an evening Susie, as you and I would walk and have
> such pleasant musings, if you were only here – perhaps we would
> have a "Reverie" after the form of "Ik Marvel," indeed I do not
> know why it would'nt be just as charming as of that lonely Bachelor,
> smoking his cigar – and it would be far more profitable as "Marvel"
> *only* marvelled, and you and I would *try* to make a little destiny to
> have for our own. Do you know that charming man is dressing
> *again*, and will wake pretty soon – so the papers say, with *another*
> Reverie – more beautiful than the first?

Having expressed her hope that she and Susie might "make a little destiny
to have for" their "own," Dickinson prays Marvel will not precede them in
death: "We will be willing to die Susie—when such as *he* have gone, for
there will be none to interpret these lives of ours." Her use of an-
tanaclasis—"'Marvel'" only "marvelled" and "We will be willing"—is
common in her letters of this period.[5] By exercising a bit of literary fun
and sporting her writerly wit, Dickinson entertains "Susie," simultaneously attempting to flatter and seduce with the proclamation that as a pair
they are extraordinary. The document ends abruptly, just after Dickinson's
attentions turn completely to a description of what her love for Sue means
and she appropriates Christian language to declare its powerful adhesive-
ness—"for what shall separate us from any whom we love—not '*hight* nor
depth' . . ." (Rom. 8:39). Perhaps it was merely lost, but probably Sue or
her daughter removed the letter's last page. As I noted at the end of the
preceding chapter, destruction of an entire document (in this instance a
sheet) is characteristic of the excisions by Sue that Bianchi described and
contrasts with the scissorings and erasures of parts of documents characteristic of "Austin's" mutilations. As is the case for the erasures in the
letters to Austin, in this epistle her writing is removed when Dickinson
begins to focus all of her attentions on expressing affections for Sue.[6]

Were it not for the self-consciousness of Dickinson herself, Sue,
Bianchi, and "Austin," and were it not for the fact that intensely loving
writings continue from Emily to Sue over the next three and a half
decades, Dickinson's early passionate writings to Sue could perhaps be
equated with those to her other female friends. However, to characterize
these passionate letters to Sue as conventional manifestations of female
love and ritual seems naive, for time and again Dickinson inscribes the

self-consciousness evident when she apologizes for writing "all these *ugly things*." As well as pleading, "I know I was very naughty to write such fretful things" (L 88), Dickinson expresses her sense that what she is writing "may be wrong, and that God will punish" her "by taking" Sue "away" (L 85) and repeatedly asks for Sue's forgiveness. "Will you forgive me . . . I cannot stay away" (L 70) and "Susie, forgive me Darling, for every word I say" (L 94) are the kinds of pleas frequently made during this period. Even in a gleeful moment, having pirated the marriage vow to echo "Till death do us part" in a letter's salutation, "Yours till death – ," Dickinson nicknames herself "*Judah*," after the lost tribe of Israel (H B 176; L 97), humorously acknowledging her secession from conventional comportment.

Four months after the altered 1851 letter, Dickinson again presents bodily evidence of her love by contrasting her excruciatingly painful feelings to the weather: ". . . I don't know how I shall bear it, when the gentle spring comes; if she should come and see me and talk to me of you, Oh it would surely kill me! While the frost clings to the windows, and the World is stern and drear; this absence is easier; the *Earth* mourns too, for all her little birds; but when they all come back again, and she sings and is so merry – pray, what will become of me?" (H L 22; L 73, February 1852). Within days, Dickinson identifies an ink blot on another letter as a sign of her transgressive behavior: "Dont see the *blot*, Susie. It's because I *broke the Sabbath!*" (H L 9; L 77, February 1852). Breaking the sabbath by staying home and writing Susie excites Dickinson to splash ink on the page, to proclaim that "the words wont come, tho' the *tears* will," and to "class" Susie "with the *angels*." By the letter's end her mood is so enlivened that she is positively giddy, and thus closes the epistle with a charming ditty written, as if by someone with vertigo, up the side of the fourth page: "Who loves you most, and loves you best, and thinks of you when others rest? t'is Emilie – ." Three months later Dickinson continues to express her physical passion with humor, to entertain as well as woo: "I have got to go out in the garden now, and whip a Crown-Imperial for presuming to hold it's head up, until you have come home, so farewell, Susie – I shall think of you at sunset, and at sunrise, again; and at noon, and forenoon, and afternoon, and always, and evermore, till this heart stops beating and is still" (H B 173; L 92, May 1852). There are three long letters dated in June 1852, the last of which ends with palpitating desire: ". . . I hope for you so much, and feel so eager for you, feel that I *cannot* wait, feel that *now* I must have you – that the expectation once more to see your face again, makes me feel hot and feverish, and my heart beats so fast . . ." (H L 7; L 96). Two years hence Dickinson has accepted that Sue and Austin will indeed marry, and the tone and descriptions of her bodily excitations change accordingly: "You need not fear to leave me lest I should be alone, for I often part with things I fancy I have loved, – sometimes to the grave, and sometimes to an oblivion rather bitterer than death – thus my heart bleeds so frequently that I shant mind the hemorrhage, and I only add an agony to several previous ones, and at the end of day remark – a bubble burst!" (H L 17; L 173, 1854). Dickinson concludes this famous "Sue – you can go or stay –" letter with the only poetic "publication" of record for the next four years. It begins:

> I have a Bird in spring
> Which for myself doth sing – . . .
>
> (P 5)

This bird flies "beyond the sea" for the poem's speaker, to learn "Melody new for me" and "return." Thus there will be no discontent and no grudge because "that Bird of mine," "though flown" and perched "in a distant tree," sings "Bright melody" only for the speaker.

Sharp contrasts—perhaps signaling ambivalence, perhaps designed to entertain or to coax Sue out of an intransigent religious position—permeate this joint presentation of letter and poem. In the letter, Dickinson refers to "the Jesus Christ *you* [Sue; emphasis added] love," claims "a darker spirit will not disown it's child," and concludes "Perhaps this is the point at which our paths diverge." Yet their religious differences were nothing new. Two years earlier, when Dickinson refers to three "sweet and true" little books that "dont *bewitch*" her any but that she is sure Susie "would love," she alludes to novels with strong religious content, one of which was published by the American Baptist Publication Society (H L 13; L 85, April 1852). Counterpointing the epistolary resignation and despair over religious and other differences with a poem optimistically predicting that apparent desertion is in fact a new sort of devotion, Dickinson belies the letter's tone. Within the letter itself she equates her hemorrhaging heart, loss of loved ones through death, and loss through separation "rather bitterer than death" with the most trivial of deprivations—a bubble bursting. By deflating her own painful exclamations, Dickinson calls overly morose interpretation of them into question or blusters to appear less hurt than she actually is or seeks to cajole her addressee through rather ludicrous juxtapositions. Yet the bibliographical note Johnson attaches to this letter and poem establishes parameters for interpretation that allow no ambiguity in tone:

There is nothing in other letters to indicate a rift between the girls at this time. The draft of a letter from Austin to Susan, 23 September 1851, alludes to some differences between the girls about which he refuses to take sides, but this letter is in the handwriting of 1854. It is placed here to follow the emotional tone of the letter to Susan of late August, though the disagreement on spiritual matters that seems to lie behind it may have no connection with the feeling of neglect shown in the earlier one.

(L 173N)

Generally this has been recognized as one of Dickinson's "bitterest" letters.[7] Johnson's description of twenty-three-year-old women as "girls" perhaps sets limits for his response, but his view need not foreclose ours. Though it appears that the letter refers to a real falling out and actual anger or hurt on Dickinson's part, the undercutting comparison of extreme physical and emotional pain to a bubble popped out of existence and playing one genre off another complicate interpretation. These strategies suggest that this young woman is beginning to take responsibility for her feelings, is determined not to let differences with loved ones defeat her into sourness, and even dares to charm her friend across the emotional distance that has apparently developed between them. The preceding letter to which Johnson refers does not have these mediating features, and its complaints about Susie not writing and its remark that "when you meet, and I meet – we'll try and forgive each other" seem both more bitter and less hopeful than the intertextual suggestions of the letter and poem. Significantly, the fact that "Baltimore," where Sue taught from 1851 to 1852, is penciled on the letter he places just before the "go or stay" letter and poem suggests that Johnson's dating may be off by at least two years. Otherwise, over these early years, Dickinson's letters inscribing physical evidences of her love appear to evolve from ones describing anticipatory palpitations causing accidents at her writing table and such ravenous reception of Susie's "precious billet" that "I am wearing the paper out, reading it over and o'er" (H L 22; L 74, February 1852) to ones that seem to mock her own histrionic exclamations that depict unrequited passion as cardiac hemorrhage.

Similarly, her fantasies about touching and kissing Sue evolve over these few years from imagining primarily physical unions to ones fusing the erotic and intellectual. In her first letter to "Dear Susie – *happy* Susie," Dickinson imagines that she will "steal a kiss from the sister" when "the darling Rover" returns (H B 131; L 38, December 1850). A little over a year later, Dickinson imagines holding Susie—"in my arms"—when the latter returns from Baltimore in July (H L 15; L 70, January 21, 1852). Continually flirting with Sue, Dickinson seems to imagine touch in everything and caresses her beloved friend with onomatopoeia: "To day it rained at home – sometimes it rained so hard that I fancied you could hear it's patter – patter, patter, as it fell upon the leaves –" (H L 5; L 56, October 1851). A few months later, she makes the kind of declaration that crops up several times in these early letters: "How vain it seems to *write*, when one know how to feel – how much more near and dear to sit beside you, talk with you, hear the tones of your voice; so hard to 'deny thyself, and take up thy cross, and follow me' – give me strength, Susie, write me of hope and love, and of hearts that *endured*, and great was their reward of 'Our Father who art in Heaven'" (H L 10, L 73, February 1852). Consonant with many of her contemporaries, Dickinson formulates a private sentimental love religion by allying her physical yearnings with scripture. For example, writing in 1852 about their mutual friend Henry Root and herself talking about the absent Sue, Dickinson urges, "You remember home and Amherst, then know, Loved One – that *they* are remembering *you*, and that 'two or three' are gathered in your name, loving, and speaking of you – and will you be there in the midst of them?" (H L 9; L 77, February 1852). The traditional interpretation of Jesus's reference to his Holy Spirit's guaranteed presence "where two or three are gathered in my name" (Matt. 18:20) does not satisfy Dickinson, but by appropriating it to express her adoration of Sue, she "create[s] new meanings" to "replace the inadequacies of the old."[8]

Over but a few months, this new sacred text evolves from enshrining remembrance of Sue to enshrining fantasies of touching her in a kind of emotional/erotic scripture. Dickinson imagines that "when you come home, darling, I shant have your letters, shall I, but I shall have *yourself*, which is more – Oh more, and better, than I can think!" (H L 13; L 85, April 1852), then "how soon I shall have you, shall hold you in my arms" (H L 20; L 93, June 1852), then "If you were here . . . , my Susie, we need not talk at all, our eyes would whisper for us, and your hand fast in mine, we would not ask for language" (H L 2; L 94, June 1852). When Dickinson adds a kiss to end this last letter, it does not seem entirely innocent, merely an exchange between friends, for she self-consciously does so "shyly, lest there is somebody there!" In the very next letter, she tells her "darling," "so near I seem to you, that I *disdain* this pen, and wait for a *warmer* language," then pleads, "Susie, will you indeed come home next Saturday, and be my own again, and kiss me as you used to?" (H L 7; L 96, June 1852). Again, she consecrates her desire by identifying it with the

Apostle Paul's rhapsody on love: "Shall I indeed behold you, not 'darkly, but face to face' or am I *fancying* so, and dreaming blessed dreams from which the day will wake me?"

By late 1854, Dickinson no longer writes as much of touching or kissing, but she has not abandoned fantasies of physical unions—of sorts. Neither does she eschew appropriation of the Bible to express her feelings, but she no longer employs scripture merely to validate eroticism. In a November–December letter written over several days, she imagines that Sue and she embrace practically identical situations, though they are miles apart: "I want to think of you each hour in the day. What you are saying – doing – I want to walk with you, as seeing yet unseen. You say you walk and sew alone. *I* walk and sew alone" (H L 6; L 176). Her fantasy of but two months later while away in Washington seductively embeds an erotic suggestion: "I'm loving you at home – I'm coming every hour to your chamber door. I'm thinking when awake, how sweet if you were with me, and to talk with you as I fall asleep, would be sweeter still" (H L 14; L 178, February 1855). In "Notes on Sleeping with Emily Dickinson," Karl Keller asserts that "Female bonding is missing in Emily Dickinson's poems because there is a female narrator but no (or very seldom a) female subject. There is a woman speaking (and generally speaking to men, I believe) but no woman loving a woman."[9] Missing from neither her poems nor her prose, female bonding and a woman speaking her love for a woman repeatedly over the decades of her adulthood are in fact central to Dickinson's work. Her notes on sleeping with someone foreground this fantasy of sharing a bed with Sue. Significantly, like the departed bird in "I have a Bird in spring" who sings for the supposedly abandoned speaker, Dickinson makes sharing language with one another central to her intimacy with Sue. Therefore, her dreams of physical intimacy with Sue evolve into reverie imagined in a setting suggesting linguistic coition.

Dickinson introduces this fantasy of sleeping and talking with Sue by scolding the latter for not writing: "Will you write to me – why hav'nt you before? I feel so tired looking for you, and still you do not come. And you love me, come soon – this is *not* forever, you know, this mortal life of our's. Which had you rather I wrote you – what I am doing here, or who I am loving *there*? Perhaps I'll tell you both, but the 'last shall be first, and the first last.'" In keeping with her habit, Dickinson cleverly appropriates Jesus's words (Matt. 19:30) to clarify and perhaps even justify her question as rhetorical: whatever Sue wants, Emily will first write about whom she is "loving *there*." As we have seen, Dickinson continually casts her love for Sue in terms of biblical metaphor, but this last revisionary statement has evolved from those made earlier which dressed her admiration. By 1854, she revises biblical text not only to assert her love, but also to assert that her desire to proclaim affection supersedes Sue's druthers.

This revisionary use of the Bible employs the familiar to mediate understanding both of her intensely affectionate expressions and her right to say such things. Whether all this offended or charmed the believing Sue cannot be clearly discerned, but this part of Dickinson's new sacred text clearly helps create a world of us versus, or different from, THEM. So does her revisionary use of literary or cultural scripture. Echoing Milton's ". . . though what if Earth / Be but the shaddow of Heav'n, and things therein / Each t' other like, more then on earth is thought?" (*Paradise Lost* 5:574–576), Dickinson proclaims that love for Sue transforms her earthly state into a heaven that may just surpass that for which all the "saved" are waiting: "'Herein is Love.' But *that* was Heaven – *this* is but *Earth*, yet Earth so *like* to heaven, that I would hesitate, should the true one call away" (H L 13; L 85, April 1852). Similarly, Dickinson's beloved is superior to any earthly resident: "'Eye hath not seen, nor ear heard, nor can the heart conceive' *my* Susie, whom I love" (H B 173; L 92, May 1852; 1 Cor. 2:9). Not surprisingly, then, Susie is not just a teacher in Baltimore, part of the common lot or one of "them," but a cultural hero, "the precious patriot at war in other lands!" (H L 10; L 73, February 1852).

As does "their" limiting interpretation of scripture, their church dissatisfies Dickinson and she attempts to dissuade Susie from conventional services: ". . . dont *you* go Susie, not to *their* meeting, but come with me this morning to the church within our hearts, where the bells are always ringing, and the preacher whose name is Love – shall intercede there for us!" (H L 9; L 77, February 1852). For this church with Sue, Emily crossdresses her emotion as "the old *king feeling*," perhaps to ally it with the power of patriarchs even as she disobeys their dicta. In "their" church, just as Dickinson decides "to wear the blue" dress for Susie, down comes "the minister's fist with a terrible rap on the counter" (H L 7; L 96, June 1852); in the church she builds for herself and Sue, Dickinson, anticipating the mooring of "Wild Nights," "would nestle close to" Susie's "warm heart, and never hear the wind blow, or the storm beat again" (H L 22; L 74, February 1852; see also H L 9; L 77). While their pastor says "Oh Heavenly Father," Dickinson says "Oh Darling Sue" (H L 18; L 88, April 1852).

"Their" sense of family as husband, wife, and children, and "their" sense of that "proper" domestic scene as nineteenth-century women's domain, differs sharply from Dickinson's conception of what will make her most happy. "They are cleaning house today, Susie, and I've made a flying retreat to my own little chamber, where with affection and you, I will spend this precious hour, most precious of all the hours which dot my flying days, and the one so dear, that for it I barter everything, and as soon as it is gone, I am sighing for it again" (H L 20; L 93, June 1852). Dickinson constructs an imaginary world insulated from society, or "them," who threaten to interfere, come between the two, and defeat her plans for their little destiny. Denying that "they" may have already succeeded, Dickinson elaborates a fantasy that she knows just how Sue feels:

> I do think it's wonderful, Susie, that our hearts dont break,
> *every day*, when I think of all the whiskers, and all the gallant men, but
> I guess I'm made with nothing but a hard heart of stone, for it dont
> break any, and dear Susie, if mine is stony, your's is stone, upon stone,
> for you never yield *any*, where *I* seem quite beflown. Are we going to
> *ossify* always, say, Susie – how will it be? When I see the Popes and
> Polloks, and the John-Milton Browns, I think we are *liable*, but I dont
> know! I am glad there's a big *future* waiting for me and you. . . .

(H L 13; L 85, APRIL 1852)

To the young men, Dickinson claims that both young women are not pliant but unyielding and that Susie is especially so. But when doubts creep into her rhetoric, she makes several pointed literary allusions. First Dickinson refers to Alexander Pope, the eighteenth-century writer whose poetic example she most certainly did not follow, though he was deeply admired during her day as exemplary for his mastery of regular verse, and whose moral and philosophical pieties she quoted but three or four times; significantly, she couples his name with that of Robert Pollock, a Scottish poet popular during her time but whose work apparently did not thrill her. Then she puns on the name of the seventeenth-century bard Milton, master of blank verse whose poetry she so deeply admired, and couples his name with that of John Brown, a Scottish divine "who wrote voluminously on religious subjects" (L 85n).[10] By this allusion, she perhaps expresses a dim view of those who would dogmatically either reduce the epic *Paradise Lost* to a religious treatise or regard it as heresy. If, as Johnson suggests, she characterizes the young men of her acquaintance, Dickinson worries that, surrounded by so many whose attitudes insist on behaviors and lifestyles predictably proper and conventional, she and Susie will succumb to peer pressure. Even in this near-giddy paragraph, as soon as she admits such possibility, she immediately asserts that instead theirs will be a "big *future.*" The literary allusions seem designed to amuse, and coded both to make fun of "them" and assert the special line of communication between herself and Sue.

Besides taking a fairly ungenerous view toward their peers, through discouraging examples, Dickinson supplies reasons for Sue to eschew the usual matrimonial course. The most famous is of course her letter written but a couple of months later contrasting their unmarried state to that of the bride "safe" in her romantic thralldom, whom she in turn compares "to the *wife*, Susie, sometimes the *wife forgotten*" (H L 20; L 93, June 1852). Significantly, wives, not just those forgotten, might well find a single woman's life "dearer than all others in the world." Rendering neither praise nor excited anticipation for a wife's role, Dickinson describes courtship in terms that make women the prizes of conquest, men mythically inhuman: "I told Mattie this morning, that I felt all taken away, without her, or Susie, and indeed I have thought today of what would become of me when the 'bold Dragon' shall bear you both away, to live in his high mountain—" (H L 15; L 70, January 1852). By presenting women's status through comic exaggeration, Dickinson both warns and seeks to delight her friend, hopefully making herself more appealing.

Over the four-year course of this early correspondence, Dickinson's letters grow more loving and more exasperated, sometimes self-mockingly so, while Sue withdraws. When Sue mentions all "the girls" in Amherst in a January 13, 1853, letter to a friend, she does not list Emily, who is there among them (*YH* 1 : 259). Two months later, Dickinson complains to Austin, "I have not heard from Sue again, tho' I've written her three times" (L 108, March 1853). Also sent in 1853, "On this wondrous sea," Dickinson's first poetic "publication" to Sue, is a letter-poem addressed to "*Susie*," signed "Emilie," with "*Write! Comrade, write!*" centered above the poem as a title would be (H B 73; L 105, P 4). Like several of Dickinson's letters to Sue, this letter-poem anticipates the images of safe, restful harbor celebrated in "Wild Nights." Significantly, this is a place constructed by Dickinson's imagination. But Dickinson does not only attempt to charm or imagine Sue out of her position of some remove from Emily's passionate entreaties. Accompanying the many lengthy, effusive expressions of the early letters, scripted with longing and filled with implicit arguments against convention, are apologies for writing and excuses for Sue's not reciprocating.

When in early 1852 Dickinson writes, "Will you forgive me, Susie, I cannot stay away," she immediately complements her apologetic plea with explanation: "it is not *me only* – that writes the note today – dear Mattie's *heart* is here, tho' her *hand* is not quite strong enough to hold a pen today" (H L 15; L 70). In the same letter, Dickinson blames failure to receive letters from Sue on the weather, not on the latter's failure to write, and again couples with Martha in her reasoning: "She [Mattie] has'nt got your letter, owing she thinks to the great snow storm, which blocked up all the railroads, and dont give us any mail – and Susie – I am so credulous, and so easily deluded by this fond heart of mine – that I am supposing snow storms have got *my* letter too, and I shant lay it to *you*, but to the wicked *snow storm*, if mine does not come *too*!" Even while Dickinson admits her delusions, she argues against them by supplying Sue with more excuses: "Never mind the letter Susie, I wont be angry with you if you don't give me any at all – for I know how busy you are, and how little of that dear strength remains when it is evening. Only *want* to write me, only sometimes sigh that you are far from me, and that will do, Susie!" (H L 10; L 73, February 1852). In her next letter, Dickinson demands more: "Never mind the letter, Susie; you have so much to do; just write me every week *one line*, and let it be, 'Emily, I love you,' and I will be satisfied!" (H L 22; L 74, February 1852).

While through comic depiction, verbal wit, or unabashed praise of "Susie," Dickinson tries to make herself more appealing, at other times she presents herself as crazy, depressed to the point of distraction, apostate or otherwise alien. Though these descriptions often feature a comic edge, they also furnish Sue with an excuse to regard Emily's loving advances as inappropriate. Besides declarations like that mentioned in the first chapter—"in thinking of those I love my reason is all gone from me, and I do fear sometimes that I must make a hospital for the hopelessly insane, and chain me up there such times, so I wont injure you" (L 77)—are those which echo the rhetorical posturing of Barrett Browning's "How do I love thee?": "Dear Susie, when you come, how many boundless blossoms among those silent beds! How I do count the days – how I do long for the time when I may count the days without incurring the charge of Femina insania!" (H B 173; L 92, May 1852). Supplementing her appropriation of a heterosexual love poem Sue would recognize by wittily making up a Latin phrase, Dickinson charmingly admits the excesses of her passion.

About this same time, she portrays herself as something of a hag and apologizes for her disheveled appearance: "Will you let me come dear Susie – looking just as I do, my dress soiled and worn, my grand old apron, and my hair – Oh Susie, time would fail me to enumerate my appearance, yet I love you just as dearly as if I was e'er so fine, so you wont care, will you?" (H L 22; L 73). In fact, Dickinson aspires to be anticonventional and unattractive, at least to "them": "I do feel gray and grim, this morning, and I feel it would be a comfort to have a piping voice, and broken back, and scare little children. Dont *you* run, Susie dear, for I wont do any harm, and I do love you dearly tho' I do feel so frightful." By 1854 and early 1855, Dickinson describes herself as depressed and even disoriented: "I do not miss you Susie – of course I do not miss you – I only sit and stare at nothing from my window, and know that all is gone – Dont *feel* it – no – any more than the stone feels, that it is very cold, or the block, that it is silent, where once 'twas warm and green, and the birds danced in it's branches" (L 172); "I miss you, mourn for you, and walk the Streets alone – often at night, beside, I fall asleep in tears, for your dear face, yet not one word comes back to me from that silent West [Sue is in Michigan]" (H L 1; L 177, late January 1855). In fact, Dickinson suggests that she may be in the process of being punished for her heretical affections: "Few have been given me, and if I love them so, that for *idolatry*, they are removed from me – I simply murmur *gone*, and the billow dies away into the boundless blue, and no one knows but me, that one went down today" (H L 17; L 173, 1854).

Perhaps intended to elicit sympathy, this last statement cues readers to a key characteristic of these letters from Emily to Sue: while she keeps declaring her love and concern for "Susie" over and over, Dickinson is finally selfishly concerned most about herself, her feelings, her desires. As we have seen, she only makes a pretense of asking what Sue wants her to write in order to declare who she is "loving *there*," no matter what Sue's preferences are. Though Austin and Emily are writing Sue simultaneously, Emily's late 1850 and early 1851 offhand remarks to her brother about "Susie," almost always accompanied with mention of Sue's sister Martha, indicate that either she chose to deny or did not know about Sue and Austin's budding romantic interest in one another (see, for example, L 37, L 42, L 43, L 44, L 46, L 47). Austin is the only correspondent of this period who, according to the surviving documents, received more letters from Emily than Sue, and in her letters to him of autumn 1851, Dickinson remarks upon how much Martha appreciates the charm he gave her (L 57), reminds him of how much "Mat" misses him (L 59) and "Martha loves you" (L 62), and how she "never comes" without inquiring about him (L 63). Sometimes Dickinson mentions Sue, but she always foregrounds Martha's affections for Austin: "Mat misses *you* so much, and her dear sister Susie" (L 59). Throughout 1852, Dickinson continues to urge his attentions toward Martha, sends Mat's love and urges him to write her

(L 76, L 87, L 95), tells him how much Martha misses him and "antici-pates" his arrival (L 82) and how much Mat appreciates his letters (L 90).

By March 1853, Dickinson realizes that Sue and Austin's romance has begun, knows about their meeting in Boston, and passes letters along for them (L 106, L 107). Even as she employs terms of sororal endearment in her letters to Sue of 1853–1855, Dickinson is not merely sanguine to know that if Sue marries Austin, she will be forever "*Sister*": willing to pass along Mother and Vinnie's love, she remarks that "Austin must carry his"; though he plans to visit Sue in Michigan, this refusal to pass along his affectionate regards seems pointed, especially since Dickinson was willing to do so earlier (H L 6; L 176, November–December 1854). Immediately after Sue and Austin's Revere meeting in 1853, Emily writes him, "I hope you have been made happy" (L 109); writes Sue, "One would hardly think I had lost you to hear this revelry" (H L 4; L 107); begins to sign her letters to Sue, "your lonely / Emilie –" (H L 4; L 107, March); and time and again complains about her loneliness to Austin (L 123, L 125, L 128). By 1855 Dickinson implicitly argues that her attentions are more lover-like than Austin's by reporting that "he had not noticed" what Sue wore, how she looked, nor how her hair was fixed, while those are the questions Emily first asks when he returns from his visit to Sue in Michigan (H L 1; L 177). In that same letter, ostensibly praising their soon-to-be in-law rela-tionship, Dickinson's phrases group Austin with Vinnie and Mat, and her-self with Sue, separated by a comma from the other three: "Why Susie – think of it – you are my precious Sister, and will be till you die, and will be still, when Austin and Vinnie and Mat, and you and I are marble – and life has forgotten us!"

Most important for our consideration is not how selfish Dickinson appears to be, but how obsessed she is with writing her desire. These his-trionic, sometimes seemingly hysterical letters are not necessarily imma-ture, sinful, or neurotic. As Pollak points out, in his letters to Sue of this period, Austin often sounds "driven to desperation," and some of his rav-ings even make "Dickinson's descriptions of her loneliness sound well-balanced by comparison."[11] Certainly his and Mabel's letters thirty years later are no less histrionic than these early ones by Dickinson, and Susan Howe has noted Austin's self-absorption after embarking on the affair. When he is well into his fifties, Austin writes Mabel that he has nothing "except for you alone" when he in fact "had a wife," who bore him a child when she was forty-five, "and two surviving children as well as his ador-ing sisters next door."[12] Such engrossment is common among lovers pas-

sionately enthralled. Thus the readily available example of Austin con-
sumed first with desire for Sue, then for Mabel, indicates not so much a
Dickinson familial trait of self-indulgence as it highlights the fact that
Emily's self-centered preoccupations in these ardent letters to Sue are characteristic of one deeply in love. Observing that the "rhetoric" that describes
the Master and Sue relationships is "surprisingly similar," Adalaide Morris
notes that the two sets of love letters are "even suspiciously similar, as if
Dickinson were writing to the Master and Sue out of some peculiarly ellip-
tic book of pattern letters." [13] Indeed, these early letters to Sue are proto-
types of the heavily revised "Master" epistles. Significantly, Dickinson's
writing desire in missives to Sue evolves from "wont that make a poem such
as can ne'er be written?" (H L 9; L 77) to actually writing poems. As we shall
see in the next section, that surely had something to do with her audience,
for Sue actively encouraged, promoted, and critiqued the poet's work; over
the next thirty years, Dickinson sent Sue more than twice as many poems as
letters, and many of the letters are in fact letter-poems. Readers may or may
not agree with Howe that Susan Gilbert evoked a "libidinal freeing of the
Imaginary" in Dickinson's poetry. What cannot be denied is that Dickinson
herself considered her correspondence with Sue to be a profound creative
wellspring and that these early letters offer scholars a glimpse at some of the
writerly evolutions of the young poet. [14]

Sue, Dear Sue, Sweet Sue, Sister

After February 1855 comes a conspicuous silence in Dickinson's correspondence to Sue that parallels the mutilations made by her and "Austin" as well as gaps in the poet's correspondence with Elizabeth Holland.
According to Johnson's dating, Emily Dickinson neither addressed a letter
nor published a poem to her friend between February 1855 and September
26, 1858. Since this was when Sue first took up residence next door, a possible explanation might be that it did not occur to Dickinson to write one
so near. But a letter dated "about 1854" (L 173) was certainly sent to Sue
while she was in Amherst, and, as was the custom, Dickinson was already
in the habit of sending notes locally (see, for example, L 162, L 163, L 164,
L 168, L 169). Pollak flatly declares that the "problematic silence of 1857
signifies something more than an accident of historiography," and reminds
us that "among the wealth of correspondence Emily exchanged with both
Sue and Austin, there is no message of congratulations on their marriage,
just the kind of letter they would have saved, as they saved so many others,

had it been written." Lillian Faderman points out that the fact that Emily Dickinson's correspondence to confidante Elizabeth Holland also either waned during 1857, the year after Austin and Sue's marriage, or is "missing" seems significant.[15] Examining Dickinson's correspondence to Sue in the three years preceding this gap, and considering it all in the context of "Austin's" mutilations, this "silence" of three and a half years suggests that, as do Pollak and John Cody, Faderman is justified to "make a connection between her loss of Sue and her ostensible silence." Faderman contends that if Dickinson's summaries of others' writings can be trusted—to Sue she writes, "Thank you for loving me, darling, and *will* you 'love me more if ever you come home'?" (L 74)—"it is also fairly clear that Sue was not simply an innocent recipient of Emily Dickinson's protestations of love," but "seems to have answered her in turn." Here Faderman quotes one of the February 1852 letters to characterize Sue's response, but, as we have seen, between 1850 and 1855, Dickinson seems increasingly romantic in her attentions toward Sue, while her declarations of love are increasingly unrequited. After March 1853, as their marriage approaches, Dickinson's letters to Austin and Sue reflect tension and her ambivalence. We can never know for certain whether Sue initially reciprocated Dickinson's erotic passions or what kind of letters from each to and about the other have been lost. However, what is important to remember is that this gap in writing—no poems are dated during these years—has been overlooked in most stories of reading Dickinson. Crucial, too, to keep in mind is that, according to the record, after 1854 Dickinson virtually stops writing her brother while she writes his wife hundreds of poems and letters.[16]

On July 1, 1856, Austin and Sue were married in Geneva, New York, in her "Aunt's dear cozy home." The wedding which Loomis Todd said Austin called his "execution" was, on May 19, a month and a half before it occurred, described as "a little cake—a little ice-cream and it is all over—the millionth wedding since the world began" by Sue (*YH* 1 : 342). The couple moved to "the new house Austin" was "building as fast as possible," the Evergreens, next to his father's Homestead. Opting not to demolish completely "General Mack's place," Austin erected his Victorian mansion around the colonial structure already on the property: the Evergreens' kitchen and dining room have the low ceilings, and the kitchen the heavy, thick, rough-hewn floors common in a period when unrefined Amherst and the Connecticut Valley were still relatively frontier. Though the Dickinson homes were "quite as attractive as any in Am—," Sue's remark on the upcoming nuptials entitling her to take up residence there does not sound like that of a young woman passionately and happily in love, and the later disavowals attributed to Austin lack even a hint of sentimentality about the newlywed years (*YH* 1:344). Thus both compose stories suggesting that the lovely appearance of the younger Dickinson's mansion and their festive evenings entertaining as a fashionable couple perhaps masked tensions between a doubtful and tentative two within.

Yet whether these stories reflect the truth of the matter is questionable. Sue's downplaying of the wedding follows a decision to marry in her "foster-Mother's" home instead of in Amherst, a change that "made great shaking among the old plans" and forced Sue to say "good-bye to some of the sweet old plans and pretend to believe the new ones are the best" (*YH* 1:342). Her remarks, then, could easily be disappointed responses to wedding arrangements, not necessarily to the marriage itself. Mabel Loomis Todd reported Austin's remarks more than three decades later. Certainly a story about his marriage for his mistress would not be likely to emphasize good times with his wife. John Evangelist Walsh has observed, "Except for the claims of those two [Loomis Todd and Bingham] there exists no hint that Sue and Austin were anything but congenial up to the arrival in Amherst of the Todds. One or two scant phrases in Emily's letters, which in reality allow and even demand the most innocuous of interpretations, are all that can be cited." More recently, Polly Longsworth has pointed out that "Mabel, much younger, less experienced, less philosophical, and intensely in love, needed a strong case to justify her radical departure from convention and to defend herself against Sue's anger and hatred, which she quickly became the target of." Most significant of all, decades after their newlywed years and a decade after his affair with Loomis Todd had begun, Austin "could not bring himself to put into writing (as Mabel urged him to do, for her protection) the counts on which he held Sue destructive of their union. Nor would he abandon Sue and start a new life elsewhere, a risky venture Mabel was prepared to undertake."[17] This is all the more reason that any characterization of the relationship between Austin and Sue rendered by Loomis Todd or Bingham must be questioned and treated as gossip, not documentation.

By anyone else's standards, accounts recorded of life in the Evergreens sound gay, culturally rich, and vibrant with fine meals and delectable conversation. Sue describes frequent visitor Samuel Bowles as one whose "range of topics was unlimited, now some plot of local politics, rousing his honest rage, now some rare effusion of fine sentiment, over an unpublished poem which he would draw from his pocket. . . . I especially remember two such, 'Pomegranate Flowers' by Harriet Prescott," and "a little unpublished poem of Mrs. Browning's which I fear I have lost" ("Annals" 3). Visiting luminaries such as Emerson, Harriet Beecher Stowe, Frederick Olmsted, and abolitionist/suffragist Wendell Phillips were also entertained in the Evergreens ("Annals" 4–11). Sue found Phillips "the most brilliant fireside talker I ever met," Emerson's "manner in talking . . . so very quiet that it quite put me out," and though she found Judge Lord's manner "bristling" from "his conviction that he alone was the embodiment of the law," she graciously describes his "kindly" taking "the head of the table" for an ill Austin and reciting "with an energy worthy himself and the subject" an entire hymn complemented by "a most remarkable artistic performance" by Vinnie ("Annals" 11, 13, 17–18). Emerson talked with Sue about Coventry Patmore's *Angel in the House* and recommended Julia Ward Howe's "Passion Flowers," while Stowe, "in a fascinating and talkative mood," "fell into some talk of her prolonged stay in Paris, and dwelt with great enthusiasms over the simple, but artistic French plays she constantly heard there, relating the plots of several, describing the stage accessories, and the audiences, with much other interesting detail" ("Annals" 13, 25).[18] Her depiction of Stowe's excitement on a drive – "the glory of the October morning was too much for her – she clapped her hands in her joy over the yellow maples, begging me to stop, now and then, that we might sit longer in the golden glory"—reveals Sue's own passion for nature. All in all, Sue's descriptions are luscious, recounting details like "fresh asparagus" and "salad from our own garden" for lunch, "arbutus" filling "the centre of the table," and "wild violets" gathered for a visitor ("Annals" 23–24).

Besides portraying a cultivated, entertaining woman, appreciative of both culture's and nature's finer things, Sue's accounts, as well as those of Kate Anthon, relate vignettes from the lives of a privileged family.[19] During the late 1850s and early 1860s, Dickinson was part of this social swirl. Whatever the relations between Emily and Sue during the years represented by the gap in the correspondence, by late spring and early summer of 1858, when Dickinson writes Mr. and Mrs. Bowles about socializing next door, daily interactions were most cordial: ". . . I think Jerusalem must be like Sue's Drawing Room, when we are talking and laughing there, and you and Mrs. Bowles are by . . ." (L 189). This is important, because it is clear that she was writing poetry during these years and was surrounded by much, in the way of people and activities, to encourage serious literary endeavors. Sue was a central figure in these domestic settings and cultural happenings, and there are perhaps some telling similarities between Emily's and Sue's composing habits, indicated by the latter's manuscript "Annals of the Evergreens." Like Emily's, Sue's shorthand to reorder words is to place numbers above them to indicate their position in a series (for example, "2" atop the word or phrase to come second). Such a method may be fairly common, and alone this is not enough to suggest significant similarities. But quotation marks in "Annals" "sashay" like Dickinson's in "Dear Master," and besides mentioning "Aunt Emily" several times and recounting a few of her astute observations ("Annals" is addressed to Austin and Sue's children), Sue echoes the famous "There's a certain Slant of light" (F 13; P 258) when she describes "a particular slant of light, falling across the parlor carpet," then alludes to an author both women relished—DeQuincey ("Annals" 7, 18). Taken all together, and with the fact that a dash in one of her letters to Emily is directed decisively down (H Box 8; see below), such likenesses in the mechanics of composition and reinscriptions of Dickinson's conversations, writings, and tastes strongly suggest Sue's intimate familiarity with Emily's work.

Significantly, by the late 1850s Dickinson has not stopped writing Sue in a loverlike fashion, but her expressions have become considerably more artful. In the letter which identifies Sue with *Vanity Fair*'s Captain Dobbin, Dickinson once again fantasizes about sleeping with Sue by offering the latter her pillow: " – How much you cost – how much Mat costs – I will never sell you for a piece of silver. I'll buy you back with red drops, when you go away. I'll keep you in a casket – I'll bury you in the garden – and keep a bird to watch the spot – perhaps my pillow's safer – Try my bosom last – That's nearest of them all, and I should hear a foot the quickest – should I hear a foot – The thought of the little *brown plumes* makes my eye awry. The pictures in the air have few visitors." (H L 3; L 194, September 26, 1858). Clearly, Dickinson misses Sue, who is away visiting Martha. Promising never to be her Judas, more than two years after Sue's marriage Dickinson suggests that Emily's may be "safer" than any other cushion. More explicitly than her earlier passionate writings, Dickinson acknowledges the difference between her fantasy of the anticipated footfall of a fashionably dressed woman and an actual visitor. Her play with inversion, rhythm, and sound—"I should hear a foot," "should I hear a foot"— shows careful manipulation of the most obvious and more subtle components of meaning and perhaps even puns on schemes of poetic meter.

Dated this same year and signed "Emilie," "One Sister have I in our house," more than almost any of her poems, plainly refers to a real person, Sue, a real house "a hedge away," the Evergreens, and an apparently real perception that Sue "did not sing as we did." Though the earlier Them-Us dichotomy in which Emily and Sue constituted "Us" has been disrupted, Dickinson does not simplistically portray their union as dissolved but claims that holding Sue's "hand the tighter" has "shortened all the miles." Interpreting this poem in the context supplied by Loomis Todd, Sewall suggests that it is not "a pledge of eternal loyalty," but "an elegy on a youthful friendship and a bitter reminder" (*Life* 1 : 169). But more interesting than gossip-informed innuendos are the connotations conveyed by shifts in poetic form and meter. Besides the move out of quatrains, the rhyme scheme is no longer an off-rhyming ABCB, but in the fifth stanza is AABBBC. Breaking the pattern, the fifth stanza's sixth line prepares readers for the sixth and final stanza, which foregrounds alliteration and abandons rhyme scheme. On cursory reading, the first four stanzas appear predictable as four-line forms that merrily recount a friendship while securely acknowledging differences and confidently asserting comradeship. However, in her iambic contract with the reader, by the poem's first two lines Dickinson prepares one to expect an iambic tetrameter or trimeter line in the third but renders instead two iambs and a bacchic (unstressed syllable followed by two stressed syllables)[20]:

> One Sister have I in our house ,
> And one, a hedge away.
> There's only one recorded,
> But both belong , to me.

Readers can of course substitute "There is" for the contraction and make an iambic tetrameter line, but Dickinson did not write one. In fact, of the first sixteen lines, seven are comprised of two iambs followed by an amphibrach (stressed syllable between two unstressed syllables) or bacchic foot:

> One came the road that I came ,
> And wore my last year's gown ,
> The other, as a bird her nest,
> Builded our hearts among.
>
> She did not , sing as we did ,
> It was a different tune ,
> Herself to her a music
> As Bumblebee of June.
>
> Today is far from childhood ,
> But up and down the hills
> I held her hand the tighter ,
> Which shortened all the miles.

Occurring in lines 3, 5, 9, 10, 11, 13, and 15, these verse disruptions conform to no pattern but subtly call attention to themselves, urging the reader's more diligent scrutiny. Rife with ambiguity, the last two stanzas break the four-line regularity of the first four:

> And still her hum
> The years among,
> Deceives the Butterfly;
> Still in her Eye
> The Violets lie
> Mouldered this many May.
>
> I spilt the dew ,
> But took the morn ,
> I chose this single star
> From out the wide night's numbers ,
> Sue— forevermore!
>   Emilie –

(H SH 1; L 197; P 14)

Since, as Paul Fussell has pointed out, "poetic meter is a prime physical and emotional constituent of poetic meaning," through these metrical surprises Dickinson fosters a reader's careful attentiveness and highlights some unusual or ambiguous key word choices: What does it mean to "deceive" a butterfly? Are the violets reclining when they "lie" or do they lack veracity? Or are they an illusion? Does she mean to pun on "mourn" or is she really talking about the time of day in which most of us take our breakfast? For one's hum to fit into a natural scene so well that a butterfly is fooled is a gay and complimentary depiction; to associate the depth of one's eyes with the richest sort of flower that may moulder into perfume, then to counterpoint a pun on mourning with alliterative phrases that stress the choice of a "single star" from all of "night's numbers" does not smack of bitterness. Instead, both the structure and content of this simple-seeming poem are in fact very complicated: positive expressions bear negative possibilities, negative connotations positive. Most significant, the last three lines emphatically affirm Dickinson's choice to write to Sue.

The record shows Dickinson writing her sister-in-law regularly from 1858 on. In the summer of 1861, when she was thirty years old, she published "Safe in their Alabaster Chambers" to Sue (H B 74, H 203; L 238), which initiated the much alluded to but still understudied exchange between them over the suitability of various second stanzas. Some important questions are raised by Sue's response to the initial presentation of this poem as well as by Dickinson's subsequent response and alternative presentations. Contrasting them with critical receptions of Sue's influence reveals significant features of Dickinson's poetic project, not the least of which is her various means of "publishing" poems to her primary audience.

On the verso of her response, Sue has written "Pony Express," an initially inscrutable nickname or phrase apparently characterizing her prompt response to the poem. However, considered in the context of other writings by Sue, the phrase appears also to refer to her sometimes acting as courier between Dickinson and the printers. When the poem was first printed March 1, 1862, Sue wrote Emily: "Never mind Emily – to-morrow will do just as well – Don't bother I'm 'not an hard master' – You know Maggie is out, and I don't like to [neglect?] my fold – There are two or three little things I wanted to talk with you about without witnesses but to-morrow will do just as well – *Has girl read Republican?* It takes as long to start our Fleet as the Burnside (H B 94).[21]

Sue compares what she plainly considers to be their mutual enterprise, making Dickinson's poetry known to the public, to a Civil War general's siege and capture of Roanoke Island a few weeks earlier. Thus "Pony Express" as well refers to Sue's "love" turned "to larceny," or so she would describe her own role as intermediary between Dickinson and the world of print in her obituary for the poet. Echoes of Dickinson's vocabulary to Higginson about "The Snake's" appearance in the *Republican*—"it was robbed of me"—in the first piece written posthumously about the poet and her work hint that Sue may even have been privy to Dickinson's correspondence with the famous editor. In an 1881 letter, Dickinson shared part of her epistolary exchange with editor Josiah Holland with Sue (H B 17; L 714). How much Sue knew about Dickinson's relationships with editors can never be precisely determined, but Bowles's letters to Sue substantiate that she was both privy to his interest in printing Dickinson's poems and cooperatively facilitated obtaining copies for him. Though Karen Dandurand conjectures that Mary, the wife of *Drum Beat* editor Reverend Richard Salter Storrs, may have carried on a correspondence with Emily and "may have played a part in obtaining" the three poems Dickinson printed in the Civil War journal between February 29 and March 11, 1864, it is just as reasonable to conclude that Sue gave the poems to the editor.[22] An appreciative, sensitive, and enthusiastic audience, possibly aware sooner than the poet was of Dickinson's genius, Sue would most likely welcome any opportunity to voice her regard to an editor and possible pub-

lisher. An Amherst College trustee from 1863 to 1898, Storrs "was a frequent commencement week guest of Austin and Susan Dickinson . . ." and
is one of the visitors Susan writes about in "Annals of the Evergreens."
Whoever delivered the poems to these editors—Sue, some other friend or
acquaintance, or the poet herself—Sue more than promoted them; at least
in the case of "Safe in their Alabaster Chambers," she critiqued the text
while Dickinson was in the process of writing and in that way participated
in the composition of the poem.

Sue liked the first stanza, but apparently was not pleased with the
new second, beginning "Grand go the Years – in the / Crescent – above
them –":

> I am not suited dear Emily with the second verse – It is
> remarkable as the chain lightening that blinds us hot nights in the
> Southern sky but it does not go with the ghostly shimmer of the first
> verse as well as the other one – It just occurs to me that the first
> verse is complete in itself it needs no other, and can't be coupled –
> Strange things always go alone – as there is only one Gabriel and
> one Sun – You never made a peer for that verse, and I *guess* you[r]
> kingdom does'nt hold one – I always go to the fire and get warm
> after thinking of it, but I never *can* again – The flowers are sweet
> and bright and look as if they would kiss one – ah, they expect a
> humming-bird – Thanks for them of course – and not thanks only
> recognition either – Did it ever occur to you that is all there is here
> after all – "Lord that I may receive my sight"—
>> Susan is tired making *bibs* for her bird – her ring-dove – he
> will paint my cheeks when I am old to pay me –
>> Sue –

(H B 74B)

Long recognized is the fact that Higginson's paraphrase of critical commentary rendered by Dickinson upon his visit to the Homestead a decade
later echoes Sue's assessment of the draft of "Safe in their Alabaster
Chambers." To him, Dickinson apparently remarked: "If I read a book
[and] it makes my whole body so cold no fire ever can warm me I know
that is poetry. If I feel physically as if the top of my head were taken off, I
know *that* is poetry. These are the only way [*sic*] I know it. Is there any
other way" (L 342a). Like Sue, Dickinson is not content to confine her
critical commentary only to poetry's mental effects, but acknowledges its
sensual power. The chills both women describe are of a different order
from the cold that heat from a fire or swaddling by a blanket will relieve.

Significantly, by acknowledging that poetry's effects are not merely mental, both women recall both Dickinson's account of transformations upon reading Elizabeth Barrett Browning—"The Dark – *felt* beautiful" [emphasis added], then "The Bees – became as / Butterflies – / The Butterflies – as Swans –" (F 29; P 593)—and the Wordsworth of "Tintern Abbey," who simultaneously feels the "wild ecstasies" (l. 138) of Dorothy and stands apart reading them. Likewise, both women acknowledge literary power as affective and implicitly state that poems are bound to readers' performances, then narrate their stories of reading—Dickinson in her poem, Sue in her paragraph of critique.[23]

Powerfully affected by the haunting beginning of "Safe in their Alabaster Chambers," Sue ruminates on whether the first stanza is not in fact a poem unto itself. In turn, Dickinson was powerfully affected by Sue's criticism and began producing alternative second stanzas. Such a response on Dickinson's part underscores her deep respect for Sue's literary views and casts serious doubt on arguments constructed to repudiate them by construing them as disingenuous. Indeed, if Dickinson's admiring remarks to Sue are insincere or sarcastic, then she expended astonishing amounts of time and energy on causticity. In profound contrast to some critical diminishments of their relationship, in the early 1860s, Dickinson does not appear to be coy or in any way conceal her appreciation of and admiration for Sue, repeatedly inscribing her respect by imaginatively bonding with Sue in erotically charged fashion through salutations like "Should I turn in / my long night, I should / murmur 'Sue'" (H B 179; L 294, September 1864) and by sending letter-poems like that uttering "Dear Sue. / Your – Riches – / taught me – poverty! . . ." (H B 44; L 258, P 299, early 1862). By addressing the letter-poem "Dear Sue," then appending it with the note, "Dear Sue – / You see I remember – ," and signing both the poem and note "Emily," Dickinson encourages Sue to receive this laudatory poem as one in which the "you" refers to Sue herself. However, the added note could be telling Sue that Dickinson remembered to forward a copy of a poem she had previously forgotten to send along as easily as it could mean that the lyric is a tribute to Sue's value and as easily as it could mean both those things or something else nonrecoverable to other audiences. Certainly her framing the lyric as a letter-poem with a specified addressee fosters assumptions different from those fostered by the score upon score of poems during this period that are signed "Emily" and sent to Sue but *not* headed with the address "Dear Sue" or "Sue." In many instances "Sue" is written on the verso and no direct address heads the poem. Important to take into account are the differences between poems specifically addressed as letters to Sue and the far greater number of poems signed and sent to her but without such direct address; different from both of these are the unsigned poems sent to Sue.[24] Recoverable and telling in all these presentations is Dickinson's acting on her trusting respect for Sue's abilities as reader.

Dickinson neither addresses "Safe in their Alabaster Chambers" directly "Dear Sue," nor signs it, though she does follow or introduce stanzas with signed notes asking Sue's opinion. In the poem's five verses—the first pleasingly powerful stanza plus the four efforts to form its "peer"—Dickinson demonstrates her poetic virtuosity as the little tippler at liberty, sober as seer and sayer, and then at play. In her story of reading the poem, Sue declares that "thinking of" the first stanza's fore-conceit or Idea creates a response in her that she cannot quell:

> Safe in their Alabaster Chambers,
> Untouched by Morning –
> And untouched by Noon –
> Lie the meek members of
> the Resurrection –
> Rafter of Satin – and Roof of
> Stone –
>
> (H B 74; P216, L 238; FACSIMILE *LIFE* 1:202)

Like Blake's crystal cabinets, these chambers are hard; unlike his, they are not prismatic and glittering but cold and translucent, transmitting light, although not radiantly.[25] In a Connecticut Valley noted for two centuries for its fervent piety, alabaster is a biblical, ceremonial word: at Bethany in the home of Simon the leper, a woman, identified only as a sinner, uses nard from an alabaster jar to anoint Jesus's body for burial (Matt. 26:6–13; Mark 14:3–9; Luke 7:36–50). These chambers' meek members "Lie," apparently waiting for a resurrection never to be realized: morning and noon, both full of light and associated with Christ's triumphant return, cannot touch them. Here, the meek shall inherit the earth, not heaven. Lie connotes falsehood as well as states of recline. That these members await the conquest of nature embodied in notions of resurrection may be a lie, like the happiness of brides, who must "lie still and be happy" (H L 20; L 93, June 1852). Concomitantly, the "Safe" shelters are made of rafters of satin supporting a roof of stone: Dickinson's impossible metaphor of the coffin echoes the absurdity of the belief that these dead wait in hope of rising to a new and better life. As she so loves to do, Dickinson calls this definitely collapsible, utterly fantastic chamber "Safe," takes the commonly held notion of nineteenth-century Amherst—that sanctified Christians are assured of afterlife—and tells what she apparently considers to be the truth about their circumstance: they wait in vain. Of course she tells it slant, ironically, and, as Charles Anderson pointed out three decades ago, mocks the faith of the "Elect" who think themselves saved.[26]

Throughout the Dickinson lexicon, and conspicuously in this poem, "Safe" reverberates with ironic connotation. In poetic publication to Sue, Dickinson had used the word *safe* only once before, in "Whose cheek is this?" (H B 186; P 82, about 1859). With this poem she sent a flower:

I found her – 'pleiad' – in the woods
And bore her safe away.

The speaker bears this flower to a safety of death; it will be preserved, but not as ebullient, colorful, flushed with life. In preservation the flower "Has lost a blush," is dried and withered in death. Interpretations of "Safe in their Alabaster Chambers" suggested by her repeated conflation of funeral and bridal symbols also render ironic the opening stressed monosyllable, "Safe," and couple a challenge to Amherst's pious conventions with one to nineteenth-century conventions of femininity.

This book's opening chapter notes how the imagery of "Title divine—is mine" connotes both bridal and funeral attire, suggesting that wedlock is a kind of deadlock. Like corpses, brides are "Shrouded" (P 1072). In "Emily Dickinson's Marriage Hearse," William Galperin argues that, using the trope of suitor masquerading as death himself in "Because I could not / stop for Death –" (F 23; P 712), Dickinson compares marriage to a kind of death.[27] Paralleling the rituals of a suitor with those of the undertaker is consistent with Dickinson's other descriptions: brides are portrayed as objects "yielded up" for sacrifice (H L 20; L 93), and the speaker of "A solemn thing – it was –" (F 14; P 271) characterizes the bridal bliss anticipated by a "woman – white" as in fact very somber. Indeed, one of Christianity's major similes—that the church subordinates itself to Christ as a bride submits to her husband—preaches that members should kill off their own desires, ambitions, and preferred behaviors and consciously assume those dictated by Jesus's example and subsequent Christian doctrine. When Dickinson considers "the life her culture expected her to live" and the roles of wife and mother to which she was expected to aspire, that "life surrounded by 'brittle ladies' and 'dimity convictions'" was, as Wendy Barker has observed, "in fact death to her."[28]

Thus arguing that among the multifarious connotations of "Safe in their Alabaster Chambers" are depictions of those shut up in the notions of true womanhood—women stilled, supposedly happy with tales of great reward for submission and surrender and with stifling fictions of duty—places it among themes and subjects repeated throughout the Dickinson canon. Though women were taught to expect nothing less than a sort of resurrection in Holy Matrimony, in her most critiqued letter to Sue, Dickinson pronounced marriage "dangerous" for women (H L 20; L 93).[29]

Dickinson's poetic speakers remark even more explicitly on the ironies of wifely status. Safe from lonely spinsterhood, one of those married members can declare:

> I'm "wife"— I've finished that—
> That other state—
> I'm Czar – I'm "Woman" now –
> It's safer so –
>
> (F 9, P 199)

Dickinson's quotation marks around "wife" and "woman" both conjoin the words and seem sarcastically to remind readers that these are appellations only. As wife, a woman is "rescued" from her relegation to second-class status as an unmarried woman and from the usually unflattering labels such as "old maid," "bachelor girl," and "spinster." If completed by a man, many suppose, a female can claim full status as Woman, can even claim royal title when entitled by the patriarchal password indicating her fulfillment, assumption of a responsible role, and maturity. But, as is underscored by Dickinson's repeated linking of bridal and funeral symbols, this presumed safety can in fact be deadening. However intended, her speakers time and again imply, the bridal veil may symbolize the disappointments of a woman who, wooed and won to be wife and wear her husband's name, finds that her new state of existence pales besides that promised by the seductive romances formulated by a suitor. Thus like Keats's lovelorn lady, wives may sing:

> Beneath my palm trees, by the riverside,
> I sat a weeping: what enamour'd bride,
> Cheated by shadowy wooer from the clouds,
>   But hides and shrouds
> Beneath dark palm trees by a river side?
>
> (*ENDYMION* 4: 189–193)[30]

According to Dickinson, however, instead of indulging in such roundelays, to maintain her happiness a wife must not reflect upon her situation, compare it to that "other" singular state, but, like the faithful Christian, must believe in its rewards:

> How odd the Girl's life looks
> Behind this soft Eclipse –
> I think that Earth feels so
> To folks in Heaven – now –
>
> This being comfort – then
> That other kind – was pain –
> But why compare?
> I'm "Wife"!   Stop there!
>
> (F 9; P 199)

In this context "soft Eclipse" connotes a total or partial obscuring of a wife's self from her former self. And since the "Girl's life" is "Behind" it, the metaphor recalls eclipse plumage, the brilliant, colorful (and covering), nuptial plumage of some male birds. Colored with a career outside the domestic chambers, the husband eclipses the wife's sense of self, dazzles her with his privilege and other life. Reassuring herself with fantasy, a wife tells herself that her state must be like that of heaven's members who feel that life on earth was "odd." Unable to be specific, she can only say that her new situation must be "comfort – then." If it is comfort, then that other solitary state was pain. But once she begins to compare the two situations, a wife cannot bear to continue doing so. She assures herself that she need not bother thinking about it, but must remember (and capitalize) her consolation, her title—"Wife." With that assertion and re-affirmation of her position she must stop both reflecting upon her position and speaking about it.

Over the past decade, this poem has been much scrutinized. As they did linking the same poems to discuss Dickinson's erotic Eden, William Shurr and Paula Bennett link the same "marriage" poems—"I'm 'wife' — I've finished that __ ," "A solemn thing – it was –" (F 14; P 271), "I am ashamed – I hide –" (F 33; P 473), "Title divine – is mine" (P 1072), and "Rearrange a 'Wife's' affection!" (F 11; P 1737)—to script psycho-biographies for the poet.[31] In these stories of reading, "I'm 'wife'" plays a central role. Though both talk about her poetic speakers, their interpretations maintain that these are not fictional characters but represent Dickinson herself. Thus, though they come to quite different conclusions regarding Dickinson's sexuality, both read the poems to discover biographical information. As do their conflicting but anxious responses to Dickinson's homoerotic expressions, their responses to "I'm 'wife'" provide telling contrasts. Relentlessly heterosexual in his conjectures, Shurr asserts Dickinson's complex celebration of a private marriage to a real male "Master," while Bennett, arguing for her lesbian as well as heterosexual desire, discusses Dickinson's ambivalences toward him. Though Shurr notices that exclamation points begin to abound in the fascicles in which three of the poems appear, he does not ponder the ambiguous suggestions of the technical details of a poem central to his argument—the quotation marks in "I'm 'wife.'" For him, the quotation marks signify Dickinson's never legalized but nonetheless passionate devotion to a flesh-and-blood suitor, leading to conclusions like Bennett's that she writes of "'marrying'-without-marrying the Master." However, as Gilbert and Gubar note about "the stops and starts of the mind" at work in the poem, so the quotation marks emphasize "Dickinson's ironic view of her speaker's anxious rationalizations." [32] While both Shurr and Bennett believe that Dickinson "married" the "Master" and that "I'm 'wife'" speaks of that, Gilbert and Gubar interpret the poem as a dramatic monologue.

Whether or not the poem depicts Dickinson's love for and devotion to a man or Sue or another woman will not take us very far in analyzing her poetic project. What is intriguing about Dickinson's poetic art here is her choice of subject—to write a poem that Bennett accurately characterizes as clearly ambivalent about wifely status was at great odds with conventional and finally conscriptional rhetoric touting marriage and motherhood as woman's highest achievement. In this way, "I'm 'wife'" articulates the general situation of wives in a nineteenth-century America in which matters like acts of domestic violence were by and large deemed private and in which public voicings of specific matrimonial displeasures were far from encouraged. One aspect of what amounted to a compulsory "consensus" was that matrimony's value for women was not even questioned. [33] In a patriarchal world, counting particular blessings and comparing them with those of unmarried women, interrogations from which the poem's speaker plainly refrains, are not necessary for wives. Anointed with the title yoking woman to man—"Mrs."—should be enough for those women to be safely muted in their bridal chambers.

If these "safe" spheres are represented by those of pure, bridal alabaster, wives are "Untouched by Morning," the birth and originary blaze of day, and "untouched by Noon – ," the time of day's most intense light and heat. Such images mirror the virtual closeting of many nineteenth-century wives, shut up, if not literally in their houses, then socially in their domestic circumference with family responsibilities. So these meek members of marriage, whose impossible hopes have been raised by the promise of satin bridal gowns, must lie down and be still if they are to perpetuate the myth of ready royal reward for women who surrender to conventional conjugal relations. Just as vitality and spontaneity go from the flower plucked and borne "safely" away, so the lives of these wifely members were all too often programmed by cultural expectations, and they were in effect dead to dawns of independent endeavors. In her previous "publication" to Sue, "A little over Jordan," Dickinson depicted morning as fertile with initiative and activity (P 59, copy to Sue lost). As Cynthia Griffin Wolff has pointed out about this poem, the morn of Jacob's "waxing strong" in his wrestling with the Angel represents for Dickinson a time burgeoning with creativity, "a starting point" for her "as artist."[34] Such independent creative initiative was not encouraged for wives. Whatever private significations these words held for Emily and Sue, and however Dickinson intended and Sue interpreted this first stanza of "Safe in their Alabaster Chambers," matters of women's problematic status were of concern to both.

In 1854 Dickinson's "Celibacy excludes me and my sister" (L 157) complains about Amherst society's compulsory coupling, and in 1869 she would ask Higginson about one of his articles on women's suffrage. Like Dickinson's early prayer, "God keep me from what they call *households*" (L 36, May 1850), one of Sue's earliest evaluations of woman's lot opined to Reverend Bartlett that domestic duties like sewing leave too little time for the important work of reading and thinking (*YH* 1 : 267). In one of the surviving documents from her to Emily, provocatively scissored beneath the words "summer __ I am sorry [square excision] *I*" and "a thorn, why not *we*'" (*Life* 1 : 203), and written in the same year in which Dickinson sent "Safe in their Alabaster Chambers" to her, Sue underscores their common plight as female sufferers:

> *Private*
>   I have intended to
> write you Emily to day but the
> quiet has not been mine __ I send
> you this, lest I should seem to
> have turned away from a kiss ,
> If you have suffered this past
> summer __ I am sorry [square excision] *I*
> Emily bear a sorrow that I
> never uncover __ If a nightingale

sings with her breast against
a thorn, why not *we* ¡   When
I can, I shall write __
                    Sue –

(H BOX 8)[35]

Using the nightingale image, or that of the secretly suffering poetess, Sue pens this rather tender note bearing two important elements also evident in her response to Dickinson's attempt at a better second stanza. As she had complained there—"Susan is tired making *bibs* for her bird"—and as she had predicted would be the case in her letter to Reverend Bartlett fretting over "no time to read or think," here Sue's "When I can" implies that there are more demands on her as wife and mother than time to meet them; just as important, a "kiss" plays a prominent role in both of her missives to Emily. These expressions emphasizing their intimate sharing of daily turmoils and affectionate gestures are a moving coda to this note in which Sue aligns their predicaments with the more general lot of women. As Dickinson does with her "sweet birds" in the first trial stanza, Sue borrows an image conventional in women's poetry of the period, perhaps indicating what interpretations she may have constructed as viable for the poem's images.

That "Safe in their Alabaster Chambers" lends itself to a multitude of interpretations, ranging from cosmic and religious reflections on literal deaths to domestic or social considerations of metaphorical deaths, of course speaks to the power Sue describes in her response. In the four trial stanzas are a variety of attempts to complement ideas suggested by the first. The most well-known stanzas, beginning "Light laughs the breeze" and "Grand go the Years," most obviously complement interrogations of immortality while the last two, "Springs – shake the Sills –" and "Springs – shake the Seals – ," pun on and critique one another, and more clearly direct readers' attentions to the more domestic connotations of earthly (not heavenly) households. Yet as we shall see, domestic significations are evident in each trial stanza. At first, Dickinson apparently sent the version bound into an 1859 packet to Sue. Juxtaposed with the first, the second stanza mocks the members' sleep of dead hope:

Light laughs the breeze
In her Castle above them –
Babbles the Bee in a stolid Ear,

Pipe the Sweet Birds in ignorant cadence –
Ah, what sagacity perished here!

(L 238; F 6)

Sue cast her critiques in metaphors of light—"shimmer," "chain lightening," "Sun." Though she is satisfied with neither, Sue considers this second verse a better complement to "the ghostly shimmer of the first" than "Grand go the years." Though critics like Karl Keller maintain that the mock sentimentality of the chuckling breeze, burbling bee, and sweetly chirping birds is lost on Sue, her assertion that these images of popular literature are well suited to the haunting, fitful, wavering images of the first stanza indicates that she understands Dickinson's ironic point and argue for Sewall's characterization of her criticism as "remarkably perceptive" (*Life* 1:201).[36] The stanza complements the meaning of the first, whether the members are actually dead or, as wives or other characters, figuratively dead. With delightful reverence the speaker personifies the usually gently refreshing breeze. Here, however, the female breeze, light as air, full of light like the "silver fleeces" or clouds lighting with dawn in "A little over Jordan," laughs down on those caught in their chambers. A disembodied feminine figure, ungirded by notions of modesty, free to revel where and as she pleases, she has no need of royal title: her residence is royal. Calling our attention to one of nature's rituals of fertility, the bee is, for Dickinson, an endlessly energetic and mighty little beast with the power to awaken pain, even through a shield of "dull Balm" (H 80b, P 156, sent to Sue). In "The Bumble of a Bee –" (H B 195, P 155), sent to Sue about the same time, the bee's babble or glossolalia casts a spell over the appreciative speaker. But over these dead members, who are without the power to savor or even to *be*, Bee has no power. Insensitive to his delightful chatter, the impassive members will never lend their "stolid" ears.

If it is wives who are sleeping in chambers of alabaster, then the male figure bee represents husbands. As befits the rhetoric, if not the realities, of Victorian marriage—that wives are pure in a dutiful sexuality, untainted by lust or passionate desire—the poem's members have no power to hear and thrill in sensual appreciation.[37] Babbling and singing, lively and sensual, the birds and bees try but cannot rouse these repressed, suppressed sleepers. Nature or the bird and bee calls of sexuality persist, but the dead members, who lie with their illusion of resurrection to a new life in heaven or "Eden" on earth, are rendered powerless to recognize these noises. In other words, the members are incapable of reception. Here life does not belong to members resurrected to pearly gates and streets of gold or to sexual bliss boundaried by marriage, but to nature's members, invisible but all encompassing, teensy to behold and apparently insignificant but bustling with seeming self-importance. The only time she uses "Pipe" as a verb in her poetry, Dickinson does so to emphasize the pied piper image of these benign birds. So the "ignorant cadences" signify not only nature's obliviousness to human religious and social conventions, but also a chorus of feminine birds, piping to one another and encouraging each other to follow usual arrangements and conform to an artificial plan for sexual experience. By using the sentimental rhetoric readers associate with the mass market of popular culture, Dickinson suggests that the words are more sound than substance. As can be the chants of church, so the professed positions on sexual mores are often recited rather than heeded.

Indeed, even the differences between what Dickinson actually wrote and what she saw printed in the *Republican* suggest that she intends for her poem to comment on conformity. Again, the editorial change is apparently minor. Dickinson saw

> Pipe the Sweet Birds in ignorant cadence –
> Ah, what sagacity perished here!

printed as

> Pipe the sweet birds in ignorant cadences:
> Ah! what sagacity perished here!

In the *Republican*'s version the birds "Pipe" independently of one another, each to her own drummer. This encourages, therefore, reading each bird's singing as an event separate, though simultaneous, from every other bird's. In Dickinson's version, however, the birds respond in unison. In their printing of "The Snake," editors were to divorce the third and fourth lines and "defeat" the poet's intention that they be read as one; here they separate what she wants unified and foil her dramatic purposes. Her birds respond chorally, emphasizing their personification and mocking their own conformity. In turn, this encourages reading the stanza as a three-part chorus—of the bee, the breeze, and the birds. Having perhaps assumed that Dickinson writes about birds actually perched atop tombs, or failing to consider the suggestive nature of the poem's every nuance, the *Republican*'s editors deemphasize the human consciousness projected upon nature's figures. Thus "their" version mutes the raillery about social conformity evident in Dickinson's figurative fowls.

When this microcosmically imaged second stanza did not please Sue, Dickinson produced an alternative, clothing her ideas in macrocosmic metaphors:

Grand go the Years – in the
Crescent – above them –
Worlds scoop their Arcs –
And Firmaments – row –
Diadems – drop – and Doges –
Surrender –
Soundless as dots – on a
Disc of Snow –

Perhaps this verse would
Please you better – Sue –
            Emily '

(*LIFE*, FACSIMILE, 1:202 AND F 10; L 238 FOR
DIFFERENT TRANSCRIPTIONS)

Ostensibly all here is on grand scale. Juxtaposed with the original stanza's images of popular poetry is this overview, probably incorporating the Dickinsons' new encyclopedia's description of the galaxy "as being shaped like 'a cloven disk.'"[38] In this vast scientific scope, years swell magnificently, presumably to decades, centuries, even ages, and parade majestically, at cosmic remove from the sleeping members. While corpses lie in their tombs and women the world over lie in their subjugated states, diadems drop and doges surrender—rulers rise and fall, kingdoms come and go.[39] The sweeping images of this stanza are the first to command readers' attentions, as most critical commentaries attest, and seem to be all that Sue has in mind when she characterizes it as "remarkable as the chain lightening that blinds us hot nights in the Southern sky." Grand scopes and crescents of time passing and of leaderships changing are all abstract, can be conceived but never handled or touched. Indeed, Sue seems to be stressing the connotations of that which is only available to our mind's eye, for in this new second stanza there appears to be nothing to feel, only ideas to ponder.

Yet as William Howard observed three decades ago, "Also involved in the imagery may be the homely experience of scooping flour out of a flour barrel or lard out of a lard stand, and the arc-like depression that is left behind in each case."[40] Thus when Sue employs "chain lightening" to describe the poem's metaphorical extensions, she may not be referring only to new observations of astronomy and science unsettling old religious beliefs. Even in an upper-middle-class household with servants, a nineteenth-century woman's world would be largely bound to the arcs and scoops of culinary duties. Firmaments, too, are not only the vaults of the sky, but are bases, firm supports or foundations, while "row" may mean to argue violently or cause a commotion as well as describe the act of falling in line or propelling a boat. "Firmaments row," then, may connote squabbles inevitable when those subscribing to conflicting epistemologies, or theories about the nature and foundations of knowledge, confront one another. Sue's "Did it ever occur to you that is all there is here after all – 'Lord that I may receive my sight'" suggests that the metaphorical implications of the poem go far beyond the obvious and that reflection upon the ways in which our theories about knowledge frame perceptions and experience are in fact central to the ideas explored by the poem. Different epistemologies of course generate varying constructions of gender, religion, and science.

Using "sight" metaphorically, Sue accentuates the fact that analogies ground all our hypotheses, a theme Dickinson explores in "We see – Comparatively –" (F 25; P 534). Such observations about thinking are as old as metaphor (i.e., language) itself, but, as Robert Frost would remark seventy years later, addressing the Amherst College Alumni Council: "We still ask boys in college to think, . . . but we seldom tell them what thinking means; we seldom tell them it is just putting this and that together; it is just saying one thing in terms of another. To tell them is to set their feet on the first rung of a ladder the top of which sticks through the sky." [41] Concordant with this idea are Dickinson's third and fourth trial stanzas, which frame reading of each other. Judging from their first lines, the fourth version is an appositive pun of the third. Dickinson first wrote:

> Springs – shake the Sills –
> But – the Echoes – stiffen –
> Hoar – is the window – and
> numb – the Door –
> Tribes – of Eclipse – in Tents –
> of Marble –
> Staples of Ages – have
> buckled – there –

And then:

> Springs – shake the seals –
> But the silence – stiffens –
> Frosts unhook – in the

Northern Zones –
Icicles – crawl from polar
Caverns –
Midnight in Marble –
Refutes – the Suns –

(H B 74C, L 238, F 10)

More than the other two trial stanzas, these versions explicitly direct considerations of the poem's meanings to domestic situations. "Springs – shake the Sills" recalls March winds rattling windows, a haunting, stir-crazy image for women housebound, shut up in household reponsibilities and in a sphere with boundaries that are literally the walls and floors of their domestic chambers. "Seals" connotes not only hermetic tombs but those sealed in wedlock and in a cult of domesticity, in "Sweet – safe – Houses – . . . Sealed so stately tight" (F 32; P 457) where window sills can seem like barricades. Spring, when hearts turn to love, represents the time romance may be revived in a relationship grown stale as well as the time romance outside wedlock's bonds may shake those holy unions, sanctioned and sealed by general consensus. In the fourth version the silence grows rigid, cold, and finally dark. In this realm there is no warm or blazing light of passion, but only frost and ice descending and ascending; here there is no wild night but only a midnight of cold, hard, impassionate surfaces. What comprises this silence remains up to the reader—it could be silence of the dead or "dead," silence of society about particular situations, or silence in a house when husband is at work and children are at school.

When Dickinson asked Sue, "Is *this frostier?*" she appended the third version, beginning "Springs – shake the Sills –" and reiterating the impossible, hopeless situation of the cold insensate inhabitants of the alabaster chambers. With sound answering only itself, shaking windowsills tease those as if an opening is imminent; evidently frozen in repetition, echoes "stiffen." Besides those twelve of Israel, the "Tribes of Eclipse," perhaps women interred in society's conventions, may recall the "tribe of decorous personages," the most upstanding "old patriarchs" and "matronly dames" of his congregation, summoned forth by his own imagination "to behold the ghost" Dimmesdale as he delivers one of his finest performances under the cover of night on the "guilty platform" (*The Scarlet Letter*, chapter 12). Like the meek members, Dickinson's tribes reside in yet another definitely collapsible, absurd notion of a domicile: tents of marble. Whether "Hoar" – a covering of minute ice crystals on a cold windowpane resembling grayish or whitish usually pubescent leaves—puns on woman's oldest profession is dubious, though with Dickinson, and especially in this correspondence rife with wordplay, readers can never be too sure. Obviously, with the buckling "Staples of Ages" Dickinson wants to emphasize collapsibility. Finally flimsy, then, these alabaster chambers are far from secure.

That Dickinson never settled on a single second stanza for "Safe in their Alabaster Chambers" reveals her attitude toward poetry as a dynamic and generative enterprise, as does the fact that she presented variations of it in multiple contexts. Evidently she considered the poem one of her finest, since the version with the second stanza beginning "Grand go the Years" was among the first four she sent Higginson (Boston Public Library Higg 4; L 260; P 216). In context of the three other poems enclosed with that initial letter—"I'll tell you how the Sun rose –" (Boston Public Library Higg 5; P 318), "The nearest Dream recedes – unrealized –" (P 319), and "We play at Paste –" (Jones Library; P 320)—the poem's cosmic and philosophical connotations are most resonant. Her selection of lyrics to introduce herself to the prominent man of letters suggests that she wanted to demonstrate that, as had Barrett Browning, she sought "to disprove the assertion that women" were only capable of occasional verse and could not "write true poetry" (*YH* 2:220).

Binding versions of this poem into two fascicles, Dickinson's concatenations first critique promises of immortality, then in the later "book" again link courtship and religious faith, seeming to satirize the promises of both. The version with the second stanza beginning "Light laughs the breeze" appears in the fascicle commencing with "Who never lost, are unprepared / A Coronet to find!" (F 6; P 73). While life after death is repeatedly questioned in this sequence—"Angels! Write 'Promoted' / On" a dead "Soldier's brow," but he does not rise to a new life (P 73); and "Going to Heaven!" sounds so "dim" that the poem's speaker declares, "I'm glad I dont believe it –" (P 79)—seasonal resurrections are time and again celebrated: "A Lady red – amid the Hill" becomes first "A Lady white," then yields to a "'Resurrection'" of "Orchard, and Buttercup, and Bird –" (P 74); after "An hour in Chrysalis" a "Stealthy Cocoon" emerges as "A Butterfly" (P 129); and "flowers from a hundred cribs / Will peep and prance again –" (P 133). In the later fascicle that begins with the poem "We – Bee and I – live / by the quaffing –" (F 10; P 230) appears the first verse accompanied by the other three trial stanzas. Surrounded by "Faith is a fine invention" (P 185), "You're right – 'the way *is* / narrow' –" (P 234), and "*One Life* of so much / Consequence!" (P 270), a poem casting

spiritual matters in capitalistic terms, the versions of "Safe in their Alabaster Chambers" presented in this sequence surely critique conventional
religious faith. Yet juxtapositions with other poems in the "book"—"The
Rose did caper on her cheek –" (P 208), one in which "thought" "as laces
just reveal the surge" (P 210), and "Come slowly – Eden!" (P 211)—also
suggest interrogative reading of conventional romantic relations. Indeed,
if "These" in "I've nothing else – to bring, / You know – / So I keep bringing These –" (P 224), the last poem in this fascicle, refers to the poems
themselves, then Dickinson describes reading as a possibility for journey-
ing, "To find our way Home –" (P 224).

Dickinson's sardonic commentary on "meek members" incapable of
active reception implicitly criticizes passivity in readers, and Dickinson
found the participatory perusal she desired in Sue. The ease with which
Sue delivers her response suggests that this exchange was a habit of their
relationship, and much about their correspondence indicates that writing
was central to their mutual concerns and that their communications constituted what might be called a "poetry workshop." From the distance of a
century and after study of Dickinson and her works has become an industry, we cannot help but approach this relationship with the assumption
that Emily was the writer and Sue the reader, always. Yet early on Dickinson wrote along the side of the first page of a letter: "I have heard all about
the journal. Oh Susie, that you should come to this! I want you to get it
bound – at my expense – Susie – so when he takes you from me, to live in
his new house, I may have *some* of you. I am sincere" (H L 18; L 88, April
1852). As it would be a decade later in response to "Safe in their Alabaster
Chambers," here Sue's writing is a vital component of their relationship.
Significantly, when Sue draws Emily's attention to the poem's publication,
she does not write "It takes as long to start *your* Fleet" but "It takes as long
to start *our* Fleet [emphasis added]." Neither does she use the singular *ship*
but the plural "Fleet." Pollak observes that the materials to write Sue's biography "may no longer exist"; more unfortunate, and a great loss to literary criticism, is that many of the materials to write critical stories about
Emily and Sue's poetry workshop probably no longer exist.[42] Nevertheless,
the correspondence of record could be studied much more exhaustively.

Not only do their statements and the remaining critical exchange
suggest that such a workshop existed, but some telling material facts about
the poems Dickinson sent Sue argue for that possibility. Already scrutinized is the experimental version of "I reason – ," which Sue had in her
possession after Dickinson died. Its exciting lineation, punctuation, and
elimination of stanza division hint that the women may have been discuss-

ing the effects of such technical nuances. Her transcript of "The Face we / choose to miss" (H 333, H ST on verso; P 1141), which precisely follows Dickinson's scheme for lineation until the last two lines, implies that Sue was sensitive to such details. Perhaps telling, too, are the facts that many of the versions of poems Dickinson sent to Sue do not have stanza divisions (e.g., P 67, 665, 669, 813, 814, 815, 820, 824, 1071, 1073, 1114, 1115, 1142, 1180, 1181, 1332—to cite a few) and are often in pencil. Likewise, Sue's transcripts of Dickinson's poems are more frequently than not without stanza division. The most obvious conclusion to draw is that Sue preferred poems that had not been broken into stanzas. Yet just as tenable is the possibility that, as were the trial stanzas for "Safe in their Alabaster Chambers," these versions without stanza divisions are still being worked through and Sue's response was a vital part of the composing process. That Sue may have thought she was still working on some of the poems she transcribed is further suggested by the version she produced of "To see her is a picture" (P 1568; H ST 23c):

> To see her is a picture
> To hear [her] is a Tune
> To know her an intemperance
> As innocent as June
> By which to be undone
> Is dearer than Redemption –
> Which never to receive
> Makes mockery of melody
> It might have been to live

This transcript befuddles Johnson: "The four final lines are not suggested in the worksheet draft, nor is line 5, which sounds very much like an alternative reading for line 4, as Mrs. Bingham conjectures in *New England Quarterly*, XX (1947), 49. ED never sent rough or semifinal drafts to her friends. Whence the transcript is not clear" (P 1568n). Contrary to his assumptions, what is implied by the transcript, especially when analyzed in the context of the other documents to Sue, is that, *with the exception of Sue*, Dickinson "never sent rough or semifinal drafts to her friends."

During this period, Dickinson signs letters "Susan's / Emily" (H B 185; L 333, 1869) and inscribes statements to Sue like the following:

> Susan's Idolator keeps
> a Shrine for Susan.
>
> (H B 71; L 325, 1868)

Punning on *value-blessed*, Dickinson thanks Sue for her affection:

> That my
> sweet Sister
> remind me
> to thank her
> for h*erself*
> is valuablest.
>   Emily '

(H B 97; L 328, 1868)

Dickinson's statements testify to the quality of Sue's presence—"To see you / unfits for staler / meetings" (H B 10; L 346, 1870)—and to the magnitude of her absence—"To miss you, Sue, / is power" (H B 184; L 364, 1871). Dickinson compares her love for Sue to the love of God, just after she praises her beloved by equating the writing of her love with that penned by great poets:

> We remind her
> we love her –
> Unimportant fact,
> though Dante
> did'nt think so
> nor Swift, nor
> Mirabeau.
> Could Pathos
> compete with
> that simple
> statement
> "Not that we
> loved him but
> that he loved
> us"?
>   Emily '

(H B 95; L 393, SUMMER 1873)

Declaring that she is "greedy to see" (L 407, 1874) this "Only Woman in the World" (L 447, 1875), Dickinson's letters to Sue of this period unequivocally continue to portray a speaker deeply in love.

In conjunction with these statements, all the physical manifestations of the poems to and transcribed by Sue argue for the possibility that she participated in Dickinson's literary project much more than has previously been suspected. To what extent remains in large part unrecoverable. Perhaps the greatest excisions of all have been those which have removed the stories of their mutual creative endeavors.

To Own a Susan of My Own

In the last ten years of their correspondence, Dickinson makes some of her most extravagant statements to Susan:

> Susan knows
> she is a Siren –
> and that at a
> word from her,
> Emily would
> forfeit Righteousness –

(H B 11; L 554, 1878)

These late "letters" not only are arranged on the page like poems, but the calligraphy is often striking, with the words and letters spaced far apart. These eye-catching physical embodiments underscore the astonishing content of many of this last decade's letter-poems. In the letter-poem urging her to cherish power before the kingdom and the glory, because it is "wilder" than either of them, Dickinson places Susan on a par with heavenly blessing:

> Susan –
> Whoever blesses –
> you always
> bless – the last –
> and often made
> the Heaven of
> Heavens – a sterile
> stimulus –

(H B 37; L 583)

About three years before her death, Dickinson extolled Susan to the highest, setting her above any muse:

> To be Susan
> is Imagination,

To have been
Susan, a Dream –
What depths
of Domingo
in that torrid
Spirit!
       Emily '

(H B 51; L 855, ABOUT 1883)

Like Manzanilla, Domingo is, in the Dickinson lexicon, fervent with activity, an exotic place of poetic inspiration (P 214). A place of dimension, it is not superficial, a façade, but offers depths to plumb. As John the Apostle finds divine revelation on Patmos, so Dickinson the poet discovers "Gibraltar" or an island strong with language in her relationship with "Siren" Susan:

It was like
a breath from
Gibraltar to hear
your voice again,
Sue – Your impregnable
syllables need
no prop, to stand –

(H B 89, L 722, LATE SUMMER 1881)

Though Higginson would have no way of comprehending her statement's full meaning, Dickinson told him of Susan's profound influence almost immediately. About two months after her correspondence with the *Atlantic Monthly* editor began, Dickinson wrote him: "Your letter gave no Drunkenness, because I tasted Rum before—Domingo comes but once—" (L 265, June 7, 1862). From the facts of her having just labored over various second stanzas trying to please Sue and of Dickinson's declarations throughout their relationship, especially the late one explicitly equating Susan with imagination itself, one can see that it is with the spirit and fact of Susan's creative thought that the poet finds herself intoxicated. By providing her with an encouraging audience who was not labeling her poetic performances "Dark" or "uncontrolled," Sue offered Dickinson a relationship that functioned as an Edenic isle in the sea of experience.

    To Sue, Emily sends not only poems interrogating immortality or women's circumstance in conventional marriage, but also nature poems,

poems about language and poetry-making, love poems, and cartoonlike layouts and drawings like the early depiction of "Music of the Spheres." With pink woods (H 255; P 6) and yellow lanes (H ST 25b; P 1650), a purple-flowered crocus, pungent and aromatic saffron exciting the nose and the palate as well as the eye (H ST 20c; P 1676), comic personifications with the sunset leaping like leopards or juggling her bonnet (P 228), Dickinson's poems to Sue sometimes seem like vignettes from the Sunday comics to today's reader. In sunsets, evenings, stars, moonrises, and the hills on the horizon she sees "cartoons," or exaggerated semblances, of the genteel life. "Hills erect their Purple Heads" and "Rivers lean" (H ST 18e; P 1688); "like Men and Women" out for a sidewalk or boardwalk stroll, with "a mighty Bow / Or trailing Courtesy," "Shadows walk / Upon the Hills . . ." as if they are players in a picture show (H 285; P 1105). A speaker proclaims the power of a magnificent dawn by "Musket" and precious, sparkling jewels, then settles in "The Parlor – of the Day –" (H 326; P 304). The sun's spectacle is "The guest . . . gold and crimson" (H 387; P 15); in autumn "The Maple wears a gayer scarf – / The field a scarlet gown –" (H 344; P 12). Comparing snowfall to sifting (H 278; P 311), the winds of an approaching storm to kneading (H 356; P 824), and Mother Nature's spring and summer ripening to baking (H B 147; P 1143), Dickinson makes their mutual experience in households an active principle of her verse. Apparently relishing the almost grotesque, often absurd images they form, the details of woman's experience govern her terms in these poems, dictating her choice of primary and delighting metaphors: a "Housewife in the Evening West," the setting sun, "sweeps with / many-colored Brooms –" (H 312; P 219); and "The Snow and Wind" sweep winter streets "Like Brooms of Steel" (H 283; P 1252). "Autumn begins to be inferred / By millinery . . . / Or . . . shawl . . ." (H ST 3; P 1682). If nature were a "mortal lady / Who had so little time," she would be at the mercy of others' "exigencies," would have to make herself constantly available to others, always allowing her business to be interruptible. Unlike Susan, who was, as wife and mother, called upon to entertain the desires and needs of others before her own, nature is one woman who determines the spending of her own time, even "To make some trifle fairer / That was too fair before—" (P 1762).

That ruminations on language are integral to their relationship is apparent from the many poems to Sue that take wordplay as their subject. "'Morning' – means 'Milking' / To the Farmer" relates morning's different connotations—of "Dawn," "Dice" (sewing in waved patterns), opportunity, breakfast, battle, and flood—to the farmer, maid, lover, epicure, hero, and miller (H 288; P 300). The astronomer sees "Arcturus," not a "Star," "*Zenith*," not "Heaven"; the botanist "stamens," not flowers; the zoologist species, instead of a butterfly at play among "Clover bells" (H 236; P 70).

Not surprisingly, then, in October 1883 when the two women face the devastating death of Susan and Austin's youngest son—formally named Gilbert in honor of his mother's maiden name, affectionately nicknamed "Gib" by his adoring family—Dickinson's letter-poems to Susan simultaneously acknowledge both the necessity to address the unfathomable senselessness of a dear joyous life so quickly cut short and language's lack when attempting to articulate the measure of the loss. Knowing that words alone will not suffice, Dickinson muses that perhaps one of nature's tokens will offer Susan at least momentary respite from pain:

> Perhaps the
> dear, grieved
> Heart would
> open to a
> flower, which
> blesses unre-
> quested, and
> serves without
> a Sound.
>
> (H L 50; L 869)

The constant memories that serve to remind Dickinson of the unrelenting absence of her little coconspirator who "rejoiced in Secrets – " (H B 79; L 868) are like heavy cargo which must be carried with no relief of a clear destination in sight. In other words, the havoc and despair wrought by Gib's succumbing to typhoid fever are the woes of sorrow unbound:

> Moving on in
> the Dark like
> Loaded Boats
> at Night, though
> there is no
> Course, there is
> Boundlessness –
>
> (H B 91; L 871)

Johnson's description of one of Dickinson's five writings to Susan in memory of little Gilbert (L 868, L 869, L 870, L 871, L 938) is an appropriate characterization of them all: "the form it takes is that of a letter, but in a truer sense it is a poem, an elegy of surpassing eloquence."[43] A year after Gib's decease, neither the miseries of missing the little boy nor a poignant sense of language's failure in the face of such family tragedies had ceased. On the verso of a draft of a letter-poem sent to Susan in October 1884 on the first anniversary of their most terrifying loss (L 938; H B 145), Dickinson inscribed the prose fragment: "'Tis a dangerous moment for any one when the meaning goes out of things and Life stands straight – and punctual – and yet no content(s) (signal) come(s)" (PF 49). However strong the will to comfort through language, meaning that will content the sufferers eludes the poet.

Though language fails to relieve Emily and Susan's agonies, Dickinson unequivocally declares that it nevertheless serves as their most reliable source for ecstasy. As her life drew to a close Dickinson continued to reiterate that Susan's command of language enticed her like no one else's:

No Words
ripple like
Sister's –
Their Silver
genealogy is
very sweet
to trace –
   Amalgams
are abundant,
but the lone
student of
the Mines
adores Alloyless
things –

(H B 134; L 913, ABOUT 1884)

Though Johnson recognizes that at least one of these late letter-poems is "in a truer sense . . . a poem," he classifies that document and all its eloquent, sometimes elegiac, always poetic, peers to Susan as letters. In one of the most recent studies of the Emily-Sue relationship, Ellen Louise Hart discusses the genre-confounding editorial practices of Johnson and Bianchi as she analyzes the letter-poem beginning "Morning / might come / by Accident – / Sister –" (H B 90; L 912, 1884) by asserting that it has been "mistakenly presented by Dickinson's editors solely as a letter and not also as a poem." I will add that all of these late letter-poems have been erroneously reproduced simply as letters and that these textual mis-representations occlude not only Susan's literary importance to Dickinson as primary audience but also limit our ability to analyze the poet's literary project. Furthering an argument similar to one made by Bennett—that Dickinson "had seen in death the one sure path to the fulfillment of her love"—Hart maintains that Emily hopes to join Sue "in the 'Costumeless Consciousness' (H 358; P 1454) of immortality, the mind without the body, limitless, free of artifice and the restrictions of gender." [44] Yet whether Dickinson believed in an afterlife or immortality will ever be open to question.

As Johnson and other editors have reformulated Dickinson's writings to conform to foreordained genres, so readers can select poems and letters and construct compelling arguments to confirm their own desires and thus demonstrate that she did or did not believe in an afterlife or God. For every letter or poem evincing belief, there is one like the early letter to Sue stating, "Sermons on unbelief ever did attract me" (H L 9; L 176, 1854) or the late one to Mrs. Henry Hills declaring, "When Jesus tells us about his Father, we distrust him. When he shows us his Home, we turn away" (L 932, 1884). About such matters, it appears that Dickinson equivocated until the very end. About one matter readers can rest assured that she never equivocated. Through all the anger, disappointments, exultations, emotional distance, and intense spiritual, intellectual, and erotic unions that inevitably accompany a deep and lasting love relationship, Dickinson equated Sue with Eden, the land of imagination:

> Sue – to be
> lovely as you
> is a touching
> Contest, though
> like the Siege
> of Eden, impracticable,
> Eden never
> capitulates –
>   Emily '

(H B 50; L 584, ABOUT 1878)

I have had a "Joan of Arc" feeling about Emilies poems from the first & their reception convinces me I was right.

—LAVINIA DICKINSON, *AB* 87

Every man has his disciples, and it is always Judas who writes his biography.

—OSCAR WILDE

Susan – The sweetest
acts both exact
and defy, gratitude,
so silence is all
the honor there is –

—EMILY DICKINSON, HB 55; L 586

Six Fame Is a Fickle Food: "Sister Sue" as Producer of Poems

As Dorothy Oberhaus points out, had it not been for Mabel Loomis Todd, Susan's obituary might have prefaced the first edition of *Poems by Emily Dickinson* (1890). Thomas Higginson wanted to use it and recommended as much to Loomis Todd, but she "seems never to have responded. At least Mrs. Bingham includes no such response, reporting only that her mother said that such a suggestion had infuriated Lavinia."[1] Though Lavinia and Susan were at odds over Dickinson's poems at the time, whether or not this accurately characterizes Lavinia's response can never be known. In fact, whether or not Higginson's suggestion was ever proposed to Vinnie will ever remain open to question, for, as we have seen, Loomis Todd's perspective on such a matter would be far from disinterested. Significantly, the last half of Lavinia's July 14, 1890, letter to Higginson expressing her wish that Loomis Todd's role in producing the first volume of poems be strictly sub-rosa is "missing" (*AB* 60–62). What she wrote to conclude the letter and whether those epistolary statements would modify Loomis Todd's account have been forever lost to us. Beginning with a December 1890 letter from Lavinia to Higginson, Susan has been roundly criticized and her character questioned for her failure to edit and produce a volume of Dickinson's poems in a timely fashion, and Loomis Todd much praised for having done so (*AB* 87–88; see below). But Lavinia did not feel forever indebted to Mabel nor was her judgment of Susan forever harsh. Later she would equivocate about her feelings toward both women and testify in court that Loomis Todd had asked to edit the poems because she thought it would be good for her literary reputation to do so, and that "it made her reputation" (*AB* 358).

Interestingly enough, Loomis Todd appears to have appreciated Susan's printed account of Dickinson's life and writing, for if one compares the former's "Introduction" for the Second Series of *Poems of Emily Dickinson* (1891) to the obituary, there are striking similarities. Like Susan,

Loomis Todd says Dickinson was "not an invalid," nor was she "disappoint[ed]"; like Susan, she says Dickinson's withdrawal was a result of her "nature"; like Susan, who says that "she seemed herself a part of the March sky" and that immortality made "her life . . . aglow," Loomis Todd goes on to mention the poet's intimacy with the "March sky" and to say that "immortality" was "close about her." If as "wife forgotten" and mistress they acrimoniously disagreed about personal matters, they concurred about the talent of Emily Dickinson.

About seeking editors for her sister's poems, Lavinia wrote Higginson:

> Mrs Dickinson was enthusiastic for a while, then indifferent & later, utterly discouraging. I naturally looked to her *first* (with you) for help, supposing 'twould be her highest pleasure, but I found my mistake. She wished the box of poems *there* constantly & was unwilling for me to borrow them for a day, as she was fond of reading them (the verses) to passing friends. Mrs Dickinson has fine ability but lacks mental energy to complete. She has many ideal plans for work worthy of her talent, but the world will (probably) not see any finished. But for Mrs Todd & your self, "the poems" would die in the box where they were found.
>
> (AB 87)

That Lavinia assumed both Susan's talents and appreciative familiarity with Dickinson's literary achievements is important. Lavinia's characterization of Susan's work habits may or may not be accurate or fair, but is crucial for understanding her impatience to see her sister's poems printed and widely disseminated. While it is sad and perhaps even infuriating that Susan, who knew Dickinson and her writing better than anyone else, could not, because of the emotional complications resulting from the Austin-Mabel affair, work with Higginson and Loomis Todd on the poems, Dickinson's readers are fortunate enough to have some key items written by Susan about the poet's work. As examining Dickinson's literary presentations of herself to her primary correspondent informs readers about her composing processes, creative evolutions, and her imaginative life, so Susan's obituary and subsequent epistolary commentaries to editors offer valuable information about the poet's project as well as their relationship.

Not surprisingly, Susan was the first to declare that Dickinson stayed at home "in the light of her own fire" and on her "own premises."[2] In her obituary for Dickinson (*Springfield Republican*, May 18, 1886), Susan, as Lavinia would do eight years later, declares that Emily was "not disappointed with the world," that "her talk and her writings were like no one's else," and spends no less than half the memorial depicting Dickinson the writer. Thus the two women most intimately involved with Emily Dickinson are unapologetic and unequivocal in their esteem of her literary performances.

Susan made the arrangements to swaddle her beloved friend's body for burial, "arranged violets and a pink cypripedium at Emily's throat and covered her white casket with violets and ground pine," "lined the grave with boughs" (*FF* 61), wrote several commemorative paragraphs within hours of the poet's last breath, and was posterity's first reader of the manuscript books. Printed in the *Republican*, Susan's obituary describes a woman she had known since adolescence (H Box 9). Publicly voicing her regard for Dickinson, Susan's memoir portrays a strong but loving, brilliant woman:

> The death of Miss Emily Dickinson, daughter of the late
> Edward Dickinson, at Amherst on Saturday, makes another sad
> inroad on the small circle so long occupying the old family mansion.
> It was for a long generation overlooked by death, and one passing
> in and out there thought of old-fashioned times, when parents and
> children grew up and passed maturity together, in lives of singular
> uneventfulness unmarked by sad or joyous crises. Very few in the
> village, except among older inhabitants, knew Miss Emily personally,
> although the facts of her seclusion and her intellectual brilliancy
> were familiar Amherst traditions.

The woman Susan sees was not completely absorbed in her family and household:

> . . . There are many houses among all classes, into which her
> treasures of fruit and flowers and ambrosial dishes for the sick and
> well were constantly sent, that will forever miss those evidences of
> her unselfish consideration, and mourn afresh that she screened
> herself from close acquaintance.

According to this perspective, this "screening" was not pathological or a result of a broken heart or of a disappointing life. Susan's depiction is of a woman given to a life of thinking:

> . . . As she passed on in life, her sensitive nature shrank from
> much personal contact with the world, and more and more turned
> to her own large wealth of individual resources for companionship,
> sitting henceforth, as some one said of her, "in the light of her own

fire." Not disappointed with the world, not an invalid until within the past two years, not from any lack of sympathy, not because she was insufficient for any mental work or social career—her endowments being so exceptional—but the "mesh of her soul," as Browning calls the body, was too rare, and the sacred quiet of her own home proved the fit atmosphere for her worth and work. All that must be inviolate.

As one might expect in an essay directed toward a nineteenth-century, "New Englandly" (F 11; P 285) readership, Susan reassures the audience that even while devoted to intellectual pursuits, Dickinson attended to good housekeeping:

> . . . One can only speak of "duties beautifully done"; of her gentle tillage of the rare flowers filling her conservatory, into which, as into the heavenly Paradise, entered nothing that could defile, and which was ever abloom in frost or sunshine, so well she knew her subtle chemistries; of her tenderness to all in the home circle; her gentlewoman's grace and courtesy to all who served in house and grounds; her quick and rich response to all who rejoiced or suffered at home, or among her wide circle of friends the world over. This side of her nature was to her the real entity in which she rested, so simple and strong was her instinct that a woman's hearthstone is her shrine.

Of primary importance, however, is the fact that the memorial repeatedly emphasizes that Dickinson was a writer with serious objectives. Just as Susan is careful to make the point that, in her own way, the poet performed the conventional womanly services which make a house a home, she also conscientiously asserts that Dickinson was not one of those writing "for Time," whose primary goal was "Fame" (F 28; P 406):

> Her talk and her writings were like no one's else, and although she never published a line, now and then some enthusiastic literary friend would turn love to larceny, and cause a few verses surreptitiously obtained to be printed. Thus, and through other natural ways, many saw and admired her verses, and in consequence frequently notable persons paid her visits, hoping to overcome the protest of her own nature and gain a promise of occasional contributions, at least, to various magazines. She withstood even the fascination of Mrs. Helen Jackson, who earnestly sought her cooperation in a novel of the No Name series, although one little

poem somehow strayed into the volume of verse which appeared in
that series. Her pages would ill have fitted even so attractive a story
as "Mercy Philbrick's Choice," unwilling though a large part of the
literary public were to believe that she had no part in it. "Her wagon
was hitched to a star"—and who could ride or write with such a
voyager?

Depicting a writer who distinguishes herself from all others, Susan appreciates Dickinson's cerebral powers. As her later comment to William
Hayes Ward, editor of the *Independent*, shows, Susan did not consider
Dickinson's "lack of rhyme and rhythm" merely eccentric, but a product
of "bold thought" (*AB* 115). The story of Mercy Philbrick, who becomes a
famous poet only after rejecting two suitors and thrives on her secret passion for one of them after he has died, is too usual a narrative, Susan
claims, to be Dickinson's. While tales speculating about "secret sorrow"
and "hidden rapture" might be convenient to explain her dear friend's passion for the word, they would never be sufficient. As we have seen, Susan's
"love to larceny" recalls Dickinson's declaration that "A narrow Fellow in
the Grass" had been "robbed" of her, and the metaphor Sue chooses to
describe the poet's unique way with words echoes both "There is a word /
Which bears a sword," a poem bound and folded as the lead poem in a
fascicle about 1858 (F 2; P 8), and "She dealt her pretty / words like
Blades," bound into a fascicle about four years later (F 22; P 479):

> . . . A Damascus blade gleaming and glancing in the sun was
> her wit. Her swift poetic rapture was like the long glistening note of
> a bird one hears in the June woods at high noon, but can never see.
> Like a magician she caught the shadowy apparitions of her brain
> and tossed them in startling picturesqueness to her friends, who,
> charmed with their simplicity and homeliness as well as profundity,
> fretted that she had so easily made palpable the tantalizing fancies
> forever eluding their bungling, fettered grasp. So intimate and
> passionate was her love of Nature, she seemed herself a part of the
> high March sky, the summer day and bird-call. Keen and eclectic in
> her literary tastes, she sifted libraries to Shakespeare and Browning;
> quick as the electric spark in her intuitions and analyses, she seized
> the kernel instantly, almost impatient of the fewest words by which
> she must make her revelation. To her life was rich, and all aglow
> with God and immortality. With no creed, no formalized faith,
> hardly knowing the names of dogmas, she walked this life with the
> gentleness and reverence of old saints, with the firm step of martyrs

who sing while they suffer. How better note the flight of this "soul of fire in a shell of pearl" than by her own words?

> Morns like these, we parted;
> Noons like these, she rose;
> Fluttering first, then firmer,
> To her fair repose.

Within days of the poet's death, through allusion Susan wields Dickinson's own words to describe her pithy power. By doing so, she publicly records her familiarity with the Dickinson canon. In "She dealt her pretty / words like Blades," a powerful female speaker is described using language that cuts to the core—every word "unbared / A Nerve / Or Wantoned with a Bone – ." "Shadowy apparitions of her brain" tossed in "startling picturesqueness" and "tantalizing fancies" "easily made palpable" echo the deifying "Magic" elements of "I think I was enchanted" (F 29; P 593), the phrases "Of Pictures, the Discloser—" and "Distills amazing sense" of "This was a Poet" (F 21; P 448), and the lines "Nor tossed my shape in / Eider Balls" of "I cannot dance upon my Toes—" (F 19; P 326). Susan beseeches readers to consider the marvelous appropriateness of Dickinson's word choices, just as the poems themselves—deceptively simple, dense, with a syntax that disrupts a reader's expectations—call one to contemplation. As Dickinson, through her poems and their perspective of gist, invites reflection, Susan concludes this allusive memorial asking the reader to ponder and calling attention to the woman as writer—"How better note the flight of this 'soul of fire in a shell of pearl' than by her own words?" Though her daughter would later claim that Dickinson "met her fate in Philadelphia" and was in fact bearing a secret sorrow (*FF* 51–53n), Susan's portrait is of a self-reliant woman who was as exceptional in her intellect and powerful poetic expression as she was in her neighborly ministrations, and whose "worth and work" was writing. The "sins" of "Madame Bianchi," an easy target who has been much maligned for her pretentiousness, stories about her aunt, and conventional poetry and fiction, should not visited upon her mother.[3]

Her constantly reiterated accentuation of Dickinson's writing and thinking demonstrate that Susan was not interested in producing a woman poet easily commodified as another Lucy Larcom or Maria Brooks, reclusive and always wearing white. As revealed by a century of recurrent speculations about the reasons for Dickinson's self-imposed withdrawal and the use of her poems as biographical data to prove yet another theory, Susan's worries that her beloved friend would be characterized as a Mercy

Philbrick were more than justified. Within weeks of the initial release of *Poems by Emily Dickinson*, Emily Fowler Ford printed "Eheu! Emily Dickinson," a poem conventionalizing her as a poetess, in the *Republican* (January 11, 1891; *YH* 2:372–373). Little more than a decade later, Higginson did something of the same when, for *A Reader's History of American Literature*, he situated Dickinson among other literary figures he deemed "secondary" like Lydia Maria Child and Catharine Sedgwick, characterized her as "morbidly sensitive" and "pitifully childlike," and proclaimed that she "never quite succeeded in grasping the notion of the importance of poetic form."[4]

The dilemma that Susan recognized immediately—how to arrange the poems and portray Emily Dickinson the poet without depicting a cliché fictional character[5]—may have been one of the reasons that she took what seemed (to Lavinia) an interminably long time editing the poems. To Ward she declared, "I was to have compiled the Poems—but as I moved slowly, dreading publicity for us all, she [Lavinia] was angry and a year ago took them from me" (H Lowell Autograph, February 8, 1891; *AB* 114–115). Yet other significant factors surely contributed to Susan's hesitations: unlike Loomis Todd, who had lost a fascinating literary acquaintance of three or four years, Susan was devastated at the loss of her most faithful and intimate correspondent of four decades, and reading through the manuscripts may well have been emotionally trying and inhibiting for her; it is highly likely, then, that Susan was angry at Emily's death, and editing the latter's poems would only exacerbate frustrations and feelings of abandonment; having referred to poems years earlier in a letter to Dickinson as "*our* Fleet" (H B 94; discussed in chapter 5), Susan may well have felt possessive of her friend's work and thus been reluctant to share the fruits of their special bond with the world; or, occasionally a poet herself and having a daughter who was a poet, Susan may have been jealous of Emily's talent; or, since we know that she read Dickinson's poems aloud to guests in the Evergreens, Susan may have taken great pride in being a hidden authority and ambivalently balked at the celebrity conventional publication might bring.

Whatever her true motives, Susan's responses to editing Dickinson's poetry for mass reproduction and distribution were complicated, contradictory, and probably confused, hence she was too slow to act as far as Lavinia was concerned. Subsequent readers have been befuddled by Susan's relative silence about Emily's poetic project in the two decades following the poet's death. However, as the object of vicious Loomis Todd gossip that accused her of drunkenness and unnatural feelings toward childbearing and having been judged by Lavinia to be incapable of sustaining work to complete a project, Susan may well have not known how to respond to such character assassinations and settled on silence as her best option. Certainly, as far as Susan was concerned, one shock had followed another in the decade preceding the discovery and printing of poems from her beloved Emily's manuscript books: in 1878, her dear family friend Samuel Bowles died, followed by the elder Emily Dickinson in 1882; in October 1883 at the age of fifty-two, Susan lost her youngest son Gib and within weeks her husband of twenty-seven years had enthusiastically embarked on an affair with a women twenty-six years younger than his wife; just two and one-half years later in May 1886, Susan found herself preparing the body of her closest friend for burial. Though it seems that Susan would be the least likely of Dickinson's contemporaries to be shocked at the existence of scores of manuscript books, she may have been transfixed or distressed or otherwise awed and immobilized by their contents. Important to keep in mind is the fact that, about most matters, Dickinson historiography has consistently failed to account for Susan's point of view and feelings with sufficient complexity. For example, Johnson and Ward's biographical blurb for Gib informs readers that "His sudden and unexpected death from typhoid fever, 5 October 1883, was a blow from which neither his father nor his Aunt Emily fully recovered" (L, p. 938). Susan's grief is completely omitted, as if a mother would not be profoundly and inconsolably saddened by the unexpected death of her youngest son. Similarly, study of her letters and obituary about Dickinson and her work has been left out of literary criticism and biography or distorted by the prejudicial interpretations of Loomis Todd, Bingham, and their critical lineage.

In any case, though Susan's failure to edit a volume of Dickinson's poems is somewhat perplexing, readers can imagine that no single reason given will explain her very complicated response and situation. Even by Millicent Todd Bingham's account, it was not simply that Susan refused to submit the poems for consideration. A letter housed in the New York Public Library shows that as early as December 31, 1886, scarcely seven months after Dickinson's death, Susan submitted "a poem of Miss Emily Dickinson's on the 'Wind' thinking you might like to print it" to an editor of the *Century* (*AB* 88). Her subsequent letters to Higginson and Ward indicate that, without a "market judgment," she was not interested in selling books of Emily Dickinson's poetry but in presenting "dear Emily's" profound poetic thoughts to the world.

Susan's "dreading publicity for us all" resonates with the fear that, once her friend's work was commodified, the "personal details" of the life of Emily Dickinson, woman poet, would be pored over time and again to explain the astonishing artistic productions. In *Swann*, contemporary novelist Carol Shields compellingly reflects on this as well as other facts of some literary criticism. In that fictional narrative, professor and biographer Morton Jimroy is positively convinced that finding deceased poet Mary Swann's notebook, "marginalia" to the literary work that would "offer a glimpse of the private person" behind the poems and would "kind of comment on" them, "would bring our graceful Swann out of the jungle of conjecture."[6] Conscious of how clamor for biographical information can impel literary study to devolve into titillating tattle about the author, Susan, while not ignoring biographical elements, focuses her letters to Higginson on Dickinson's literary productions. Significantly, her first letter to him reveals that she had been thinking about how to compile a volume that did not take for its organizational principle the all too familiar scheme for divisions—"Life," "Love," "Nature," "Time and Eternity." In this December 1890 letter Susan presumes to thank Higginson for his help editing and publishing Dickinson's poetry, "for her as well as for myself":

> My Dear Col. Higginson
>   Thanks for your kind letter duly received. I have not answered it before, because I was so dazed, by the announcement of Emily's poems in the Xtian Union that I do not rally easily. It was my first intimation that stranger hands were preparing them for publication. I planned to give my winter, with my daughter's aid, to the arrangement of a vol. to be printed at my own expense sometime during the year, subject to your approval of course, with an introduction also by yourself, to make the setting perfect. The volume would have been rather more full, and varied, than yours as I should have used many bits of her prose—passages from early letters quite surpassing the correspondence of Gunderodi[e] with Bettine—quaint bits to my children &c &c. Of course I should have forestalled criticism by only printing them. I have been held back from arranging them to be published the past years by your verdict of "un-presentable." My own taste must be my own, but a market judgment I have none of, and shrank from going contrary to your practical opinion in the matter. I think this much is due myself—my life long intimacy with Emily, my equally long deep appreciation of her genius. I am told Miss Lavinia is saying that I *refused* to arrange them. Emily knows that is not true. You are generous enough to be patient with my exegesis even if tedious to you.

Though she was not one of Dickinson's "official" editors, Susan makes no attempt to conceal the fact that she is thoroughly acquainted with the poet's corpus. Without reservation, she proclaims that Dickinson's early letters to her rival those of the German poet Karoline von Gunderode with writer Bettina von Arnim. Since Margaret Fuller translated von Arnim's *Gunderode* into English, and since an account of von Armin's relationship with Gunderode had been written at his request and incorporated into *Goethe's Correspondence with a Child*, Susan draws Higginson's attention not only to the intensity of her relationship with Dickinson but also underscores the importance of its literary component.[7] Susan writes as if Emily is still alive—Emily "knows"—then expresses her hope that Higginson will protect Dickinson's privacy:

> . . . "The Poems" will ever be to me marvellous whether in
> manuscript or type. Most of your titles are perfect—a few I don't
> happen to fancy. I want to thank you, for her as well as myself for
> the perfect way in which you have led her before the curtain—but
> for that, her verses would have waited a long time for the recogni-
> tion your name and fame have won for them. I trust there will be no
> more personal detail in the newspaper articles. She hated her pecu-
> liarities and shrank from any notice of them as a nerve from the
> knife. I sometimes shudder when I think of the world reading her
> thoughts minted in deep heartbroken convictions. In her own words
> (after all the intoxicating fascination of creation) she as deeply real-
> ized that for her, as for all of us women not fame but "Love and
> home and certainty are best."

Interestingly, in her concluding quotation Susan misrepresents, perhaps intentionally, the last stanza of Dickinson's "The Robin is the One" (Set 6c; P 828). In Dickinson's poem, the robin does not celebrate domesticity, but is forced to accept it as an unavoidable fact of her existence:

> The Robin is the One
> That Speechless from
> her Nest
> Submit that Home
> And Certainty
> And Sanctity, are best

When Susan Huntington Dickinson speaks for Emily Dickinson, it is to assure the liberal but conventional Thomas Higginson that Dickinson's "peculiarities" did not interfere with her femininity. Yet she does not close the letter here, but with a declaration of her love for Emily followed by a criticism of the selection of poems for the inaugural print edition:

> . . . I find myself always saying "poor Emily." And so I go up in the snow to-morrow to put a wreath of her own mountain laurel on her grave. I will only add that I missed many favorites among the collection which knowing your taste I wonder over. I fear you have no time to read so long a letter, but my own self respect and regard for yourself seemed to demand just this.
>
> Yours as ever cordially
S. H. Dickinson

(AB 86–87)

When she writes Higginson a couple of weeks later on January 4, 1891, Susan boldly corrects the editing of "I know some lonely Houses off the Road" (F 13; P 289) and relates an amusing anecdote about the poet's ingenuities:

> Dear Col. Higginson
>
> I forgot in my letter to you to speak of a blunder (of the printer I suppose) in Emily's robber poem. In the verse, "An alma-nac's aware" &c. the vol. has it "the spectacles *afar*." Emily wrote and meant it, "ajar." I wish it might be changed for her sake. Sitting up late at night long after her family had retired, I can easily see, as she came on the unclasped spectacles of her Father, how that, and the other expressions came. I meant to have told you too of a funny bit. One of our Prof's returning the Library copy of the Poems said to my son, Col. H. is a famous literary man but does not know much about typography. "I have made a correction in the poem about the approaching shower" ["A drop fell on the apple-tree" (*Poems*, 1890, 81)]. The book has it, "*hoisted* roads." Of course it should be *moisted*, "there is no sense in the other." Need I add that I sent for the vol. erased his "*m*," and said Prof. E. is a fine geologist but no poet. I did not mean this to be so long. Do not trouble to reply.
>
> Very sincerely yours
S. H. Dickinson

(AB 92)

Claiming to strike a deferential pose, ostensibly wishing most not to be too much of a bother, and telling anecdotes to defuse the fact that she is really quite brisk are strategies very similar, of course, to Dickinson's own approaches to Higginson. In a later letter to Ward, Susan maintains this pose, claiming that her daughter resists publication because "she is im-movable, having a most feminine horror of print" (H Lowell Autograph, March 23, 1891; *AB* 117–118). Addressing editors, Susan assumes the same tactics as had Dickinson; and like Dickinson, though she clothes her judgment in deferential dress, she finally declares it without apology. To Higginson she authoritatively cites an anecdote that exemplifies her ap-preciation of Dickinson's practically oxymoronic use of an adjectival verb which, like the *Pequod*'s deck, recalls for readers both questing voyage and the stage: sails and curtains, not roads, are "hoisted." Connotations of movement and theatricality mimic the activity and appearance of the storm. In apparent response to it, and in the peculiar light of a turbulent, threatening sky, the road appears to rise.

After publication of the first edition by Higginson and Loomis Todd, Susan writes Ward with authority: "I have a little article in mind, with illustrations of her [Emily's] own, showing her witty humorous side, which has all been left out of her [Lavinia's (as Susan called that first edi-tion)] vol." (*AB* 118). Susan has been the only critic to make such a point of the cartoonlike little sketches and layouts that are sometimes found in Dickinson's correspondence, one of which is reproduced above in chap-ter 3.[8] Had Susan influenced the earliest printings of her poems, Dickin-son's lighter side would probably, from the beginning of critical study, have received much more attention. According to Macgregor Jenkins, who as a young man was acquainted with Dickinson, her sly humorous side was well-known: "Miss Emily was apt with a pencil and in a tiny sketch of Amherst, sent my mother, everything was covered with snow except the parsonage. With it came a line saying: 'I omitted the snow on the roof, distrusting the premonition, Emily'" (*YH* 2:284). Undoubtedly, had Susan helped produce the earliest volumes of Emily Dickinson's works, our pat-terns of reading would have been decidedly altered. Though Bianchi edited quite a few editions of her aunt's poetry, we cannot determine from those how her mother would have executed a similar enterprise. Of course to speculate what Susan would have done quickly becomes a pointless ex-ercise, but there is still plenty of critical work to study what she did do—handling Dickinson's manuscripts, serving as primary audience for nine-teenth-century America's most outstanding poet.

Only after a century are readers beginning to understand the multi-tude of implications—for study of her works as well as for literature in general—when, like Blake, Dickinson privatized "the roles of author, edi-tor, illustrator, publisher, printer, and distributor," making of herself and her highly responsive audience, Sue, a literary institution unto themselves.⁹ What Sue intended when she marked poems in the fascicles with the notations "D, F, L, N, P, S, W" and "x, xx, xxx," "x2," and "xx3" (F 12, F 14, F 15, F 16, F 18, F 25, F 27, F 29) is probably unrecoverable. Perhaps they are, as Ralph Franklin suggests, thematic or topical—the *W* on "The Wind – tapped like / a tired Man – " for "Wind" (F 29; P 436), the *D* on "'Twas warm – at first – like / Us – " and "What care the Dead, for / Chanticleer – " for "Death" (F 29; P 519, P 592), and the *N* on "From Cocoon forth a Butterfly" for "Nature" (F 29; P 354). Is the *P* at the top of "The Day that I was crowned" (F 29; P 356), "Inconceivably solemn! / Things so gay," "A shady friend – for Torrid days," "It ceased to hurt me, though / so slow," and "Give little Anguish" for "Poetry" or "Poets" and do the letters always stand for the same thing (F 14; P 582, P 278, P 584, P 310)? Does the *P* on "Prayer is the little implement" not signify "Prayer" (F 29; P 437)? Or is poetry being equated with prayer or something altogether different being denoted? What might Susan have had in mind when she wrote *P* on "The Battle fought between the Soul" (F 29; P 594)? Is the *L* on "Ah ' Moon—and Star!" for "Love" (F 14; P 240)? If that is an *S* atop "The Months have Ends – the Years – a Knot – " (F 14; P 423), "Her Sweet Weight on my / Heart a Night," and "'Tis Opposites – Entice – " (F 29; P 518, P 355), what might it represent and are those poems being linked together by Susan? If *F* heads "I think I was enchanted," is it for "Foreign," "Forerunner," "Femme" (F 29; P 593)? Was Susan simply titling the poems when she wrote "Sun" on "To interrupt His Yellow / Plan" and "Love" atop "Forget! The lady with the / Amulet" (F 29; P 591, P 438)? Why was Susan's title or critical commentary beginning "Sto[?]" erased from "It always felt to me – a / wrong" (F 24; P 597)? As one can see perusing the *Manuscript Books*, more of Susan's marks appear throughout the fascicles and what Franklin calls "sets"; efforts to formulate analyses of them are in their rudimentary stages and should not be abandoned.

Somewhat ironically, the ever-changing material reproductions of Dickinson's poems, letters, and letter-poems demonstrate what Hans Robert Jauss avers: that "a literary work is not an object that stands by itself and that offers the same view to each reader in each period," nor "a monument that monologically reveals its timeless essence," but "is much more like an orchestration that strikes ever new resonances among its readers and that frees the text from the material of the words and brings it to a contemporary existence."¹⁰ Over the past decade, technological advances in textual reproduction like the photographic representations of the fascicles which show Susan's marks on the poems have worked hand in hand with critical advances like the development of feminist analyses to reveal more clearly Susan's immense importance as a participatory reader of Dickinson's works. What the costs to Dickinson's readers have been of the first and then many of the subsequent literary institutions diminishing this primary relationship of hers can never be measured. What is certain is that the gains of exploring this relationship and its importance to Dickinson's literary production are inestimable.

Notes

Introduction

1. Karl Keller, *The Only Kangaroo among the Beauty: Emily Dickinson and America*, p. 26. Though he is interpreting a poem, Keller uses it to interpret Dickinson's life, too; see his statement about her "willing submission" to men on p. 35. One of the more recent (and insightfully literary) studies of her friendships with Charles Wadsworth and Thomas Wentworth Higginson is Benjamin Lease's *Emily Dickinson's Readings of Men and Books: Sacred Soundings*.

2. Jonathan Arac, *Critical Genealogies: Historical Situations for Postmodern Literary Studies*, p. 206. As we embark on a new era of critical methods, that Dickinson comprehended and controlled more than she was compelled beyond control is a major consequence of the woman-centered shift in the course of criticism. Arac also observes that "to write by hand and to preserve manuscripts would be absolutely normal for a monastic poet of the Middle Ages; to circulate poetry in manuscript among a few chosen associates would be perfectly normal in a Renaissance court; but for Dickinson these modes were part of an unusual . . . strategy. . . . For the criticism of Dickinson, the overwhelming issue is that she was a woman," and for "our particular relation to Dickinson, the special force that binds our moment to hers, again the issues of women's lives are paramount."

3. Bonnie Zimmerman has pointed out that lesbian critics and critics of lesbian texts often pose similar questions: "How, for example, does the lesbian's sense of outlaw status affect her literary vision? Might lesbian writing, because of the lesbian's position on the boundaries, be characterized by a particular sense of freedom and flexibility or, rather, by images of violently imposed barriers, the closet? Or, in fact, is there a dialectic between freedom and imprisonment that is unique to lesbian writing?" See "What Has Never Been: An Overview of Lesbian Feminist Literary Criticism," *Feminist Studies* 7, no. 3 (1981): 470.

4. Patrocinio Schweikart, "Toward a Feminist Theory of Reading," in *Gender and Reading: Essays on Readers, Texts, and Contexts*, ed. Elizabeth A. Flynn and Patrocinio Schweikart, p. 39. Dickinson's self-consciousness about gender-determined differences in speaking and writing to members of each sex is most obvious in the doubling of productions like "Going to Him! Happy letter! / Tell

Him –" (A 689; P 494); "Going – to – Her! / Happy– Letter! Tell Her –" (A 197; P 494). Woman's relationship to patriarchal language has generated many debates, and the focus of this study does not pretend to answer the many complex questions attending those. However, as Andrea Nye observes, "That the categories of patriarchal language distort what she [the woman speaker] might like to say is no longer in question." See "Woman Clothed with the Sun: Julia Kristeva and the Escape from/to Language," *Signs* 12 (1987): 665.

5. Rebecca Patterson, *Emily Dickinson's Imagery*, ed. Margaret Freeman, p. 17.

6. Silvia Dobson, "Woof and Heave and Surge and Wave and Flow," *H.D.: Woman and Poet*, p. 37.

7. Domna C. Stanton, *The Female Autograph: Theory and Practice of Autobiography from the Tenth to the Twentieth Century*, p. vii.

8. See Marianne Moore, "Author's Note," *The Complete Poems of Marianne Moore*, p. vii.

9. Gayatri Chakravorty Spivak reproducing Jacques Derrida in "Translator's Preface," *Of Grammatology*, p. xii.

10. See Adrienne Rich, "The Spirit of Place," *A Wild Patience Has Taken Me This Far*, p. 42.

11. Walter Benjamin, "The Work of Art in the Age of Mechanical Reproduction," *Illuminations*, trans. Harry Zohn, ed. Hannah Arendt, p. 223.

12. Jerome McGann, *A Critique of Modern Textual Criticism*, p. 121.

13. Ibid., p. 102. The transmissions of Dickinson's letter-poem prove its own point: no holograph survives and the words have been arranged in various ways when printed (see P 1212n for publication history and chapter 2 for more thorough discussion of its implications).

1. To Fill a Gap: Erasures, Disguises, Definitions

1. Should the reader wonder why I edit out the last sentence of this "paragraph," she might contrast Johnson's representation of it in his edition of *Letters* to his representation in *Poems*. The discrepancy between those reproductions indicates the larger problem of decisively paragraphing Dickinson's prose. To a great degree, beginnings and endings of paragraphs are left up to the reader; in fact, as we shall see in the following chapter, paragraphing her prose may be a misleading strategy for reading.

2. The *Springfield Republican* was Samuel Bowles's newspaper; editors were J. G. Holland and Thomas Niles.

"The Snake" was printed in both the weekly and daily *Republican*. To the weekly version, which Dickinson sent to Higginson, they added a question mark after the third line; to the daily version, they added a comma. No mark of punctuation appears in either manuscript copy. See David Higgins, *Portrait of Emily Dickinson: The Poet and Her Prose*, pp. 162–163, or John L. Spicer, "The Poems of

Emily Dickinson," *Boston Public Library Quarterly* 8 (July 1956): 142. See *YH* 2:110 for a facsimile of the version featuring the question mark. Both the question mark and the comma determine interpretations for the reader that Dickinson did not wish to impose.

Since Johnson completed his edition in 1955, poems have been added to the list of those published during Dickinson's lifetime: "Nobody knows this little Rose –" (P 35) was published in 1858; "Blazing in Gold and quenching in Purple" (P 228), "Flowers – Well – if anybody" (P 137), "These are the days when Birds come back –" (P 130), "Some keep the Sabbath going to Church" (P 324), and "Success is counted sweetest" (P 67) were all published in New York in 1864. See Karen Dandurand, "Another Dickinson Poem Published in Her Lifetime," *American Literature* 54 (1982): 434–437; and "New Dickinson Civil War Publications," *American Literature* 56 (1984): 17–27.

3. The variant in *Manuscript Books* (Set 6) reads "His notice sudden is" in the last line, first stanza. As one can see from Johnson's notes, only the variant to Sue (H B 193) and the version Dickinson saw published read "His notice instant is" in that line. This and "the fact that Sue lacked a copy" of this poem tend "to confirm" that it was Dickinson's sister-in-law Sue who forwarded a copy to the *Republican* to be printed (see P 986n and chapter 5). For extended analysis of transmission of poems with variant versions and particular problems with lineation, see my discussion of "I reason – / Earth is short –" (F 20; P 301) in chapter 2.

4. As quoted by Barbara Herrnstein Smith, *Poetic Closure: A Study of How Poems End*, p. 9.

5. Joanne Dobson, *Dickinson and the Strategies of Reticence: The Woman Writer in Nineteenth-Century America*, p. xiv.

6. Hans Robert Jauss, *Question and Answer: Forms of Dialogic Understanding*, ed. and trans. Michael Hays, p. 205.

7. Clark Griffith, *The Long Shadow: Emily Dickinson's Tragic Poetry*, p. 208; Cynthia Griffin Wolff, "The Women in My Life," *Massachusetts Review* 24 (1983): 438–452; Adrienne Rich, "Vesuvius at Home: The Power of Emily Dickinson," *On Lies, Secrets, and Silence: Selected Prose 1966–1978*, pp. 157–183; John Hollander's remarks are from "Great American Writers: Emily Dickinson," *Pen Newsletter* 68 (May 1989): 3–14, esp. p. 8. Comments from Hollander and Rich in the paragraphs that follow are from these articles.

I could have chosen at least another hundred Emily Dickinsons represented by critical commentaries over the last century. These were selected because their range of emphasis—on her sexuality, her psyche, the role of religion in her life, her circumstance as a woman, and her poetic technique—represents the major categories of Dickinson studies.

8. Though this discussion does not pretend to answer the many complex questions raised, thus to "fix" the roles of the reader, the author, and the text, I draw on a large body of reader-response and poststructuralist criticism. The dialogues among those who locate the text in the reader and those who posit a deter-

minate text which induces particular responses, as well as deconstructive assertions that readers play out roles dramatized in the text, serve as clarifying backdrop for my discussion of the dynamic exchange between Dickinson's readers and her texts. See especially Roland Barthes, *The Pleasure of the Text*; David Bleich, *Subjective Criticism*; Jonathan Culler, *On Deconstruction*; Jacques Derrida, "The Purveyor of Truth," *Yale French Studies* 52 (1975): 31–113; Umberto Eco, *The Role of the Reader: Explorations in the Semiotics of Texts*; Judith Fetterley, *The Resisting Reader: A Feminist Approach to American Fiction*; Stanley Fish, *Is There a Text in This Class? The Authority of Interpretive Communities*; Elizabeth Flynn and Patrocinio P. Schweickart, eds., *Gender and Reading: Essays on Readers, Texts, and Contexts*; Wolfgang Iser, *The Act of Reading: A Theory of Aesthetic Response*; Hans Robert Jauss, "Literary History as a Challenge to Literary Theory," *Toward an Aesthetic of Reception*, trans. Timothy Bahti; David H. Richter, *The Reader, the Text, the Poem: The Transactional Theory of the Literary Work*; Michael Steig, *Stories of Reading: Subjectivity and Literary Understanding*. Cristanne Miller's discussion of compression and ellipsis in *Emily Dickinson: A Poet's Grammar* attends somewhat to the roles of the reader; however, Miller's critique focuses primarily on the strategies of the author Dickinson.

9. See Hollander, "Great American Writers"; John Updike, "To the Editors," *New York Review of Books* 35 (August 1988): 63.

10. Ralph Waldo Emerson, *Emerson in His Journals*, ed. Joel Porte, p. 271; see also David Leverenz, "The Politics of Emerson's Man-Making Words," in *Speaking of Gender*, ed. Elaine Showalter, pp. 134–162.

11. Thomas Wentworth Higginson, *Women and the Alphabet*, p. 50. It should be noted that though Higginson uses a French example here, he speaks elsewhere in the book of the feminine pronoun following the masculine and is clearly aware of the fact that woman is subordinated in English, too.

12. Both Emily and Sue Dickinson consistently apply this distinction. In three other letters to Ward, Sue uses "print" for mass reproduction and distribution of poetry (H Lowell Autograph, February 8, 1891, March 14, 1891, March 23, 1891). In the 1890s when Sue or her daughter Martha marks one of Dickinson's manuscripts to indicate that the poem has already appeared in print, she writes "printed" (not "published") on the document; see, for example, Sue's copy of "Except to Heaven – she is nought" (H 251; P 154), which had been printed in *Poems by Emily Dickinson* (1890). In a letter to her brother, Emily writes, "I should be pleased with a line when you've published your work to Father . . ." (L 108, March 18, 1853). In "It would never be Common – / more – I said –" (F 19; P 430), the poem's speaker writes that her joy was such that she "felt it publish–in my Eye." One is of course also reminded of Milton's use of the term:

> . . . Suppose he should relent
> And publish Grace to all, and to his Godhead sing
> Forc't Hallelujahs; . . .

> (*PARADISE LOST* 2:237–239)

As late as 1876, book publishers at the U.S. Centennial in Philadelphia were debating the meaning of the term *publish*. See John Tebbel, *A History of Book Publishing in the United States: The Expansion of an Industry 1865–1919*, 2:36.

13. If this request came from Elizabeth Stuart Phelps, as has been suggested, it is probable that she knew about Dickinson from Thomas Higginson; Higginson and Phelps were acquainted with one another and both published in *Scribner's* in 1871 (*YH* 2:181).

14. In "The Illogic of Sumptuary Values," a slide lecture presented at "Companions of the Flame: Emily Dickinson–H.D. Dual Centennial Colloquium," San Jose Poetry Center, San Jose State University, October 22–25, 1986, Susan Howe first called my attention to the visual effects of this particular poem. In conversation with Martha Lindblom O'Keefe (who in 1986 privately published *This Edifice*, a study of the structure of Dickinson's fascicles) my reading of this holograph has also been enhanced. See chapter 2.

15. See "Great American Writers," p. 11.

16. According to Thomas Johnson, this is the second Master letter; according to R. W. Franklin, it is the third. See "Introduction" (ML 5–10) for extended discussion of the dating of these letters. The penciled handwriting of what Franklin calls "Letter 2" (L 248; A 829) matches that of drafts supposedly written to Judge Lord (L 559; A 735). Since Johnson said these documents were written at least a decade apart, all sorts of questions arise and need to be addressed about the dating of Dickinson's manuscripts. Dating has been determined in part by the type of stationery used. Yet Dickinson herself points out a problem with this method. Writing her cousin Louise Norcross about 1870, she notes: "This little sheet of paper has lain for several years in my Shakespeare, and though it is blotted and antiquated is endeared by its resting-place" (L 340).

17. Johnson's brackets and parentheses indicate that some lines are crossed out and that some words have alternative readings, hence that the copies we have of these letters do not indicate final choices made ready for posting, but only possibilities drafted. The facsimile of the letter in question here (*Home* 423–429) shows clearly that the copies are drafts, and I knew that Jay Leyda and Richard Sewall were right when they pointed out that the bit of verse printed at the end of this "Master" letter really belongs in the middle of the text. The lines

> No Rose. yet felt myself
> a'bloom,
> No Bird–yet rode in Ether.
>
> (A 828c)

should be printed just after the letter's speaker has mused on the result of Master having given something other than "Redemption" and says, "I forgot the Redemption and tired – no more –" (A 828aᵛ). See *YH* 2:22, *Life* 2:514, and chapter 3.

18. John Cody, *After Great Pain: The Inner Life of Emily Dickinson*,

pp. 379–381; Richard Chase, *Emily Dickinson*, pp. 158–159; Charles Anderson, *Emily Dickinson's Poetry: Stairway of Surprise*, pp. 168, 179; see also Rebecca Patterson, *The Riddle of Emily Dickinson*.

19. John Crowe Ransom, "A Poet Restored," in *Emily Dickinson: A Collection of Critical Essays*, ed. Richard B. Sewall, p. 91.

20. Susan Howe, *My Emily Dickinson*, p. 27. David Copperfield's nickname, it should be remembered, was, like that of the speaker of the Master letters, "Daisy." Likewise, Margaret Homans has noted "a literary source in the manipulation of power [similar to that evinced by the speaker of the Master letters] in the relationship between Jane Eyre and Mr. Rochester." See *Women Writers and Poetic Identity: Dorothy Wordsworth, Emily Bronte, and Emily Dickinson*, p. 205.

21. See *LF* 2–7. Wylder suggests that Dickinson appropriated rhetorical notation to make her punctuation more poetically suggestive. This will be discussed more thoroughly in chapter 2.

22. Franklin evidently assumes that the stanza is primary, as is shown by his remarks in a June 5, 1985, letter to Susan Howe: "Doesn't much of your argument depend on your assumption that one (she) reads in lines or parts of lines? What happens to it if the form lurking in the mind is the stanza? Personally I am not convinced that the placement of run on lines is more than arbitrary convenience." See Susan Howe, "Some Notes on Visual Intentionality in Emily Dickinson," *HOW(ever)* 3, no. 4 (1986): 11.

23. I examined this fascicle before beginning to study the letters because I was familiar with the facsimile in Franklin's *Manuscript Books* and wanted to see if the extensive mutilations of this poem would yield any clues about the mutilations of the letters to Austin. Franklin's notes on F 2 state: "Intact when transcribed in 1889 and 1891, this fascicle when indexed about August 1891 had been mutilated, apparently by Mabel Todd, and six poems were missing: 147, 56, 14, 1730, 57, and 1729." Several others have discussed Todd's rewriting the record left by Dickinson. See, for example, R. W. Franklin, "Three Additional Manuscripts," *American Literature* 50 (1978): 113–116; Dorothy Huff Oberhaus, "In Defense of Sue," *Dickinson Studies* 48 (1983): 1–25; Anna Mary Wells, "ED Forgeries," *Dickinson Studies* 35 (1979): 12–16. Though she downplays her mother's alterations, even Bingham admits that in preparing them for publication Loomis Todd "did alter the wording of some of the poems" (*AB* 335).

24. Of the period 1851–1854, seventy-two of Dickinson's letters to her brother survive; of these, twenty-nine are mutilated. Since my primary subject is Dickinson's relationship with Sue, I focus on Dickinson's writings to and about her. There are two important factors for readers to keep in mind: first, Austin saved nearly all of his letters and only parts of them were mutilated, while the plain statements of Sue and her daughter suggest that quite a few of Dickinson's letters to the former were destroyed; second, after their marriage, the record shows that Emily sent only three pieces of her writing to Austin while she sent four hundred and five letters and poems to Sue. See chapter 5, n16.

25. Interpreting this letter, Jane Eberwein states that Dickinson seems "gleeful over his secret engagement to Susan"; see *Dickinson: Strategies of Limitation*, p. 52. However, analyzing the various tones of this letter, Eberwein does not consider Dickinson's characterizing herself as fox and Austin as hound, nor the ways in which the letter has been mutilated. In chapter 4 I discuss problems inherent in assessing Dickinson's tone. Of their meeting in Boston Austin within a month writes Sue: " . . . & no one shall know that you have ever given yourself to me—except those of whom you yourself have told—for *I have never lisped it*" (*YH* 1:268). Whether he refers simply to their engagement (as some parts of the letter suggest) or also to their physical intimacy (as other parts suggest) is debatable.

26. Carroll Smith-Rosenberg, *Disorderly Conduct: Visions of Gender in Victorian America*, p. 39.

27. Ruth Bleier, *Science and Gender: A Critique of Biology and Its Theories on Women*, p. 172. See also Lillian Faderman, *Surpassing the Love of Men: Romantic Friendship and Love between Women from the Renaissance to the Present*, pp. 239–253, for descriptions of how this attitude changed in the late nineteenth century. Thomas Higginson's remark about the speculations of "the malignant" is quoted by Millicent Todd Bingham (*AB* 127).

28. John D'Emilio and Estelle B. Freedman, *Intimate Matters: A History of Sexuality in America*. All quotations are from the "Same-Sex Intimacy" section of "Outside the Family," pp. 121–130.

29. In both her article "Emily Dickinson's Letters to Sue Gilbert," *Massachusetts Review* 18 (Summer 1977): 197–225, esp. p. 213, and *Surpassing the Love of Men*, p. 175, Faderman edits out the self-conscious ". . . all these *ugly thing*s." Although I am discussing a problem with Faderman's essay, I consider her work invaluable and essential to lesbian/feminist studies; her analysis of Bianchi's anxious editing is particularly elucidating, as is Patterson's in *The Riddle of Emily Dickinson*. For further analysis of Faderman, see also Vivian Pollak, *Dickinson: The Anxiety of Gender*, p. 79n: "Faderman contends that 'Emily's love letters to Sue were not simply an example of Victorian rhetoric, but neither was this a lesbian relationship as such relationships have been lived through much of our century.' Her argument hinges, however, on the assumption that this relationship was free of guilt and anxiety and 'the need to keep secrets from family and friends.' In essence, she represents Dickinson as an asexual woman."

As I point out in the following paragraph, Dickinson uses a calligraphic strategy for underlining here, in effect italicizing "*ugly thing*s." In both words, an elaborate tail for the *g* underscores the letters that precede it, calling attention to the words as if they were underlined. Both study of the strokes of the pen and reflection on the content convince me that this calligraphic underlining was deliberate.

30. See particularly Faderman, "Emily Dickinson's Letters to Sue Gilbert," pp. 200–201, 207, 209.

31. Peter Gay, *Education of the Senses*, vol. 1 of *The Bourgeois Experience: Victoria to Freud*, esp. pp. 90–106; Karen Lystra, *Searching the Heart: Women, Men, and*

Romantic Love in Nineteenth-Century America. Readers might also consult Ellen K. Rothman, *Hands and Hearts: A History of Courtship in America.*

32. One might think of Stimpson and Rich as representing opposite poles of a continuum of lesbian interpretation. See Adrienne Rich, "Compulsory Heterosexuality and Lesbian Existence," in *Women: Sex and Sexuality,* ed. Catharine R. Stimpson and Ethel Spector Person, pp. 62–91; and Catharine R. Stimpson, "Zero Degree Deviancy: The Lesbian Novel in English," in *Writing and Sexual Difference,* ed. Elizabeth Abel, pp. 243–259. Estelle B. Freedman, Barbara C. Gelpi, Susan L. Johnson, and Kathleen M. Weston, eds., *The Lesbian Issue: Essays from SIGNS,* is a useful source for beginning to survey recent lesbian literature. Pollak also considers Stimpson's definitions for *lesbian* and concludes, "'Carnality,' however, was not the major focus of her relationship with Sue" (*Dickinson,* p. 79); however, Pollak does not take into account the carnal desire expressed in many of Dickinson's letters to Sue (two of which I mention in this paragraph), nor does she modify Stimpson's proposals by pondering them in dialogue with those of Rich, Friedman, Farwell (all considered below).

33. This and the subsequent quotation are from Susan Stanford Friedman, *Psyche Reborn: The Emergence of H.D.,* pp. 45–46.

34. Rachel Blau DuPlessis, *H.D.: The Career of That Struggle,* p. 103. See also Susan Stanford Friedman and Rachel Blau DuPlessis, "'I had two loves separate': The Sexualities of H.D.'s *HER,*" in *Signets: Reading H.D.,* ed. Friedman and DuPlessis, pp. 205–232.

35. "In Defense of Sue," p. 4. Oberhaus echoes Sue's obituary for Dickinson (*Springfield Republican,* May 18, 1886). No less than half the memorial depicts Dickinson the writer. The obituary is quoted by Bianchi in *LL* 100–103.

36. Marilyn Farwell, "Toward a Definition of the Lesbian Literary Imagination," *Signs* 14 (Autumn 1988): 100–118.

37. Though this is by no means an exhaustive list, Dickinson critics whose work seeks to develop a better understanding of the poet's erotic relationships with women include, first, Patterson, *The Riddle of Emily Dickinson* and *Emily Dickinson's Imagery*; and in subsequent decades (listed in alphabetical order), Paula Bennett, "The Language of Love: Emily Dickinson's Homoerotic Poetry," *Gai Saber* 1, no. 1 (1977): 13–17, "'The Pea That Duty Locks': Lesbian and Feminist-Heterosexual Readings of Emily Dickinson's Poetry," in *Lesbian Texts and Contexts: Radical Revisions,* ed. Karla Jay and Joanne Glasgow, pp. 104–125, her fifth chapter in *Emily Dickinson: Woman Poet,* and, though most of her discussion focuses on Dickinson's supposed relationship with a male master, *My Life a Loaded Gun: Female Creativity and Feminist Poetics,* pp. 15–94; Nadean Bishop, "Renunciation in the Bridal Poems of Emily Dickinson" (paper presented at the National Women's Studies Association Conference, Bloomington, Indiana, May 16–20, 1980); Faderman, "Emily Dickinson's Letters to Sue Gilbert" and *Surpassing the Love of Men*; Judith Farr, "Emily Dickinson's 'Engulfing' Play: *Antony and Cleopatra,*" *Tulsa Studies in Women's Literature* 9, no. 2 (Fall 1990): 231–250; Judy Grahn, "A Heart-Shaped

Journey to a Similar Place," *The Highest Apple: Sappho and the Lesbian Poetic Tradition*, pp. 3–22; Ellen Louise Hart, "The Encoding of Homoerotic Desire: Emily Dickinson's Letters and Poems to Susan Dickinson, 1850–1886," *Tulsa Studies in Women's Literature* 9, no. 2 (Fall 1990): 251–272; Susan Howe, "Women and Their Effect in the Distance," *Ironwood* 28 (1986): 58–91; Adalaide Morris, "Two Sisters Have I: Emily Dickinson's Vinnie and Susan," *Massachusetts Review* 22 (1981): 323–332, and "'The Love of Thee – a Prism Be': Men and Women in the Love Poetry of Emily Dickinson," in *Feminist Critics Read Emily Dickinson*, ed. Suzanne Juhasz, pp. 98–113; Jean McClure Mudge, "Emily Dickinson and 'Sister Sue,'" *Prairie Schooner* 52 (Spring 1977): 90–108; Vivian Pollak, *Dickinson*, esp. pp. 59–82; and Martha Nell Smith, "To Fill a Gap," *San Jose Studies* 13, no. 3 (1987): 3–25, and "Gender Issues in Textual Editing of Emily Dickinson," *Women's Studies Quarterly* 19, nos. 3 and 4 (Fall/Winter 1991): 78–111.

38. This and the subsequent quotation in this paragraph are from Rachel Blau DuPlessis, *Writing Beyond the Ending: Narrative Strategies of Twentieth-Century Women Writers*, p. 66.

39. See Cheryl Walker's discussion of this common subject, "secret sorrow," in nineteenth-century women's poetry in *The Nightingale's Burden: Women Poets and American Culture before 1900*, pp. 87–116. David S. Reynolds uses Samuel Bowles's phrase "literature of misery" to categorize and analyze primarily prose writings by women of this period. Characterizing women's literature in the American Renaissance, he delineates three categories as most important—"Conventional literature, women's rights fiction, and the literature of misery." Most important, however, he stresses the "ironic, stylized" nature of much of the "literature of misery" and discusses how many women writers used conventional poses to mask expressions of radically subversive ideas. See *Beneath the American Renaissance: The Subversive Imagination in the Age of Emerson and Melville*, pp. 387–437, especially his critique of Fern's *Ruth Hall* and Alcott's *Behind a Mask; or, A Woman's Power* (both recently reprinted by Rutgers Univ. Press). The quotation explaining Dickinson's use of stereotypes is from Reynolds, p. 424. See also Sandra M. Gilbert and Susan Gubar's discussion of the literary significance and "Victorian iconography of whiteness which underlies Dickinson's metaphorical white dress" in *The Madwoman in the Attic: The Woman Writer and the Nineteenth-Century Literary Imagination*, p. 620.

40. Thomas Johnson says that "Mrs. Todd mistook the alternate for 'timid' as one for 'blameless' in the line preceding." A glance at the facsimile in the *Manuscript Books* calls this point into serious question. Like the variants for "mystic" and "until," "hallowed" is written directly above (and quite close to) "timid." See F 14, p. 289, and P 271n. On Dickinson's "self-mythologizing" in this poem, see Sandra Gilbert, "The Wayward Nun beneath the Hill: Emily Dickinson and the Mysteries of Womanhood," in *Feminist Critics Read Emily Dickinson*, ed. Juhasz, pp. 22–44.

41. See, for example, Sandra M. Gilbert and Susan Gubar, eds., "Emily

Dickinson," in *The Norton Anthology of Literature by Women*, ed. Gilbert and Gubar, pp. 867–873. One might compare their selections, which make it seem as if "Master" and Higginson are Dickinson's primary correspondents, with those made by Peggy McIntosh and Ellen Louise Hart for the *Heath Anthology*, ed. Paul Lauter, 1:2838–2921. However, Gilbert and Gubar's bibliography (pp. 2399–2400) is far more extensive than that supplied in the *Heath* collection.

42. That Sue was a powerful political influence is plausible when one considers the printings of Dickinson's poems during her lifetime. If we compare the printings Dickinson witnessed to the versions that Sue had in her possession after the poet's death and remember that Sue hosted many an editor at her home, the Evergreens, some of whom printed Dickinson's verse (specifically those of the *Drum Beat*, the *Republican*, and the volume *A Masque of Poets*), it is reasonable to conclude that it was Sue who "turned love to larceny" (see Sue's obituary) and "robbed" (see L 316) Dickinson of select poems, forwarding them to publications. The *Drum Beat* was a Civil War publication used to raise support for Union soldiers. This will be discussed in the chapters that follow.

43. In Cynthia Griffin Wolff's *Emily Dickinson*, the degree of Sue's importance is not acknowledged, although the overprivileging of Mabel Loomis Todd is: "This all-too-well documented love affair between Austin and Mabel is of such vivid human interest that it occasionally threatens to obscure the cold truth: Mrs. Todd never met Emily Dickinson face to face . . . and although she played a central role in preserving Dickinson's work for future readers, neither her character nor her relationship with Austin had any bearing on his sister's poetry" (p. 6). The spectre of Mabel Loomis Todd hangs over most responses to Sue. In "The Upper Story," *Atlantic Monthly*, January 1989, pp. 70–71, Mary Jo Salter concludes her poem by reminding readers of Dickinson's love for Sue, yet in an earlier stanza Loomis Todd is mentioned as if she was a primary correspondent. Though a primary player in the posthumous affairs of Dickinson, Loomis Todd cannot be considered an intimate of the poet.

44. Gilbert and Gubar, *The Madwoman in the Attic*, p. 569.

45. Stressing the erotic symbolism of Dickinson's imagery, Patterson discusses this poem in *Emily Dickinson's Imagery*, pp. 81–82.

46. See Bennett, *My Life a Loaded Gun*, pp. 64–94.

47. See Reynolds, *Beneath the American Renaissance*, p. 422. In his analysis of this poem, he points out that Dickinson joins peers like Alice Cary and Lillie Devereux Blake in portraying the suffering of wives.

48. Ibid., p. 395.

49. Walker, *Nightingale's Burden*, p. 88.

50. Richard Sewall, as quoted by Patterson, *Emily Dickinson's Imagery*, pp. xv.

51. Tillie Olsen, *Silences*, p. 6.

52. Willis J. Buckingham, *Emily Dickinson's Reception in the 1890s: A Documentary History*, p. xii.

53. Hans Robert Jauss, "Literary History as a Challenge to Literary Theory," *Toward an Aesthetic of Reception*, trans. Timothy Bahti.

54. Gwendolyn Brooks, "A Celebration of Emily Dickinson and American Women's Poetry," produced by John Harrington, Poetry-in-the-Round at Seton Hall University, April 10–11, 1986.

55. Jerome Loving, *Emily Dickinson: The Poet on the Second Story*. See Dorothy Oberhaus's review in *American Literature* 61 (1988): 661–663.

56. Rich, *A Wild Patience*, pp. 40–45.

57. Walker, *Nightingale's Burden*, p. 87. For subsequent references in this discussion, see pp. 87–116. The one-woman show is William Luce's *The Belle of Amherst*; Charles Kuralt narrated the sixty-second spot for CBS (it has not been shown, though he has referred to the poet on "CBS Sunday Morning," spring 1985); one of the recordings is a reading by Julie Harris, *Emily Dickinson—A Self-Portrait*; the murder mystery is Jane Langton's *Emily Dickinson Is Dead*; and the cookbook is by Guides at the Dickinson Homestead, *Profile of Emily Dickinson as Cook*.

58. Paul Simon, "The Dangling Conversation," *Parsley, Sage, Rosemary & Thyme*; William H. Shurr, *The Marriage of Emily Dickinson*.

59. See Marilee Lindemann's analysis in "Women Writers and the American Romance: Studies in Jewett and Cather," (Ph.D. diss., Rutgers Univ., 1991), pp. 1–71.

60. Reynolds, *Beneath the American Renaissance*, p. 414.

61. For an illuminating discussion about sexual difference, see Janice Doane and Devon Hodges, *Nostalgia and Sexual Difference: The Resistance to Contemporary Feminism*, pp. 3–14. Doane and Hodges focus on differences between male and female, but many of their insights enrich analysis when transposed to discuss the uses of ideologies of difference to evaluate heterosexual and homosexual desires.

62. See the Helms Amendment to the Fiscal Year 1990 Interior and Related Agencies Appropriations Bill, H.R. 2788. In an astounding denial of its own intolerant agenda, Specifications 2 and 3 proceed, by association, to parallel homoeroticism with various bigotries (denigration of adherents of a particular religion or nonreligion and denigration of a group or class of citizens on the basis of race, creed, sex, handicap, age, or national origin). For a similar argument exposing the ideological oversimplifications of this amendment, see Catharine R. Stimpson, "President's Column," *MLA Newsletter* 22 (Summer 1990): 3.

63. I have neither the time nor space to cite all the literary examples of homoeroticism (some of Shakespeare's sonnets [e.g., Sonnet 33]), Huck and Jim, the *Pequod*'s crew) and sadomasochism (the death of Marlowe's Edward II and the tyranny of Captain Ahab, as well as, if we also refer to psychological brutality, Gilbert Osmond) that would be excluded by this amendment.

64. Heather Findlay, "Is There a Lesbian in This Text? Derrida, Wittig, and the Politics of the Three Women," in *Coming to Terms: Feminism, Theory, Politics*, ed. Elizabeth Weed, pp. 59–69.

65. Here I draw on the ideas of M. M. Bakhtin; see especially *The Dialogic Imagination*, ed. Michael Holquist, trans. Caryl Emerson.

66. Doane and Hodges, *Nostalgia and Sexual Difference*, pp. 3, 12.

2. Rowing in Eden: Reading Dickinson Reading

1. See, for example, Myra Jehlen, *American Incarnation: The Individual, The Nation, and The Continent*, or Annette Kolodny, *The Lay of the Land: Metaphor as Experience and History in American Life and Letters* and *The Land Before Her: Fantasy and Experience of the American Frontiers, 1630–1860*. For poems exploring various physical, emotional, psychic, and mental metaphors of exploration, see, on geography, "We pray – to Heaven –" (F 22; P 489), "Volcanoes be in Sicily" (P 1705); on exploration, "Baffled for just a day or two –" (F 2; P 17), "Who never lost, are unprepared / A Coronet to find!" (F 6; P 73), "Soto! Explore Thyself!" (Set 5; P 832), "I play at Riches – to appease / The Clamoring for Gold –" (F 38; P 801); on discovery, "Taking up the fair Ideal," (F 19; P 428), "Not to discover weak – / ness is" (Set 7; P 1054), "His Mansion in the Pool" (P 1379), "Eden is that old-fashioned House" (P 1657), "The largest Fire ever / known" (Set 7; P 1114), "Had we known the Ton she bore" (P 1124, variant fourth line), "This Consciousness that / is aware" (Set 6a; P 822), "Finding is the first / Act" (Set 5; P 870), "How far is it to Heaven?" (Set 7; P 929), "Because that you are going" (P 1260); and on that undiscovered, "Soto! Explore Thyself" and "You cannot take itself" (P 1351).

2. Joan DeJean, *Fictions of Sappho 1546–1937*, pp. 317–325.

3. See Roland Barthes, *Image—Music—Text*, trans. Stephen Heath, and *S/Z*, trans. Richard Miller, p. 4.

4. Miller, *Emily Dickinson*, p. 178.

5. Willis Barnstone, *The Poetic of Ecstasy: Varieties of Ekstasis from Sappho to Borges*, p. 1.

6. Gwendolyn Brooks's remarks are from her reading at "A Celebration of Emily Dickinson and American Women's Poetry," Poetry-in-the-Round at Seton Hall University, April 10, 1986. In the sentence about Dickinson that follows, contemporary poet Susan Howe extends Brooks's observation in *My Emily Dickinson*, p. 29. Highly allusive, Dickinson often uses reference to the Bible, Milton, Shakespeare, Barrett Browning, or some other literary work to illustrate or elaborate her own expression. Sometimes she actually cuts others' texts and glues or fastens them to her own to create new, humorous texts (see chapter 3 for my critique of the "cartoon" she fashioned by attaching engravings from Dickens's *The Old Curiosity Shop* to "A poor – torn Heart").

7. Alicia Ostriker, *Stealing the Language: The Emergence of Women's Poetry in America*, p. 11.

8. Richard Poirier, *The Renewal of Literature: Emersonian Reflections*, p. 139. "Each and all" purposely echoes Emerson's poem. Betsy Erkkila has recently ar-

gued that "elitist, antidemocratic values were at the very center" of Dickinson's work. However, Erkkila relies on the Higginson-Todd-Bingham view of Dickinson and predicates her argument on what Higginson reported about his 1870 visit to the Homestead (L 342a). The liberal Higginson's elitist views regarding culture are well known, and Erkkila may be conflating his projections with Dickinson's own attitudes. See "Emily Dickinson and Class," pp. 14, 23.

9. For some basic information about women's poetry and the publishing industry, see Emily Stipes Watts, *The Poetry of American Women from 1632 to 1945*, p. 65. Also, for extended discussion of Dickinson's cliched, conventional poetry, see Dobson, *Dickinson and the Strategies of Reticence*, pp. 3–5, 131–134.

10. Jauss, *Question and Answer*, pp. 200, 207; for purposes of introducing these ideas to students, see also "Literary History as a Challenge to Literary Theory," most recently anthologized in *The Critical Tradition: Classic Texts and Contemporary Trends*, ed. David H. Richter (New York: St. Martin's Press, 1989), pp. 1198–1218.

11. Shurr, *The Marriage of Emily Dickinson*, pp. 18–23. Rebecca West also exemplifies literary equation of sexual experience with another, paradisaical realm:

> I was amazed at lovemaking. It was so strange to come, when I was
> nearly middle-aged, on the knowledge that there was another state
> of being than any I had known, and that it was the state normal for
> humanity, that I was a minority who did not know it. It was as if I
> had learned that there was a sixth continent, which nearly everybody
> but me and a few others had visited and in which, now I had come to
> it, I felt like a native, or as if there was another art as well as music
> and painting and literature, which was not only preached, but actu-
> ally practised, by nearly everybody, though they were silent about
> their accomplishment. It was fantastic that nobody should speak of
> what pervaded life and determined it, yet it was inevitable, for
> language could not describe it.

From West's novel, *Cousin Rosamund*, quoted in *The Oxford Book of Marriage*, ed. Helge Rubinstein (Oxford: Oxford Univ. Press, 1990), pp. 162–163.

12. See, for example, Juhasz, *"The Undiscovered Continent": Emily Dickinson and the Space of the Mind*, esp. pp. 175–178.

13. Commenting on the "dance mix" versions of his own songs, which some of his fans thought violated their integrity, popular poet Bruce Springsteen unwittingly elucidates the situation of Dickinson's texts: "I was always so protective of my music that I was hesitant to do much with it at all. Now [post–Arthur Baker's dance mix production of "Dancing in the Dark"] I feel my stuff isn't as fragile as I thought." See Dave Marsh, *Glory Days: Bruce Springsteen in the 1980s* (New York: Pantheon Books, 1987), p. 231. So Dickinson's poetry, remixed by many an editor, biographer, and critic is not so fragile as Thomas Higginson thought. He re-

marked that her poems "reminded him of skeleton leaves so pretty but *too delicate*, —not strong enough to publish— . . ." (*YH* 2 : 193).

14. The definitions of *glossolalia* and *heteroglossia* are taken from Mae Gwendolyn Henderson, "Speaking in Tongues," in *Changing Our Own Words: Essays on Criticism, Theory, and Writing*, ed. Cheryl A. Wall, p. 22.

15. See Michel Foucault, *The Archaeology of Knowledge* and *The Order of Things: An Archaeology of the Human Sciences*; Tania Modleski, "Feminism and the Power of Interpretation: Some Critical Readings," in *Feminist Studies/Critical Studies*, ed. Teresa de Lauretis, pp. 121–138; Modleski refers to Nancy K. Miller, "The Text's Heroine: A Feminist Critic and Her Fictions," *Diacritics* 12 (Summer 1982): 53. Biddy Martin discusses the dilemma a loss of identity poses especially for lesbians, "given the institutional privileges enjoyed by those who can afford to disavow 'identity'"; see "Lesbian Identity and Autobiographical Difference," *Life/Lines: Theorizing Women's Autobiography*, ed. Bella Brodzki and Celeste Schenck, p. 80. Barton St. Armand comments on Dickinson too often being viewed as an abstraction in this "Age of Theory" when he compliments Shurr's book.

16. Culler, *On Deconstruction*, pp. 72–73.

17. In "Intention," Annabel Patterson astutely discusses ideas of Foucault, Derrida, and de Man to trace recent evolutions in attitudes toward the author and notes that "even among deconstructive critics the suspicion lurks that intention cannot so easily be banished." See *Critical Terms for Literary Study*, ed. Frank Lentricchia and Thomas McLaughlin, p. 145.

18. This and the quotation in the next paragraph are from Mark Schulman, "Gender and Typographic Culture: Beginning to Unravel the 500-Year Mystery," in *Technology and Women's Voices: Keeping in Touch*, ed. Cheris Kramarae, pp. 98–115.

19. Here I am indebted to Alicia Ostriker who, in her forthcoming *Nakedness of the Fathers*, discusses both a "hermeneutics of suspicion" and a "hermeneutics of indeterminacy." An excerpt from that work was presented as "Genesis, Exodus, and the Feminist Imagination," at the annual meeting of the Modern Language Association, Washington, D.C., December 27–30, 1989.

20. See Barnstone, "Eve: The Mother of Ecstasy," *The Poetics of Ecstasy*, pp. 1–2. Appropriately, the epigraph he chooses for the book is from Emily Dickinson. Also, whatever her intention, the first two words mirror the last in Dickinson's simple declarative sentence, for *Hawwah*, Hebrew for Eve, derives from the verb "to be." I thank Alicia Ostriker, whose *Nakedness of the Fathers* brought the meaning of Eve's name to my attention.

21. Keller, *The Only Kangaroo*, p. 334.

22. Jerome McGann, *Social Values and Poetic Acts: The Historical Judgment of Literary Work*, pp. 32–49. McGann declares Blake's poetics "contestatory," but ends this part of his discussion suggesting that the critique may well be adapted to the case of Dickinson.

23. Nina Baym, "Melodramas of Beset Manhood: How Theories of American Fiction Exclude Women Writers," *American Quarterly* 33 (1981): 123–139.

24. David Porter, *Dickinson: The Modern Idiom*, p. 2. See also Benjamin, "The Work of Art in the Age of Mechanical Reproduction," p. 226: "When the age of mechanical reproduction separated art from its basis in cult, the semblance of its autonomy disappeared forever."

25. See, for example, Hastings' poem "To Critics," *Poems on Different Subjects* (Lancaster, Penn.: William Dickson, 1808), p. 1. It begins

> PRAY, learned Critic, don't in haste
>   The little Warbler fright:
> If she's at your tribunal cast,
>   'Twill disconcert her quite.

I am indebted to Susan Stanford Friedman for calling my attention to this poem.

26. Taking his cue from Emerson, who declared "that the most interesting department of poetry would hereafter be found in what might be called 'The Poetry of the Portfolio,'" or "the work . . . of persons who wrote for relief of their own minds, and without thought of publication," Thomas Higginson titled his first essay on Dickinson "An Open Portfolio." See *The Recognition of Emily Dickinson*, ed. Caesar R. Blake and Carlton F. Wells, pp. 3–10. See especially his first paragraph. See also Wolff, *Emily Dickinson*, p. 9.

27. Sharon Cameron, *Lyric Time: Dickinson and the Limits of Genre*, p. 14. See also the critics she cites, esp. Inder Nath Kher, Austin Warren, Herbert Read, Charles Anderson, and David Porter, who declares that Dickinson's "art in its range and technique never altered over three decades of writing" (*Dickinson*, p. 83).

28. Howe, "Some Notes on Visual Intentionality in Emily Dickinson," pp. 11–13; such "innocence" is of course a state informed by literature ushered through the processes of mechanical reproduction which simultaneously has more possibilities (for example, of reaching a wider audience) and more limitations (for example, foreclosing experimentations to only those techniques which can be typeset). See also Howe's "Women and Their Effect in the Distance."

29. G. Thomas Tanselle, "The Editorial Problem of Final Authorial Intention," *Selected Studies in Bibliography*, p. 309.

30. McGann, *A Critique of Modern Textual Criticism*, p. 100. While Tanselle is more concerned with the individual author and her intentions (though he recognizes the collaborative nature of printed works), McGann focuses more on literary sociology and critiques "the ideology of final intentions." Both are concerned that the material corporealization of a text not be confused with the text itself.

31. Lillian Faderman has pointed out that the addressee of this poem might well be female. See "Emily Dickinson's Homoerotic Poetry," *Higginson Journal* 18 (1978): 19–27. For speculation that the poem may be about a stormy night Dickinson spent with Kate Anthon, see Patterson, *Emily Dickinson's Imagery*, p. 28.

32. One of the most recent examples repeating the commonplace about Dickinson's form is in A. R. C. Finch, "Dickinson and Patriarchal Meter: A Theory of Metrical Codes," *PMLA* 102 (1987): 166–176. This article is an excellent

analysis of Dickinson's print translations (readers should note, however, that Finch mistakenly refers to Clark Griffith as "Griffin," both in the article and her bibliography).

33. G. Thomas Tanselle, "Response to John Sutherland," *Literature and Social Practice*, ed. Philippe Desan, Priscilla Parkhurst Ferguson, and Wendy Griswold, pp. 284, 286. Sutherland's "Publishing History: A Hole at the Centre of Literary Sociology" originally appeared in *Critical Inquiry* 14 (Spring 1988): 574–589.

34. Miller, *Emily Dickinson*, p. 49.

35. "Great American Writers," p. 8.

36. Steig, *Stories of Reading*, p. xiv.

37. It seems most appropriate that this poetic statement does not survive in holograph. Her beloved Norcross cousins passed it along to Mabel Loomis Todd for publication in *Letters of Emily Dickinson* (1894).

38. Eco, *The Role of the Reader*, p. 4.

39. Gary Lee Stonum, *The Dickinson Sublime*, esp. pp. 3–21; for elaboration of the "Dickinson sublime," see pp. 110–148. For further elaboration of Faulkner's remarks, see Joseph Blotner and Frederick L. Gwynn, eds., *Faulkner in the University*.

40. Thomas H. Johnson, "Establishing a Text: The Emily Dickinson Papers," *Studies in Bibliography* 5 (1952–1953): 31–32.

41. Ransom, "Emily Dickinson: A Poet Restored," p. 89; for Ostriker's commentary on this, see *Stealing the Language*, p. 5; R. P. Blackmur, "Emily Dickinson: Notes on Prejudice and Fact," in *The Recognition of Emily Dickinson*, ed. Caesar R. Blake and Carlton F. Wells, pp. 201–223; Porter, *Dickinson*, pp. 83, 152. Instead of finding Dickinson's freedom enabling, Porter finds it disabling; see pp. 105–142. The fact that many, even most, find liberty formidable, even terrifying, has been widely discussed; see, for example, Erich Fromm, *Escape from Freedom* (New York: Holt, Rinehart & Winston, 1941).

42. Cheryl Walker, "Feminist Literary Criticism and the Author," *Critical Inquiry* 16 (Spring 1990): 551–571. Subsequent quotations of Walker in this and the next few paragraphs are from this article. See also Nancy K. Miller, "Changing the Subject: Authorship, Writing, and the Reader," in *Feminist Studies/Critical Studies*, ed. Teresa de Lauretis, pp. 102–120, and, especially for discussion of concepts of author's rights and copyright law emerging in the eighteenth century, see Peggy Kamuf, *Signature Pieces: On the Institution of Authorship*.

43. Stonum critiques this position in *The Dickinson Sublime*, p. 15; this and the subsequent quotations are from his first chapter, "A Poet without a Project? A Poetry without Scope or Structure?" pp. 3–21.

44. For Lukacs' commentary, see *The Theory of the Novel: A Historico-philosophical Essay on the Form of Great Epic Literature*, trans. Anna Bostock; on the homosexual lyric, see Thomas E. Yingling, *Hart Crane and the Homosexual Text: New Thresholds, New Anatomies*; on Dickinson and the lyric, see Cameron, *Lyric*

Time, and Margaret Dickie, *Lyric Contingencies: Emily Dickinson and Wallace Stevens*.

45. Linda Kauffman, *Discourses of Desire: Gender, Genre, and Epistolary Fictions*, pp. 21–22, 293.

46. This and the subsequent commentaries by M. L. Rosenthal are from "Poems by the Packet," a review of Franklin's *Manuscript Books* and Porter's *Dickinson*, *Times Literary Supplement*, March 26, 1982, p. 357.

47. Cameron, *Lyric Time*, pp. 13–14.

48. Cristanne Miller, *Emily Dickinson*, pp. 50–51.

49. McGann, *A Critique of Modern Textual Criticism*, pp. 107–109.

50. This is quoted by Carlton Lowenberg in *Emily Dickinson's Textbooks*, ed. Territa A. Lowenberg and Carla L. Brown, p. 80.

51. This and the following quotation are from R. P. Blackmur, "Emily Dickinson's Notation," in *Emily Dickinson*, ed. Sewall, pp. 78–87.

52. Cristanne Miller, "'A Letter is a Joy of Earth': Dickinson's Communication with the World," *Legacy* 3 (Spring 1986): 29–39.

53. Howe recently elaborated this lecture for print. See "These Flames and Generosities of the Heart: Emily Dickinson and the Illogic of Sumptuary Values."

54. From Thomas Higginson's 1891 essay on Dickinson, written for a curious public; quoted in Robert N. Linscott, ed., *Selected Poems and Letters of Emily Dickinson*, pp. 5–24. The facsimile copy Loomis Todd and he reproduced is probably that sent to Higginson.

55. For more discussion of Chicago, see Sandra Caruso Mortola Gilbert and Susan Dreyfuss David Gubar, "Ceremonies of the Alphabet: Female Grandmatologies and the Female Authorgraph," in *The Female Autograph: Theory and Practice of Autobiography from the Tenth to the Twentieth Century*, ed. Domna C. Stanton, pp. 21–48. Also cited is Olga Broumas, "Artemis," *Beginning with O*, p. 23.

56. Examples of such print conventions are far too numerous to mention, but *The Poetical Works of Alice and Phoebe Cary* and Whitman's *Leaves of Grass* show what I mean.

57. James Wright's paraphrase of Frost is quoted by Neil Fraistat, *The Poem and the Book: Interpreting Collections of Romantic Poetry*, p. 3. Though she does not approach the fascicles in the way I do, Ruth Miller in *Emily Dickinson* proposed that we see them as integral units two decades ago.

58. Neil Fraistat, ed., *Poems in Their Place: The Intertextuality and Order of Poetic Collections*, p. 8.

59. Joseph Wittreich, "'Strange Text!': 'Paradise Regain'd . . . to which is added *Samson Agonistes*,'" in *Poems in Their Place*, ed. Fraistat, p. 164.

60. St. Armand, *Emily Dickinson and Her Culture*, p. 9.

61. Fraistat, *Poem and the Book*, p. 7. The reader might also consult John Van Sickle, "The Book-Roll and Some Conventions of the Poetic Book," *Arethusa* 13 (1980): 5–42.

62. It may be of interest for the reader to note that in this fascicle in particu-

lar, many, even most, of the dashes are directed down by the poet. In a poem like "It was given to me by," such strategy creates an especially resonant irony. My readers should consult the *Manuscript Books*.

63. Harold Bloom, ed., *Emily Dickinson: Modern Critical Views*, p. 7.

64. J. A. Leo Lemay and P. M. Zall, eds., *Benjamin Franklin's Autobiography*, pp. 3–4.

65. Marjorie Perloff, "The Two *Ariels*: The (Re)Making of the Sylvia Plath Canon," in *Poems in Their Place*, ed. Fraistat, pp. 308–333; Dale Spender, "Margaret Fuller," *Women of Ideas (And What Men Have Done to Them)*, pp. 197–212.

3. All Men Say "What" to Me: Sexual Identity and Problems of Literary Creativity

1. Sewall may have been wrong to "correct" Lavinia here. Perhaps she was, like her sister, using the dash to say "friends" are "the most delight." Lavinia mentions that she was with Emily in Washington and pointedly remarks on their pleasurable time and the lack of any particular reason for her sister's withdrawal because many, like her niece, Martha Dickinson Bianchi, maintained that the poet "met the fate she had instinctively shunned" on that trip. That fate "doomed" her, "once and forever by her own heart" (*LL* 46–47).

2. On four leaves, Franklin's first two letters (L 187, L 248) are each on one folded sheet (A 827, A 827a, A 829, A 829a), his third (L 233) on two (A 828, A 828a, A 828b, A 828c).

3. See Gilbert and Gubar, *The Madwoman in the Attic*, pp. 600–606; Cody, *After Great Pain*, p. 356; Wolff, *Emily Dickinson*, pp. 406–411; St. Armand, *Emily Dickinson and Her Culture*, p. 51; Pollak, *Dickinson*, p. 84; Shurr, *The Marriage of Emily Dickinson*, pp. 8–10; Bennett, *My Life a Loaded Gun*, p. 55.

4. Ellen Louise Hart and I are currently working on *With the Exception of Shakespeare*, an edition of the "publication" to Sue.

5. Loomis Todd's production and alteration of this poem were discussed at length in chapter 1. Compare the copy of Dickinson's holograph (F 14; P 271) with "Wedded" in Mabel Loomis Todd, ed., *Poems by Emily Dickinson*, Third Series, p. 97.

6. The term is Rachel DuPlessis's. See *Writing Beyond the Ending: Narrative Strategies of Twentieth-Century Women Writers* and my discussions in chapter 1.

7. This term is used by Martha Dickinson Bianchi; see her preface to *The Single Hound*, p. v. As Faderman points out, post-Freudian Bianchi is quite self-conscious about her mother's "romantic friendship" with Dickinson and uses this term to emphasize their sororal, familial ties.

8. Polly Longsworth, "'Was Mr. Dudley Dear?': Emily Dickinson and John Langdon Dudley," *Massachusetts Review* 26 (1985): 360–372. In the section of the letter Longsworth quotes, Dickinson asks about four other acquaintances. Since she begins that part of the letter—"Clara and Anna [Newman] came to see me and

brought beautiful flowers. Do you know what made them remember me?"—and the Newman sisters were staying with Sue and Austin, the reader might more logically infer that Dickinson is as concerned with Sue or Austin's possible remembrance of her as she is with asking after any acquaintance.

9. Willa Cather, *Alexander's Bridge*, p. 131. I would like to thank Marilee Lindemann for bringing this to my attention.

10. Miller, "'A Letter is a Joy of Earth,'" p. 35.

11. See Karl J. Weintraub, "Autobiography and Historical Consciousness," *Critical Inquiry* 1 (Summer 1975): 821–848. For various perspectives on women's autobiographies, see Shari Benstock, ed., *The Private Self: Theory and Practice of Women's Autobiographical Writings*, esp. Susan Stanford Friedman, "Women's Autobiographical Selves: Theory and Practice," pp. 34–62, and Nancy Walker, "'Wider Than the Sky': Public Presence and Private Self in Dickinson, James, and Woolf," pp. 272–303; Brodzki and Schenck, eds., *Life/Lines*, esp. Martin, "Lesbian Identity and Autobiographical Difference[s]," pp. 77–103, and Celeste Schenck, "All of a Piece: Women's Poetry and Autobiography," pp. 281–305; Sidonie Smith, *A Poetics of Women's Autobiography: Marginality and the Fictions of Self-Representation*. On women's poetry and writing one's selves, see Ostriker, *Stealing the Language*.

12. Suzanne Juhasz, "Reading Emily Dickinson's Letters," *ESQ: Journal of the American Renaissance* 30 (1984): 170–192.

13. When Jonathan Auerbach refers to Dickinson's "confessional lyrics," he does not mean that the poems tell stories of the poet's life, but refers to tensions between the first-person form and constitutions and constrictions of personal identity. See *The Romance of Failure: Poe, Hawthorne, and James*, pp. 18–19, 180 nn. 18, 20.

14. Schenck, "All of a Piece," p. 286. For important observations about women poets' interrogations, appropriations, and revisionary use of literary forms, see Rachel Blau DuPlessis, *The Pink Guitar: Writing as Feminist Practice*.

15. The Master letters can be dated only by Emily Dickinson's handwriting. "Dear Master" seems to be in the script of the late 1850s; "Master" in the hand of the early 1860s. "Oh' did I offend it" is in pencil, not pen, and matches her rough-draft holograph in notes said to be written in the late 1870s, as well as penciled drafts in the 1860s. This will be more thoroughly discussed at the end of this section. That the emendations to "Master" are in pencil and in a hand that more closely resembles the pencil draft of "Oh' did I offend it" may indicate that the changes were made by Dickinson quite a while after the letter was penned; or the difference in handwriting may simply reflect that she was in a very different mood. The handwriting may even belong to someone else; since the letters passed through the hands of Austin, Mabel, and Millicent Todd Bingham, the changes may have been made by them (Bingham appears to have written on "Oh' did I offend it"). In any case, it is important to note what is penned and what penciled, what is crossed out, and what is not; indicating cancellations by brackets obscures the marks' impact.

16. Stonum, *The Dickinson Sublime*, esp. pp. 149–187.

17. In "ED Forgeries," Wells suggested that Mabel Loomis Todd may have forged Dickinson's supposed love letters to Otis Lord. If anything has been forged, I think it might be the "like you," though I am most comfortable with the conclusion that Dickinson made the revision herself. However, comparing the "like" of this phrase with that of other Dickinson holographs (e.g., "It's like the light," F 12; P 297), it may be significant that the *e* ending the pencil revision in the letter is distinctly separated from the word, while it is joined to the word all five times in the poem and is joined to the word when Dickinson writes it on the verso (A 828 b^V, ML 42); and it may be significant that the "like" in the phrase resembles the word written by Loomis Todd as much as it does the word written by Dickinson (see, e.g., the Loomis Todd holograph photographically reproduced by Franklin in *Editing*, fig. 20, p. 103). Taking exception to an earlier version of my argument, Lease says that the two representations of "like" in this letter are "identically written," but he fails to note the distinctly separated *e* of the pencil revision; see *Emily Dickinson's Readings of Men and Books*, pp. 135–136. As matters of intrigue, these suggestive details are fascinating, but they detract from the most important issues for critical contemplation—apparently anxious revision of passionate expression.

18. To read about the loss of "Rearrange a 'Wife's' affection," see Franklin, *Editing*, pp. 46–47. For notes on Susan's marks on the fascicles, see F, p. xvi, and discussion below in chapter 6. The original of this poem is "missing," apparently removed by Austin or Loomis Todd. According to Franklin, it was copied into a fascicle about 1860, a provocative date since it falls about seven years after Dickinson fell in love with Sue.

19. Wendy Barker interrogates Dickinson's subversive appropriations of these conventional metaphors that equate sun and light with men, and, in sharp contrast, equate moon and dark with women. See *Lunacy of Light: Emily Dickinson and the Experience of Metaphor*, esp. pp. 1–30 and pp. 51–73.

20. Morris, "'The Love of Thee—a Prism Be,'" esp. pp. 99–103.

21. Homans, *Women Writers and Poetic Identity*, p. 209; the subsequent quotation of Homans near the end of this paragraph is from p. 201.

22. Gilbert and Gubar, *The Madwoman in the Attic*, p. 611.

23. St. Armand, *Emily Dickinson and Her Culture*, pp. 80–115, 137–147.

24. Howe, *My Emily Dickinson*, pp. 24–27.

25. *Comic Power in Emily Dickinson*, a book I have coauthored with Suzanne Juhasz and Cristanne Miller, critiques this and other of Dickinson's cartoons at length and discusses how her layouts comment on interactive, "writerly" reading. For extensive analysis of writerly activities on the part of early nineteenth-century American readers, see Cathy Davidson, *Revolution and the Word: The Rise of the Novel in America*, esp. pp. 55–79.

26. Pollak, *Dickinson*, p. 84.

27. See Aristotle, *Rhetoric*, trans. W. Rhys Robarts (Oxford: Oxford Univ. Press, 1924); Bakhtin, *The Dialogic Imagination*, pp. 331–366; Roland Barthes, *A Lover's Discourse: Fragments*, trans. Richard Howard. A historian of the literary love

letter, Kauffman synthesizes these critiques and formulates analyses of particular interest to feminist scholars; see *Discourses of Desire*, esp. pp. 17–36. Also enlightening are Jauss's commentaries on "dialogic understanding" in literary communication in *Question and Answer*, pp. 207–218, especially for analyzing our role as interpreters of the "Master" documents. I echo David Porter's proclamation that, particularly in her letters to Higginson, "Dickinson earnestly meant what she said"; see *Dickinson*, p. 3. What Porter does not factor into account are her highly developed rhetorical skills.

28. See especially "Mute thy Coronation –" (P 151), "Sexton! My Master's sleeping here" (F 3; P 96), "Sunset at night – is natural –" (F 15; P 415), "The face I carry with / me – last –" (F 19; P 336), "A Wife – at Daybreak – / I shall be –" (F 32; P 461), "Why make it doubt – it / hurts it so –" (F 32; P 462), and "My Life had stood – a / Loaded Gun –" (F 34; P 754).

29. Jauss, *Question and Answer*, p. 200. Much in these concluding paragraphs summarizes aspects of Jauss's arguments, especially those on pp. 51–94 and pp. 197–231.

4. With the Exception of Shakespeare: Reconstructing Dickinson's Relationship with Susan Huntington Gilbert Dickinson

1. When referring to Susan Gilbert, I try to use the name she seems to have preferred at the time about which I am writing, though in referring to her as a correspondent of Dickinson's (and not at a particular time), I often use Sue, the name she used throughout most of her adult years, to emphasize her intimacy with Emily. To conjecture Susan's preference, I have observed how she signs her name to letters and in the front of books. A late December 1890 letter to Higginson, for example, is signed "S. H. Dickinson" (see *AB* 86); I conclude, therefore, that at that time she preferred to be addressed with Huntington as her middle name. Similarly, in late letters to her, Dickinson begins to use "Susan" more frequently. A few paragraphs below I discuss the significance of Sue's struggles with naming.

2. See Walker, *The Nightingale's Burden*, esp. pp. 105, 107; and Oberhaus, "In Defense of Sue," esp. p. 4.

3. Modleski, "Feminism and the Power of Interpretation," pp. 121–138. Wendy Martin recognizes the importance of Dickinson's correspondences with women and calls for extended analyses of them. See *An American Triptych: Anne Bradstreet, Emily Dickinson, Adrienne Rich*, esp. pp. 148–164.

4. The most recent critique of the relationship between the mother and daughter pair of Emilys is Wolff's biography, *Emily Dickinson*; see esp. pp. 36–65. For illuminating presentation and discussion of the elder Emily Dickinson's letters, see Vivian Pollak, ed., *A Poet's Parents: The Courtship Letters of Emily Norcross and Edward Dickinson*.

5. Camille Paglia, *Sexual Personae: Art and Decadence from Nefertiti to Emily Dickinson*, pp. 12, 672; the quotation in the paragraph immediately following is on

p. 653. Paglia devotes her last chapter to Emily Dickinson, and concludes the book with a sentence declaring that "Amherst's Madame de Sade still waits for her readers to know her." While Paglia points out many problems with general critical views, the most important being criticism's tendency to sentimentalize authorial relations (whether with "Master" or in naive reconstruction of Dickinson's place in nineteenth-century female culture), she writes as if it is primarily feminists who fall into such reductive traps. Unfortunately, as her notes make plain, she either chooses to ignore or is not familiar with the vast body of feminist criticism on Dickinson and reductively characterizes woman-centered analyses. No Dickinson criticism is mentioned besides that by R. P. Blackmur, Jack Capps, Richard Chase, John Cody, Rebecca Patterson, and George Whicher; thus Paglia, appearing uninformed or unwilling to address the complexities of the last twenty years of scholarship (much of it feminist), undercuts her own analyses. Paglia seems to believe that feminist inquiry tends to be sentimental, simplistically portraying the victimization of good, sensitive women by bad, power-hungry men. Believing in biological determinism, she goes so far as to say that "Women have a more accurate sense of reality; they are physically and spiritually more complete" (p. 20). Thus she argues that women, not made perpetually anxious by feeling overwhelmed by the mother, do not need, as do men, to escape into philosophical and artistic achievement (culture). Though she repeatedly attacks feminists for being sentimental, her totalizing views of the feminist enterprise and of male creativity are sentimental, especially in valorizing men.

6. Weedon, "Language and Subjectivity," *Feminist Practice and Poststructuralist Theory*, p. 101.

7. Gilbert and Gubar, "Ceremonies of the Alphabet," p. 24; Ruth Stone, "Names," *Second-Hand Coat: Poems New and Selected*, p. 23.

8. Gerda Lerner, *The Creation of Patriarchy*, p. 181.

9. Keller, *The Only Kangaroo*, pp. 188–191.

10. A recent three-volume study, which analyzes the debates about woman's nature and place, problematizes and refutes the traditional model of a single Victorian attitude toward women; however, for the matters of reception under discussion here, the most widely held perceptions are more important than the facts. See Elizabeth K. Helsinger, Robin Lauterbach Sheets, and William Veeder, *The Woman Question*.

11. Barker, *Lunacy of Light*, p. 6.

12. Watts, *The Poetry of American Women*, p. 71.

13. *Democratic Review* 24 (1849): 232–241.

14. Ann D. Gordon, Mari Jo Buhle, and Nancy Shrom Dye, "The Problem of Women's History," in *Liberating Women's History*, ed. Berenice Carroll (Urbana: Univ. of Illinois Press, 1976), p. 89; quoted by Joan W. Scott, "Gender: A Useful Category of Historical Analysis," in *Coming to Terms: Feminism, Theory, Politics*, ed. Elizabeth Weed, p. 82.

15. Forty years ago, Elizabeth Bishop, a lesbian, launched a rather strident

attack on Patterson's "infuriating book." See "Unseemly Deductions," review of *The Riddle of Emily Dickinson*, by Rebecca Patterson, *New Republic* 127 (August 18, 1952): 20. Readers might contrast her review with Laurence Perrine's far more favorable response, "Emily's Beloved Friend," *Southwest Review* 37 (Winter 1952): 81–83.

16. Walker, "'Wider Than the Sky,'" p. 275.

17. Pollak, *Dickinson*, p. 64.

18. Joanne Feit Diehl, *Dickinson and the Romantic Imagination*, p. 15.

19. Margaret Homans, "'Oh, Vision of Language!': Dickinson's Poems of Love and Death," in *Feminist Critics Read Emily Dickinson*, ed. Juhasz, pp. 114–133; Patterson, *The Riddle of Emily Dickinson*, pp. 126, 177, 225, 229, 383; Morris, "'The Love of Thee – a Prism Be,'" pp. 98–113.

20. Dobson, *Dickinson and the Strategies of Reticence*, p. xvi.

21. H.D., *Tribute to Freud*, pp. 48–49.

22. Louise Bernikow, *Among Women*, p. 192. See also Mary K. DeShazer, *Inspiring Women: Reimagining the Muse*, esp. pp. 1–44.

23. Keller, *The Only Kangaroo*, p. 187, 26. See the first note of the "Preface" for his psychobiographical interpretation of gender hierarchies and their relation to Dickinson's poetic production.

24. As Heather Findlay recently pointed out, extenuations and complications of philosophical and psychoanalytic paradigms continue to privilege heterosexuality: "Derrida stresses that heterogeneity, the privileged mode of deconstructive theory, is not to be confused with or inhabited by homogeneity or sameness." See "Is There a Lesbian in This Text?" p. 59.

25. Howe, "Women and Their Effect in the Distance," esp. pp. 79–85.

26. Sandra M. Gilbert and Susan Gubar, *No Man's Land 2: Sexchanges*, pp. 215–257. The list I adduce does not pretend to be comprehensive, but serves to demonstrate the wide range of intense, primary relationships between women. See also Shari Benstock, *Women of the Left Bank: Paris, 1900–1940*.

27. Mudge, "Emily Dickinson and 'Sister Sue,'" pp. 90–108; for additional commentary on Sue's involvement with the printing of "A narrow Fellow" and the writing of "Safe in their Alabaster Chambers," see Thomas A. Davis, ed., *14 by Emily Dickinson with Selected Criticism*, pp. 19–30. Bowles's letters to Sue are discussed at the beginning of the next chapter.

28. For a different interpretation of this which alludes to the creation story in Genesis, see Paglia, *Sexual Personae*, pp. 671–672. Paglia believes that Dickinson's "homoerotic flirtations were integral to her masculine poetic identity." Also see "Like Some Old fashioned Miracle," which was sent to Sue and addressed "Combined Girl" (H B 178; P 302).

29. In her chapter "Susan Gilbert," Vivian Pollak concurs with Lillian Faderman, and I in turn obviously agree with them, that Dickinson's correspondence to Sue is markedly different from that to other women with whom she was good friends; see *Dickinson*, pp. 59–82. As we shall see in the next chapter, this

distinction characterizes the entire corpus of their correspondence, from the earliest missive to the latest.

30. Gary Scharnhorst, "A Glimpse of Dickinson at Work," *American Literature* 57 (October 1985): 192. When he disputes that "she wrote poetry only for the eye and never for the voice," he argues with David Porter, who claims that " . . . she could not have spoken these poems or anything like them. . . . Not in speech but only in writing could the Dickinson words wield power"; see *Dickinson*, p. 141. Manuscript review corroborates the account of "L.N.'s" letter. Many poems are drafted on wrapping paper, shopping bags, the backs of used envelopes, and other pieces of scrap paper, though, with the exception of some sent to Sue, when Dickinson sent her poems out to correspondents, she copied them onto formal stationery.

31. Derrida, *Of Grammatology.*

32. Paglia, *Sexual Personae*, p. 671.

33. Thomas H. Johnson, *Emily Dickinson: An Interpretive Biography*, p. 41; "Safe in their Alabaster Chambers" is discussed on pp. 106–108 and p. 117. Sue's poems are filled with clichéd religious metaphors. She describes lives blurred by sin and grief, and writes:

> What offering can I bring
> thee Lord
> To show I am thy child . . .

One poem was inspired by Job:

> —IRONY—
>
> A myth in velvet dust,
> Frail devotee of light
> So bent on idle quest!
> Waif of the Summer night;
> Tinted with Tyrian dyes,
> A hint of tropic heat—
> Faint in the morning's dawn,
> Thy silly life complete.
>
> O man of pride and boast,
> Is this the stronger host?
> Thou'rt "crushed before the moth."

(H BOX 9)

34. The signature on the letter beginning "Dear Sue – / The Supper was delicate and strange" (H B 66; L 1025) was "taken out to give to a begging friend" (see note on ms. and description in *FF* 269). This was a common practice; Thomas Higginson also had a "tendency to give away" Dickinson's "manuscript poems"

(*YH* 2:214), and in fact gave away "Before I got my eye put out" and "I cannot dance upon my Toes," the poems enclosed in the "All men say 'What' to me" letter (L 271, 1862).

35. Judy Jo Small, *Positive as Sound: Emily Dickinson's Rhyme*.

36. Paglia, *Sexual Personae*, pp. 670–671; Judith Farr's *The Passion of Emily Dickinson* is to be published by Harvard University Press; Paula Bennett makes a similar argument for autobiographical interpretation in "'The Orient is in the West': Emily Dickinson's Reading of *Antony and Cleopatra*," in *Women's Revisions of Shakespeare*, ed. Marianne Novy, pp. 108–122.

37. Though letters from Emily to Mabel that very possibly refer to Sue's attitudes toward the "other woman" may augment our understanding of Emily's protective feelings for Sue, the correspondence produced by the melodramatic love affair between Austin and Mabel had no bearing on Dickinson's literary production (see Wolff, *Emily Dickinson*, p. 6). Dickinson's letter to Mabel—"Why should we censure Othello, when the Criterion Lover says, 'Thou shalt have no other Gods before Me'?" (L 1016, late 1885)—could well be Emily defending the "*wife forgotten*" (L 93), Sue. Sue's bitterness toward Mabel, who appeared to be flaunting her affair with Austin by driving around Amherst with him, seems a little matter when one remembers Othello, who out of unfounded jealousy smothered Desdemona. Important for critical formulations is understanding how characterizations of Sue by Mabel and her daughter have profoundly influenced critical receptions of Emily and Sue's relationship.

38. In the last section of the following chapter I discuss more thoroughly how various selections of Dickinson's documents may be arranged to prove both her belief and disbelief in God and the afterlife.

39. See Sewall's commentary in "The Problem of the Biographer": "She can be known as a person not through what she *did* (excluding for the moment her poems and letters as forms of doing) so much as through her relationships with people, events, books, ideas—but mostly, being an intensely personal person, with people. Like Jamesian 'reflectors,' each relationship gives back a phase, or facet, of her character, her personality, and her literary purpose" (*Life* 1:12). Though Sewall has done a most impressive job of compiling and collating information and hearsay from accounts of people who knew or knew of Emily Dickinson, he seems well aware of the limits of constructing a "true" image of the poet through these and only purports to know more *about* her, not to know her thoroughly. I am perhaps even more skeptical than he of our ability to reconstruct accurate evaluations of her relationships.

40. Paul De Man, *The Resistance to Theory*, p. 29.

5. To Be Susan Is Imagination: Dickinson's Poetry Workshop

1. Mudge, "Emily Dickinson and 'Sister Sue'," p. 105; in an 1851 letter to Austin, Dickinson calls Sue "Twin *Susan*" (L 49).

2. See Franklin's notes on dating (ML 7–9): "Early in this period, almost without exception, Dickinson's form for *the* (lower case) consisted of two parts, a *t* separate from a linked *he*, but in 1861 she shifted to a form in which all three letters were linked. . . . The linked form is unknown before 1861. The earlier form appears occasionally thereafter, but the later one dominates, often accouting for more than ninety per cent of the instances." By his account, which plainly describes both inconsistencies and identifiable evolutions, readers can see how tricky it is to assign any document to a particular year solely on the basis of handwriting.

3. Carroll Smith-Rosenberg, *Disorderly Conduct*, pp. 53–76. A version of this chapter, "The Female World of Love and Ritual," originally appeared in *Signs: Journal of Women in Culture and Society* 1 (1975): 1–29. Pollak, *Dickinson*, p. 59.

4. See chapter 3 for discussion of "discourses of desire" and of Linda Kauffman's work in the field.

5. A letter to Austin sports similar wordplay: "Mary Warner and her friend Abbie Adams, made a call. . . . They had been *taking a walk*. I think any sentiment must be consecrated by an interview in the mud. There would be certainly, a correspondence in *depth*" (L 157, March 1854).

6. As my first chapter contends, the mutilations to Dickinson's writings were not only made in acts of editorial translation to produce what Barton St. Armand has called "user-friendly" poems for a late nineteenth-century audience, but most of the scissorings and erasures were made to excise affectionate references to Sue. St. Armand made the remark in a talk delivered at the Dickinson Homestead in October 1989, quoted by Jane Eberwein in "Amherst Conference: 'Emily Dickinson in Public,'" *EDIS Bulletin* 1 [1989]: 5. Loomis Todd also produced a "user-friendly" book on astronomy, *Total Eclipses of the Sun*, by rewriting her husband's work; see Oberhaus's "In Defense of Sue," p. 6, and *AB* 214. These popularizing productions are evidence that Loomis Todd was anxious to achieve publishing celebrity, as the fact of her privately printed *Foot Prints* (Amherst, 1883, before her involvement with the Dickinsons) appears to be.

7. In her excellent handling of the Emily-Sue relationship, Eberwein describes this letter as Dickinson's "bitterest." See *Dickinson*, p. 284 n.10.

8. Susan Stanford Friedman, "'I go where I love': An Intertextual Study of H.D. and Adrienne Rich," *Signs* 9 (Winter 1983): 228–245. Revisionary mythmaking is a strategy common to many women poets. See Ostriker's excellent discussion in "Thieves of Language: Women Poets and Revisionist Mythology," *Stealing the Language*, pp. 210–238; a version of this chapter originally appeared in *Signs* 8 (Autumn 1982): 68–90. For more discussion of sentimental love religion, see chapter 3, and for extensive analysis see St. Armand, *Emily Dickinson and Her Culture*.

9. Karl Keller, "Notes on Sleeping with Emily Dickinson," in *Feminist Critics Read Emily Dickinson*, ed. Juhasz, pp. 67–79.

10. Dickinson refers to Milton throughout her correspondence; perhaps her most famous poetic response to him is "Before I got my Eye put out –" (F 16; P 327), which alludes to *Samson Agonistes*.

11. Pollak, *Dickinson*, p. 74.

12. This and the following quotation are from Howe, "Women and Their Effect in the Distance," pp. 81–82.

13. Morris, "'The Love of Thee – a Prism Be,'" p. 99.

14. Eberwein discusses some aspects of these evolutions; see especially her chapter "'An Enlarged Ability for Missing': Artistic Exploitation of Limits," *Strategies of Limitation*, pp. 47–69.

15. Pollak, *Dickinson*, pp. 78, 74; Faderman, "Emily Dickinson's Letters to Susan Gilbert," pp. 219, 217. In *After Great Pain*, Cody, who asserts that Dickinson was crushed when she lost Susan to Austin, also calls attention to this significant silence. See "The Earl, the Malay, and the Pearl," pp. 185–258, esp. p. 249. Though Cody is writing about women well into their twenties, he calls them "girls" (see p. 244). Especially since it occurs in a book which recognizes Susan's power, but reads Dickinson's life as that of a never fully matured woman, this label bespeaks his judgmental attitude which sees Dickinson more as patient than poet, and in turn fosters a finally negative evaluation of her relationship with Sue.

16. The record of surviving documents suggests that between 1850 and 1855 Dickinson wrote Austin twice as often as she wrote Sue, while between 1858 and 1886 she wrote Sue one hundred and thirty-five times as many letters and poems as she sent to Austin (four hundred and five items to Sue, three to Austin). The number of her letters to him testifies to her strong, possibly even incestuous, feelings for Austin, which may in turn have contributed to her attraction to Sue. Conversely, Dickinson's attractions to Sue may have encouraged Austin to turn his attentions entirely to the younger Gilbert daughter (during this period he also wrote and flirted with Sue's older sister Martha). Readers interested in speculations about incestuous feelings among the Dickinsons should consult Cody, *After Great Pain*, and Norbert Hirschhorn, "A Bandaged Secret: Emily Dickinson and Incest," *Journal of Psychohistory* 18 (Winter 1991): 251–281.

17. John Evangelist Walsh, *The Hidden Life of Emily Dickinson*, p. 241; and Polly Longsworth, *Austin and Mabel: The Amherst Affair and Love Letters of Austin Dickinson and Mabel Loomis Todd*, pp. 67–124, esp. pp. 110–111. Among other things, Longsworth reminds us that it was Mabel who charged that Sue had "a morbid fear," an "unnatural, cowardly horror of having children." Sue was forty-five when she gave birth to Gilbert.

18. On Stowe's visit, see Pollak, *Dickinson*, p. 195.

19. Scholars are beginning to analyze the long overlooked significance of Dickinson's privileged economic and social status; see Betsy Erkkila, "Emily Dickinson and Class," *American Literary History* 4 (Spring 1992): 1–27. Erkkila's story of reading might be called a "romance of elitism" that serves to normalize Dickinson. See chapter 2, n8.

20. Paul Fussell mentions that John Hollander has spoken of "'the metrical contract' which every poet undertakes with his reader from the first few words of his poem." See Fussell's *Poetic Meter and Poetic Form*, p. 18. To formulate critique here, I draw on many of Fussell's analyses. The quotation below is from his book's first sentence.

21. Interestingly, though Johnson quotes this letter in his biography and connects it directly to the publication of "Safe in their Alabaster Chambers," he does not refer to it in the variorum or complete letters. See *Emily Dickinson*, p. 117. A note by Martha Dickinson Bianchi on the envelope housing Sue's missive says "after appearance of Snake in the Republican"; however, since Sue alludes to Ned's bibs, this most likely refers to the earlier publication of "Safe in their Alabaster Chambers," when he was a baby instead of to the publication of "A narrow Fellow" when he was five.

22. Dandurand maintains that the three poems Storrs published "were Dickinson's contribution to the war effort" and not, therefore, "robbed" of her. See "New Dickinson Civil War Publications," pp. 22–24. See also Dandurand's "Another Dickinson Poem Published in Her Lifetime," p. 437.

23. For a superb discussion of her poetics and concern with audience see Stonum, *The Dickinson Sublime*, esp. pp. 3–21 and pp. 110–187.

24. Readers of the variorum must be especially diligent to note that Johnson's descriptions only subtly distinguish between these different modes of address; he will describe a poem addressed only on the verso as "addressed 'Sue' and signed 'Emily'" (P 316n), while describing a letter-poem like that discussed above "It is headed, 'Dear Sue,'" (P 299n). Since all this information is described in notes but not visually represented in the printed forms, the distinctions may easily elude readers and become conflated with one another.

25. Perhaps like Yale's "alabaster chamber," the Beinecke Library.

26. Anderson, *Emily Dickinson's Poetry*, pp. 269–275. Anderson situates his interpretation of the poem in the context of encyclopedias and a book in the Dickinson family library by Felix Eberty, *The Stars and the Earth*, "written for the avowed purpose of reconciling the latest scientific theories with religious belief" (p. 271). Anderson's commentary on "Safe in their Alabaster Chambers" is reprinted in *14 by Emily Dickinson*, ed. David, pp. 26–30. Readers should consult the entire collection of critical commentary on the poem, pp. 19–30.

27. William Galperin, "Emily Dickinson's Marriage Hearse," *Denver Quarterly* 18 (1984): 62–73.

28. Barker, *Lunacy of Light*, p. 89.

29. This theme, likening marriage to death, is prevalent in many writings by women. The reader might consult Annis Pratt, *Archetypal Patterns in Women's Fiction*. Readers who assume little disjunction between the speaker of Dickinson's poems and the poet will want to consider whether the domestic alabaster chamber to which she refers is located on the west side of the Homestead. Bianchi described the Homestead parlor as something of an "alabaster chamber":

> The walls were hung with heavily gold-framed engravings: 'The Forester's Family,' 'The Stag at Bay,' 'Arctic Nights,' and other chastely cold subjects. The piano was an old-fashioned square in an elaborately carved mahogany case, and the carpet a fabulous Brussels, woven in a pattern. It had in the centre a great basket of flowers at the edge. It enjoyed a reputation of its own; and the day of my grandmother's funeral two old ladies came an hour ahead of the service 'to get a last look at the carpet before the mourners broke up the pattern.'
>
> The wallpaper was white with large figures. The white marble mantels and the marble-topped tables added a chill even on hot midsummer afternoons.

(*FF* 34)

30. Dickinson's familiarity with *Endymion* is well documented (see L 261, L 1034).

31. For discussion of the Eden poems, see Shurr, *The Marriage of Emily Dickinson*, pp. 18–23, Bennett, *Emily Dickinson*, and my second chapter. For discussion of the marriage poems, see Shurr, *The Marriage of Emily Dickinson*, pp. 12–16, 23–26, 32, 60, 80, 109, 133, 138–139, 174, and Bennett, *My Life a Loaded Gun*, pp. 72–90.

32. Gilbert and Gubar, *The Madwoman in the Attic*, p. 589.

33. See *YH* 1:283 and 291 for accounts of Edward Dickinson defending a reverend charged with violence against his wife. Whatever the truth of this matter, the fact that the case was an exception, the community's near hysteria over the trial, and accounts of women (the "Sewing Society") testifying against the wife show how little countenance was given to any analysis that the institution of patriarchal marriage itself may have been the root of the problem. In such a world, unwed mothers could be driven to suicide (*YH* 2:187).

34. Wolff, *Emily Dickinson*, p. 151. Contextualized by the popular literature Dickinson preferred, the poem is also a commentary on the writerly activities of readers. At the end of Henry Wadsworth Longfellow's *Kavanagh*, a Dickinson family favorite, and in answer to questions such as "And shall all these lofty aspirations [of his friend Mr. Churchill to write a romance] end in nothing? . . . ," these lines of poetry come to Kavanagh's mind:

> Stay, stay the present instant!
> Imprint the marks of wisdom on its wings!
> O, let it not elude thy grasp, but like
> The good old patriarch upon record,
> Hold the fleet angel fast until he bless thee!

Writing creates or "imprint[s]" the illusion that we "stay" the present instant in the "marks" made to record, interrogate, or comment upon lived events, emotions, experiences. In Longfellow's terms, the writer whom this opportunity does not elude is like Jacob, who, after wrestling with the angel all night, finally relaxed to be blessed by God's messenger, and demanded, "I will not let thee go, except thou bless me" (Gen. 32:26). To produce literature is, therefore, equivalent to receiving divine blessing. In this instance, reading Dickinson reading reveals how multilayered and complex are her allusions, characteristics of her literary art that are vital components of the creative exchange she anticipates with readers.

Dickinson refers to this biblical story not only in her famous poem, but also in two letters written within a couple of months of her death. In contrast to Longfellow, Dickinson revises the biblical account by altering the pronouns even as she pretends to quote precisely. In the first allusive "quotation," the angel speaks the line; in the second, Jacob utters it: "I will not let thee go, except I bless thee" (L 1035, L 1042). Important in the parable for literary production Dickinson makes from scripture is not whether the angel or Jacob represents the reader or author nor which one speaks, but that they both do. In her terms, then, and in continuing juxtaposition to Longfellow, not only does the author become a reader as soon as she begins to write, but the reader becomes a writer as soon as she begins to read. Challenging nineteenth-century presuppositions about what literature is and the receptions that would compare a text to an art object (a poem to an urn), Dickinson compares writing and reading to contact sports.

35. A photographic reproduction of this letter appears in Polly Longsworth, *The World of Emily Dickinson*, p. 71. There one can see that the second scissoring of this letter goes up and around the word "When" in the next to last line and that only one square bit of the document has been removed. Also see Walker, *The Nightingale's Burden*, p. 90, for discussion of the nightingale imagery in this letter.

36. Keller, *The Only Kangaroo*, pp. 187–191. As has already been noted in chapter 4, Keller was ambivalent toward Dickinson's relationship with Sue and concluded that she "found herself stimulated [by Sue] . . . but struggling to transcend the limits Sue represented" (p. 187).

37. As we saw in chapter 1, studies like D'Emilio and Freedman's *Intimate Matters*, Gay's *Education of the Senses*, and Lystra's *Searching the Heart* amply document the fact that sexual practices were quite different from the period's chaste rhetoric.

38. Anderson, *Stairway of Surprise*, pp. 269–275.

39. When fighting either for freedom or to control aggression, the leaders of the United States have never concerned themselves with systemic abuses of women. A contemporary example is our defense of Saudi Arabia, where women are not allowed to drive a car and must wear veils in public. That Dickinson was sometimes piqued over the pervasive subordination of women is obvious from her frequent comments and queries. In one she complains about both the public and private consequences of her confining disenfranchisement: "Why cant *I* be a

Delegate to the great Whig Convention? – dont I know all about Daniel Webster, and the Tariff, and the Law? Then, Susie I could see you, during a pause in the session – but I don't like this country at all, and I shant stay here any longer! 'Delenda est' America, Massachusetts and all!" (H L 2; L 94, 1852).

40. William Howard, "Dickinson's 'Safe in their Alabaster Chambers,'" in *14 by Emily Dickinson*, ed. David, pp. 23–24. See also his "Emily Dickinson's Poetic Vocabulary," *PMLA* 72 (March 1957): 236–238.

41. Robert Frost, "Education by Poetry," *Robert Frost: Poetry and Prose*, ed. Edward Connery Lathem and Lawrance Thompson, pp. 329–340. Frost's "After Apple Picking" powerfully explores this proposition. Theories about thinking and metaphor are myriad, far too many to mention here. Readers might consult Sheldon Sacks, ed., *On Metaphor*; George Lakoff and Mark Johnson, *Metaphors We Live By*; George Lakoff and Mark Turner, *More Than Cool Reason: A Field Guide to Poetic Metaphor*.

42. Pollak, *Dickinson*, p. 82 n.19.

43. Johnson, *Emily Dickinson*, p. 43.

44. Hart, "The Encoding of Homoerotic Desire," pp. 252, 264. Bennett's argument is in *My Life a Loaded Gun*, pp. 90–91. Dickinson's mingling of genres is discussed above in chapters 2 and 3. Examples abound showing that editors have arbitrarily made poems; see "Silence is all we dread," a poem extrapolated by Johnson which, "arranged as prose, conclude[s] a letter" (H B 123; P 1251n; L 397, autumn 1873).

6. *Fame Is a Fickle Food: "Sister Sue" as Producer of Poems*

1. Oberhaus, "In Defense of Sue," *Dickinson Studies* 48 (1983): 6.

2. Three-quarters of a century later, Adrienne Rich picks up the analysis Susan renders in her obituary in "I am in Danger – Sir –," *Necessities of Life*. See also "Vesuvius at Home."

3. Loomis Todd, Bingham, and subsequent biographers and critics too often conflate the personalities of Susan and Martha. What has not received much critical attention is the fact that mother scolded daughter for her arrogance. For example, when Martha proposed to come home from school because she was not as well liked as she wanted to be, Susan wrote: "Some of your trials with the girls come from your rash speaking I have no doubt, and much as I deplore it, bitter as the lesson is for your dear self if it is a salutary one, it may prove the best experience of your life—There can be no turning back—You must make the most of each day instead of living perpetually in the dread of the next thirteen weeks. You would be covered with shame to leave in a sort of disgrace" (*YH* 2:438).

4. Thomas Wentworth Higginson and Henry Walcott Boynton, *A Reader's History of American Literature*, pp. 125–131. Higginson reproduced a facsimile of his copy of "Safe in their Alabaster Chambers" but offered no critical reason for doing so.

5. Upon hearing Dickinson described as "a lady whom people call the *Myth*," Loomis Todd wrote her parents, "Isn't that like a book? So interesting" (*YH* 2:357).

6. Carol Shields, *Swann*, pp. 269, 26. This novel also renders a lucid, exciting critique of the misguided reverence (in search of originary moments) for manuscripts discussed in my preface and chapter 2; see ibid., pp. 192, 310–313.

7. For brief reference to this, see Patterson, *Emily Dickinson's Imagery*, p. 167. For a more exhaustive analysis of the Gunderode-von Armin relationship, see Elke Fredericksen and Monika Shafi, "'Sich im Unbekannten suchen gehen': Bettina von Arnims 'Die Gunderode' als weibliche Utopie," *Frauenspache— Frauenliteratur?: Fur und Wider einer Psychoanalyse literarischer Werke*, pp. 54–61.

8. In *Comic Power*, coauthored with Juhasz and Miller, I interrogate Dickinson's "cartooning" at length.

9. McGann, *A Critique of Modern Textual Criticism*, p. 47.

10. Jauss, "Literary History as a Challenge to Literary Theory," p. 21.

Bibliography

Anderson, Charles. *Emily Dickinson's Poetry: Stairway of Surprise*. New York: Holt, Rinehart & Winston, 1960.

Arac, Jonathan. *Critical Genealogies: Historical Situations for Postmodern Literary Studies*. New York: Columbia Univ. Press, 1989.

Auerbach, Jonathan. *The Romance of Failure: Poe, Hawthorne, & James*. New York and Oxford: Oxford Univ. Press, 1989.

Bakhtin, M. M. *The Dialogic Imagination*. Ed. Michael Holquist. Trans. Caryl Emerson. Austin: Univ. of Texas Press, 1981.

Barker, Wendy. *Lunacy of Light: Emily Dickinson and the Experience of Metaphor*. Carbondale: Southern Illinois Univ. Press, 1987.

Barnstone, Willis. *The Poetic of Ecstasy: Varieties of Ekstasis from Sappho to Borges*. New York and London: Holmes and Meir, 1983.

Barthes, Roland. *Image—Music—Text*. Trans. Stephen Heath. New York: Hill & Wang, 1977.

———. *A Lover's Discourse: Fragments*. Trans. Richard Howard. New York: Hill & Wang, 1978.

———. *The Pleasure of the Text*. Trans. Richard Miller. New York: Hill & Wang, 1975.

———. *S/Z*. Trans. Richard Miller. New York: Farrar, Straus and Giroux, Noonday Press, 1974.

Baym, Nina. "Melodramas of Beset Manhood: How Theories of American Fiction Exclude Women Writers." *American Quarterly* 33 (1981): 123–139.

Benjamin, Walter. "The Work of Art in the Age of Mechanical Reproduction." *Illuminations*. Trans. Harry Zohn. Ed. Hannah Arendt. New York: Harcourt Brace Jovanovich, 1968.

Bennett, Paula. *Emily Dickinson: Woman Poet*. Iowa City: Univ. of Iowa Press, 1991.

———. "The Language of Love: Emily Dickinson's Homoerotic Poetry." *Gai Saber* 1, no. 1 (1977): 13–17.

———. *My Life a Loaded Gun: Female Creativity and Feminist Poetics*. Boston: Beacon Press, 1986.

———. "'The Orient is in the West': Emily Dickinson's Reading of *Antony and*

Cleopatra." In *Women's Revisions of Shakespeare.* Ed. Marianne Novy, pp. 108–122. Urbana and Chicago: Univ. of Illinois Press, 1990.

———. "'The Pea That Duty Locks': Lesbian and Feminist-Heterosexual Readings of Emily Dickinson's Poetry." In *Lesbian Texts and Contexts: Radical Revisions.* Ed. Karla Jay and Joanne Glasgow. New York and London: New York Univ. Press, 1990.

Benstock, Shari, ed. *The Private Self: Theory and Practice of Women's Autobiographical Writings.* Chapel Hill and London: Univ. of North Carolina Press, 1988.

———. *Women of the Left Bank: Paris, 1900–1940.* Austin and London: Univ. of Texas Press, 1986.

Bernikow, Louise. *Among Women.* New York: Harper & Row, 1980.

Bianchi, Martha Dickinson. *Emily Dickinson Face to Face: Unpublished Letters with Notes and Reminiscences.* Boston: Houghton Mifflin, 1932.

———. *The Life and Letters of Emily Dickinson.* Boston: Houghton Mifflin, 1924.

———. *The Single Hound.* Boston: S. J. Parkhill, 1914.

Bingham, Millicent Todd. *Ancestors' Brocades: The Literary Debut of Emily Dickinson.* New York: Harper & Brothers, 1945.

———. *Emily Dickinson: A Revelation.* New York: Harper & Brothers, 1954.

———. *Emily Dickinson's Home: Letters of Edward Dickinson and His Family.* New York: Harper & Brothers, 1955.

Bishop, Elizabeth. "Unseemly Deductions." Review of *The Riddle of Emily Dickinson* by Rebecca Patterson. *New Republic* 127 (August 18, 1952): 20.

Bishop, Nadean. "Renunciation in the Bridal Poems of Emily Dickinson." Paper presented at the National Women's Studies Association Conference, Bloomington, Indiana, May 16–20, 1980.

Blackmur, R. P. "Emily Dickinson: Notes on Prejudice and Fact." In *The Recognition of Emily Dickinson.* Ed. Caesar R. Blake and Carlton F. Wells, pp. 201–223. Ann Arbor: Univ. of Michigan Press, 1964.

———. "Emily Dickinson's Notation." In *Emily Dickinson: A Collection of Critical Essays.* Ed. Richard B. Sewall, pp. 78–87. Englewood Cliffs, N.J.: Prentice-Hall, 1963.

Bleich, David. *Subjective Criticism.* Baltimore and London: Johns Hopkins Univ. Press, 1978.

Bleier, Ruth. *Science and Gender: A Critique of Biology and Its Theories on Women.* New York: Pergamon, 1984.

Bloom, Harold, ed. *Emily Dickinson: Modern Critical Views.* New York: Chelsea House, 1985.

Blotner, Joseph, and Frederick L. Gwynn, eds. *Faulkner in the University.* 1959. Reprint. New York: Random House, 1965.

Brodzki, Bella, and Celeste Schenck, eds. *Life/Lines: Theorizing Women's Autobiography.* Ithaca and London: Cornell Univ. Press, 1988.

Broumas, Olga. *Beginning with O.* Yale Series of Younger Poets, vol. 72. New Haven and London: Yale Univ. Press, 1977.

Buckingham, Willis J. *Emily Dickinson's Reception in the 1890s: A Documentary History*. Pittsburgh and London: Univ. of Pittsburgh Press, 1989.

Cameron, Sharon. *Lyric Time: Dickinson and the Limits of Genre*. Baltimore and London: Johns Hopkins Univ. Press, 1979.

Cary, Alice, and Phoebe Cary. *The Poetical Works of Alice and Phoebe Cary*. Boston: Houghton, Mifflin, 1882.

Cather, Willa. *Alexander's Bridge*. 1912. Reprint. Lincoln and London: Univ. of Nebraska Press, 1977.

Chase, Richard. *Emily Dickinson*. New York: William Sloan, 1951.

Cody, John. *After Great Pain: The Inner Life of Emily Dickinson*. Cambridge, Mass.: Harvard Univ. Press, Belknap Press, 1971.

Culler, Jonathan. *On Deconstruction: Theory and Criticism after Structuralism*. Ithaca: Cornell Univ. Press, 1982.

Dandurand, Karen. "Another Dickinson Poem Published in Her Lifetime." *American Literature* 54 (1982): 434–437.

———. "New Dickinson Civil War Publications." *American Literature* 56 (1984): 17–27.

David, Thomas A., ed. *14 by Emily Dickinson with Selected Criticism*. Chicago: Scott, Foresman, 1964.

Davidson, Cathy. *Revolution and the Word: The Rise of the Novel in America*. New York and Oxford: Oxford Univ. Press, 1986.

DeJean, Joan. *Fictions of Sappho 1546–1937*. Chicago and London: Univ. of Chicago Press, 1989.

De Man, Paul. *The Resistance to Theory*. Minneapolis: Univ. of Minnesota Press, 1986.

D'Emilio, John, and Estelle B. Freedman. *Intimate Matters: A History of Sexuality in America*. New York: Harper & Row, 1988.

Derrida, Jacques. *Of Grammatology*. Trans. by Gayatri Chakravorty Spivak. Baltimore and London: Johns Hopkins Univ. Press, 1974.

———. "The Purveyor of Truth," *Yale French Studies* 52 (1975): 31–113.

DeShazer, Mary K. *Inspiring Women: Reimagining the Muse*. New York: Pergamon, 1986.

Dickie, Margaret. *Lyric Contingencies: Emily Dickinson and Wallace Stevens*. Philadelphia: Univ. of Pennsylvania Press, 1991.

Dickinson, Emily Elizabeth. Dickinson Papers. Amherst College Library Special Collections, Amherst, Mass.

———. Dickinson Papers. Houghton Library, Harvard University, Cambridge, Mass.

———. *Letters of Emily Dickinson*. Ed. Mabel Loomis Todd. New York: Harper Brothers, 1894.

Dickinson, Susan Huntington Gilbert. "Annals of the Evergreens." Box 9. Dickinson Papers. Houghton Library, Harvard University, Cambridge, Mass.

Diehl, Joanne Feit. *Dickinson and the Romantic Imagination*. Princeton: Princeton Univ. Press, 1981.

Doane, Janice, and Devon Hodges. *Nostalgia and Sexual Difference: The Resistance to Contemporary Feminism*. New York and London: Methuen, 1987.

Dobson, Joanne. *Dickinson and the Strategies of Reticence: The Woman Writer in Nineteenth-Century America*. Bloomington and Indianapolis: Indiana Univ. Press, 1989.

Dobson, Silvia. "Woof and Heave and Surge and Wave and Flow." *H. D.: Woman and Poet*. Orono: National Poetry Foundation, University of Maine at Orono, 1986.

DuPlessis, Rachel Blau. *H.D.: The Career of That Struggle*. Bloomington and Indianapolis: Indiana Univ. Press, 1986.

———. *The Pink Guitar: Writing as Feminist Practice*. New York and London: Routledge, 1990.

———. *Writing Beyond the Ending: Narrative Strategies of Twentieth-Century Women Writers*. Bloomington: Indiana Univ. Press, 1985.

Eberwein, Jane. "Amherst Conference: 'Emily Dickinson in Public.'" *EDIS Bulletin* 1 [1989]: 5.

———. *Dickinson: Strategies of Limitation*. Amherst: Univ. of Massachusetts Press, 1985.

Eco, Umberto. *The Role of the Reader: Explorations in the Semiotics of Texts*. Bloomington: Indiana Univ. Press, 1979.

Emerson, Ralph Waldo. *Emerson in His Journals*. Ed. Joel Porte. Cambridge, Mass: Harvard Univ. Press, Belknap Press, 1982.

Erkkila, Betsy. "Emily Dickinson and Class." *American Literary History* 4 (Spring 1992).

Faderman, Lillian. "Emily Dickinson's Homoerotic Poetry." *Higginson Journal* 18 (1978): 19–27.

———. "Emily Dickinson's Letters to Sue Gilbert." *Massachusetts Review* 18 (Summer 1977): 197–225.

———. *Surpassing the Love of Men: Romantic Friendship and Love between Women from the Renaissance to the Present*. New York: William Morrow, 1981.

Farwell, Marilyn. "Toward a Definition of the Lesbian Literary Imagination." *Signs* 14 (Autumn 1988): 100–118.

Farr, Judith. "Emily Dickinson's 'Engulfing' Play: *Antony and Cleopatra*." *Tulsa Studies in Women's Literature* 9, no. 2 (Fall 1990): 231–250.

Fetterley, Judith. *The Resisting Reader: A Feminist Approach to American Fiction*. Bloomington: Indiana Univ. Press, 1978.

Finch, A. R. C. "Dickinson and Patriarchal Meter: A Theory of Metrical Codes," *PMLA* 102 (1987): 166–176.

Findlay, Heather. "Is There a Lesbian in This Text? Derrida, Wittig, and the Politics of the Three Women." In *Coming to Terms: Feminism, Theory, Politics*. Ed. Elizabeth Weed, pp. 59–69. New York and London: Routledge, 1989.

Fish, Stanley. *Is There a Text in This Class? The Authority of Interpretive Communities*. Cambridge, Mass.: Harvard Univ. Press, 1980.

Flynn, Elizabeth, and Patrocinio P. Schweickart, eds. *Gender and Reading: Essays on*

Readers, Texts, and Contexts. Baltimore and London: Johns Hopkins Univ. Press, 1986.

Foucault, Michel. *The Archaeology of Knowledge*. New York: Random House, 1969.

———. *The History of Sexuality*. 2 vols. Trans. Robert Hurley. New York: Random House, 1980.

———. *The Order of Things: An Archaeology of the Human Sciences*. New York: Random House, 1966. Originally published as *Les mots et les choses*.

Fraistat, Neil. *The Poem and the Book: Interpreting Collections of Romantic Poetry*. Chapel Hill and London: Univ. of North Carolina Press, 1985.

———, ed. *Poems in Their Place: The Intertextuality and Order of Poetic Collections*. Chapel Hill and London: Univ. of North Carolina Press, 1986.

Franklin, R. W. *The Editing of Emily Dickinson: A Reconsideration*. Madison: University of Wisconsin Press, 1967.

———. "The Emily Dickinson Fascicles." *Studies in Bibliography* 36 (1983): 1–20.

———. "Three Additional Manuscripts." *American Literature* 50 (1978): 113–116.

———, ed. *The Manuscript Books of Emily Dickinson*. Cambridge, Mass: Harvard Univ. Press, Belknap Press, 1980.

———, ed. *The Master Letters of Emily Dickinson*. Amherst, Mass.: Amherst College Press, 1986.

Fredericksen, Elke, and Monika Shafi. "'Sich im Unbekannten suchen gehen': Bettina von Arnims 'Die Gunderode' als weibliche Utopie." *Frauenspache— Frauenliteratur? Fur und Wider einer Psychoanalyse literarischer Werke*, pp. 54–61. Tubingen: Max Niemeyer Verlag, 1986.

Freedman, Estelle B., Barbara C. Gelpi, Susan L. Johnson, and Kathleen M. Weston, eds. *The Lesbian Issue: Essays from SIGNS*. Chicago: Univ. of Chicago Press, 1985.

Friedman, Susan Stanford. "'I go where I love': An Intertextual Study of H. D. and Adrienne Rich." *Signs* 9 (Winter 1983): 228–245.

———. *Psyche Reborn: The Emergence of H. D.* Bloomington: Indiana Univ. Press, 1981.

———. "Women's Autobiographical Selves: Theory and Practice." In *The Private Self: Theory and Practice of Women's Autobiographical Writings*, ed. Shari Benstock, pp. 34–62. Chapel Hill and London: Univ. of North Carolina Press, 1988.

Friedman, Susan Stanford, and Rachel Blau DuPlessis, "'I had two loves separate': The Sexualities of H.D.'s *HER*." In *Signets: Reading H.D.*. Eds. Susan Stanford Friedman and Rachel Blau DuPlessis, pp. 205–232. Madison and London: Univ. of Wisconsin Press, 1990.

Frost, Robert. *Robert Frost: Poetry and Prose*. Eds. Edward Connery Lathem and Lawrance Thompson. New York: Holt, Rinehart and Winston, 1972.

Fussell, Paul. *Poetic Meter and Poetic Form*. New York: Random House, 1965.

Galperin, William. "Emily Dickinson's Marriage Hearse." *Denver Quarterly* 18 (1984): 62–73.

Gay, Peter. *Education of the Senses*. Vol. 1 of *The Bourgeois Experience: Victoria to Freud*. New York and Oxford: Oxford Univ. Press, 1984.

Gilbert, Sandra. "The Wayward Nun beneath the Hill: Emily Dickinson and the Mysteries of Womanhood." In *Feminist Critics Read Emily Dickinson*. Ed. Suzanne Juhasz, pp. 22–44. Bloomington: Indiana Univ. Press, 1983.

———, and Susan Dreyfuss David Gubar. "Ceremonies of the Alphabet: Female Grandmatologies and the Female Authorgraph." In *The Female Autograph: Theory and Practice of Autobiography from the Tenth to the Twentieth Century*. Ed. Domna C. Stanton, pp. 21–48. Chicago and London: Univ. of Chicago Press, 1987.

———. *The Madwoman in the Attic: The Woman Writer and the Nineteenth-Century Literary Imagination*. New Haven and London: Yale Univ. Press, 1979.

———. *No Man's Land 2: Sexchanges*. New Haven and London: Yale Univ. Press, 1989.

———, eds. "Emily Dickinson." *The Norton Anthology of Literature by Women*, Ed. Sandra M. Gilbert and Susan Gubar, pp. 839–872. New York: W. W. Norton, 1985.

Grahn, Judy. "A Heart-Shaped Journey to a Similar Place." *The Highest Apple: Sappho and the Lesbian Poetic Tradition*. San Francisco: Spinsters, Ink, 1985.

"Great American Writers: Emily Dickinson." Second in a series of symposia, held October 9, 1988, with participants Amy Clampitt, John Hollander, Susan Stewart, and moderator Susan Sontag. *PEN Newsletter* 68 (May 1989): 3–14.

Griffith, Clark. *The Long Shadow: Emily Dickinson's Tragic Poetry*. Princeton: Princeton Univ. Press, 1964.

Guides at the Dickinson Homestead. *Profile of Emily Dickinson as Cook*. Amherst, Mass.: Hamilton I. Newell, 1976.

Harris, Julie. *Emily Dickinson—A Self-Portrait*. New York: Caedmon Records, 1968.

Hart, Ellen Louise. "The Encoding of Homoerotic Desire: Emily Dickinson's Letters and Poems to Susan Dickinson, 1850–1886." *Tulsa Studies in Women's Literature* 9, no. 2 (Fall 1990): 251–272.

H.D. [Hilda Doolittle]. *Tribute to Freud*. New York: McGraw-Hill, 1956.

Helsinger, Elizabeth K., Robin Lauterbach Sheets, and William Veeder. *The Woman Question*. 3 vols. Chicago and London: Univ. of Chicago Press, 1983.

Henderson, Mae Gwendolyn. "Speaking in Tongues." *Changing Our Own Words: Essays on Criticism, Theory, and Writing*. Ed. Cheryl A. Wall, pp. 16–37. New Brunswick and London: Rutgers Univ. Press, 1989.

Higgins, David. *Portrait of Emily Dickinson: The Poet and Her Prose*. New Brunswick, N.J.: Rutgers Univ. Press, 1967.

Higginson, Thomas Wentworth. "An Open Portfolio." In *The Recognition of Emily Dickinson*. Ed. Caesar R. Blake and Carlton F. Wells, pp. 3–10. Ann Arbor: Univ. of Michigan Press, 1964. First published in *Christian Union* 42 (September 25, 1890): 392–393.

———. *Women and the Alphabet*. Boston: Houghton Mifflin, 1881.

————, and Henry Walcott Boynton. *A Reader's History of American Literature*. Boston: Houghton Mifflin, 1903.

Hirschhorn, Norbert. "A Bandaged Secret: Emily Dickinson and Incest." *Journal of Psychohistory* 18 (Winter 1991): 251–281.

Homans, Margaret. "'Oh, Vision of Language!': Dickinson's Poems of Love and Death." In *Feminist Critics Read Emily Dickinson*. Ed. Suzanne Juhasz, pp. 114–133. Bloomington: Indiana Univ. Press, 1983.

————. *Women Writers and Poetic Identity: Dorothy Wordsworth, Emily Bronte, and Emily Dickinson*. Princeton: Princeton Univ. Press, 1980.

Howard, William. "Dickinson's 'Safe in their Alabaster Chambers.'" In *14 by Emily Dickinson with Selected Criticism*. Ed. Thomas A. David, pp. 23–24. Chicago: Scott, Foresman, 1964.

————. "Emily Dickinson's Poetic Vocabulary." *PMLA* 72 (March 1957): 236–238.

Howe, Susan. *My Emily Dickinson*. Berkeley: North Atlantic Books, 1985.

————. "Some Notes on Visual Intentionality in Emily Dickinson." *HOW(ever)* 3, no. 4 (1986): 11–13.

————. "These Flames and Generosities of the Heart: Emily Dickinson and the Illogic of Sumptuary Values," *Sulfur* 28 (Spring 1991): 134–155.

————. "Women and Their Effect in the Distance." *Ironwood* 28 (1986): 58–91.

Iser, Wolfgang. *The Act of Reading: A Theory of Aesthetic Response*. Baltimore and London: Johns Hopkins Univ. Press, 1978.

Jauss, Hans Robert. "Literary History as a Challenge to Literary Theory." *Toward an Aesthetic of Reception*. Trans. Timothy Bahti. Minneapolis: Univ. of Minnesota Press, 1982.

————. *Question and Answer: Forms of Dialogic Understanding*. Ed. and trans. Michael Hays. Minneapolis: Univ. of Minnesota Press, 1989.

Jehlen, Myra. *American Incarnation: The Individual, The Nation, and The Continent*. Cambridge and London: Harvard Univ. Press, 1986.

Johnson, Thomas H. *Emily Dickinson: An Interpretive Biography*. Cambridge, Mass.: Harvard Univ. Press, Belknap Press, 1966.

————. "Establishing a Text: The Emily Dickinson Papers." *Studies in Bibliography* 5 (1952–1953): 31–32.

————, ed. *The Poems of Emily Dickinson*. Cambridge, Mass.: Harvard Univ. Press, Belknap Press, 1955.

————, and Theodora Ward, eds. *The Letters of Emily Dickinson*. Cambridge, Mass.: Harvard Univ. Press, Belknap Press, 1958.

Juhasz, Suzanne. "Reading Emily Dickinson's Letters." *ESQ: Journal of the American Renaissance* 30 (1984): 170–192.

————. *"The Undiscovered Continent": Emily Dickinson and the Space of the Mind*. Bloomington: Indiana Univ. Press, 1983.

————, Cristanne Miller, and Martha Nell Smith. *Comic Power in Emily Dickinson*. Austin: Univ. of Texas Press, 1993.

————, ed. *Feminist Critics Read Emily Dickinson*. Bloomington: Indiana Univ. Press, 1983.

Kamuf, Peggy. *Signature Pieces: On the Institution of Authorship*. Ithaca and London: Cornell Univ. Press, 1988.

Kauffman, Linda. *Discourses of Desire: Gender, Genre, and Epistolary Fictions*. Ithaca and London: Cornell Univ. Press, 1986.

Keller, Karl. "Notes on Sleeping with Emily Dickinson." In *Feminist Critics Read Emily Dickinson*. Ed. Suzanne Juhasz, pp. 67–79. Bloomington: Indiana Univ. Press, 1983.

———. *The Only Kangaroo among the Beauty: Emily Dickinson and America*. Baltimore and London: Johns Hopkins Univ. Press, 1979.

Kolodny, Annette. *The Land Before Her: Fantasy and Experience of the American Frontiers, 1630–1860*. Chapel Hill and London: Univ. of North Carolina Press, 1984.

———. *The Lay of the Land: Metaphor as Experience and History in American Life and Letters*. Chapel Hill: Univ. of North Carolina Press, 1975.

Lakoff, George, and Mark Johnson. *Metaphors We Live By*. Chicago and London: Univ. of Chicago Press, 1980.

———, and Mark Turner. *More Than Cool Reason: A Field Guide to Poetic Metaphor*. Chicago and London: Univ. of Chicago Press, 1988.

Langton, Jane. *Emily Dickinson Is Dead*. New York: St. Martin's, 1984.

Lease, Benjamin. *Emily Dickinson's Readings of Men and Books: Sacred Soundings*. New York: St. Martin's Press, 1990.

Lemay, J. A. Leo, and P. M. Zall, eds. *Benjamin Franklin's Autobiography*. New York and London: W. W. Norton, 1986.

Lerner, Gerda. *The Creation of Patriarchy*. New York and Oxford: Oxford Univ. Press, 1986.

Leverenz, David. "The Politics of Emerson's Man-Making Words." In *Speaking of Gender*. Ed. Elaine Showalter, pp. 134–162. New York and London: Routledge, Chapman & Hall, 1989.

Leyda, Jay. *The Years and Hours of Emily Dickinson*. New Haven and London: Yale Univ. Press, 1960.

Lindemann, Marilee. "Women Writers and the American Romance: Studies in Jewett and Cather." Ph.D. diss., Rutgers Univ., 1991.

Linscott, Robert N., ed. *Selected Poems and Letters of Emily Dickinson*. Garden City, N.Y.: Doubleday & Co., 1959.

Longsworth, Polly. *Austin and Mabel: The Amherst Affair and Love Letters of Austin Dickinson and Mabel Loomis Todd*. New York: Holt, Rinehart, Winston, 1984.

———. *The World of Emily Dickinson*. New York: W. W. Norton, 1990.

———. "'Was Mr. Dudley Dear?': Emily Dickinson and John Langdon Dudley." *Massachusetts Review* 26 (1985): 360–372.

Loving, Jerome. *Emily Dickinson: The Poet on the Second Story*. New York: Cambridge Univ. Press, 1986.

Lowenberg, Carlton. *Emily Dickinson's Textbooks*. Ed. Territa A. Lowenberg and Carla L. Brown. Berkeley, Calif.: West Coast Print Center, 1986.

Luce, William. *The Belle of Amherst*. Boston: Houghton Mifflin, 1976.

Lukacs, Georg. *The Theory of the Novel: A Historico-philosophical Essay on the Form of Great Epic Literature*. Trans. Anna Bostock. Cambridge, Mass.: MIT Press, 1971.

Lystra, Karen. *Searching the Heart: Women, Men, and Romantic Love in Nineteenth-Century America*. New York: Oxford Univ. Press, 1989.

Martin, Biddy. "Lesbian Identity and Autobiographical Difference[s]." In *Life/Lines: Theorizing Women's Autobiography*. Ed. Bella Brodzki and Celeste Schenck, pp. 77–103. Ithaca and London: Cornell Univ. Press, 1988.

Martin, Wendy. *An American Triptych: Anne Bradstreet, Emily Dickinson, Adrienne Rich*. Chapel Hill and London: Univ. of North Carolina Press, 1984.

McGann, Jerome. *A Critique of Modern Textual Criticism*. Chicago and London: Univ. of Chicago Press, 1983.

———. *Social Values and Poetic Acts: The Historical Judgment of Literary Work*. Cambridge, Mass. and London: Harvard Univ. Press, 1988.

McIntosh, Peggy, and Ellen Louise Hart. "Emily Dickinson." *Heath Anthology of American Literature*. Ed. Paul Lauter, 1:2838–2921. Lexington, Mass. and Toronto: D. C. Heath & Co., 1990.

Miller, Cristanne. *Emily Dickinson: A Poet's Grammar*. Cambridge, Mass., and London: Harvard Univ. Press, 1987.

———. "'A Letter is a Joy of Earth': Dickinson's Communication with the World." *Legacy* 3 (Spring 1986): 29–39.

Miller, Nancy K. "Changing the Subject: Authorship, Writing, and the Reader." In *Feminist Studies/Critical Studies*. Ed. Teresa de Lauretis, pp. 102–120. Bloomington: Indiana Univ. Press, 1986.

———. "The Text's Heroine: A Feminist Critic and Her Fictions." *Diacritics* 12 (Summer 1982): 53.

Miller, Ruth. *Emily Dickinson*. Middletown, Conn.: Wesleyan Univ. Press, 1968.

Modleski, Tania. "Feminism and the Power of Interpretation: Some Critical Readings." In *Feminist Studies/Critical Studies*. Ed. Teresa de Lauretis, pp. 121–138. Bloomington: Indiana Univ. Press, 1986.

Moore, Marianne. *The Complete Poems of Marianne Moore*. New York: Macmillan/Viking Press, 1967.

Morris, Adalaide. "'The Love of Thee – a Prism Be': Men and Women in the Love Poetry of Emily Dickinson." In *Feminist Critics Read Emily Dickinson*. Ed. Suzanne Juhasz, pp. 98–113. Bloomington: Indiana Univ. Press, 1983.

———. "Two Sisters Have I: Emily Dickinson's Vinnie and Susan." *Massachusetts Review* 22 (1981): 323–332.

Mudge, Jean McClure. "Emily Dickinson and 'Sister Sue.'" *Prairie Schooner* 52 (Spring 1977): 90–108.

Nye, Andrea. "Woman Clothed with the Sun: Julia Kristeva and the Escape from/to Language." *Signs* 12 (1987): 664–686.

Oberhaus, Dorothy Huff. "In Defense of Sue." *Dickinson Studies* 48 (1983): 1–25.

Olsen, Tillie. *Silences.* New York: Delacorte, 1978.

Ostriker, Alicia. *Stealing the Language: The Emergence of Women's Poetry in America.* Boston: Beacon Press, 1986.

Paglia, Camille. *Sexual Personae: Art and Decadence from Nefertiti to Emily Dickinson.* London and New Haven: Yale Univ. Press, 1990.

Patterson, Annabel. "Intention." In *Critical Terms for Literary Study.* Ed. Frank Lentricchia and Thomas McLaughlin, pp. 135–146. Chicago and London: Univ. of Chicago Press, 1990.

Patterson, Rebecca. *Emily Dickinson's Imagery.* Ed. Margaret Freeman. Amherst: Univ. of Massachusetts Press, 1979.

———. *The Riddle of Emily Dickinson.* Boston: Houghton Mifflin, 1951.

Perloff, Marjorie. "The Two *Ariel*s: The (Re)Making of the Sylvia Plath Canon." In *Poems in Their Place: The Intertextuality and Order of Poetic Collections.* Ed. Neil Fraistat, pp. 308–333. Chapel Hill and London: Univ. of North Carolina Press, 1986.

Perrine, Laurence. "Emily's Beloved Friend," *Southwest Review* 37 (Winter 1952): 81–83.

Poirier, Richard. *The Renewal of Literature: Emersonian Reflections.* New York: Random House, 1987.

Pollak, Vivian. *Dickinson: The Anxiety of Gender.* Ithaca and London: Cornell Univ. Press, 1984.

———, ed. *A Poet's Parents: The Courtship Letters of Emily Norcross and Edward Dickinson.* Chapel Hill and London: Univ. of North Carolina Press, 1988.

Porter, David. *Dickinson: The Modern Idiom.* Cambridge, Mass. and London: Harvard Univ. Press, 1981.

Pratt, Annis. *Archetypal Patterns in Women's Fiction.* Bloomington: Indiana Univ. Press, 1981.

Ransom, John Crowe. "Emily Dickinson: A Poet Restored." In *Emily Dickinson: A Collection of Critical Essays.* Ed. Richard B. Sewall, pp. 88–100. Englewood Cliffs, N.J.: Prentice-Hall, 1963.

Reynolds, David S. *Beneath the American Renaissance: The Subversive Imagination in the Age of Emerson and Melville.* Cambridge, Mass. and London: Harvard Univ. Press, 1989.

Rich, Adrienne. "Compulsory Heterosexuality and Lesbian Existence." In *Women: Sex and Sexuality.* Ed. Catharine R. Stimpson and Ethel Spector Person, pp. 62–91. Chicago and London: Univ. of Chicago Press, 1980.

———. "I am in Danger—Sir—." *Necessities of Life.* New York: W. W. Norton, 1966.

———. "Vesuvius at Home: The Power of Emily Dickinson." In *On Lies, Secrets, and Silence: Selected Prose 1966–1978*, pp. 157–183. New York: W. W. Norton & Co., 1979.

———. *A Wild Patience Has Taken Me This Far.* New York: W. W. Norton, 1981.

Richter, David H. *The Reader, the Text, the Poem: The Transactional Theory of the Literary Work.* Carbondale: Southern Illinois Univ. Press, 1978.

———, ed. *The Critical Tradition: Classic Texts and Contemporary Trends*. New York: St. Martin's, 1989.

Rosenthal, M. L. "Poems by the Packet." Review of Franklin's *The Manuscript Books of Emily Dickinson* and Porter's *Dickinson: The Modern Idiom*. *Times Literary Supplement*, March 26, 1982, p. 357.

Rothman, Ellen K. *Hands and Hearts: A History of Courtship in America*. Cambridge and London: Harvard Univ. Press, 1987.

Sacks, Sheldon, ed. *On Metaphor*. Chicago and London: Univ. of Chicago Press, 1979.

St. Armand, Barton Levi. *Emily Dickinson and Her Culture: The Soul's Society*. Cambridge: Cambridge Univ. Press, 1984.

Scharnhorst, Gary. "A Glimpse of Dickinson at Work." *American Literature* 57 (October 1985): 190–192.

Schenck, Celeste. "All of a Piece: Women's Poetry and Autobiography." In *Life/Lines: Theorizing Women's Autobiography*. Ed. Bella Brodzki and Celeste Schenck, pp. 281–305. Ithaca and London: Cornell Univ. Press, 1988.

Schulman, Mark. "Gender and Typographic Culture: Beginning to Unravel the 500-Year Mystery." In *Technology and Women's Voices: Keeping in Touch*. Ed. Cheris Kramarae, pp. 98–115. New York and London: Routledge & Kegan Paul, 1988.

Schweikart, Patrocinio. "Reading Ourselves: Toward a Feminist Theory of Reading." In *Gender and Reading: Essays on Readers, Texts, and Contexts*. Ed. Elizabeth A. Flynn and Patrocinio Schweikart, pp. 31–62. Baltimore and London: Johns Hopkins Univ. Press, 1986.

Scott, Joan W. "Gender: A Useful Category of Historical Analysis." *Coming to Terms: Feminism, Theory, Politics*. Ed. Elizabeth Weed, pp. 81–100. New York and London: Routledge, 1989.

Sewall, Richard B. *The Life of Emily Dickinson*. New York: Farrar, Straus and Giroux, 1974.

———, ed. *Emily Dickinson: A Collection of Critical Essays*. Englewood Cliffs, N.J.: Prentice-Hall, 1963.

Shields, Carol. *Swann*. New York: Viking Penguin, 1987.

Showalter, Elaine, ed. *Alternative Alcott*. New Brunswick and London: Rutgers Univ. Press, 1988.

———, ed. *Speaking of Gender*. New York and London: Routledge, Chapman & Hall, 1989.

Shurr, William H. *The Marriage of Emily Dickinson: A Study of the Fascicles*. Lexington: Univ. of Kentucky Press, 1983.

Small, Judy Jo. *Positive as Sound: Emily Dickinson's Rhyme*. Athens and London: Univ. of Georgia Press, 1990.

Simon, Paul. "The Dangling Conversation." *Parsley, Sage, Rosemary & Thyme*. New York: Columbia Records, 1966.

Smith, Barbara Herrnstein. *Poetic Closure: A Study of How Poems End*. Chicago and London: Univ. of Chicago Press, 1968.

Smith, Martha Nell. "Gender Issues in Textual Editing of Emily Dickinson." *Women's Studies Quarterly* 19, nos. 3 and 4 (Fall/Winter 1991): 78–111.

———. "To Fill a Gap." *San Jose Studies* 13, no. 3 (1987): 3–25.

Smith, Sidonie. *A Poetics of Women's Autobiography: Marginality and the Fictions of Self-Representation*. Bloomington and Indianapolis: Indiana Univ. Press, 1987.

Smith-Rosenberg, Carroll. *Disorderly Conduct: Visions of Gender in Victorian America*. New York: Alfred A. Knopf, 1985.

Spender, Dale. "Margaret Fuller." *Women of Ideas (And What Men Have Done to Them)*. London: Routledge & Kegan Paul, 1982.

Spicer, John L. "The Poems of Emily Dickinson." *Boston Public Library Quarterly* 8 (July 1956): 135–143.

Stanton, Domna C. *The Female Autograph: Theory and Practice of Autobiography from the Tenth to the Twentieth Century*. Chicago and London: Univ. of Chicago Press, 1987.

Steig, Michael. *Stories of Reading: Subjectivity and Literary Understanding*. Baltimore and London: Johns Hopkins Univ. Press, 1989.

Stimpson, Catharine R. "President's Column." *MLA Newsletter* 22 (Summer 1990): 3.

———. "Zero Degree Deviancy: The Lesbian Novel in English." In *Writing and Sexual Difference*. Ed. Elizabeth Abel, pp. 243–259. Chicago and London: Univ. of Chicago Press, 1982.

Stone, Ruth. *Second-Hand Coat: Poems New and Selected*. Boston: David R. Godine, 1987.

Stonum, Gary Lee. *The Dickinson Sublime*. Madison and London: Univ. of Wisconsin Press, 1990.

Sutherland, John. "Publishing History: A Hole at the Centre of Literary Sociology." *Critical Inquiry* 14 (Spring 1988): 574–589.

Tanselle, G. Thomas. "The Editorial Problem of Final Authorial Intention." *Selected Studies in Bibliography*. Charlottesville: Univ. Press of Virginia for the Bibliographical Society of the Univ. of Virginia, 1979.

———. "Response to John Sutherland." In *Literature and Social Practice*. Ed. Philippe Desan, Priscilla Parkhurst Ferguson, and Wendy Griswold, pp. 169–175. Chicago and London: Univ. of Chicago Press, 1989.

Tebbel, John. *A History of Book Publishing in the United States: The Expansion of an Industry 1865–1919*. Vol. 2. New York and London: R. R. Bowker, 1975.

Todd, Mabel Loomis, *Total Eclipses of the Sun*. Boston: Roberts Brothers, 1884.

———, ed. *Poems by Emily Dickinson*. Third Series. Boston: Roberts Brothers, 1896.

Updike, John. "To the Editors." *New York Review of Books* 35 (August 18, 1988): 63.

Walker, Cheryl. "Feminist Literary Criticism and the Author." *Critical Inquiry* 16 (Spring 1990): 551–571.

———. *The Nightingale's Burden: Women Poets and American Culture before 1900*. Bloomington: Indiana Univ. Press, 1982.

Walker, Nancy. "'Wider Than the Sky': Public Presence and Private Self in Dickinson, James, and Woolf." In *The Private Self: Theory and Practice of Women's Autobiographical Writings*. Ed. Shari Benstock, pp. 272–303. Chapel Hill and London: Univ. of North Carolina Press, 1988.

Walsh, John Evangelist. *The Hidden Life of Emily Dickinson*. New York: Simon and Schuster, 1971.

Warren, Joyce W., ed. *Ruth Hall and Other Writings*. By Fanny Fern. New Brunswick, N.J.: Rutgers Univ. Press, 1986.

Watts, Emily Stipes. *The Poetry of American Women from 1632 to 1945*. Austin and London: Univ. of Texas Press, 1977.

Weedon, Chris. *Feminist Practice and Poststructuralist Theory*. Oxford and New York: Basil Blackwell, 1987.

Weintraub, Karl J. "Autobiography and Historical Consciousness." *Critical Inquiry* 1 (Summer 1975): 821–848.

Wells, Anna Mary. "ED Forgeries." *Dickinson Studies* 35 (1979): 12–16.

Whitman, Walt. *Leaves of Grass*. Ed. Sculley Bradley and Harold W. Blodgett. New York: W. W. Norton, 1973.

Wittreich, Joseph. "'Strange Text!': 'Paradise Regain'd . . . to which is added *Samson Agonistes*.'" In *Poems in Their Place: The Intertextuality and Order of Poetic Collections*. Ed. Neil Fraistat, pp. 164–194. Chapel Hill and London: Univ. of North Carolina Press, 1986.

Wolff, Cynthia Griffin. *Emily Dickinson*. New York: Alfred A. Knopf, 1986.

———. "The Women in My Life." *Massachusetts Review* 24 (1983): 438–452.

Wylder, Edith. *The Last Face: Emily Dickinson's Manuscripts*. Albuquerque: Univ. of New Mexico Press, 1971.

Yingling, Thomas E. *Hart Crane and the Homosexual Text: New Thresholds, New Anatomies*. Chicago and London: Univ. of Chicago Press, 1990.

Zimmerman, Bonnie. "What Has Never Been: An Overview of Lesbian Feminist Literary Criticism." *Feminist Studies* 7, no. 3 (1981): 451–475.

I _ndex_

Index to Groups of Poems Cited

"Calvary of Love" poems, 37
F 6, critiquing promises of immortality, 196
F 10, linking courtship and religious faith, 196–197
F 21, on poetrymaking and subverting conventional order, 90–92
"Master" poems, 241n28
"New World" poems of exploration, 232n1
poems sent to Sue without stanza divisions, 198
printed during ED's lifetime, 223n2

Index of Poems by First Lines

* _Denotes poems sent to Sue Dickinson; readers should consult text to ascertain other recipients and/or inclusion in fascicle._

* A Death blow – is a Life blow –
  (P 816 in L 316), 62, 147
A Drop fell on the Apple Tree
  (P 794), 217
Ah ' Moon – and Star! (P 240), 219
* A Lady red – amid the Hill (P 74),
  196

* A lane of Yellow led the eye
  (P 1650), 202
* A little over Jordan (P 59), 189
* A narrow Fellow in the Grass
  (P 986), 11, 13, 154–155; as
  "The Snake," 11–12, 59, 181,
  192
A Pit – but Heaven over it – (P 1712),
  93
* A poor – torn Heart – a tattered
  heart – (P 78), 119–121, 124,
  232n6, 240n25; photograph of,
  Fig. 5, 120
* "Arcturus" is his other name –
  (P 70), 203
As Children bid the Guest "Good
  Night" (P 133), 196
A shady friend – for Torrid days
  (P 278), 219
A solemn thing – it was – (P 271),
  30–31, 63, 185, 187; as "Wedded," 31, 100
A word is dead, when it is said
  (P 1212), 8, 71, 222n13, 236n37
* A Word made flesh (P 1651), 33

Because I could not stop for Death
  (P 712), 185; used to appeal for
  organ donors, 42
Before I got my eye put out (P 327),
  247n10

Index of Letter-Poems and Letters (by recipient and first line[s] or important words)

General Index